Mass Uprisings
IN THE USSR

The New Russian History

Series Editor: Donald J. Raleigh,
University of North Carolina, Chapel Hill

This series makes examples of the finest work of the most eminent historians in Russia today available to English-language readers. Each volume has been specially prepared with an international audience in mind, and each is introduced by an outstanding Western scholar in the same field.

**THE REFORMS OF
PETER THE GREAT**
Progress Through Coercion in Russia
Evgenii V. Anisimov
Translated with an introduction by
John T. Alexander

IN STALIN'S SHADOW
The Career of "Sergo" Ordzhonikidze
Oleg V. Khlevniuk
Translated by David Nordlander
Edited with an introduction by
Donald J. Raleigh,
with the assistance of Kathy S. Transchel

**THE EMPERORS AND EMPRESSES
OF RUSSIA**
Rediscovering the Romanovs
Edited by Donald J. Raleigh
Compiled by Akhmed A. Iskenderov

WOMAN IN RUSSIAN HISTORY
From the Tenth to the Twentieth
Century
Natalia Pushkareva
Translated and edited by Eve Levin

**THE RUSSIAN EMPIRE IN THE
EIGHTEENTH CENTURY**
Searching for a Place in the World
Aleksandr B. Kamenskii
Translated and edited by David Griffiths

RUSSIA AFTER THE WAR
Hopes, Illusions, and Disappointments,
1945–1957
Elena Zubkova
Translated and edited by Hugh Ragsdale

LABOR CAMP SOCIALISM
The Gulag in the Soviet
Totalitarian System
Galina Mikhailovna Ivanova
Edited by Donald J. Raleigh
Translated by Carol Flath

OUR DAILY BREAD
Socialist Distribution and the
Art of Survival in Stalin's Russia
Elena Osokina
Translated and edited by
Kate Transchel
and Greta Bucher

MASS UPRISINGS IN THE USSR
Protest and Rebellion in the
Post-Stalin Years
Vladimir A. Kozlov
Translated and edited by
Elaine McClarnand MacKinnon

Mass Uprisings in the USSR

Protest and Rebellion in the Post-Stalin Years

Vladimir A. Kozlov

Translated and Edited by
Elaine McClarnand MacKinnon

M.E. Sharpe
Armonk, New York
London, England

English translation, editorial matter, introduction © 2002 by M. E. Sharpe, Inc.
An earlier version of this work was published in Novosibirsk in 1999 by Sibirskii
Khronograf under the title "Massovye Besporiadki v SSSR: pri Khrushcheve i Brezhneve,
1953–nachalo 1980-kh gg." © 1999 by V.A. Kozlov and "Russkii khronograf."

The author gratefully acknowledges the support of the Harry F. Guggenheim Foundation.

Library of Congress Cataloging-in-Publication Data

Kozlov, V.A. (Vladimir Aleksandrovich)
    [Massovye besporiadki v SSSR. English]
    Mass uprisings in the USSR : protest and rebellion in the post-Stalin years / by
Vladimir A. Kozlov ; translated and edited by Elaine McClarnand MacKinnon.
        p. cm. — (New Russian history)
    Includes index.
    ISBN 0-7656-0667-4 (alk. paper); ISBN 0-7656-0668-2 (pbk.)
        1. Soviet Union—Politics and government—1953–1985. 2. Government, Resistance
to—Soviet Union. 3. Insurgency—Soviet Union. 4. Riots—Soviet Union. 5. Social
conflict—Soviet Union. I. McClarnand MacKinnon, Elaine. II. Title. III. Series.

DK274.K6513 2002
947.085—dc21   2001049843

Printed in the United States of America

The paper used in this publication meets the minimum requirements of
American National Standard for Information Sciences
Permanence of Paper for Printed Library Materials,
ANSI Z 39.48-1984.

∞

MV (c)   10   9   8   7   6   5   4   3   2   1
MV (p)   10   9   8   7   6   5   4   3   2   1

To Marina

Contents

Translator's Note

Elaine McClarnand MacKinnon

The death of Stalin in 1953 gave rise to a new period in Soviet history, one marked by reform and recovery from the trauma of forced modernization, mass terror, and a world war. Yet this was also an era of turbulent social conflict that witnessed numerous strikes, riots, and other forms of mass uprisings, particularly in provincial towns and cities. From time to time, Westerners received tantalizing glimpses of such events, as information seeped out through dissident and émigré channels and was picked up by Western news outlets such as Radio Liberty, the *New York Times*, *Washington Post*, and *Posev*, an émigré journal published in Germany. In this way the outside world learned about disturbances in exotic-sounding places such as Temir-Tau, Alexandrov, Kemerovo, and Novocherkassk during the late 1950s and early 1960s.[1] The information, however, tended to be secondhand, often based on rumor, and limited in scope, with many details shrouded in mystery or unsupported by hard evidence.

Consequently, as with most topics related to Soviet history and society, the dearth of reliable sources, compounded by the lack of access to Soviet archives and official state censorship, inhibited in-depth scholarly analysis of mass unrest.[2] Beginning in 1985, Mikhail S. Gorbachev's *glasnost* and the subsequent opening of Soviet archives unleashed a veritable flood of new information about riots, strikes, and demonstrations, followed by the publication in Russia and the former Soviet Union of numerous memoirs and documentary collections. In the West, however, the study of social conflict continued to focus primarily on peasant and Gulag rebellions or covered periods prior to 1953.[3] Only recently has the first monograph on popular uprisings emerged, Samuel Baron's book on the Novocherkassk events of 1962, *Bloody Saturday in the Soviet Union*.[4]

Thus, Vladimir A. Kozlov's pioneering work breaks new ground in its comprehensive analysis of mass social unrest during the eras of Nikita S. Khrushchev and Leonid I. Brezhnev. Penetrating the smoke screens thrown up by Soviet propaganda and state mythology, Kozlov is the first historian to use previously inaccessible police, party, and state documents to examine a broad range of popular disturbances ranging from soldiers' riots to workers' strikes, from ethnic pogroms to revolts among Orthodox believers. With his extensive use of archival materials, the author clarifies and substantiates many details that in the past were based solely on rumor or secondary sources. Although some of the uprisings he covers are known to Western scholars, he provides stunning new facts and thorough documentation. In addition, Kozlov introduces Western readers to lesser-known riots and disturbances, thereby revealing the broader context of mass unrest in the post-Stalinist Soviet Union. The psychological profiles he draws of participants in the disturbances illuminate the dynamics of social conflict and provide a human dimension to what otherwise might seem like random and brutal acts of violence.

Kozlov's research is a valuable complement to studies recently published on Soviet society and mass consciousness after World War II. While Elena Zubkova does not examine specific uprisings in her book *Russia After the War*, she does highlight many of the same frustrations, social problems, and heightened expectations that spurred popular unrest in the post-Stalinist era. The divided and conflictive society Zubkova uncovers, marked by a vast chasm that developed after 1953 between the government and the people, is the same one that produced the riots, strikes, and uprisings analyzed by Kozlov. Likewise in a recent article, Iurii Aksiutin examines mass unrest as part of a larger study of popular attitudes toward Khrushchev. Aksiutin briefly discusses the March 1956 demonstrations in Tbilisi, which saw thousands take to the streets to protest Khrushchev's criticism of Stalin at the 1956 Twentieth Party Congress of the Communist Party of the Soviet Union (CPSU), and records as well public opposition to the Soviet invasion of Hungary that same year. Like Kozlov, he finds anti-Khrushchev, pro-Stalinist sympathies running strong among the common people along with a propensity for rallying behind leaders removed from power.[5]

None of the works published thus far, though, provides coverage of mass uprisings comparable to that of Kozlov. He offers an impressively panoramic survey of multiple cases of unrest, which allows him to determine distinctive patterns of social consciousness and behavior. Kozlov's analysis of these patterns, based upon a broad range of sources, both confirms and expands upon that of earlier studies, many of which had to rely chiefly upon interviews with émigrés. Moreover, he provides substantive material for comparative studies of popular unrest in other societies and time periods, particularly his discussions of crowd behavior, motives of individual leaders, the "ideology," and the largely localized nature of mass protest in the Union of Soviet Socialist Republics (USSR).

The significance of this book, however, goes beyond the historiographical gap it fills, for its portrait of the post-Stalinist era brings fresh insight to critical questions concerning the nature of the state-society relationship and the appropriateness of "totalitarianism" as a model for understanding the Soviet system. Although the author does not place himself in any particular scholarly "camp," his research certainly reveals the recurrent difficulties faced by the Soviet regime in its attempt to be "totalitarian." What emerges is a sense both of the harsh brutality of the state and its inherent inability to achieve any degree of truly "totalitarian" control over its populace.

Kozlov repeatedly illustrates the repressive nature of the Soviet regime, which ruthlessly punished participants in mass disturbances, typically caring little for the truth in its search for convenient scapegoats. In several cases Kozlov even raises the possibility that Soviet authorities themselves sometimes manipulated social unrest to serve their own selfish purposes, readily sacrificing the lives of those individuals gullible enough to serve as their puppets. Particularly vivid are the visible scars of Stalinism, the devastating legacy of arbitrary policies that broke innocent human beings, rendering them incapable of productive lives and service. Many of those who became the catalysts or leaders of mass disturbances were victims either directly or indirectly of the Stalinist era. Some had fallen prey under Stalin to harsh laws criminalizing minor infractions such as absenteeism, while others were exploited by the regime's incessant drive to industrialize and develop remote areas at all costs, regardless of the harsh conditions. Kozlov reveals the difficulties many Stalinist victims had in trying to reintegrate into Soviet society. Passport and registration regulations often forced former convicts to settle in small towns and rural areas lacking in amenities and services. During outbreaks of unrest, they were often easy targets for police investigators. Kozlov documents as well the traumatic legacy of Stalin's forced exile during World War II of Chechens, Ingush, and other non-Russian nationalities. Repatriation led to tremendous instability and ethnic tension, resulting in major outbreaks of unrest such as the 1959 riots in Grozny.

Yet, despite being ruled by a regime that possessed powerful mechanisms of control and manipulation, this was a society of people who questioned and criticized authority, willfully broke laws, and often sought violent avenues for expressing frustration. The state was repressive and cruel in its policies, but it lacked absolute control. It made mistakes; its massive bureaucratic structures often failed to provide for popular needs. Mass disturbances, as Kozlov reveals, actually served as a type of reciprocal connection between the state and society, allowing people to express grievances and emotions that otherwise might have been censored or suppressed. A rather complex interrelationship developed between an unruly populace and a state that sought but failed to be all-controlling and instead ended up using violence to bring citizens back into line. But people continued to engage in activities beyond the regime's ability to control, from drinking to vandalism to "antisocial" mob violence.

Kozlov reveals here a seamier side of Soviet life, one not often visible to Western eyes, marked by poverty, frustration, wanton cruelty, and widespread drunkenness. Here are people who have fallen through the cracks, who have not assimilated the values of the regime, who do not work, but rather spend their days in idleness and drinking—former convicts drifting aimlessly, drunken soldiers terrorizing railroad stations and villages, "hooligans" and delinquents who do not conform to the image of *homo Sovieticus*.

At the same time, Kozlov also shows that these uprisings were not necessarily propelled by criminality nor by any rejection of the Soviet system. Among the leaders of mass disturbances were many deeply loyal Soviet citizens who were acting on the basis of official values, not against them. Far from being predominantly antiregime, anti-Stalinist, or anticommunist upheavals, the majority of the uprisings treated by Kozlov were conservative in nature, directed not against the system itself but against local injustices or the disruptions caused by Khrushchev's impetuous and often destabilizing reforms. The targets of mass protest and violence were often those whom people believed to be corrupting the original ideals of Soviet communism. Kozlov's research confirms the constancy of older patterns of popular consciousness—faith in the "good tsar" and hatred for corrupt local officials, coupled with a determination to inform the center of the wrongdoing, which then will assuredly be corrected.

Ironically, the author suggests that the riots, strikes, and pogroms of the Khrushchev era were actually a sign of regime stability, evidence that people still believed in the original vision of Soviet communism and felt that it could yet be realized. Kozlov points out that mass unrest reached its peak under Khrushchev in the early 1960s, during a time of reform, renewed idealism, and raised expectations, and that it virtually came to a standstill during the conservative and "stagnant" years of Brezhnev's rule. The latter produced new "rules of the game"—renewed populist policies, such as artificial price decreases and higher wages—which satisfied popular demands and lessened social volatility. But, above all, Kozlov links the decline in mass unrest to growing disillusionment with "romantic communist utopias." People were less likely to risk their lives and security for the sake of beliefs or dubious ideals, and therefore growing ethnic tension and social pathologies such as

excessive drinking and street hooliganism rarely provoked large-scale uprisings. This situation, however, held disturbing implications for the future of
Soviet socialism. As Kozlov stresses, society was disintegrating, weakened
by chronic social diseases and ideological ambivalence, which hardly provided the proper foundation for Gorbachev's attempt to renew and strengthen
the Soviet system. Kozlov's research raises the question, therefore, of what
was more dangerous for the regime and for Gorbachev's goals, volatile and
violent popular uprisings or cynical disillusionment?

Each chapter examines either a specific disturbance or a range of related
uprisings in a particular region. Chapter 1 treats unrest in areas targeted for
rapid development by the Soviet regime, particularly the Virgin Lands, which
were previously uncultivated territories in Kazakhstan newly opened up in
1954 for growing crops, and large-scale construction and mining projects.
Here workers would be sent into areas totally lacking in infrastructure and
amenities, producing appalling conditions conducive to social conflict. The
chapter concludes with an in-depth examination of the 1959 revolt at Temirtau,
a vivid example of how easily mass unrest could explode under such circumstances. Chapter 2 focuses on uprisings and disturbances involving regular
soldiers as well as those mobilized for construction and mining work. The
extensive use of militarized labor was considered necessary by the regime,
but created as many problems as it solved. What seemed to matter most to
the authorities was amassing human material to exploit. Meeting the needs
of that same human mass, however, was not a priority, at least not until people
were pushed to the brink of desperation and rose up in protest.

Chapters 3 and 4 both deal with the problems created by Stalin's 1944
exile from the Northern Caucasus of non-Russian nationalities such as the
Chechens, Ingush, Kalmyks, and Balkars, who were charged with treason
and collaboration with the German invaders and who eventually were repatriated during the mid-to-late 1950s. Government actions, or lack of action,
exacerbated ethnic tensions both in the areas of exile and in the homelands
of the exiled peoples, where often the state had moved in new settlers. Chapter 3 focuses on problems arising for the Chechens and Ingush in their exile,
and zooms in on a brutal and tragic attack upon an Ingush family in the
Kazakh city of Dzhetygar. Chapter 4 highlights the tensions and conflict
generated by repatriation of the Chechen and Ingush peoples back to the
newly restored Chechen-Ingush Autonomous Soviet Socialist Republic
(ASSR), culminating in the bloody 1959 riots in Grozny. Chapter 5 considers how nationalism merged with pro-Stalinist sentiments to produce one of
the largest disturbances treated in the book—the March 1956 riots in Tbilisi
and in other Georgian cities. The author explores the troubled reactions of
ordinary Georgians as well as Georgian party leaders to the 1956 CPSU

Twentieth Party Congress. Many could not comprehend the dethroning of their former communist "god" while others perceived the attack on Stalin as an anti-Georgian act.

In chapter 6, the author focuses on hooliganism and the role of marginalized urban masses in a series of disturbances that occurred between 1953 and 1958. The last section in the chapter analyzes the "ideology" behind popular unrest, which often represented an irrational mixture of contradictory values, symbols, or glorification of past leaders, usually those deposed or denigrated by the Khrushchev leadership. Chapter 7 explores unrest among religious believers incited by Khrushchev's antireligious campaign of the late 1950s. Although the protests of believers failed to halt the campaign, they nonetheless forced the regime to make compromises to placate popular indignation.

Chapter 8 explains the reasons for the outbreak of a series of uprisings, strikes, and disturbances during the early 1960s, which are subsequently treated in chapters 9–14. Khrushchev's attempt to reform the Soviet economy led to unpopular increases in prices and simultaneous decreases in wages, while efforts to restore order by clamping down on street crimes produced new waves of hooligan violence. The expectations raised by reform and by propagandistic claims concerning the achievement of socialism clashed with the harsh reality of Soviet life, particularly in regions far from Moscow and Leningrad. The hardships engendered by Khrushchev's policies seemed the last straw, a betrayal of the regime's promised consideration of the people's interests and needs. The result was social tension and heightened conflict among urban masses leading to a series of disorders, covered in chapters 9–11, that broke out between 1960 and 1962 in the cities of Krasnodar, Murom, Alexandrov, and Biisk. Motivating factors in all of these riots and disturbances were frustrations with state policies and a sense of betrayal by local authorities, particularly the police, who frequently became the targets of mob violence.

The subject of chapters 12 and 13 is the workers' strike in Novocherkassk that lasted from June 1 to 3, 1962, and represented the height of popular dissatisfaction with Khrushchev's wage and price policies. The author recounts the principal events day by day and profiles many of the leading strike participants. Kozlov considers the strike not as an exceptional or unique occurrence, nor as a specifically anticommunist protest, but as an internal systemic disorder led largely by individuals who believed that they were acting to save the regime and the ideals they believed to be its foundation. Putting the Novocherkassk uprising in the context of other popular upheavals in the Soviet Union brings needed balance to interpretations that view it as an extraordinary rebellion directed specifically against the Soviet system.

Chapter 14 covers mass disturbances during the last two years of

Khrushchev's rule, spotlighting a workers' strike in Primorskii Krai, pro-Stalinist riots in Sumgait, and a disturbance involving Chechen exiles seeking to return to their former homes in Dagestan ASSR. In chapter 15, the author discusses the relative stability of the Brezhnev era and the factors that led to the decline of mass unrest. Ultimately, as Kozlov states, the stability proved to be costly, and Gorbachev came to power in a society torn by growing social and ethnic problems and no longer believing in communist ideals. The study of mass unrest, therefore, offers fresh insight into the ultimate failure of Gorbachev's perestroika and of the Soviet system in general.

At the heart of much of the conflict portrayed in this book is the Soviet *militsia*, translated here as police. In the Soviet Union, the militsia were under the jurisdiction of the USSR Ministry of Internal Affairs (MVD) and were the nonsecurity police, i.e., they were in charge of keeping order and enforcing laws within Soviet borders, and were distinguished from the security police, the USSR Committee for State Security (KGB), which handled exceptionally dangerous and state crimes, such as treason, espionage, anti-Soviet activities, and mass disorders. On a day-to-day basis, the regular police were the most visible representation of state authority and at the same time, as Kozlov shows, were the most frequent target for popular resentment and violence. This tension was perhaps rooted in the ubiquitous role played by police in the daily lives of Soviet citizens, and in the lack of viable legal protections against the abuses of law enforcement agencies. As agents of the state, the police were required to force compliance with its ideological objectives, including restricting citizen mobility through the passport system, enforcing strict laws related to the economy, protecting state property, and identifying unemployed "parasites" and placing them in jobs. Therefore police controls affected every aspect of citizens' daily lives, from taking a vacation to registering an automobile. Police were continually monitoring forms of behavior that in the West would not have been considered illegal, such as moving freely from place to place or selling goods privately or in public markets. To catch illegal traders and black marketeers, police regularly patrolled open-air markets and were stationed at bus and train stations. It also fell to the police to carry out state campaigns against hooliganism and drunkenness, which, as the author shows, created deep personal grievances and grudges. Further abuses stemmed from the fact that police did not need warrants to enter homes, schools, or workplaces to obtain information on suspected violators, even if the latter had not committed any crime.

Frustrations with police regulation of people's day-to-day lives were exacerbated by the rampant corruption that permeated the law enforcement system. Many laws and regulations regarding citizens' activities, particularly mobility, were unpublished, so police had arbitrary powers to define criminality and to determine who could register in particular regions. Bribery was endemic, partly due to low wages. Police brutality was also a factor in many mass disturbances, although the use of weapons was not as widespread as in the West, due to the fact that the Soviet police had to give a warning cry before using a gun and then file a written report every time a shot was fired. But officers often used nightsticks to beat suspects, especially since handcuffs were not allowed and beatings were at times the only way to gain control over a suspect. All of these problems contributed to the extremely caustic relations between the populace and the police during the 1950s and 1960s.[6]

Moreover, this book graphically exposes the often biased nature of criminal investigations in the USSR.[7] Either the police, the USSR Procuracy (which supervised the MVD and prosecuted criminal offenders), or the KGB would conduct the investigation; but as Kozlov shows, mass uprisings and disturbances usually meant that the KGB would be involved. There would be two types of investigation, an inquiry and a preliminary investigation, each of which would gather evidence and produce a written report. The reports were submitted to a judge, who decided whether the case would be tried. The purpose of the investigations was not so much to uncover the truth as it was to prepare a case that would bring a conviction, although in most instances this was assured if the matter went to trial. In the majority of cases examined by Kozlov, the guilt of defendants seemed predetermined, although some would later have sentences reduced or repealed as a result of appeals through the Procuracy. Perjury and the fabrication of evidence were common tactics employed by investigators to ensure that the case would go to trial and would end in a conviction. Physical abuse of defendants and witnesses occurred frequently. Citizens charged with a crime were not allowed access to defense attorneys until the criminal investigation (often lasting up to nine months) was completed, thus making it even more difficult to protect defendants. Those depicted in this book appear to be caught up in an endless cycle of abuse, outrage, and cruel recrimination, which eventually produced a populace plagued by social apathy and chronic social pathologies.

With his research, Kozlov opens a long-closed window into the Soviet past, one that is not always easy to look through, but one that will indelibly alter historical understanding of Soviet society. Social conflict, ethnic tensions, and mob violence were much more a part of the Soviet landscape than has often been acknowledged. Even before the 1970s and 1980s, there were signs of crisis in the capacity of the Soviet welfare state to satisfy popular needs and to combat chronic social problems such as alcoholism, with the consequences graphically depicted here. But Kozlov has also convincingly demonstrated that these forms of mass protest, violence, and vandalism cannot be fully understood using Western political, sociological, or psychological formulas. They must be examined within the context of Soviet and Russian history, culture, and society, and with an understanding that social protest in the USSR was often a product of strong grass-roots support for the overall values and ideals of Soviet communism. Yet it was just this support that the regime squandered. Throughout this book there are recurring examples of betrayal, despair, and ideological confusion, and of the Soviet leadership's inadequate grasp of popular consciousness. The distorted forms of reciprocal ties between the state and society in the USSR precluded truly mutual understanding, and, as Kozlov reveals, both the people and the government eventually paid a heavy price for this circumstance.

In sum, the New Russian History Series is pleased to bring to English-speaking readers this richly detailed and thought-provoking study. There is much here for scholars and students to digest, ponder, and debate, manifestly demonstrating the value and significance of post–Cold War linkages between Russian and Western scholarship.

I would like to thank the author, Vladimir A. Kozlov, for his cooperation in making it possible to publish a revised version of his monograph in English translation. He was invaluably helpful and responsive to my many inquiries, and it was a great pleasure to work with him. I want to thank as well Donald J. Raleigh, who commissioned me to do the translation and has mentored the project from start to finish. I am extremely grateful for his constant support and insightful editorial comments. I am deeply indebted to my colleague, Dr. Steve Goodson, for his critical reading of the manuscript and his always valuable editorial advice and to Martha Goodson for her expertise and skill in designing the index. In addition, I thank Sharon Kowalsky for her careful reading and critical comments on the text. I must thank Julie Gauchman and the Slavic Reference Service at the University of Illinois Library, Jennifer Wynot, Rashyd A. Latypov, Natia Jokhadze, and Ekaterina Kristesashvili for their help in translating especially difficult Russian words and expressions. I appreciate greatly the assistance from subscribers to H-Russia who responded to historiographical queries, particularly Alison Rowley, Bob Arnot, and Abbott Gleason. I also want to express my gratitude to Patricia A. Kolb at M.E. Sharpe for her support of both this publication and of the New Russian History Series, and to Elizabeth Granda, Ana Erlic and Irina Belenky for their expert assistance. Above all, I must thank my husband, Dr. Aran MacKinnon, for his steadfast support of my work as well as his invaluable advice and critical commentary on the manuscript. He is my eternal source of inspiration.

Acknowledgments

Much time and effort have gone into this book. Its publication would have been impossible without support from the Harry F. Guggenheim Foundation, which in 1997 approved the project "Urban Unrest in Soviet Russia, 1960–1963." The book was originally published in Russian by Sibirskii Khronograf, a publishing company based in Novosibirsk. Now it is coming out in a revised and shortened English-language version.

The first reader of the manuscript was my close friend of many years, Timothy McDaniel, professor of sociology at the University of California (San Diego). He was also its first critic—good-natured, wise, and fair. I am greatly beholden to this remarkable individual. At various stages of the work, I have received moral and professional support from my assistants Olga Edelman and Elina Zavadskaia; from professors Sheila Fitzpatrick, Arch Getty, and Jeffrey Burds of the United States; Francesco Benvenuti of Italy; Dr. S.V. Mironenko and Dr. O.V. Khlevniuk of Russia; the historian and member of the "Memorial" society, N. Petrov; and the former deputy director of the State Archive of the Russian Federation (GARF), Aliia Barkovets. D.N. Nokhotovich rendered invaluable assistance in the search and selection of materials in GARF. For discovering a number of important documents on the history of uprisings in Grozny and Tblisi, I am indebted to T.V. Tsarevskaia-Diakina.

This book is dedicated to my wife, Marina Kozlova. She has not only inspired me (indeed, this was the easiest part of her burden) but has also endured my caprices, pushed me when I have been lazy, and, above all, has helped me to live by the simple fact of her own existence on this earth.

V.A. Kozlov

Mass Uprisings
IN THE USSR

Introduction

Vladimir A. Kozlov

From the mid-1990s, broad layers of Russian society, including both the winners and losers of liberal reforms, were increasingly dissatisfied with the spontaneity of the new political, social, and economic processes. Furthermore, they became nostalgic for old notions of order and for a "firm hand" capable of introducing and maintaining this order. For their part, politicians and government officials tended to blame stalemated reforms and the absence of a positive social dynamic on the "lack of civilization among the people," the "malicious conniving of our enemies," and hostile "forces."

In reality, all of these and similar explanations for the failure of reform in the USSR only mask the real reasons for "what happened." These reasons are actually rooted in the steadfast "structures of everyday life," in traditional models of mass behavior, in the functioning of state institutions, as well as in the historical relationship (which is itself embedded in culture, traditions, and ways of life) between people and the state. In truth, what occurred during the last ten years is a normal attempt of society and the state to adapt to the fundamental, long-term consequences of revolution, forced modernization, and urbanization. Likewise, Khrushchev's indecisive reforms and cosmetic changes in the political technology of power represented similar attempts to overcome the crisis of modernization, which had been exacerbated by the postrevolutionary syndrome of the Stalinist "Great Terror," by ethnic and social purges, and by the destructive consequences of World War II. The failure of Khrushchev's reforms led in turn to Brezhnev's "stagnation," which was marked by temporary conservatism and the smoothing over of acute problems. In the end, all of these relatively old contradictions interacted with the postcommunist politics of Yeltsin and with the interests of Russian capitalism to determine the current shape of the country.

In modern times, the Russian state and its social elites, who had successfully mobilized the masses to change the former tsarist and Soviet social foundations under similar slogans of a "rejected legacy," almost immediately collided with this very legacy. They themselves, as well as society as a whole, could not reject this legacy, and, in fact, they did not even want to reject it. The emergence in Russia of a new political regime could not resolve the conflict between the people and the state, nor could it alter the potential predisposition of Russian social consciousness toward spontaneous unrest and mass disorders. The historical experience of the USSR has shown that conflict between the populace and political authority could and did develop into spontaneous uprisings, despite police control and harsh penalties to intimidate potential rebels.

In contemporary Russia, it would seem as though the use of violence in resolving conflicts is being replaced by more moderate and organized means of struggle: through institutions of civil society, strikes, demonstrations, meetings, and protest marches. At the same time, however, under certain conditions—the marginalization of the populace, the discrediting and loss of legitimacy of local or federal power, the ineffectiveness of institutions of civil society, heightened ethnic competition—conflicts between legal authority and social or ethnic groups can engender phenomena that essentially resemble traditional rebellions and popular disturbances.

In principle, one can talk about a definite set of conditions in which the transformation of social or ethnic tension into violent conflict becomes almost inevitable. There are standard mistakes committed by the state that provoke mass unrest, as well as standard models of behavior for groups in conflict. Furthermore, crowds and their self-appointed leaders follow established formulas of behavior. All of this imparts a special timeliness to research on mass unrest and urban disorders. Such historical reconstructions have significance that can be applied to increasing the effectiveness of state rule and improving its capacity to diagnose and preempt illegal mass actions.

This book represents one of the first attempts to study Soviet history from the 1950s to the beginning of the 1980s within a conceptual framework new to Russian historiography: the study of historical conflict. The subject of my research is the history of violent social and ethnic conflict under Khrushchev and Brezhnev, and the specific characteristics of conflict between the people and the state in authoritarian-bureaucratic systems that are undergoing modernization. The book gives special attention to historical forms of influence exercised by the people over decision-making. It focuses on the contradictory "symbiotic" relationship between people and the state, within which unresolved social and ethnic contradictions result in specific "signals" to the state—mass riots, spontaneous uprisings, and ethnic disturbances.

Social and nationalist tensions grew throughout the USSR during the 1950s. Simultaneously, traditional norms and models of conflict broke down and were replaced by new ones. In addition, ethnic competition and nationalism heightened and became more organized. In a number of cases, social and ethnic conflicts developed into bloody confrontations that inevitably involved the active participation of the state and its police forces. The most acute and painful conflicts occurred in regions experiencing industrial construction and mass migrations of people, as well as in the Northern Caucasus and Transcaucasus. In the course of these turbulent conflicts, the people and the state worked out new forms of coexistence, changed the rules of the game, and thereby reformed the political course and the mechanisms of mass action. Both the common people and the elites formed new models of the world; both the "bosses" and the populace adapted to the new historical reality.

This monograph examines traditional Russian models of rebellious antisocial mass behavior: "hooligan wars" and "occupations," pogroms,* spontaneous revolts against local authorities, and ethnic riots. In addition, it covers more conscious forms of protest that had a relatively distinct political direction. The book gives special attention to paradoxical forms of the popular "communist dream," which often acted as an ideological shell for mass disturbances and rejected the existing "real socialism" as "despoiled truth." It also puts particular focus on models of mass conflict, on psychological profiles of participants and leaders of mass disorders, and on cultural and ethnic stereotypes that worked both for and against the regime in crisis situations.

Chronologically, the study encompasses the period from the death of Stalin in 1953 to Mikhail Gorbachev's rise to power in 1985. The author conditionally uses the term "liberal communism" to designate the rule of Khrushchev and Brezhnev. The qualitative unity of this period can, above all, be conceived as a *definitio per negatio*—a definition by negation. The difference between the epoch of Khrushchev and Brezhnev and the repressive dictatorship of the 1930s and 1940s is as completely obvious as the difference between the former and Gorbachev's attempt to reform Soviet socialism, which ended in the collapse of the entire system.

---

*A pogrom is an organized local massacre, usually directed at a specific ethnic or religious group, particularly Jews. In this monograph, the author uses the term in a broad sense to encompass looting, vandalism, and violent attacks against specifically targeted objects such as police departments, party and government office buildings, stores, and markets.—E.M.

But an even more pertinent argument for choosing this chronological framework is the evaluation of the whole epoch of liberal communism as an arena of struggle. The demands of an already relatively modernized and, in terms of technology, a very modern Soviet society collided with traditions of patriarchy and bureaucratic tyranny rooted in the institutions of power and management, as well as in ideology and mass psychology. Instead of a modern model of democratic interaction between society and the government, a traditional dichotomy of "people–state" prevailed. The search for an optimal social-political mechanism, or at least one adequate for a new postindustrial epoch, went on spontaneously under both Khrushchev and Brezhnev. But the ruling hierarchy only learned about the existence of social and ethnic conflicts and popular reactions to their decisions in the inevitably distorted form of uprisings and mass disorders or illegal "anti-Soviet phenomena." Gorbachev's endeavor to modernize this patriarchal mechanism of interrelationships led in 1991 to the collapse of the entire Soviet system, to the degradation, though not the disappearance, of the paternalistic tradition, and to the rise of civil society. It is the weakness of the latter that has contributed to the continual crises of legitimacy of the new order and the threat of a return to paternalist forms of ruling the country.

The historiography of conflict in Soviet society under Khrushchev and Brezhnev has been limited by both structural and conceptual constraints. Western researchers of this period did not have access to Soviet sources comparable to the collections of Leon Trotsky, Boris Nicolaevsky, or the Smolensk archive.* They had to be satisfied with the materials of the official Soviet press, with rumors filtered through the Iron Curtain, with superficial impressions of Western journalists, or with dissident writings, most of which were memoirs or were highly ideological in character. Attempts to historically reconstruct events hushed up by Soviet authorities began after the uprising in Novocherkassk. Interestingly, however, in early 1963, while commenting on Western press coverage of the Novocherkassk events, a certain unnamed high-level Soviet official admitted to a French journalist that there had been a large number of mass protests of workers analogous to Novocherkassk that were completely unknown in the West.

The 1964 article of Albert Boiter, "When the Kettle Boils Over," reflected

---

* The Trotsky Archive, containing personal papers and writings, is at Harvard University. Boris L. Nicolaevsky, an exiled Menshevik, collected hundreds of thousands of documents relating to the Russian Revolution, which are located at the Hoover Institute on War, Revolution, and Peace. The Smolensk archive consists of thousands of pages of Communist Party files that were seized by the Germans in 1941 and later ended up in the hands of American troops.–E.M.

the heightened interest in this "secret" theme.[1] The author had gathered together scraps of information that had seeped out through the Iron Curtain. According to contemporary criteria, this work does not meet scholarly standards. Boiter based the article exclusively on rumors and oral testimonies, but even this is not the main criticism, since he simply did not have access to any other information. What is most problematic is the biased nature of the analysis and the unwarranted faith of the author in his own sources, which were essentially rumors retold to Western correspondents and stories from anonymous Soviet tourists.

Boiter's research was limited to a discussion of two cases of mass disorders (Novocherkassk in 1962 and Krivoi Rog in October 1963). Ten other episodes were mentioned in passing. For the next thirty years, Boiter was the main source of information about rebellions and workers' protests from 1960 to 1964. Often quoted, his preliminary and very inaccurate account of events in the end became universally accepted in the West and was incorporated into general works and textbooks on Soviet history. Sometimes Boiter's material has been used without even a citation, since his information was accepted as common knowledge. The second most authoritative source for Western information about mass disorders of the Khrushchev period was Alexander Solzhenitsyn's *The Gulag Archipelago*. In addition to mentioning the disorders in Murom and Aleksandrov in 1961, Solzhenitsyn in his third volume focused on the riots in Novocherkassk. He called these events, with great exaggeration, a turning point in Soviet history and the beginning of the struggle of the people against the communist yoke.

Conceptually speaking, Western historical literature dealing either directly or tangentially with the theme of mass protest in the Soviet Union has greatly simplified events. The Novocherkassk uprising, for example, has been understood almost exclusively as a "struggle with communism," or at best as the *beginning* (after a long interruption) of the working-class struggle for economic rights.[2] Yet as Jeffrey Burds has intelligently noted, to examine mass riots in the USSR exclusively in an anticommunist context is just as naive as it would be to label, for example, an uprising in a Los Angeles ghetto a "struggle against capitalism."[3]

Soviet historians, who in their day wrote mountains of books and articles on the history of "developed socialism," not only lacked access to information about mass riots and disorders in the USSR, but found the very theme of conflict between the people and the state to be off limits. Since the dissolution of the USSR, therefore, a paradoxical situation has developed. Russian historians have been forced against their will to rewrite this history, despite the fact that they themselves have only a superficial conception of it. For more than ten years, there has been under way what some have termed a "rethinking of the past", but this process has been, figuratively speaking, *publicistic* (popular or journalistic) in nature. Consequently, the rethinking of old historiographical myths has often been subverted by the creation of "antimyths" that may be useful ideologically but bear no relation to historical science.

Nonetheless, Russian historians have been able to advance substantially the known facts of Soviet history as well as its meaning, thanks to the opening of archives and special collections and the declassification of millions of archival files. Western Sovietologists have also contributed with critical self-analysis of their own historiographical experience as well as their research. Such advances are particularly visible in research on the history of the first half of the twentieth century. But in the study of the postwar history of the USSR, both Russian and Western historians basically have had to begin anew by tapping and analyzing new sources. This, in turn, means confronting the problem of the partial declassification of entire collections of documents.

Even serious authors who have written about the postwar period have often fallen into a methodological trap. Interpreting the communist past as an "inferior present" and often relying on a liberal Western model of development, they have been inclined to examine the epoch of Khrushchev and Brezhnev in the context of a certain readiness (or lack of readiness) of society and the state for reform. The fact that such reforms each time led to a dead end has been evaluated as exclusively the fault of communist rulers who suffered either from doctrinal blindness or from bureaucratic idiocy. In essence, some interpretations of the thaw and stagnation that were widespread in the late 1980s and early 1990s oversimplified the real interrelationships between the people and the state in authoritarian political systems.

The response to such journalistic simplifications was the move of serious historians into the sphere of "positive empiricism" at the beginning of the 1990s.[4] The analysis of completely new factual material has resulted in the appearance of a number of professional investigations into the history of the state and society in the USSR. Both political and social historians have examined such themes as the specific characteristics of liberal communism as a system of politics, ideology, and power; the mechanisms for policy-making and for processing significant social-political information in administrative structures; the dynamic of interaction between rulers and the ruled; changes in mass psychology and in elite consciousness; and the history of intellectual dissidence.[5]

Simultaneously, the contours of new problems have emerged. These are primarily concerned with the crisis in state-society relations engendered by the stress of accelerated modernization, as well as by the consequences of the Stalinist Great Terror and World War II. Such problems, however, have not yet received serious analysis. In the majority of cases, the study of events and processes that communist oligarchs had deliberately pushed to the periphery of official history demands long and laborious archival research. There were also other problems besides these obvious professional difficulties, not as overt perhaps, but more substantial. Amid the tumultuous political storms of the last decade, it has been quite hard for researchers to get excited over histories of events that seem to lack political or moral value in the current context. In many cases, the line between antisocialist and antisocial was so blurred that mass disorders as a form of social protest appeared insufficiently respectable. Consequently, they simply dropped out of the mainstream of historical rethinking. It is not surprising that Russian researchers have much more enthusiastically devoted their works to organized and politically unambiguous forms of resistance to communist power: the anti-Soviet mutinies during the Civil War period and the transition to the New Economic Policy,[6] the peasant riots during collectivization,[7] and events such as the mutiny on the antisubmarine carrier *Storozhevoi* (The Guard) in 1975.[8]

Yet, although Russian historians have taken it upon themselves to write professionally about oppositionist attitudes among the peoples of the USSR, some have made completely unforgivable mistakes. For example, having come across in the documents a mention of the large-scale mass riots in Murom in 1961, one of the authors of the book *Vlast' i Oppozitsiia: Rossiiskii politicheskii protsess XX stoletiia* [The State and Opposition: The Russian Political Process in the Twentieth Century] for some reason decided that the reference was to "the shootings by Soviet authorities of the participants in the uprising of July 10, 1918, in defense of the Constituent Assembly."[9] Such conjectures prove once more that in the study of the postwar USSR, the deficiency in the knowledge of elementary facts is at times even greater than the deficiency of new theoretical conceptions.

The noted exception is the uprising at Novocherkassk in 1962, which has been a popular subject of research since the end of the 1980s.[10] The first conceptualization of these events was the official Communist Party version formulated at the time of the unrest in the speech of Presidium* member F.R. Kozlov** that was transmitted over Novocherkassk radio on June 3, 1962,

---

*The Political Bureau of the Central Committee, or Politburo, was known as the Presidium from 1952 to 1966. This was the foremost policy-making body of the Soviet Union.—E.M.

** Frol Romanovich Kozlov (1908–1965) until 1963 was regarded by Khrushchev as his likely successor. In 1960 he became secretary for cadres in the Central Committee Secretariat and was effectively number two to Khrushchev until Koslov suffered a debilitating stroke in April 1963.—E.M.

as well as in the indictments and sentences presented at the two trials of participants in the disorders. This simplistic and unconvincing version blamed hooligans and criminal elements, secret and overt anti-Soviet forces, drunks and marginalized persons, who, using provocations, threats, and force, led astray a crowd of naive workers lacking in political consciousness. But the uprising at Novocherkassk, as well as other popular riots similar in scale and direction, did not end up in the history books. The leaders were convinced, and not without reason, that the less the populace knew about events such as Novocherkassk, the longer the great Soviet myth about the "inviolable unity of party and people" could serve the needs of the regime.

It was only in the late 1980s that the first documentary research and collections of documents about Novocherkassk began to appear in Russia. The publication of R.G. Pikhoia, N.A. Krivova, S.V. Popov, and N.Ia. Emelianenko, "Novocherkasskaia tragediia, 1962" (The Tragedy of Novocherkassk 1962) made a serious contribution.[11] The authors of this professional work rightfully rejected the thirteen-year-old official version of the 1962 events, calling it "biased, but useful for the CPSU (Communist Party of the Soviet Union)."[12] But in their evaluation of the rioters' behavior at Novocherkassk, these authors reveal their own biases. In reality, the Novocherkassk events represented a smorgasbord of reasons, motives, programs, and models of behavior. Therefore a one-sided interpretation is not appropriate: neither the Communist version of events, which depicts hooligans and criminal elements who fooled the "unconscious" masses into following them, nor the liberal version of a peaceful demonstration of agitated workers who were not inclined to violence is satisfactory.[13]

The short work of journalist I. Mardar, *Khronika neob"iavlennogo ubiistva* (Chronicle of an Undeclared Murder), which is based primarily on materials of the USSR chief military procurator and on the recollections of participants in the events, appears to be less ideological and more objective. Although written without features mandatory in the works of professional historians (there are no footnotes or endnotes citing sources), this book represents one of the first reconstructions of events, day by day and hour by hour. However, Mardar, an investigative journalist at the end of the 1980s and the beginning of the 1990s, could not use a number of important sources that were at the time inaccessible. It is possible, therefore, that in the work there are many small factual errors, though the correction of these in principle would not substantially alter the truth of the author's portrait of the Novocherkassk events. The book's objectivity did not prevent Mardar from both expressing empathy for the victims of tyranny and displaying understanding for those rank-and-file participants who simply by the will of fate (military service, an oath of loyalty) became the executors of the evil will of authorities. Historians know far less about the many other mass riots, disorders, and violent ethnic conflicts of the period from the 1950s to the 1980s than they do about Novocherkassk. There have been several documentary publications about the political riots in 1956 in Tbilisi;[14] various scholarly and memoir-style works, largely inspired by the books of Alexander Solzhenitsyn, about mass uprisings of prisoners in the Gulag;[15] and articles on the uprising of young workers in Temirtau in 1959.[16] But this is basically all that exists in contemporary Russian historiography about the history of conflict between the people and the state during the post-Stalinist years.

Until now, historians have simply not written about or described the majority of events. These include the numerous uprisings in the Virgin Lands during the 1950s and 1960s (with the exception of Temirtau), soldiers' mutinies, and the violent ethnic conflicts in the areas where the "punished peoples"* had been exiled as well as in the areas to which they returned after the death of Stalin. Historians have also not examined the riots of religious believers who protested the closing of monasteries and cathedrals, hooligan uprisings in the 1950s and 1960s, and such predecessors to Novocherkassk as the Krasnodar disorders of 1961, the Murom "funeral" uprising, and the riots in Aleksandrov and Biisk. There is barely even a mention in the histori cal literature of the majority of the disorders of the late Khrushchev period, such as the pro-Stalinist riots in Sumgait and the riots in Krivoi Rog, or of the early Brezhnev period. For the purpose of comparison and contrast, it is possible to draw upon a small number of works that have appeared on various popular mutinies of the twentieth century, such as, for example, the 1912 riots in the Lena gold fields,[17] the mass protests over high prices during World War I,[18] or the uprising of Ivanovo textile workers during the fall of 1941.[19]

The current state of the historiography requires, therefore, the simultaneous resolution of two groups of research problems. It is necessary to combine the labor-intensive factual reconstruction of events, based on archival investigations, with elaboration of the theoretical and methodological problems involved in studying state-society conflict in the context of the sociopolitical history of the postwar period.

The rebellious activity of the Soviet population, which proceeded within the strict boundaries of a regime sufficiently stable and viable at that time, is interpreted in this book as part of a crisis of modernization. It represents the

---

*The "punished peoples" included nationalities whose loyalty was questioned by Stalin. During World War II Stalin ordered the deportation of national groups accused of collaboration with the Germans, including the Ingush, Chechens, Kalmyks, Balkars, and Crimean Tatars.—E.M.

agony of traditional Russian society as well as the attempt of the state and the populace to adapt to post-Stalinist society. The analysis of conflict between the people and the regime that arose in this context relies on a so-called "broad" understanding of conflict proposed by Ralf Dahrendorf,[20] who considered conflict to be any relation between individuals or groups in which there are incompatible goals. In light of this definition, this monograph examines conflict not only as the *actions* of sides that have incompatible goals, but above all as a definite *social condition*,[21] which grows into open and active confrontation or resistance.

In accordance with the work of Lewis Coser,[22] the monograph takes as a basic premise the fact that conflict exerts a positive influence on society. This occurs not only in elastic, democratic systems, but also in rigid, authoritarian ones. It is clear that authoritarian regimes and dictatorships in situations of conflict do not seek a constructive compromise. Rather, they seek to destroy the opponent, if the conflict is between the state and some social group. Or, they suppress both sides of an intergroup conflict, because independence is considered to be a violation of the regime's prerogative. Yet, paradoxically, in nondemocratic social systems that lack legal channels for the expression of dissatisfaction and for the defense of group interests, which have ineffective reciprocal ties with the people due to bureaucratic interference, it is precisely mass unrest, spontaneous mutinies, and riots that realize this reciprocal connection. They bypass the bureaucratic machine and give the political bosses a direct and harsh signal about the presence of conflict. Even when there are severe punishments for violations of law and the social order, the state is nonetheless forced to seek explanations and to make changes in policy. In the end, the state must find a more or less acceptable balance of interests.

The global antagonism between communism and capitalism during the Cold War forced Soviet communists and Western leftists, as well as their liberal opponents, basically to ignore the specific functions of uprisings and riots and interpret such actions as a direct attack on the Soviet system. The communists connected mass disorders with the "lack of consciousness among the people," the influence of "bourgeois remnants," and so on. Western leftists (Trotskyists, in particular) saw them as acts of the working people against a degenerate regime, while anticommunists and liberals were inclined to examine such phenomena as essentially a struggle for democratic values. Whether the ideological protagonists evaluated these events positively or negatively is not significant, for the majority of them did not doubt that popular uprisings during the Khrushchev and Brezhnev eras were antisystem in nature.

The historical and philosophical conceptions worked out by A.S. Akhiezer[23] and A.V. Obolonskii during the 1970s and 1980s and published at the beginning of the 1990s represent a different view of the social-political and social-psychological symbiosis between the people and the state at various stages in the development of Russian society. These conceptualizations present a unique Russian version of the theory of modernization, laid out on the basis of Albert Toynbee's idea of the cyclical development of civilizations. Obolonskii delineated systemcentric and personcentric genotypes in Russian cultural-ethical and social-psychological tradition. Having defined "systemcentrism" as the dominant genotype, he concluded:

> The basis of the worldview for the 'system-centric genotype' is the traditional evaluation of stability within the System as the highest value. This leads to an immaturity of individualistic consciousness and a tendency toward equating individual interests with the interests of the social whole—families, tribes, communes or even broader formations. The internal equilibrium for members of such a collective is achieved only through full harmony with the System, which, in its own order, preserves stability only due to the proper behavior of its members.[24]

In the opinion of Obolonskii, power in a society with such a worldview:

> by no means guarantees against mutinies and similar social cataclysms. History knows many bloody uprisings in traditional societies. But these movements are directed not against the System as such, but against individual persons and groupings, who have abused, in the opinion of the masses, their own privileged position and by this have threatened the System's stability. It is not coincidental that popular uprisings in traditional societies, as a rule, occur under the flag of the "good tsar," and when the dust of the battle has settled, the basic bastions of the system turn out not only to be unharmed, but at times become even stronger.[25]

Such a view of the ideology of popular mutinies and uprisings is not original. The English historian E.P. Thompson, for example, showed that the English crowd even at the end of the eighteenth and the beginning of the nineteenth century continued to act in accordance with an innate myth of plebeian culture—faith in the "good king."[26] Obolonskii's thesis about the systemic loyalty of participants in mass unrest could also be extended to many mass uprisings of modern times. Spontaneous leaders of the disorders of the 1950s and 1960s usually did not attack the foundations of the communist system. Their actions were directed either against "bad officials" in the provinces or the "bad Khrushchev" at the very top.

It is extremely rare to find in the unclear and barely comprehensible statements of agitated participants in disorders any counterposing of the "bad system" (communist) to the "good system" (capitalist). If, in the confusion of the events, any persons actually uttered such sacrilegious declarations, then arrested participants in the disorders were quick to dissociate themselves from them, preferring instead to confess to purely criminal transgressions. Even in Novocherkassk, the demonstrators held aloft portraits of Lenin, clearly demonstrating their ideological loyalty and "faith in the cause of communism."

In truth, the diversity of conflicts cannot be encompassed in a single classification schema, no matter how detailed. Nonetheless, it is obvious that any theory of conflict is forced to operate "with something resembling the 'two-class model' " (Darendorf). But in each concrete case, the opposing sides in the conflict must be clearly defined. In practice, this simple question turns out to be far more complex than it appears at first glance. When tension moves from a latent or hidden state to the form of open and sharp opposition, this inevitably leads to government intervention, even in the most ordinary, everyday conflict. The state's monopoly on violence has been violated and there is a threat to the social order. Individuals and social groups in authoritarian systems are thus caught in a perpetually spinning vicious circle: Legal paths for expressing their dissatisfaction are closed, and illegal ones are naturally criminalized. It is not surprising, therefore, that there are many examples of intergroup conflicts turning into acts of insubordination toward local authorities. In the eyes of participants in the confrontations, such officials have lost their right to be the arbiters of the people's fates. In this context, even a group fight that ends in a confrontation with the police or in attempts to liberate detained hooligans could be examined as part of the more general conflict between the people and the state.

The range of spontaneous violent actions was very wide, from commonplace group fights, marketplace riots, and attacks on police departments to mass ethnic pogroms and urban uprisings with unclear (possibly anti-Soviet) political demands. It is necessary to emphasize that conflict between the state and the people cannot be limited to purely mass disorders as defined in Soviet criminal law. If one follows only the Criminal Code and categorizes events according to Article 79 of the Criminal Code of the Russian Soviet Federated Socialist Republic (RSFSR) or Article 14 of the Law "On Criminal Responsibility for State Crimes," then numerous actions are lost to analysis that were closely connected with mass uprisings in terms of motives, forms of expression, and the particular behavior of participants. Therefore, this monograph analyzes many other forms of conflict, regardless of whether any article qualified these actions as such in Soviet jurisprudence. It also examines forms of group behavior that the Criminal Code in general did not recognize, such as strikes.

In Soviet society the majority of social groups were atomized and, as a result of the monopoly of the CPSU on power, did not have any legal outlets for organized expression and defense of their own special interests. Therefore, I am compelled to use the very vague but more encompassing term "people" (or populace) instead of group or class. For the same reasons, I prefer to use the term "state" or "state power" rather than "government" to define the other side of the conflict. The strict use of the term government would impart to many spontaneous riots and disturbances a more purposeful and conscious character then they in reality had.

For Soviet society, which was organized more primitively, or in any case, differently than Western civil society, the antonym "people–state" conveys the specific features of these conflicts more accurately than the terms accepted in Western sociology, such as "group-society" and "group-government." In other words, the vocabulary for describing conflicts must not contradict the historical and cultural uniqueness of one or another social milieu. Terminology must be appropriate for the traditions and the language in which the representatives of the given social milieu describe their actions and behavior. Imposing on one society concepts and categories worked out to describe another society not only substantially distorts the general picture, but weakens analysis of these events and their development.

For the Soviet population, state power began with the first policeman one met and ended with the general secretary of the CPSU Central Committee. The same policeman in situations of conflict was often perceived, especially by marginal layers of the population, not as the representative of the government, and thereby subordinate to its laws, but as a force acting independently against the people, accountable to justice only at the very top. But again, unlike his or her Western counterpart, no Soviet citizen would have thought to seek justice in a court. He would have been more likely to trust the "highest arbitrator" in Moscow than a people's court in his own district or city.

The criteria for classifying conflictive situations, and consequently for the choice of research topics, were in the first place the mass scale and duration of the confrontations; second, the level of violence and brutality displayed by participants, including the use of firearms by authorities or participants; and third, the forms of resistance to state power—attacks on policemen, KGB personnel, *druzhinniki*,* and military personnel, attacks on police departments or stations,

---

*Established in March 1959, *druzhinniki* were auxiliary civilian police volunteers enrolled in so-called People's Squads. Their purpose was to "maintain public order" by patrolling streets and public places, and they were to be composed of outstanding workers, employees, collective farmers, students, and pensioners. In 1964, there were over 6 million citizens enrolled as *druzhinniki*. The term will be translated as civilian police volunteers or People's Squads.—E.M.

destruction of KGB or police documents, attempts to free prisoners from custody, and attacks on party committee offices and state institutions causing material damage.

The sources for studying conflict between the people and the state during the period of liberal communism are as extensive as they are little known. This is explained as much by the secretive character of events in the Soviet era as by the incomplete declassification in the 1990s of documents illuminating these events. From the beginning of the 1950s to the beginning of the 1980s, the Soviet periodical press did not publish any interesting or useful information. The only exceptions are short notices about the trials of participants in mass disturbances, which were published sometimes in local newspapers or more rarely in the central press. The majority of these propagandistic and completely uninformative materials appeared in newspapers at the beginning of the 1960s, when the Khrushchev leadership was attempting to use a new tactic in its struggle with state crimes—publicly intimidating the population by publishing harsh sentences. This method of deterrence turned out to be ineffective and was soon rejected. The veil of secrecy was again lowered over mass disorders.

The first professional publication of documents about mass unrest under Khrushchev and Brezhnev began to appear in Russian scientific periodicals in the first half of the 1990s. A particularly significant publication appeared in the journal *Istochnik* (Source): "Spravka o massovykh besporiadkakh, imevshikh mesto v strane c 1957 g," (Information on Mass Disturbances in the Country since 1957), which had been prepared in March 1988 by the KGB chairman, Viktor Chebrikov, for the CPSU general secretary, Mikhail Gorbachev.[27] The journal was limited to printing only the "bare" text of the document, that is, without any commentary or notes. However, the systematized KGB information is significant in and of itself. It is particularly important that this brief listing (time, place, number of participants) contains information about several events of the Khrushchev period about which there is little or no material in other sources, including, for example, the mass disorders in Podolsk in 1957 and Bronnitsy in 1964, located in the greater Moscow region, and in the city of Breslan in the North Ossetian Autonomous Soviet Socialist Republic (ASSR). Sometimes the list is the single source of reliable information about the various uprisings of the Brezhnev period that are discussed in the last chapter of the monograph.

At the same time, not all of the known cases of mass disturbances during the period 1957 to 1987 are included in this KGB document, which is partly due to the formal criteria for inclusion in the list. As a rule, the selection includes events with no less than three hundred participants and probably only those in which the actions of instigators and organizers were classified as mass disturbances or riots according to the Criminal Code of the RSFSR and of other union republics. A number of important events were simply left out by the compilers of the document, including, in particular, the Chechen pogrom in Grozny and the uprising of young workers in Temirtau, Kazakh Soviet Socialist Republic (SSR), in 1958.

In the first half of the 1990s, document collections appeared that were devoted to significant individual episodes of mass unrest. The work of R.G. Pikhoia, N.A. Krivova, S.V. Popov, and N.Ia. Emelianenko on events in Novocherkassk cited above included KGB memoranda sent to the Central Committee; the text of the speech by F.R. Kozlov on June 3, 1962; the indictment for case No. 22 (the first trial of participants in the unrest); several directives of the Presidium, of the USSR Council of Ministers, and of the KGB about measures taken in connection with the Novocherkassk events; and KGB materials as well as notes of the Central Committee Department of Propaganda and Agitation about the first trial, which took place on August 20, 1962.[28] V. Lebedev also published a significant work providing KGB information about the reactions of the population to the increase in food prices in 1962, which illuminated the popular attitudes informing the Novocherkassk riots.[29]

In 1995, M. Zezina published an interesting selection of documents on the riots in Tbilisi in 1956, including a secret letter from a correspondent of the newspaper *Trud* (Labor) to its chief editor; the "Appeal of the Georgian Central Committee and the Central Committee of the Komsomol to Communists, Komsomol members, Workers and Employees, and to All Laborers of Tbilisi"; and the order of the head of the Tbilisi garrison from March 9, 1956.[30] From the small number of memoir sources, particularly noteworthy are the recollections of P. Siuda, a participant in the Novocherkassk events,[31] and the testimony of F. Baazova, an eyewitness to the political riots in Tbilisi in 1956. Baazova's account first appeared in print abroad in 1978 and was reprinted in Russia in 1992.[32]

On the whole, however, the published sources fail to give a full and detailed picture of popular unrest during the period of liberal communism, nor do they facilitate even a chronological reconstruction of the rebellious activism of the Soviet population. Therefore, 90 percent of the sources used for this book are recently declassified archival documents, the majority of which are for the first time being introduced into scholarly circulation.

Party documents that reflect the reaction of the top leadership to popular riots and uprisings are particularly significant. But it must be noted that examination of such problems in the Central Committee was completely top secret. Only once did the issue of mass disorders reach the level of a Central

Committee plenum—in September 1958, when a resolution was prepared about the riots in Grozny. But even then the matter was limited to a short report during a session of party secretaries from the republican, district, and regional levels of the CPSU that took place after the actual Central Committee plenum.[33] A more frequently used source is informational documents received by the Central Committee from local party organs, ministries, and departments, as well as concrete, finely chiseled resolutions of party-state organs on various difficult issues. Also important is the collection of materials declassified in connection with the preparations for the trial of the CPSU in 1993, which are presently located in the Russian State Archive of Modern History (RGANI).

The KGB, the USSR Ministry of Internal Affairs (MVD), and the USSR Procuracy* regularly sent materials to the Central Committee. Only part of the materials received by the Central Committee from the KGB during the period from 1953 to the beginning of the 1980s are deposited in RGANI. Party archivists habitually extracted documents about the most important cases from the files of the General Department of the Central Committee and deposited them in the Politburo Archive (now the Presidential Archive of the Russian Federation). The materials of this archive for the years 1953 to 1985 are only very slowly being transferred to government storage. In a number of cases, the KGB and the Procuracy jointly prepared analytical documents on mass uprisings or related themes (statistics on crime and the prosecution of political crimes, the mood of the population, the struggle with dissidents, and so on). These materials are found in the files of the USSR procurator-general** in the State Archive of the Russian Federation (GARF).

Informational gaps in party and KGB documents have been filled by memoranda and special reports of the Ministry of Internal Affairs that were sent to the Central Committee and personally to Khrushchev. There is a full collection in GARF of such documents for the period 1954 to 1960. It is possible to assert with confidence that everything the MVD communicated at this time to higher party levels about mass uprisings and unrest is known. Unfortunately, though, the documents from the period after 1960 have not yet been transferred to state archives from the Russian Federation Ministry of Internal Affairs, and since the majority have not been declassified, they

*The Procuracy was part of the Soviet legal apparatus. There is no close equivalent to this agency in Western legal systems, and I will use the term Procuracy (procurator) rather than translate it. Its two main functions were "supervising" the execution of the law within Soviet institutions as well as investigating and prosecuting crimes.—E.M.
**The top position in the Procuracy was the procurator-general, who supervised the regulatory and investigative powers of the agency.—E.M.

are practically inaccessible to the average researcher. The most important collection of documents is the files of the Procuracy's Department of Surveillance over Investigations in the Organs of State Security. These materials, the majority of which have been declassified and are preserved in GARF, encompass practically the entire period of this study, from 1953 to the beginning of the 1980s. In order to evaluate the fullness, the reliability, and the representative nature of these sources, it is necessary to keep in mind the following: Participation in mass disorders was considered a state crime, as defined by Article 16 of the USSR Law "On Criminal Responsibility for State Crimes" and by Article 79 of the RSFSR Criminal Code (there were analogous articles in the criminal codes of other union republics). Evidence of mass unrest included, in particular, actions such as pogroms, vandalism, and arson.

Some individual participants in such disorders were also tried on charges of "anti-Soviet agitation and propaganda" (Article 58 and then Article 70 of the RSFSR Criminal Code, 1960 edition; analogous articles of the union republic criminal codes), as well as for hooliganism (Article 206 of the RSFSR and union republic criminal codes). In the case of the latter, information about those convicted of hooliganism would not have ended up in the Procuracy's Department of Surveillance over Investigations in the Organs of State Security. Usually these were cases of group fights that did not involve confrontations with authorities, pogroms, and the like, or actions during an urban uprising or riot that were defined as hooliganism (the rest were prosecuted under Article 79 of the RSFSR Criminal Code and analogous articles in the criminal codes of other union republics). Qualifying the actions of participants in disorders according to Articles 70 and 79 signified that the KGB would conduct the preliminary inquest and the criminal investigation. The Department of Surveillance over Investigations in Organs of State Security and corresponding procuracy departments in the union republics would supervise the investigation and examine the appeals and petitions for pardon sent both from defendants and from their relatives.

Beginning in the early 1960s, local public procurators had to inform the Procuracy about all matters falling under their jurisdiction. Ideally, special communications were to be sent to the procurator-general immediately after events occurred and would serve as the basis for opening the surveillance process. Comparison of surveillance procedures involving state crimes with other sources shows that most of the major uprisings of the 1960s in which participants were accused of mass disorders, banditry, or anti-Soviet agitation are represented in the files of the Procuracy.

The situation is somewhat worse regarding documentation for events in the second half of the 1950s. Judging by the Procuracy files, it was standard practice at this time for local procurators to send reports on public disorders to the office of the procurator-general. But the local procurators often disregarded this rule, and the Department of Surveillance itself was at this time overburdened with other matters, particularly the rehabilitation of victims of Stalinist repressions. As a result, for example, the original surveillance procedures for the cases of participants in the Tbilisi riots in 1956, the Chechen pogrom in Grozny in 1958, and the protests against the closing of monasteries and churches at the end of the 1950s could not be located. Thus, the necessary information for these cases was found either in the materials of the Ministry of Internal Affairs or in the files of the Council on Matters of the Russian Orthodox Church under the USSR Council of Ministers.

On the whole, the research I have undertaken in the former archive of the Central Committee's General Department (now the RGANI) and in GARF (collections of the MVD, Procuracy, and the Council on Religious Issues under the Council of Ministers) has produced an extensive collection of documents. With the addition of documents and memoirs published in the last decade, this body of materials constitutes a representative compilation of reliable sources on the history of social and ethnic conflicts and urban unrest within the territory of the USSR during the Khrushchev and Brezhnev eras.

PART I

Social Conflict in the USSR After the Death of Stalin, 1953–1960

Chapter 1

Mastering New Territories in Kazakhstan and Siberia: The Crisis of Modernization and the Heritage of the Gulag in the 1950s

The "Virgin Lands Syndrome"

During the first half of the 1950s, the Khrushchev leadership experienced significant problems supplying food to cities, particularly bread, which was the most important food item for the Soviet people. Therefore, the regime decided to expand agricultural production by developing virgin, previously uncultivated lands in Kazakhstan* (the Altai Krai**). Simultaneously it continued an ambitious program of industrial construction in scarcely populated and undeveloped regions of the country, including but not limited to Siberia, a process that had begun earlier under Stalin. These virgin land regions and the new industrial construction sites subsequently became zones of conflict.

---

*Originally drafted as a temporary measure, the campaign to develop unused or underused land in Kazakhstan began in 1954, and within three years 36 million hectares of additional land was being used to grow grain. In 1956, the Virgin Lands initiative contributed to an unprecedented wheat harvest, though thereafter it encountered serious problems.—E.M.

**Large republics in the Soviet Union, such as Russia, Ukraine, and Kazakhstan were divided into regional units known as oblasts (regions) or krais (territories). These terms will not be translated.—E.M.

Rapid urbanization (at the end of the 1950s and the beginning of the 1960s, the urban population for the first time in Soviet history exceeded the number of rural inhabitants), and the mass migration of young people, who were cut off from familiar surroundings and the influence of customary family and local networks, created a volatile environment fraught with social tension. Many young people arrived at the new construction sites and the Virgin Lands from the countryside and from small towns, where social controls over individual behavior were traditionally strong.* Some of the young people came under the auspices of the Komsomol (League of Communist Youth). Filled with enthusiasm, they hardly realized the monumental problems and trials of everyday life that awaited them: an unsettled existence, which often began in a lonely and virtually empty place; tent settlements, which looked romantic only in the propaganda publications of newspapers and in lofty Soviet films about the new industrial cities; interruptions in the supply of food, shortages of drinking water, and a gender imbalance (more males than females among the recruits). In truth, the promised romance of taming the Virgin Lands and constructing new cities differed sharply from the reality of life in these undeveloped regions.

These workers in the Virgin Lands and on the new construction sites suffered marginalization, but nonetheless remained relatively resilient against various criminal influences. Instead, the young people tended to come under the control of party, trade union, and Komsomol organizations. However, if they came to see the repeated, long-term disruptions not as objective difficulties connected with new construction projects but rather as subjective abuses of bosses and bureaucrats, these youth groups could turn into an aggressive and unruly crowd, determined to restore social justice with the help of criminal and half-criminal collective actions.

Dissatisfaction with the situation could be expressed both through internal conflict, which poisoned the functioning of the collective, as well as through conflict among groups. In a number of cases, the attempts of authorities to restore order in the course of such intergroup confrontations brought angry attacks upon representatives of the state, especially the police. Even less manageable were temporary collectives formed in the Virgin Lands or at the new industrial construction sites by individuals mobilized through military enlistment offices, factories and plants (usually to help with the harvest), teams of military personnel used for agricultural and construction projects, and also groups of adult workers recruited for labor in undeveloped

---

*In the first year alone of the Virgin Lands campaign, 300,000 young volunteers went to Northern Kazakhstan, the Altai, and southern Siberia. Migration of entire families was also encouraged.—E.M.

regions. Among these were people with a criminal past or simply people who had led unsettled lives.

Thus, an enormous flood of people torn from their customary social milieu poured into an unstable social environment characterized by weakened collective ties and relationships, as well as by ineffective regulations over individual and group behavior. Consequently, the weak forms of social regulation and administrative control were often replaced by spontaneously organized groups that defended their members from the aggressive actions of strangers. In return, these groups demanded the subordination of the weak to the strong, and the adherence of all to the principle of "mutual or collective responsibility" [krugovaia poruka].* These spontaneously arising collectives provided an alternative form of self-regulation, for they were only weakly controlled by official institutions and propaganda.

In principle, a smart boss or party leader could cope with dissatisfaction and outbursts of mass aggressiveness by displaying concern over the organization of labor and supply as well as over entertainment opportunities. It was also critical to control the supply of alcohol to the construction site. But the heightened sensitivity of temporary collectives to any outside influences and irritants kept them continually on the threshold of spontaneous social protest and mass disorder.

The legacy of the Stalinist regime exacerbated the volatile social situation in the Virgin Lands and in the regions of new construction. Kazakhstan and Siberia, which before 1917 had been places of exile and punishment, continued to serve this purpose under Stalin and became regions with a vast concentration of forced labor camps. Many prisoners, both political and criminal, remained in these areas after their release, either to serve out their term of exile or to live permanently in places now familiar to them. Concentrated among the former prisoners in these regions were numerous special settlers: former kulaks,** whose legal rights had only been partially restored in 1946; family members of Ukrainian and Lithuanian nationalists; people who had worked for the Germans during their occupation of Soviet territory in World War II and "members of families of active German collaborators"; people exiled "for habitual evasion of work in agriculture and antisocial, parasitic

---

*Krugovaia poruka was a principle dating back to medieval Russia. It was customary for peasant communes to be collectively responsible for labor and money obligations owed to the state or to a landowner, even if some members had to make up for those who defaulted or who could not work.—E.M.
**By definition, kulaks were those peasants who used hired labor and therefore were capitalist exploiters. But this opprobrious term came to be applied to anyone who was a prosperous farmer or who opposed collectivization. Up to 5 million kulaks were shot, exiled, or sent to forced labor camps during the Stalinist collectivization drive.—E.M.

ways of life"; participants in religious sects; and the "punished peoples" deported from the Crimea and the Caucasus before and during World War II. At the end of the 1940s, according to the records of the Ministry of Internal Affairs, there were 2,307,410 exiles and special settlers (including their family members).[1]

The fever for new construction in the 1950s and the Virgin Lands campaign struck blow after blow to the customary way of life of the local population and continually created tension between the locals and the new arrivals, that is, between "Us" and "Them." In these conditions, any individual conflict could by means of "mutual responsibility" develop into mass riots or fights.

The "Police" Crisis in the Virgin Lands and the New Construction Projects

In the new construction areas and the Virgin Lands, the volatile situation and the criminalization of group behavior, such as mass hooliganism, gang fights, and riots, were aggravated even more by the fact that the Ministry of Internal Affairs clearly lacked sufficient personnel to secure social order and fulfill routine police functions in the new regions. The internal operative forces under the command of the MVD, whose task was to suppress uprisings among the populace, decreased in size by more than three times from 1953 to 1956. Thus, during the initial period of developing the Virgin Lands and widespread industrial construction, especially from 1954 to 1959 and above all in Kazakhstan, in the Southern Urals, and in Siberia, there were in general no operative MVD forces equal to those in the majority of cities in central Russia. Ironically, central authorities did not view riots in the regions of the Virgin Lands and the new construction projects as a serious danger. Poor communication, as well as geographical remoteness and isolation, prevented unrest from spreading, even in Kazakhstan itself. The majority of local intragroup conflicts ended even before any serious intervention by the police— right after the "first blood." Under certain conditions, however, the absence of police forces in the areas of risk facilitated the swift transformation of local conflicts into mass riots, bloody uprisings, looting, and so on. Failure to suppress the flaring conflict at the moment of its inception meant that authorities often had to deal with acute forms of mass opposition. Such disturbances could in turn provoke antigovernment slogans, which constituted an especially serious state crime.

From this boiling cauldron of passionate strife and tension, spontaneous forms of self-organization headed by home-grown, alternative leaders emerged. Through such channels the people demonstrated to the state their dissatisfaction and sometimes formulated complaints. The more destructive these events were, the more quickly the signal of reciprocal ties reached the authorities. It would then force them to take measures and "correct the situation," though usually in combination with harsh repression of the instigators of the riots.

The most common form of resolving intergroup conflict was the collective or group fight. In principle, these involved ordinary criminal acts. An important feature of such conflicts, however, was the element of self-organization— group hierarchy, spontaneously promoted leaders, "mutual responsibility," and opposition to outsiders. There was as well a heightened tendency toward violent behavior, which reflects specific experiences of opposition (against authorities, bosses, parents, society) and the activation of traditional forms of asocial behavior. These elements constituted an obligatory precondition for mass unrest. Those active in the disorders were not simply inclined to violence. Rather, it is as if they somehow knew and remembered how to act in such situations, and felt liberated from strictures that normally limit the aggression of law-abiding citizens. Conflict could weaken social constraints even among loyal citizens. But the instigators of violent behavior, those who rallied the crowd, were people in whom such constraints had already shut down. They typically had already taken part in asocial actions and had thereby fallen from their conventional social milieu.

The First Conflicts in the New Construction Sites After the Death of Stalin

Increasing tensions and quarrels between the new settlers and the local population surfaced almost immediately after the recruitment of young people for the Virgin Lands and new construction projects began. In the spring of 1954 about five hundred Komsomol volunteers from Moscow arrived at the Kaztsik State Farm, which was located in the Shostandinsk district of the Akmolinsk Oblast, Kazakh SSR. On the first day off from work, a fight broke out in the recreational club of the state farm between three local workers and some of the young people from Moscow. Both groups had been drinking. One of the participants in the fight received a fatal knife wound.

The report on these events went directly to the CPSU Central Committee, bypassing the usual channels of the Ministry of Internal Affairs. The Central Committee gave the command to investigate the incident, raising a flurry of bureaucratic activity. The MVD began setting up permanent police subdivisions to maintain order in the areas where newcomers to the Virgin Lands were concentrated. The Chief Directorate of the MVD police force also sent personnel to these same regions.[2]

Nonetheless, the increased expenditure of personnel and resources for stabilizing the region did not always alleviate the tensions or prevent violence. It proved difficult to maintain order during the mass relocation of new settlers and the mobilization of harvest workers along the transportation arteries of the country. Practically every cohort heading eastward carried with it the potential for conflict. Some were essentially drunken hordes riding on the railroad, among whom an individual could easily lose himself along with any sense of personal responsibility and any capacity for self-control.

On August 15, 1954, a freight train arrived at the Kupino Omsk railroad station with automobiles and drivers who were to carry grain to the Altai Krai. The drivers had been drinking throughout the train ride. At Kupino they began to pester the people around them; they belted out obscene songs, and assailed those passing by the train. Next they went to the city gardens, where they picked a fight with local youth. Several people were beaten, and two received serious knife wounds. Afterward they broke into the railway station office and started a brawl, disrupting the work of the station for some time. Four policemen tried to bring order, but met with resistance and began to fire. One of the hooligans was killed and another was wounded. The rest ran away in fright.[3]

After the events of 1954, the Virgin Lands territories enjoyed a certain degree of calm, but it was impossible to organize the harvest using local manpower. Consequently, the demand for seasonal transfers of a significant number of laborers imported from other regions of the USSR, such as students, military personnel, and workers, made harvest work a constant headache for officials at all levels. In the middle of 1955, the Ministry of Internal Affairs by order of the Central Committee took measures to restore order at the Piatigorskii State Farm, Akmolinsk Oblast, Kazakh SSR, which had been disrupted by hooliganism fueled by drinking, truancy, and everyday disorganization.[4] In August 1956, the ministry made a special report before the Central Committee about the investigation and indictment of participants in fights between local inhabitants and harvest workers who had come to Kazakhstan from different regions of the country.[5]

Confrontations on the Railroads

Part of the collective experience of violent actions that later informed large-scale urban uprisings involved rioting and looting in railroad stations, outbreaks of which became more frequent during 1956 to 1958. As a rule, two social groups took part in them—either Soviet army recruits on the way to their permanent posting or workers and students mobilized to harvest crops, primarily cotton, in either Kazakhstan or Uzbekistan.

In July 1956, at the Orenburg station, mass unrest broke out among young workers from Armenia going to harvest grain in the Kustanaisk Oblast. The cause of the disturbances was the fact that there was no food market located in the station. As a result, 1,700 workers wandered off to the city. Some began to behave like hooligans, pestering women and railroad workers and even picking fights with one another. Accompanying the train were high-ranking Armenian party and state leaders, as well as MVD police operatives, but they were unable to stop the spreading conflict. When the police detained one of the hooligans, a large crowd of the Armenian workers surrounded police headquarters and demanded his release. The police showed sound judgment and decided to compromise, freeing the prisoner "in order to prevent further excesses." But the unrest did not stop with this. The contingent of young workers did not leave Orenburg until sixteen hours after the disorders had begun.[6]

Of even greater scale were riots in November-December 1957 involving students from technical and vocational schools who were returning from harvesting cotton at state farms in Uzbekistan and Kazakhstan. The reason for the unrest was the fact that the authorities failed to provide either food or money for the young people on their journey. The hungry crowd during one of the stops stole food from the vendors at the markets around the station and robbed produce kiosks, cafes, and stores.[7] The young people resisted the police and at one of the stations beat up two policemen.

1958: Intensification of the "Virgin Lands Syndrome" and the Temir-Tau Uprising

During 1958, clear signs emerged that the situation in certain regions was becoming explosive. Several of the newly constructed settlements had been practically taken over by hooligans. On June 17, the CPSU Central Committee received a letter addressed to N.S. Khrushchev from the secretary of the party organization of the Kishinev Construction Academy No. 1. The letter reported numerous cases of hooliganistic terror at the construction site, which was located in the Saran settlement in the Karaganda Oblast. This appeal to the highest person in the state virtually guaranteed special attention from all organs of authority, state as well as party. Furthermore, the author of the letter touched the most sensitive chord for the Communist Party hierarchy when he implied that vulgar hooliganism at the construction site had been accompanied by anti-Soviet statements ("they slung mud at different members of the party and the government").

This time the demand to restore order at the new construction site actually had an impact. A commission of the Karaganda regional party committee, along with representatives of the Procuracy and the Main Board of the Police under the Ministry of Internal Affairs, went to the site. Their investigation revealed an unpleasant but nonetheless common picture of social demoralization in the new settlements due to the complete negligence of local officials. The USSR procurator-general, R. Rudenko, reported to the CPSU Central Committee on July 14, 1958, that the construction area had been engulfed by a wave of lawless hooliganism that had gone unpunished.[8] These outbreaks tended to occur on days when wages were paid and when new workers arrived. In Rudenko's opinion, the situation was aggravated by the passivity of police, whose numbers should have been adequate for controlling the situation.[9]

As a result of the commission's investigation, the construction bosses received party reprimands, criminal charges were brought against various participants, and an additional police worker was sent to the site. The alleged "anti-Soviet statements" of the Saran hooligans were either not corroborated or the commission preferred to stifle the matter. But no matter what had occurred in the workers' settlement at Saran, the authorities in both Moscow and Kazakhstan viewed the situation only as an extraordinary incident and not as the manifestation of a dangerous social disease—the criminalization of entire new construction and Virgin Lands social groupings caused by a vacuum of power and the failure of economic leaders to resolve pressing social problems. What Moscow saw as a unique, though indeed scandalous, development was in reality only the first sign of a newly exploding wave of mass hooligan actions and uprisings.

On July 2, 1958, mass fighting broke out in the city of Krivoi Rog in the Ukraine SSR between groups of young workers at an industrial plant and local Komsomol members. The brawling continued for two days. Initially about a hundred people took part in the fight between these rival youth groups. A couple of workers were injured as well as a policeman who had headed a six-man detail that tried to stop the hooligan activities. The next day the fight flared up anew, injuring four more people. The police detained nine of the participants.[10]

At the beginning of September 1958, a report described how the police had averted a major fight in the city of Taiga, Kemerov Oblast. The cause was the same—hostile relations between local youth and newly arrived young construction workers. In all, up to four hundred people on both sides were prepared to take part in the fight. In order to prevent a bloody encounter, the police fired up to sixty warning shots in the air. No one was killed or wounded this time, for the hooligans prudently refrained from fighting the police.[11] After these events, according to the established ritual, representatives of the Kemerov regional party committee and an MVD operative group came to the scene "to conduct the investigation and carry out prophylactic work." [12]

At the end of September 1958, during the harvest of crops in the Komsomol territory of Stalingrad Oblast, a similar conflict developed between new arrivals from Stalingrad and local inhabitants. A group of eighty young people who had just arrived robbed the recreation center of a neighboring state farm. They broke a window, burst into the premises, and began to beat up those who were inside the club. The rampaging youth injured eight people, two seriously.[13]

In October 1958, a conflict between two groups of young people who had arrived in the area to harvest crops ended in murder. The events began with a fight between two young men over a girl. The aggrieved youth gathered twelve people and proceeded to hold court and inflict punishment. During the night of October 16, local students from a mechanical school approached the barracks in which the workers of the Barnaul Factory lived and set it on fire. As the workers ran out from the burning barracks, the hooligans beat them mercilessly with sticks. One worker was killed, and three received serious injuries.[14]

The intervention of authorities in these mass disturbances and conflicts in 1958 was distinguished by an important feature. The police increasingly applied firearms to suppress social conflict.[15] Yet, it was not normal policy for police to use firearms against participants in group conflicts, which were generally commonplace though expanding in scale. Rather, it reflected the growing aggression of informal youth gangs. The threat of force was no longer enough to stop hooligans, for any fear of authority was overcome by a readiness to resist. Participants in these conflicts tended to move from passive resistance against authorities to attacks on police, who increasingly turned up ready to fire.

In 1959 the Virgin Lands again came into the spotlight, owing to increasing cases of gang rapes and fights in a number of regions in the Kazakh SSR.[16] Matters were significantly worse, however, than MVD leaders realized. The tensions in various Virgin Lands regions reached a crescendo, as mass dissatisfaction no longer was limited to fights and ordinary hooliganism. The distinguishing feature of conflicts in the Virgin Lands and the new construction sites during 1954 to 1958 had been the fact that "the people were silent" or even supported the efforts of authorities to restore order. Hooligan gangs and spontaneously arising half-criminal associations were resisted not only by the state but by the people as well. Conflicts in these regions usually broke out between locals and newcomers, or between different groups of workers at the new construction sites. The populace viewed the police as their defender, resisting the harmful invasion of the outsiders. Even hooligan gangs for a long time showed relative loyalty to authorities, whom they attacked mostly as an annoying obstacle blocking the path of their spontaneous aggression.

The situation would be somewhat different in Temirtau, the culmination of the new construction site riots. In some respects, the Temirtau events of 1959 differed from all of the cases discussed above, although the basic scenario, the means and methods of crowd action, and the capacity for self-organization were the same. Each separate episode of mass rioting in Temirtau, as well as the sequence of events, had an analogy in the conflicts of the preceding years, and from this point of view does not represent anything new and original. But in these disorders, local bosses became the object of direct aggression. Moreover, it was not simply an individual group, but the population of the entire settlement that was involved in the violence.

Prehistory of the Uprising in Temirtau

As background, between May and July 1959, a large number of young people from different regions of the USSR, most between the ages of seventeen and twenty, arrived at the construction site of the Karaganda Metal Works. But the factory managers were not ready for this mass influx of workers in the so-called "tent settlement" (palatochnyi gorodok). Two thousand of the new arrivals were quartered in communal tents, including workers who had families. Many tents were torn and leaked in rainy weather. Elementary amenities were lacking—chairs, dining tables, tables for personal items. There was not even enough water for drinking, to say nothing of bathing. Sometimes the inhabitants of the tent settlement had to go three to five days without being able to bathe themselves. The young workers washed their underclothes near the barrel that held drinking water, but there was no place to dry them, so people often had to wear wet underwear. Bed linen at times went unchanged for twenty days. The lighting worked poorly, there was no radio, and the newspapers came irregularly. In some cases people were supplied with rotten meat, spoiled produce, and food crawling with worms. The work front was simply not prepared for the arrival of the young people. Generally speaking, many did not go to work for two to three weeks, and consequently their wages were lower than the minimum needed for subsistence. This idleness and instability spawned alcoholism, gambling, and fighting. On the eve of the Temirtau events, the Ministry of Internal Affairs informed the CPSU Central Committee about two of the larger fights, which had involved one hundred and two hundred participants respectively.

The local leadership not only did not want to or did not know how to improve working and living conditions, but even refused to listen to workers' grievances. Usually those registering complaints were rudely expelled from the boss's office. Certain leaders even posted security guards who simply did not allow workers to enter.[17] Indeed, in Temirtau, the system of reciprocal ties with the populace, which was absolutely essential for supporting the stability and viability of the Soviet bureaucratic state, had completely shut down. The failure of the authorities to respond to the complaints closed off the last legal avenue by which people might have improved their situation.

The criminalization of the tent settlement quickly acquired momentum. For example, in the department of workers' supplies of the trust* *Kazmetallurgstroi*, the usual concerns were embezzlement and misappropriations. In the first half of 1959, the amount embezzled and misappropriated was two times more than that for the whole of 1958.[18] In 1958 five people were taken to court for misappropriating supplies, whereas the year before there had been no such cases.[19] The workers were also incensed by reports that police personnel had been assaulting citizens.[20]

Not only was the situation in Temirtau growing increasingly tense, but there emerged a potential catalyst for mass uprisings—a group of unemployed youths living in the tent settlement who were former prisoners sent to the site after completing their terms. They not only organized drinking bouts and hooliganism, but even terrorized the young volunteer-enthusiasts, beating them at cards, stealing personal items, and so on. The main thing, however, was that they were able to influence the behavior of some of the young workers while forcing the rest to subordinate themselves to an informal group hierarchy and laws of "mutual responsibility." Besides this, they had personal experience with confronting authorities, and had serious reasons for hating the police and for seeking their own kind of social revenge. Driven to fury by the senseless trials and difficulties of everyday life and by harassment from the bosses, the youth of Temirtau were thus receptive to ready-made leaders, particularly those who were aggressive, fearless, and already accustomed to having the construction site community submit to their will. In this situation, mass riots could flare up at any moment and for the most trivial of reasons. One such reason came on August 1, 1959, when the workers living in the first tent settlement returned from the work site to find there was not enough water for washing and for drinking.

Although water shortages were a recurring problem, this time the lack of water provoked a volatile reaction. That evening, a crowd of irritated young workers, filled with a sense of their own righteousness and enraged at the bosses, broke the lock and began to drink *kvas*** from a cistern located near the cafeteria. Several went and woke up friends, inviting them to join their "collective." Confusion and much crowding resulted. Truly tortured by thirst,

---

*In the USSR, a trust was a conglomeration of enterprises with similar output or raw materials.—E.M.
***Kvas* is a dark, sour drink made from sugar, yeast, water, and toasted rye bread crumbs, very popular during the summer months.—E.M.

some of the young people ended up in a fight by the kvas barrel. The remaining kvas was poured out onto the ground. Therefore, when a large group of fresh workers from the first and second tent settlements arrived on the scene, nothing was left for them to drink. It is not surprising that the eyes of the crowd turned eventually to the cafeteria. Rioters beat up the night watchman, forced open the window latches, and broke into the building, where they stole the contents of the buffet and scattered what was left along the hallway.

While some of the participants in the riot simply satisfied their thirst and at the most carried out petty vandalism, half-criminalized elements entered the fray for purely selfish goals. Someone secretly looted the dry goods kiosk and tried to get into the store where household goods were sold, despite the fact that there was obviously no water to be found there. At the same time, firebrands emerged, calling provocatively for people to burn down the cafeteria, obviously in order to cover up all traces of the crime. The crowd, however, did not immediately respond to this appeal. The cafeteria was burned down only later.

For the most part, participants in the disorders—even some of the most active ones—did not seek to escalate the violence and did not pursue any kind of mercenary goals. For them, the broken barrel with the kvas, the looted cafeteria, the lemonade and the *kefir* [a yogurt drink—E.M.] taken from the stall represented the natural restoration of justice and harmony in their social microcosm, which had a calming effect on many of the rioters. Although the aggression of the faceless crowd continually grew, individual behavior did not necessarily follow this pattern. Many young people joined in for a short time and then dropped out. They became part of the angry mob, then they reacquired their own autonomous existence, going off either to sleep or to dance, to go swimming, or even to watch a movie. In other words, the ordinary routine of a day off from work proceeded parallel to the unfolding riot. Therefore, what the reports of the Ministry of Internal Affairs to the Central Committee described as an unbroken chain of aggressive actions were for many of the participants separate and insignificant episodes.[21]

Around three o'clock in the morning, more police appeared on the scene (until this time there had only been five policemen, all of whom remained prudently passive) and began to disperse the crowd. The mass of people was clearly not prepared for a direct confrontation with the authorities, and they simply scattered. At this stage no clear leaders had emerged, and even the influence of "provocateurs" and petty criminals ready to take advantage of a riot was not yet felt.

The first episode of the events in Temirtau—typical hooliganism found in the Virgin Lands and new construction sites, provoked by the stupidity and mismanagement of the local leaders—could easily have amounted to nothing. A small disturbance, transformed into a symbol of social revenge against the bosses, could for a time have restored harmony. The overwhelming majority of the participants in the riots were fully loyal and had actually lost the desire to continue the aggression. But the situation changed markedly when the police, inspired by the crowd's passivity and full of official zeal to expose the guilty, arrested two fellows who had only by accident turned up at the scene. The subsequent investigation failed to establish their specific guilt.

The reaction of the young Temirtau workers to the detention of their two comrades was fully predictable. Often in such situations the participants in riots demonstrate group solidarity and try to liberate the prisoners. So it happened in this case. Simultaneously a new factor appeared on the scene—a nucleus of people ready to serve as ringleaders. From this moment it was precisely their actions and behavior that increasingly shaped the physiognomy of events.

After the destruction of the cafeteria and the appearance of the additional police forces, the crowd gradually dissipated. Many went to sleep. According to the testimony of witnesses, however, between 5:00 A.M. and 6:00 A.M. on August 2, 1959, someone summoned the crowd to go and liberate the two imprisoned comrades. No actual meeting, though, took place to spur the crowd to attack the police. Instead, the authoritative will of the active nucleus of participants directed the disorders at this moment, determining the goals and direction of subsequent actions. The remaining 500 to 1,500 participants seemed to submit easily to these appeals, which corresponded to their own growing sense that what had happened was unjust.

At this point, however, the crowd appeared to choose a more acceptable "slogan of the day." Simultaneously with the cries to liberate the prisoners, other, purely criminal appeals had rung out to go to the hardware store and rob it.[22] But when faced with a choice, the crowd acted to restore justice and not to loot. Only a small number of the participants broke away and robbed the manufactured goods stall. The rest rioted for unselfish reasons. Once again growing in size, the crowd moved toward the city's police department to liberate the detained comrades. But the main forces of the police were at that time concentrated at the cafeteria, leaving the police department building without any serious security. The crowd turned over and then destroyed a police car, in addition to pelting the building with sticks and stones. Not meeting any resistance, the participants broke into police premises, snapped the telephone lines in the staff room, and smashed the typewriter.[23]

Finally, N.A. Karpich, a policeman, appeared on the street and easily pacified the crowd by saying that the prisoners had already been taken away. The provocative cries to rout the police did not work, for the crowd was still partially manageable and not yet tied to any single leader or voice. It did not view the police as hostile, and willingly entered into a peaceful dialogue with the officer.

In the morning, soldiers arrived on the scene. The police posted a guard around the cafeteria and the stall selling manufactured goods. At the same time, the manager of Kazmetallurgstroi and the local party boss arrived at the tent settlement. They held a meeting with the workers and listened to complaints, thereby creating a legal channel for expressing dissatisfaction. In principle this could have brought an end to the riots, for the bosses promised to investigate and take measures. The young people, tired from the night's adventures, began to drift off to the tents. Some went to bathe in the lake, for it was Sunday morning. The authorities breathed a sigh of relief, assuming that the conflict had exhausted itself.

But the unrest flared up anew about three o'clock in the afternoon, when a cistern of drinking water was brought to the settlement. It turned out that the water had an unusual pale pink coloring (it is possible that a weak solution of manganese had been added to the water as a disinfectant). Witnesses raised such an uproar that a crowd began to gather again. This time the instigators were immediately aggressive. One of them, armed with a bed rod, ran out, calling, "Everyone, come out onto the street." On the whole, though, the crowd was at first inclined to compromise. Once again the issue of releasing the detained comrades surfaced, since they had not yet been freed. Afterward, someone recalled the reason for the tumult and cried out: "Look at what they have given us to drink!" The tank of water was then loaded onto the car and taken to the hospital for an expert appraisal. No doctor, however, could be found, so the participants threw the tank into the hospital and headed for the police station. Their goal now was to liberate the prisoners.

At this point, some of the participants began stopping cars on the street. They placed one of them across the road and blocked traffic. The crowd again began to grow and, inspired by the aggressive appeals of spontaneously emerging leaders, moved toward police headquarters. Ultimately about 1,000 people gathered there, the majority of whom had already forgotten about the suspicious water and were again demanding the liberation of their comrades.

About thirty soldiers were guarding the police station at this time. At first, those at the head of the crowd stopped at the sight of weapons. But then someone ran forward and cried out that the soldiers would not dare to shoot at the people. Those in the back began to push the people in the front. The crowd went right up to the soldiers. Shots rang out. Initially people rushed away from the danger, but then someone yelled that the soldiers were shooting blank cartridges. The crowd turned back and threw stones at the guards, who subsequently retreated into the police building. The rioters broke into the first floor, knocked out the glass in the windows, and destroyed telephones.

A short spontaneous meeting arose near the porch, during which a conflict emerged between "criminals" and "romantics." Both groups spoke. Apparently one group, the "romantics," repeated the call to liberate the prisoners, while the other, the "criminals," called for robbing the department store as well. The brief discussion ended with the crowd electing three persons to negotiate with the police. The guards allowed the three to go up to the second floor.

A man by the name of Manyshin appointed himself as leader of the delegation and delivered an ultimatum that the prisoners be freed by 11:00 PM on August 2 or else the police station would be destroyed. At first the police rejected the ultimatum. After the delegation reported this to the crowd, a vote was held on the liberation of the prisoners, and the participants decided to repeat their demands. Subsequently, the same Manyshin for the second time went into the police headquarters and began to insist that the ultimatum be honored. Finally the police personnel promised to bring the young people to the tent settlement before midnight (this demand was in fact fulfilled).

The promise to free the prisoners, however, did not pacify everyone. The attack on the police building continued for some time until an unidentified person with sound judgment climbed onto a window sill and called for people to stop throwing stones. Accompanied by soldiers, the policeman Karpich came out and began to admonish the remaining crowd. At about this time (or possibly earlier), one of the activists volunteered to bring explosives and blow up the building. In the end, the rioters began to disperse. Reacting to a rumor that the whole police force had gone to the tent settlement, the more active and aggressive participants who remained at the scene rushed there to continue the riot. Even the more loyal workers went, although some of them probably also wanted to watch the movie that was playing at the settlement clubhouse.

On the road to the tent settlement, part of the crowd stopped near the city's department store. Here another spontaneous meeting took place, during which a new conflict surfaced between "criminals" and "romantics." Someone called for robbing the store, while another person called for a new attack on the police to liberate the prisoners. Others said that it was necessary to return to the tents and wait there, since the police had promised to bring the prisoners. The discussion grew heated as mutual accusations were exchanged.

The leadership nucleus finally split apart. The "moderate romantics" waited for the liberation of their comrades, while the "aggressive romantics" tried to organize a continuation of the riots. In the end, the "criminals" gained their objective and provoked the looting and destruction of the department store. But the criminal elements then dissolved anonymously into the crowd and acted surreptitiously. Apparently none of the active organizers of the store looting were identified in the investigation. Those who took the blame for everything were either people accidentally on the scene or "aggressive romantics" who were continually in full view throughout the events.

At midnight a large crowd vandalized Kazmetallurgstroi, and then carried out an assault on the department store. The initiative seemed now to have shifted to the "criminals." The police were in the process of setting free the two imprisoned comrades, thereby negating the previous motive of restoring justice. Now the crowd either sought revenge (among the participants in the uprisings there were sufficient numbers of people with a criminal record who wanted to settle scores with the police) or blatant self-interest.

One group set off for the tent settlement and remained there, convinced that the arrested prisoners had been freed. Some came running from the store, crying that a People's Squad (*druzhinniki*) of volunteer police were approaching the settlement. Twice the volunteers were pelted with stones, which forced them to turn back. After this a new split occurred. The crowd standing closest to the store hurled stones. Then looting began, and a real battle unfolded when the soldiers tried to clear the store building. Those pillaging the building called for reprisals against the military personnel. Someone urged the soldiers to join the riots. The troops answered by firing their weapons. One of the participants in the attack on the store brought out a truck from the garage and tried to ram the chain of soldiers, but he was killed. Stones were thrown at the police and at the military personnel, along with jars of food and wine bottles. Several of the hooligans had hunting rifles, some of which had been taken from the guards, and they shot at the soldiers and policemen. In addition, rioters broke into the weapons stockpile, seizing rifles as well as some explosives. A group of people who had participated in the attack on the department store and on the trust ran to the tent settlement after the beginning of the battle, crying out that the soldiers had come and that they were going to shoot anyone in and around the store. Then the wounded were brought to the tents, and this information sparked further unrest.

During the early hours of August 3, the Temirtau market was attacked, and the cafeteria building and vegetable stalls were set on fire. Looting, vandalism, and arson coincided with attacks on military personnel, police, and civilian police volunteers who were trying to restore order. Participants in the riots again threw stones and other items, and fired the rifles and other guns. The police detail and soldiers dispersed the crowd around the department store and carted away the dead, the wounded, and those who had been arrested. Around noon, the soldiers left the department store, but a small crowd gathered anew and went to rob the store. People threw stones at the civilian police volunteers, but then soldiers arrived at the tents.

By evening, order was largely restored in the city, although several leaders of the riots tried to continue the unrest. Three of them, who had thus far avoided arrest, attempted to provoke an uprising in the Komsomol settlement. They stole gas from cars with the aim of setting fire to buildings, including the one housing the headquarters for the volunteer police squad. Moreover, one of the leaders went to the Komsomol dormitory and called upon the young people to continue the struggle. Then all three sent a note to a comrade in the tent settlement, and proposed that he spur the young people to rise up anew. The aggressiveness of the rioters, however, had ebbed by this point. People were genuinely frightened by the arrests, the shootings, and the bloodshed and rebuffed the three leaders who had gone to the Komsomol settlement.

In the course of the mass unrest in Temirtau, 109 soldiers and officers were wounded, including 32 who were shot. Among the rioters, 11 were killed and 32 were wounded, 5 of whom subsequently died. In the suppression of the riots, 190 people were detained, most of whom were young workers age 18 to 21 who had recently come to the construction site. Among them were 75 Komsomol members. The majority were released after a brief investigation. Of those detained, 42 were arrested and criminal proceedings were brought against them. The inquiry conducted by the local KGB held 7 active participants in the riots in Temirtau criminally responsible, defining their offenses as banditry and mass disorders (Articles 14 and 16 of the Law on Criminal Responsibility for State Crimes). Later the charge of banditry was dropped. Other persons arrested were prosecuted only for participation in mass riots (without the charge of banditry), and several were convicted conditionally—"taking into account personal circumstances." A number of criminal procedures against participants were dropped "due to the lesser degree of their guilt."[24]

The investigation pointed to seven persons as the more active participants in the riots. In addition, among the young workers who died during the riots were several other organizers. One, who was killed at the department store, was an initiator of the attacks on the police station and had called for reprisals against the military. Another young worker at the time of the attack on the department store had encouraged the crowd to resist the soldiers and continue the looting. In addition, he had called on the soldiers to join the rioters and then tried to ram the soldiers while driving a truck he had taken from the garage.

Yet, one could hardly call these young people "organizers of mass riots."

They had distinguished themselves from the masses, but in truth they did not lead the crowd. On the morning of August 2, the wave of events carried the crowd, not individual leaders. An active organizing role became noticeable only in the second half of the day, when the crowd promoted three representatives to present the ultimatum concerning the liberation of the two prisoners. The self-proclaimed head of the delegation was Manyshin, the initiator of the spontaneous meeting and the voting to free the prisoners. Manyshin clearly transformed himself into a leader of the rioters. During the morning of August 3, wounded by a bayonet in the attack on the soldiers, he was carried to the tent settlement with a knife in his hands, where he implored the young people to continue the riots. It was he who said: "No matter where you go, the blood of young people is flowing there, and yet here you hide. Go there or we ourselves will kill you." In the opinion of the investigators, Manyshin ideally fit the role of the main perpetrator, and the court sentenced him and another man to execution by shooting, although in December 1959 the Presidium of the Supreme Court of Kazakhstan commuted the sentence to fifteen years in prison.[25]

The effort to identify the leaders of the uprisings revealed two more candidates—Aplotsin and Zhiriakov, who had sent a note to a friend with the following contents: "Oleg, gather the youth, 500 to 600 people, and come to 'Taiwan' [this is young peoples' slang for the Komsomol settlement.—V.K.]; there are cops here and it is necessary to take care of them' [meaning it was necessary to kill them—V.K.]. These two, having stolen a car, drove to the neighboring Komsomol settlement 'to stir up the people.' " The formation of a conscious leadership nucleus, however, clearly lagged behind the actions of the authorities in suppressing the riots. In fact, leaders only began to organize the riots after the suppression of the uprising in the tent settlement. On August 3, there were still several chances for success, for on that day almost 25,000 workers did not go to work. But on the next day, only about 1,500 people did not go to work.

Were the instigators distinguished by particular social experiences and background from other participants in the riots? Among the instigators were six Russians, one Latvian, one Jew, and one Ukrainian. Two were Komsomol members. Three had a criminal past. One, the oldest of the nine at age twenty-six, had been tried three times: for forgery, for embezzlement, and for possession of a weapon. The second defendant had been sentenced to two years in prison for corrupting a minor (the details are unknown, but judging by the light sentence, the matter may have involved sexual relations between two minors; the parents of the girl brought the charges against the defendant). The third defendant with a criminal record had been tried earlier for petty hooliganism. One other instigator did not have any previous convictions, but he had ties with the petty criminal elements who were the majority at the construction site and who knew how to use *blat* [meaning influence and personal connections used for individual or collective advancement.—E.M.]. In June 1959 he had voluntarily quit work, and then had begun to drink and pick fights.

These people had personal reasons for hating the police and had a clear tendency toward aggressive actions. But while they called for pogroms and arson, they did not try to encourage the crowd to loot. They were driven by their hatred for police, by an intoxicating feeling of power over the crowd, and by a thirst for justice. In all probability, those who provoked the crowd to rob simply dissolved into the mass of young construction workers, disappearing without a trace along with the stolen goods. Five of the activists lacked any criminal experience, nor did they have personal motives for participating in the riots. It was specifically these young people who had tried to organize the riots on August 3 and 4.

Of the four instigators who had comprised something similar to a committee and had tried to spur the Komsomol settlement to join the riots, three lacked a criminal record. They had just arrived at the construction site and could not have developed solid ties with the already existing half-criminalized gangs. These spontaneously created leaders modeled their actions on vague recollections of revolutionary heroes from Soviet-era propaganda films. At the same time, these leaders were obviously in no position to control either the spontaneous revolt of young workers or even their own behavior. Expressing their protest against the injustice of local authorities, the instigators were in reality not the leaders of the unrest, but rather its voice. It is not surprising that the rather infantile insurgents almost literally reproduced the famous episode (the "meat with maggots" sequence) from Sergei Eisenstein's film *The Battleship Potemkin* and poured the "pinkish water" on the ground with the cry: "Look at what you are drinking!" Nor is it surprising that, having joined with the crowd in looting the department store, they did not then know what to do with the stolen goods.

The Results and Lessons of the Riots in Temirtau

Fortunately the state did more than merely seek harsh punishments for active participants. It actually drew lessons from these events. Immediately after the Temirtau riots, the procurator-general and the minister of internal affairs for the Kazakh SSR visited a similar workers' settlement in Ten-Tek, where they held meetings with young Komsomol workers from different regions of the Soviet Union who had come to construct a mine. The situation here was almost a mirror image of Temirtau on the eve of the riots. This time, however, the authorities acted preemptively. The procurator-general and the Kazakh minister of internal affairs, out of fear of criminal responsibility, demanded that the local enterprise bosses bring in electricity, establish an adequate number of washbasins, and so on. The deputy minister of trade for the republic and the deputy chairman of the regional executive committee took measures to improve the supply of food and consumer goods. The Kazakh Communist Party regional committee sent a whole group of party workers to organize party and propaganda work.[26] To prepare in case new riots broke out, the MVD brigade stationed in Karaganda was increased to eighty-five people. In addition, it was proposed that some personnel in the MVD detachment secure the nearby prison.[27]

On October 17, 1959, the Central Committee Presidium discussed the situation at the Karaganda Metal Works. The resulting resolution, "On the Situation at the Construction Site of the Karaganda Metal Works," noted:

> The Central Committee of the Kazakh Communist Party did not correctly evaluate the political situation developing at the construction site; in the course of two months none of the members of the Central Committee bureau was at the construction site, and necessary measures were not taken to improve the organization of production and the cultural and everyday social services for the laborers. The bureau of the Kazakh Communist Party Central Committee showed a lack of discipline, manifested in the fact that it did not immediately report the events in Temirtau to the CPSU Central Committee.[28]

The first secretary of the Karaganda regional committee of the Kazakh Communist Party, P.I. Isaev, was not only fired but was even expelled from the party, although with the stipulation that he might be reinstated after only one year.[29] Other Kazakh regional party leaders as well as the head of the regional *sovnarkhoz* (council of the national economy)* also received party reprimands. A.S. Vishnevskii, the manager of the firm Kazmetallurgstroi, lost his post and was expelled from the party. The administrative leadership of the construction site was strengthened. The Kazakh SSR minister of construction, A.P. Krotov, was appointed manager of Kazmetallurgstroi, and a

---

*In 1957, Khrushchev switched to a territorial principle of industrial organization and divided the country into 105 regions administered by councils known as sovnarkhozes, each of which was to organize production and distribution of goods and services within the region. Khrushchev's successors later dismantled the sovnarkhozes and reestablished branch management.—E.M.

member of the USSR State Planning Committee, B.F. Bratchenko, became the chairman of the regional sovnarkhoz.[30]

At the end of 1959, new reports came from the Ministry of Internal Affairs to the CPSU Central Committee about individual episodes of unrest in the Virgin Lands.[31] However, the situation on the whole had been stabilized. There were no further disturbances similar to the riots in Temirtau either in the Virgin Lands or in other regions of new industrial construction. The state had successfully overcome the crisis.

Chapter 2

Unrest in the Military: Soldiers' Riots and Disorders

The Dynamics of Military Unrest in the 1950s

Riots and disorders involving soldiers[1] are a traditional form of mass unrest that can occur in any army or under any regime. They signal to authorities lapses in military organization and discipline, declining morale, the incompetence of commanders, and so on. The army forces soldiers to stay within rigid boundaries of legal restrictions and military discipline, and it has its own mechanisms for behavioral control that are not comparable to civilian ones. At the same time, the stifling nature of army discipline, combined with the unbelievable congestion of large groups of people and an abnormal gender balance, can, under certain circumstances, produce socially explosive situations that expose the fault lines unexpectedly emerging in the military system.

Military commanders are familiar with situations that can cause breakdowns in military discipline: conscription, demobilization of soldiers who have completed their service, and the transporting of military units. They also understand that reckless drinking and the weakening or full loss of control by the commanders over the behavior of their subordinates can spawn mass hooliganism, riots, and disorders. Cases of criminal behavior among military personnel are not only traditional, but timeless. Usually the motives for, as well as the roots of, criminal behavior among soldiers are only indirectly connected with politics and with social problems. More often they represent a means for relieving psychological tension under conditions of limited personal freedom and a strictly regimented way of life.

Nonetheless, the particular significance of military unrest during the period 1953 to 1959 lies in the fact that soldiers became one of the most vola-tile groups in the Soviet population. Out of ninety-four violent conflicts re-ported to high party officials by the USSR Ministry of Internal Affairs and Procuracy, forty-four involved soldiers. Such conflicts often developed into confrontations with authorities,[2] meaning not only random violence against police carried out by hooligans, but also direct aggression. Soldiers' con-flicts often involved the use of firearms, whether by authorities acting to suppress mass disorders or by groups engaged in the confrontation. Looting and the destruction of housing and administrative buildings, shops, and stores often accompanied fights and mass hooliganism.[3]

Much more rarely did latent ethnic tensions influence soldiers' conflicts.[4] Furthermore, in terms of political motives and goals, these events appear practically sterile. Anti-Soviet outcries and the destruction of portraits of party and government leaders surfaced in just three episodes out of forty-four. Only in Kemerovo in 1955 did mass riots involving soldiers become distinctly political in content. The Kemerovo disturbances were directed against a government decree that had postponed demobilization for certain categories of military construction workers. The unrest continued for many days and was characterized by a high level of spontaneous self-organization among the workers.

"Garrison" Riots and Conflicts

The year 1953 was distinguished by heightened conflict among outlying garrisons stationed in the union republics and by symptoms of declining discipline in military units. At least twice that year, representatives of the center (the apparatus of the chief military procurator for the Soviet Army and the Ministry of Internal Affairs) had to investigate mass violations of military discipline and order, as well as criminal acts by servicemen in the Leninabad garrison and among troops in the Estonian SSR. Both cases in-volved serious demoralization and conflict among a significant group of people who had weapons. Such situations, of course, were not specifically post-Stalinist or uniquely Khrushchevian. Even under Stalin, there had been reports to the highest Soviet leaders about numerous crimes committed by servicemen in units stationed in Moldavia (November 1945),[5] about "hooli-gan phenomena" and banditry involving personnel in local garrisons in Alma-Ata and other regional centers in Kazakhstan (December 1945),[6] and also about the criminalization of various military units.[7]

In the 1953 case of the Leninabad garrison, there were widespread and unwarranted absences, evasion of military service under various pretexts, and abuse of military property.[8] Rumors about the soldiers' outrageous acts undoubtedly spread through the city, frequently exaggerating the real situation. In a number of instances, police were unable to stop soldiers engaging in hooliganism. Periodically, fights broke out between local citizens and servicemen, some of which even involved police officers. The scenario for such fights included calls for help and to avenge the wounded. The tense situation in Leninabad spurred retaliatory actions by the civilian population, though apparently the military bosses took timely measures to stop the conflict from exploding into mass disturbances.

Apart from punishing the guilty, authorities identified reasons for the heightened volatility of the garrison, which included three antiaircraft divisions and one construction battalion. The procuracy's investigation concluded that an important principle had been violated in staffing the antiaircraft divisions. Usually it was young people from Russia, Ukraine, and Belorussia who went into such units. But this garrison had personnel from the outer and western regions that were considered less reliable. Moreover, the garrison had a dangerous multiethnic composition (in one division there were twenty-five representatives of non-Russian nationalities, and in the other, twenty). Obviously, the procurator considered the multiethnic units difficult to manage due to the different levels and types of culture, language problems, and varying degrees of adaptability to military service. In addition, there was the possibility that internal ethnic associations could develop, which would be divisive and which would bear dangerous similarity to criminal gangs.

A purely bureaucratic and extremely trivial reason for the criminalization of the Leninabad garrison also emerged during the investigation. Fearing responsibility for numerous extraordinary incidents, the commanders had sometimes simply hidden the facts of criminal acts by military personnel from the military procurator in order to keep the police away from the units. The guilty often went unpunished.[9] Inquiries were not conducted, which effectively blocked any further treatment of the matter.

The situation in Leninabad did not develop into mass disturbances, but in another border garrison, in the city of Chardzhou, a conflict in February 1953 between soldiers in a tank division and local residents ended in tragedy. Seventeen people were wounded and nine hospitalized, although according to other data, the number of injuries was higher.[10] Ethnic tensions may have aggravated the situation, but the violent behavior of the servicemen, who were linked by principles of "mutual responsibility" (subsequently no one wanted to identify the perpetrators of the fight), was largely provoked by the actions of another group, students from a local medical institute for training surgical assistants. The investigation revealed, in fact, that the students were the main instigators of the constant fighting in the city, for they had more than once assaulted individual soldiers. In all, twenty students were expelled for fighting and hooliganism, but this was not enough for the soldiers, who were determined to settle the score.[11]

The catalyst for the fight in Chardzhou was news of the first "blood-spilling." On February 12, 1953, during an ordinary tussle between two drunken soldiers and several medical students, one of the soldiers somehow ended up smeared with blood. He claimed that he had been knifed by one of the students. Later that evening, the two servicemen began to challenge their fellow soldiers to take revenge on the students. In response, a group of "avengers" gathered, headed by a master sergeant. The newly found leader of the soldier-avengers left the barracks and started a fight with students from the medical institute. Soon other soldiers from the same regiment joined them. They drove the students back to the dormitory of the local pedagogical institute and smashed the glass in the doors. Then, after breaking down the gate to the medical institute, the soldiers chased the students into the building and continued the assault. The following day, police identified the instigators and arrested them. In this case the authorities apparently were able to avoid using weapons.

Garrison disorders followed a similar pattern in the city of Gorky (September 1953, a group fight and pogrom against workers' dormitories),[12] in the village of Ureche (Slutsk district, Bobruisk Oblast, October 1953, a fight between soldiers in armored divisions and local residents, with one person killed),[13] in the city of Perm (August 1958, a fight between officer trainees and local residents),[14] and in the Kiakhtin district of the Buriatsk ASSR (December 1958, a fight in a woman's dormitory between servicemen and students of the local agro-technical school).[15]

On the whole, such garrison disorders were vulgar group fights without any serious underlying social cause. One exception was a fight involving military trainees at the Artik station in the Armenian SSR in July 1957, in which there were "insulting remarks addressed to one of the leaders of the Soviet government."[16] But it can hardly alter this general conclusion. The intervention of authorities, as a rule, quickly ended any outbreak of violence without spurring an aggressive response against the bosses. Participants in mass hooliganism and group fights tended to disappear from the scene of events. Only one attack on a policeman is known, in Nakhodka, during April 1955.[17] Since garrison disturbances did not generally raise political demands, they did not pose any threat for the regime, and therefore did not require any kind of reaction except to punish the guilty and to "reestablish order."

"Railroad" Disorders

Just as senseless, but much more brutal, were railroad disturbances involving servicemen. The year 1953 was particularly distinguished by such cases.

There were four railroad conflicts that drew the attention of Moscow authorities, and each saw the spilling of blood and the use of weapons. In three episodes there was a confrontation with the police or with representatives of the military commandant.

At the end of April 1953, soldiers of the Leningrad district antiaircraft defenses were converted into railroad troops by a directive of the General Staff. Soon thereafter, serious unrest developed. On April 30, 1953, 184 military personnel were transferred to the Alakurta Station of the Kirov Railroad. This was done in spite of a prohibition against dispatching military trains from Leningrad during holidays, in this case May 1, a national celebration traditionally honoring labor and the working class. Authorities justifiably feared the worst during such times, due to the potential volatility of servicemen on the railroad and the increased danger of mass drunkenness during holidays.

A second mistake followed the first. Some of the soldiers received money instead of a food ration and, taking advantage of their situation, they began to get drunk even before leaving the railroad station in Leningrad. In fact, a fight had already broken out before the train had left, with fifteen servicemen suffering light wounds and beatings. Yet, the officers simply loaded the instigators of the fight onto the train along with the other drunken soldiers and, together with the remaining personnel, set out on their journey.

On May 1, the train had a long layover at the Volkhovstroi Station. While waiting, a group of servicemen picked a fight with local residents and began to loot. A patrol of twenty-six soldiers from the local antiaircraft defense battalion (PVO) arrived at the station, but could not restore order. When military authorities ordered the railroad police unit to begin arresting the looting soldiers, the drunken crowd demanded the liberation of their comrades and, armed with stones and military belts, attacked the police. The head of the military patrol shot three times in the air as a warning, and then the police opened fire, killing two soldiers and wounding four others. But even this did not pacify the soldiers, who tried to block a fire brigade coming to assist the police. Again the officers opened fire and wounded still another man. Meanwhile, in honor of the May Day holiday, official demonstrations were under way at the other end of the city. Eventually local party officials arrived to act as arbitrators in the conflict. They prohibited the further use of weapons by the police and convinced the soldiers to calm down.[18]

On that same day at the Elisenvara Station of the October railroad line, a group of about a hundred servicemen went on a rampage, beating up the engineer's assistant and then robbing him. They stole watches from two other persons. At the moment of arrest, the drunken soldiers tried to disarm the police, who responded with gunfire that wounded one of the attackers in the arm.

This enraged the soldiers still more. They broke into the room of the station's duty officer, [*dezhurnyi*]* shattered the glass in the windows, damaged the telephone line, and inflicted blows on a railway worker who had accidentally turned up on the premises. They then tried to disarm two border guards, who in self-defense began to shoot into the air with their automatic weapons.[19]

A somewhat different pattern marked events at the Khabarovsk Station on September 16, 1953, yet with the same scenario of mass drunkenness and a loss of control by officers over the situation. A conflict arose between military conscripts who were traveling to the Far East in two military trains— one from Novosibirsk and one from Tashkent. One of the officers accompanying the Tashkent train got drunk and shot at the Novosibirsk contingent, killing one of the conscripts. Disturbances lasting for several hours then ensued, ending only after the intervention of the Khabarovsk garrison. During the fracas, the conscripts disarmed some of the servicemen accompanying the trains, which turned the fight into a bloody battle. Four people were killed and six received serious, life-threatening wounds. About a hundred of the active participants were detained, which in and of itself attests to the scale of the disturbances.

The last railroad episode of 1953 was a confrontation in November at the Barzhava Station in Georgia between groups of drunken conscripts and passengers of a suburban train. Seventeen passengers received knife wounds and five were sent to the hospital. Only the intervention of the commander of the border guards prevented this violence from expanding in scale.[20]

Four more railroad disorders have been documented as occurring between 1954 and 1959. One involved a conflict between conscripts and another volatile social group—young people from the city of Baku in Azerbaijan who were returning home from having worked on the harvest (Novosibirsk, September 1956). A second one involved petty hooliganism by conscripts, who threw stones and bottles at passing trains (Georgian SSR, the Trans-Caucasus Railroad, September 1958).[21]

Two other conflicts were more serious in nature, involving vandalism and confrontations with police. In December 1955, servicemen traveling by train from the Belorussian Military District to do lumbering work in the Arkhangelsk region engaged in mass disorders, hooliganism, and robbery. Along the way they robbed a store, mugged the family of a railroad worker, and stole a suitcase from a passenger. At the Medvedevo Station, they broke into two freight cars and stole cotton fabric and ammunition.

---

*Duty officers were the only police personnel who manned the police stations and posts during the evening hours. Until the 1970s, Soviet police mainly worked day shifts from 9:00 A.M. to 6:00 P.M.—E.M.

When police tried to detain two suspicious-looking soldiers with large packages, a group of seventy to a hundred servicemen intervened and liberated them by force. In the struggle, the soldiers wounded five policemen and took a loaded pistol from one of them. Using the stolen weapon, the agitated servicemen wounded a railroad inspector. After liberating the detained soldiers, participants in the disorders scattered throughout the cars and the military train set off.

By order of the head of the Iaroslav garrison, however, a reinforced military detail along with the police surrounded the train at the Vspole Station. But attempts to find and arrest the instigators provoked retaliatory actions. About a hundred soldiers got off the train. When the police detained sixteen people, some sought to liberate them by force. The police then killed two soldiers, but even this did not deter the crowd. Servicemen beat up three policemen and disarmed two of them. Not only did the head of the Iaroslav garrison have to designate a new director of the train, but he even had to assign a car with fifty machine gunners. Along the scheduled route, authorities strengthened security at the various stations and prohibited the selling of alcoholic drinks in station restaurants and snack bars.[22]

In July 1958, Moscow received news of disturbances involving conscripts on the North Caucasus Railroad. Along the route of a military train, which contained about 2,000 soldiers and 25 officers, conscripts robbed food stores and stalls, flung bottles out of windows, and then threw stones at police units. The outburst only came to an end when a group of machine gunners was placed on the train at the Rostov Iaroslav Station.[23]

The majority, if not all, of the soldiers' conflicts examined above could hardly be considered conscious collective actions. Despite the confrontations with military authorities and with police, participants in these disturbances were not rebelling against the regime. At the same time, however, these spontaneous mass actions revealed a willingness of the population to defy the law. They also point to the existence in Soviet society of potentially dangerous informal groups that could easily slip out of state control. This constant readiness to rebel forced the authorities to show exceptional sensitivity toward such events.

Military Construction Workers: A High-Risk Group

It would seem that soldiers' disturbances are too ordinary to be considered within the framework of political history, but instead constitute an exclusively managerial-administrative problem. In other words, the resolution of each conflict demands not a political reaction, but a restoration of order. At the same time, analysis of the specific features of such phenomena and of their dynamics and frequency during different periods provides deep insight into social history. It also illuminates how the conflict becomes part of collective social consciousness and then is manifested in other situations.

The Khrushchev period witnessed numerous conflicts of this type, particularly disturbances involving servicemen in military construction battalions, workers mobilized for industrial labor through the military registration and enlistment office, or soldiers demobilized early for these same purposes. To a certain degree, disturbances connected with the militarization of labor signaled to authorities that a crisis caused by rapid urbanization was developing. The disturbances also revealed an unresolved contradiction: Repression of society had weakened, but the pressure to implement strategically important or politically ambitious economic programs continued unabated. Measures employed to recruit the labor force required to realize these programs, such as organized enlistment and ideological campaigns mobilizing young enthusiasts, were only partially successful. In addition, forced labor was in decline. The rehabilitation of political prisoners and mass amnesties contributed to an enormous gap in the country's labor balance (already exhausted by the 30 million casualties from World War II). Consequently, labor policy during the Khrushchev period focused less on the use of prisoners and prisoners of war and more on soldiers mobilized to work in industry and mining.

Army commanders who now faced orders to transfer soldiers into construction battalions responded to the new policy with a mass dumping of physically weak personnel. They also sent soldiers with a criminal past or who presented disciplinary problems. Thus, the military registration and enlistment offices, which had to mobilize workers for construction sites, mines, and the gathering of harvests in the Virgin Lands, had to worry not only about the required numbers but also about the quality of the recruited workers. As a result, in the 1950s, along with the traditional soldiers' disorders, a new arena of social tension emerged—militarized labor during peacetime. It was precisely in this sphere that the greatest number of documented cases of military disorders, mass hooliganism, and collective fights, twenty-five out of forty-four episodes, occurred during 1953 to 1960.

The use of militarized labor in peacetime had already been problematic during the Stalinist period. However, judging from the People's Commissariat of Internal Affairs (NKVD)* documents found in the "special files" of Stalin and Khrushchev, the scale of conflict and the means used to resolve it

---

*The NKVD administered regular police organizations from 1917 to 1946. When the Unified State Political Directorate (OGPU) was abolished in 1934, the NKVD took over the security police organization as well. The NKVD was succeeded by the MVD and the Ministry of State Security (MGB).—E.M.

are not comparable. The Stalinist leadership, in contrast to that of Khrushchev, faced only traditional soldiers' disturbances, and did not have to confront unrest involving military construction units and soldiers mobilized to work in industry. Certain construction battalions in the new construction sites and in the Virgin Lands territories were particularly prone to conflict. Initially they were collectives with weakened or immature internal social ties, and with informal, half-criminal self-organization. For example, in the city of Usole-Sibirskoe, disorders broke out in August 1953 among soldiers in a construction battalion. The investigation revealed that the volatile unit, only in existence for two weeks, had from the very beginning served as a peculiar "dumping ground" to which commanders sent their worst soldiers. Out of 650 soldiers in the battalion, 350 had received disciplinary reprimands (172 people had from two to ten such reprimands), and 38 people had prior convictions for hooliganism, theft, etc. In addition, 498 of the servicemen suffered from various diseases, including dysentery, gastritis, gonorrhea, and tuberculosis.

In a word, the composition of the construction battalion provided soil for informal, half-criminal self-organization. On the one hand, there were incorrigible soldiers, who had actively rejected military discipline and who even had a criminal record. On the other hand, there were the "losers," who were ill-suited for military service and incapable of resistance, in addition to the sick and physically weakened servicemen. Not surprisingly, in the process of forming the battalion, not a single day passed without problems. Officers were beaten up and robbed. Soldiers were brought home drunk and dumped out of cars.[24] The "incorrigibles" were the dominant force in the battalion. Quickly subordinating the other soldiers to their rules, they created an informal hierarchy protected by "mutual responsibility" and suppressed all preexisting social ties. Consequently, in the investigation of the unrest, not even one of the 242 members of the Komsomol and the 14 Communists in the battalion would give the names of the organizers of the disorders—they were too afraid.

The situation was exacerbated by the usual difficulties of new construction sites, which were capable of driving even young Komsomol romantics to take part in mass disorders, to say nothing of military units that were disintegrating due to poor supplies, difficult living conditions, food shortages, and the lack of such facilities as kitchens, cafeterias, medical stations, and recreation centers. The battalion lived in summer tents at the edge of the city in an open area. Mass absenteeism developed. The stockade became a "daily place of rest" where soldiers who had been arrested for disciplinary violations took advantage of languid guards to go off freely to the city at night and to catch up on their sleep during the day.[25]

In February 1954, Procurator-General Rudenko prepared a special report for G.M. Malenkov* about the unfavorable situation in the construction battalions that had been transferred by the Ministry of Defense to various branch ministries for use in industrial labor. The soldiers were being quartered in crowded and stuffy housing, without a room for washing and drying clothes. Colds as well as diseases spread among the soldiers, along with frostbite and lice. The work of the construction battalions was poorly organized and wages were often late. Soldiers habitually left their units without permission, and engaged in heavy drinking and fighting in nearby towns. There had been cases of murder, rapes, and robbery of local citizens. Despite Rudenko's report, the military construction workers continued to demonstrate a heightened predisposition for disorderly and conflictive behavior.[26]

The Scenario for "Construction Battalion" Disturbances

The behavioral model for participants in construction battalion disturbances differed little from that for participation in traditional soldiers' disorders. Cases of direct conflict with military bosses and internal "barracks" unrest were the exception. One of the few examples of such conflicts was the disturbance in one of the companies of a construction battalion operated by the Ministry of Internal Affairs in Ashkhabad (Turkmenistan) in April 1954.[27] Usually the aggression of construction battalion workers was directed outward—toward the civilian population or toward police personnel—and developed according to two possible scenarios.[28]

In the first scenario, aggressive behavior or criminal actions of military construction workers, who were not subject to the regular norms of military discipline, would arouse a defensive reaction and aggressive retaliation from the civilian population. The conflict, which had lain dormant for a long time, would in the end be resolved by gang fights and sometimes by pogroms. The unique feature of this scenario was the absence of aggression against representatives of authority.

Although these disturbances did not attack the foundations of the system or the sacred inviolability of authority, they nonetheless required a quick response from above. A typical episode involved a confrontation between construction battalion soldiers and construction workers in the city of Kstov, Gorkov Oblast, in February 1955. An insignificant event triggered a virtual avalanche when four soldiers took a bottle of vodka from a worker and beat

---

*Georgy Maksimilianovich Malenkov (1902–1988) served as prime minister from 1953 to 1955. He had been close to Stalin but found himself outmaneuvered by Khrushchev after Stalin's death and was forced to resign his post.—E.M.

him. In response, a crowd of about forty to fifty workers, armed with knives, sticks, and crowbars, went looking for revenge. They broke into a women's dormitory and attacked a group of soldiers, three of whom suffered serious wounds. A soldier who had participated in the conflict got away from the dormitory and reported to his colleagues in the construction battalion. Subsequently a hundred soldiers, also armed with iron pipes, shovel handles, sticks, and crowbars, attacked the workers' dormitory. The assault lasted several hours and resulted in broken doors and shattered windows. Fifteen workers and five soldiers were seriously wounded.[29] After these events in Kstov, the Gorkov regional party committee discussed the reasons for the extraordinary incident and "measures to strengthen military discipline."[30]

In spite of the efforts of the authorities, incidents involving military construction units continued to occur. A group fight between construction battalion workers and factory workers in the city of Molotovsk, Arkhangelsk Oblast, in January 1955 ended in a seizure of weapons, guns being fired, the wounding of eleven persons, and one murder.[31] A similar confrontation of the local populace with construction battalions in the city of Biisk in December 1955[32] tore open a long developing abscess—the spread of crime and mass hooliganism—and demanded a more radical solution. This time the authorities actually removed the "source of the conflict." Local inhabitants could rejoice as five hundred construction battalion workers were immediately demobilized and dispatched from Biisk.

The second scenario for construction battalion disturbances involved the transformation of intergroup conflict into direct aggression against local authorities. This occurred when military commanders as well as the police failed to take the initiative at the beginning of events. They would try belatedly to arrest instigators, and would then become the object of attack themselves. Once the police were seen as being "with Them—the enemies," they could no longer count on being untouchable. This psychological transformation was facilitated by the fact that in Russia, even in educated society, it was considered unacceptable to "love the bosses," and even more so the police.[33]

The paradox of such situations lies in the fact that the negative emotions were directed against "bad" policemen and sometimes against local bosses. But as a rule, the negativity and aggression were not extended to the higher authorities. Also present in the spontaneous actions of the crowd was a high level of self-organization. The typical motive for continuing the disorders in a new form was the cry that "they have taken our guys to the police!" In order to overcome their subconscious fear of the state, the crowd required much more authoritative leadership than was needed for a simple fight. But such leaders were sufficiently easy to find, for inevitably within the disintegrating formal collectives, criminal and semilegal self-organization emerged.

Collective solidarity and "mutual responsibility" counterposed the informal soldierly "We" to the rest of the world. Moreover, relations between the rambunctious military construction workers and the police were already quite strained. When the latter intervened in a conflict, they became the ally of the "enemy."

The police simply were caught between a rock and a hard place. If they tried to break up a fight, they faced blows from both sides. Yet the police appeared more as an annoying obstacle, preventing one from laying hands on the real opponents, than as a specific target of aggression. Mass disorders in the city of Barnaul followed this pattern. On August 22, 1954, two soldiers picked a fight with a construction worker. A little later, about forty soldiers from two construction battalions located nearby broke into a workers' club, beat those present with their belt buckles, damaged the film projector, destroyed furniture, and then disappeared. A three-man police patrol was unable to stop the soldiers. During the night, the city police and military authorities detained forty soldiers who had taken leave without permission. Meanwhile, false rumors spread through the city that during the fight in the club the soldiers had killed a child.*

These rumors agitated workers at the construction site and in nearby factories. During the next morning, they began to assault lone soldiers. By noon a large crowd of workers had gathered at the *Teploelektrotsentral'-2* (TETs-2, a station for the centralized supply of heating and electricity) construction site. The workers then moved to the soldiers' barracks, goaded on by unidentified "tipsy persons." Sweeping aside a group of sixty police personnel, the agitated crowd broke into the premises.

A massive fight broke out, in the course of which both sides threw rocks at each other. About a hundred soldiers, in spite of warning shots, broke through the cordoned-off residential sections of the city, where they smashed windows, committed outrageous acts, and picked fights. On August 23, the workers continued to gather in groups and beat up individual soldiers they encountered. In turn, small groups of soldiers slipped into the city and went around assaulting workers. To stop the disorders, authorities had to use additional forces. Eventually they restored order, and augmented patrols were set up to cover the barracks as well as the residential and industrial quarters of the town. In the districts adjoining the construction site, authorities picked

---

*In general, the theme of the "murdered child" often acted as a catalyst even among peaceful inhabitants. At least three cases are known when such a rumor prompted peaceful citizens to carry out mass disturbances. In one case, the actual murder of a child led to nonviolent demonstrations by residents of a small town, who demanded the death penalty for the murderer.—V.K.

up twenty-two soldiers from the construction battalion who had been beaten or taken away during the assault. Five of the soldiers had died by the morning of August 24. Two workers also entered the local hospital for treatment.[34]

Owing to the tense situation in the city, the Ministry of Internal Affairs requested that the Central Committee discuss the removal of the construction battalions from Barnaul. Thus, the workers, who obviously had been upset for a long time over the behavior of the military construction workers, achieved their goal. It is telling that in the memoranda of the MVD and the Central Committee, the events were interpreted entirely as a confrontation between two groups, neither of which targeted its aggression directly against police officers or representatives of the state. Both groups simply swept aside any annoying obstacle between them and their genuine antagonist.

However, it was more often the case that, as soon as the situation developed into a direct confrontation with police and military bosses, events followed the more harsh scenario, and sometimes ended in a bloody uprising. On July 14, 1953, at the city of Rustavi in the Georgian SSR, two construction battalions of the Soviet Army from Odessa and Tiraspol arrived to work on the construction of a chemical factory. They were housed in a settlement near Rustavi by the name of Mdavari-Arkhi. The new arrivals, agitated by their trip, tried to assert their status. During the evening of that same day, a group of drunken soldiers went on a rampage in Rustavi. At first they simply roamed about the settlement, harassing the local inhabitants, but later, false rumors spread that "soldiers had been knifed and taken to the police."

A group of servicemen, who had armed themselves with sticks, iron rods, and rocks, attacked a police station, breaking down the door and beating up two policemen. Other police officers, who had saved themselves by running away, fired randomly and wounded one soldier. Under cries that "they are attacking our guys," almost all of the entire personnel (about 1,000 soldiers) of one of the construction battalions joined in the conflict. In their hunt for the policemen who were hiding, the soldiers wrecked the apartments of two local inhabitants. In the confusion, a watch as well as money was stolen.

Police who had come to restore order were beaten with sticks and rocks, and then were fired upon when they tried to get away from the assault. The soldiers also fired upon the representatives of the Tbilisi and Rustavi military command who had been called out to the scene. The servicemen's outrageous actions did not come to an end until the next morning. In the course of these disorders, two policemen received serious wounds and eight local residents were badly beaten.[35]

The theme of the wounded soldier, this time real and not imaginary, was the catalyst for riots involving military construction battalions in the city of

Usole-Sibirskoe in August 1953. During the night of August 9, an unknown group stabbed a serviceman who was returning to his unit from a leave of absence in the city. Two friends reported to the battalion that civilians had knifed their comrade and called for taking revenge. They decided to meet at the city gardens, and determined that the signal to begin the fight would be the command "Air" (this signal was typically used during an air raid.—V.K.)

On August 12, while military personnel were watching a film in the barracks, one of the soldiers returned from the city garden on a bicycle and reported: "Hey, our guys are being attacked." Someone cried out, "Air," and the rest picked up on the agreed-upon signal. The soldiers rushed off, and on the way they were joined by military personnel of a different construction battalion. The soldiers burst into the city gardens armed with belts, sticks, and knives. They broke off rods and strips from the fence and garden benches, ran in groups along the streets adjacent to the gardens, and assaulted local inhabitants. On the way the soldiers smashed the windows in the city movie theater and the store. Twice the mob of soldiers tried to break into the building of the local MVD, where many had hidden in search of shelter. In all, about 350 to 400 people took part in the disorders. Six local residents received serious knife wounds, among them the director of the evening school for young workers, who subsequently died. Forty-five people suffered less serious wounds.

Subsequent events provide a detailed psychological profile of the inveterate instigators of these public disorders. On August 15, the military command sent a group of the "most undisciplined soldiers," fifty in number, to a different infantry brigade. Even there, though, they were not humbled. The determination of these relentless rebels and "free spirits" to preserve their high status in their informal association outweighed even the natural impulse to avoid further difficulties. Two of the newly arriving soldiers insolently declared to the temporary commander of the brigade and to the head of the military counterintelligence that "they must not be admitted to the brigade, because they will bring many problems, that they would not serve the cause but would only steal and 'knife people' if they remained in the brigade."

Even when they ended up in the guardhouse, the informal ringleaders were not pacified. They began to break down the partitions and windows as well as the bars, and called for the soldiers on guard to join with them. Sensing that it would be difficult to weaken the mechanisms of psychological self-defense and obedience to the law in normal soldiers, the unrepentant provocateurs tried to use a simple but effective psychological device that was built upon an improvised image of the "enemy": "Do not obey the officers, attack them, for they are traitors and thugs who are only masquerading in officers' uniforms." After this ploy, the arrested men burned down the guardhouse.[36]

In Vladivostok in November 1953, a conflict between drunken military construction workers and city residents turned into an attack on the authorities. Local youths were involved, and the situation ended up with an attack on those who had stood up for the young people. Police and military personnel detained two hooligans. The rest fled and enlisted the help of about sixty soldiers. The crowd demanded liberation of the detained individuals and then, armed with rocks, attacked the police department. Order was restored only with the help of additional military and special section police forces.[37]

After these tumultuous events, no serious confrontations between military construction workers and police occurred until July 1958. At this time in the village of Perovo, located close to Moscow, an ordinary conflict erupted between soldier-construction workers assigned to build military installations and workers of the Karacharov Machine Factory. The events began when drunken soldiers left their unit without permission and headed for the workers' dormitory. There they began to quarrel among themselves. When the workers tried to intervene, a fight broke out. Outnumbered, the soldiers sent for help from the barracks. Soon a group of sixty to seventy servicemen surrounded the four-storied dormitory. They began to hurl stones at the windows and to break down the closed doors. Seven workers were wounded, and one of them ended up in the hospital with a concussion.

Fifteen policemen arrived on the scene, but the soldiers resisted, threatening violence. Eventually the entire city police force had to be called out, as well as on-duty troops from nearby military units. Only after this did the soldiers' outrages cease. The majority of the soldiers detained had been inebriated.

In these Perovo military construction battalion disturbances, politics entered the picture for the first time. According to reports sent by the Ministry of Internal Affairs to the Central Committee, during the attack on the dormitory "pictures and portraits in the Lenin Room were torn down and smashed," that is, portraits of Lenin and of other party leaders and government leaders. From other sources, it is known that the defilement of portraits was a typical form of spontaneous protest against the state. Particularly targeted at this time were portraits of Khrushchev, which were hung out during holidays. Unidentified vandals defaced them with insulting graffiti or, if artistic talent allowed, by transforming the portraits into caricatures. By the end of the 1950s, such symbolic acts intended to insult the state began to accompany even ordinary group conflicts. Thus, there emerged in vulgar hooliganism a rare hint of anarchistic protest against the state and its political symbols.

The Year 1955: Disturbances Among Mobilized Workers

The Legal Status and Composition of Mobilized Workers

A specific type of soldiers' disturbance involved a special category of military personnel—workers eligible for military conscription who were mobilized through military enlistment offices or soldiers who were transferred from military units to work on civilian construction sites or in industry. All nine of the known cases occurred in 1955 and posed a serious problem for the Khrushchev leadership. Circumstances as well as an entire array of clumsy administrative acts committed by state officials provoked and even predetermined them. At their height (represented by the mass disorders at Kemerovo, which lasted for many days), the events of 1955 graphically demonstrated to Moscow the mutinous potential of the people, as well as the extensive capacity for spontaneous self-organization characteristic of the crowd in mass protests.

During both the Stalinist and post-Stalinist periods, the Council of Ministers allowed workers to be conscripted and sent to specific enterprises and construction sites in order to fill the gap in labor for high-priority strategic sectors of the economy. But it had a negative impact, engendering juridical tangles and a dissonance of legal interpretations. For example, it was not clear what forms of criminal punishment and disciplinary action could generally be applied to mobilized workers. Was it possible to consider leaving early from work without permission to be desertion, and truancy to be a shirking of military service? Or were softer, civilian measures of responsibility to be applied?[38]

Military enlistment officials considered acting as labor recruiters to be secondary and outside their normal purview. They tended to make slighting references to a "quasi-army" and did not put much thought into the selection of the conscripts, often recruiting people with convictions, illnesses, etc.[39] The post-Stalinist leadership also engaged in new bureaucratic improvisations. Suffering a deficit of workers in the regions of new strategic construction, it began to disband military construction battalions and transfer soldiers with a fixed term of service to civilian construction organizations "to be utilized for work until the end of their term for obligatory military service."[40] In light of this development, the military personnel acquired a formal status as demobilized. As such, they received a wage and could dispose of their own free time as desired. It was proposed that they should be allowed to return home when their term of service ended.[41]

"Half-mobilized" soldiers endured the typical problems of construction workers but, unlike the latter, were deprived of the freedom to relocate. Thus, in the literal sense of the word, they were chained to the construction site. This new "serfdom," of course, did not have any concrete legal foundations. It put both the individual and groups in a marginal position, placing them in a zone of special anarchistic freedom. Moreover, a kind of dual marginalization was taking place: the marginalization caused by working in a new construction site, and that engendered by the ambiguity of being both military and civilian personnel. This situation meant in turn a dual predisposition toward conflict, that is, a state of hypervolatility, aggravated by the half-criminal composition of the military-construction contingent.

This unwise attempt, more spontaneous than calculated, of the Khrushchev leadership to transform soldier-construction workers into "half-soldier–half-civilian" workers turned against the state. In 1955, three waves of riots and disorders swept through regions where militarized construction units were employed. The specific circumstances of place and time produced various forms of conflict—from vulgar mass hooliganism, group fights, and criminal aggressions against the local populace to conscious social protest and direct resistance to the state.

March: Disorders in Kamensk Oblast

In March 1955, the first wave of violence and mass hooliganism swept through the towns and villages of Kamensk Oblast, a region already suffering high crime rates. In January 1955, two potentially conflictive groups arrived simultaneously at the site of the local coal industry and a mine under construction. About 30,000 people were conscripted through a special enlistment campaign along with almost 10,000 workers who were conscripted through military enlistment offices or who were "conditionally demobilized."[42] The militarized contingent included a significant number of people with a criminal past. A large part of these conscripts ended up in the city of Novoshakhtinsk and in the villages of Gukovo and Sholokhovka.[43] Not coincidentally, this is precisely where disorders subsequently erupted.

As Procurator-General Rudenko wrote in a memorandum to the Central Committee on June 2, 1955, both the Ministry of Defense and the Ministry of the Coal Industry had done a poor job of organizing the conscription.[44] There were no regulations defining the rights and responsibilities of the mobilized workers. The construction managers in the provinces were not prepared to receive this numerous and potentially explosive group. Of course, the new arrivals expected the habitual discomforts of new construction sites— dormitories not yet built, poor food, long lines in the cafeteria, poor medical service, a shortage of doctors and pharmacies, and the absence of leisure time and recreational facilities. There did exist a certain reserve of social solidity and endurance that enabled new workers in the first stages to fulfill work norms, even without additional supervision. Soon, however, desertion at the construction site began to occur, and drunkenness and hooliganism became widespread.[45]

It was not long before the mobilized workers began terrorizing the local population. In several towns and villages, a struggle for dominance erupted among the new arrivals themselves. The suppression of internal competition functioned according to the harsh laws developed within criminal associations. All this unfolded against a backdrop of stress that was experienced by the greater part of the new construction site population in trying to adapt to conditions. There was also an environment of growing dissatisfaction among different groups of local workers.

Criminal self-organization within the mobilized contingent had already begun along the journey to its appointed workplace. Consequently, problems arose as soon as the military train arrived in the Kamensk Oblast. During the night of March 1, 1,000 soldiers mobilized to work in the coal industry arrived at Novoshakhtinsk. The regional office of internal affairs reported that "economic organizations could not quickly place those who had arrived into dormitories, and consequently some of the people from the train were sent to different places in the town."

Drunken mobilized workers attacked a policeman who interrupted their attempted robbery of a food store. The officer used his gun in self-defense and wounded one of the perpetrators, who was then taken to the hospital. A group of up to sixty mobilized workers, headed by a former criminal, appeared at the town police department and raised a ruckus, demanding that the wounded man be handed over to them. The police managed to stop the disturbances and arrest the main instigator. They also took measures to detain others who had committed crimes.[46]

On that same day, March 1, in the village of Sholokhovka, some of the conscripts from the Belorussian Military District did not go to work, engaging instead in drinking and hooliganism. Several persons, headed by a former criminal, appeared at the office of the construction manager, and, threatening the administration with reprisals, demanded higher advances, clothing, and free food. After this, having gathered around them about a hundred conscripts, they picked a fight with servicemen in the construction battalion that had been stationed at the village of Sholokhovka. Armed with knives, iron rods and stones, the conscripts broke into the headquarters of the construction battalion, broke the windows, disarmed the sentry, and beat up eight of the military personnel on duty.

On March 5, 1955, a confrontation occurred between two groups of mobilized workers in the village of Sokolovka, Novoshakhtinsk district. On March

18, led by two former criminals (with convictions for robbery), several drunken conscripts picked a fight with people who were standing in line at a store. The conscripts severely beat three civilians. Indignant workers detained the hooligans and carried out spontaneous mob court proceedings against them. The triumph of this primitive justice cost the lives of both ringleaders. Three of the conscripts were seriously wounded.

On March 23, 1955, the excesses and hooliganism of the militarized contingent in the village of Gukovka, Zverev district, acquired ethnic overtones. A group of conscripts decided to take revenge for old grievances and, armed with iron rods and sticks, beat up mobilized Uzbek workers. Three people were killed and forty-eight were seriously wounded.

All of these incidents took place against a background of rampant criminality.[47] The regional police panicked and at some point in time lost control over the situation in the workers' settlements. Only the intervention of Moscow could stabilize the situation and restore calm. Therefore on March 28, 1955, the Council of Ministers issued a special, secret order to investigate violations of social order by people mobilized to work in the coal industry in Kamensk Oblast. Several ministers served on the government's investigating commission, which decided to prosecute those guilty of crimes in an open trial. The sentences given were demonstratively harsh (Soviet courts always correctly understood their "political task") and immediately deflated the criminal ardor of the conscripts. In the settlements of Gukovka and Sholokhovka, authorities created operative police units with 130 personnel, and in the cities of Shakhty and Novoshakhtinsk increased the regular and operative staff of the police. In the areas where conscripts had been settled, the sentry and patrol units were strengthened.[48] In addition to purely punitive actions, the authorities also increased the supply of food to the turbulent districts.[49] However, having slightly corrected the situation in Kamensk Oblast, Moscow bosses failed to see the problem underlying these unpleasant episodes.

May: The Outbreak of "Holiday" Disturbances

On May 1 and 2, 1955, in various regions of the USSR, disorders broke out anew involving former soldiers now assigned to civilian construction battalions and military conscripts transferred to the coal industry for purposes of construction. Two episodes occurred in direct proximity to Moscow—the village of Sokolniki and the town of Kimovsk in Moscow Oblast. Another occurred in the town of Ekibastuz in Pavlodarsk Oblast of the Kazakh SSR. In Kimovsk, a genuine battle unfolded between local residents and former construction battalion soldiers who had been transferred to industry. Several thousand people, most of whom were drunk, took part on both sides. Rumors about the murder of women and children, as well as ethnic antagonisms (among the former construction battalion soldiers were Azerbaijanis, Uzbeks, and Georgians), were additional catalysts. As a result, the typical conflict between "We" and "Them" was strengthened many times over by the appeal of mob leaders to ethnic solidarity. The shocking cruelty of the violence was ostensibly justified by the thought that the death of innocents required revenge.

In reality, there were no murders of women and children, and the ethnic argument turned out to be specious. More than half of the former military construction workers were Russian and Ukrainian, and they experienced the same number of injuries as the Azerbaijanis, Uzbeks, and Georgians. Among the rumors inflaming the crowd were vague allegations of anti-Soviet outbursts by former construction battalion soldiers. Local residents, who were determined to destroy this constant source of fear and aggression, were prepared to believe everything and to respond to any provocation. At the same time, they were ready to take advantage of any additional political argument that decisively transformed an opponent into the devil incarnate. Their logic went as follows: Look at what "They" had done—killed a woman and spoken out against Soviet power—and what is more, "They" were *chuchmeki* (this was an insulting ethnic slur used by the participants in the disorders against both the Kazakhs and Uzbeks.—V.K.). With that one word, the crowd and its leaders subconsciously turned their enemies into nonpersons, thereby placing "Them" outside the framework of morality and justifying inhumanity and cruelty.

The subsequent official investigation established that 377 former construction battalion soldiers had arrived in the town of Kimovsk on February 22, 1955. They worked well, but behaved poorly, engaging in hooliganism, fighting, and breaking into the women's dormitory, where they tried to rape the female residents.[50] Over the course of two months, local citizens came to hate these newcomers. Even the local hooligan "elite" clearly sought an opportunity to suppress their competition. Events began on the afternoon of May 2, 1955, with an ordinary drunken brawl in Kimovsk. Local hooligans came out the victors, while three Azerbaijani workers were severely beaten. Escaping pursuit, the workers prepared their comrades to avenge the attack. Armed with sticks and straps, they failed to find the instigator of the fight, so they beat up his comrade instead.

Soon, however, the instigator returned and with him were several more local hooligans. Rocks and knives now entered the picture. Once again the locals had the better of the fight and the former construction battalion soldiers had to hide in the dormitory. When the police arrived at the scene of the brawl, they closed the entrance to the building and pushed back the crowd that had gathered there. At four o'clock an ambulance arrived at the dormitory to pick up the wounded, but hooligans surrounded it. A group of construction workers came out from the dormitory with sticks and belts and tried to disperse those who had gathered. But with cries of "beat the Chuchmeki," the crowd began to throw rocks, and the counterattack disintegrated.

At this point, rumors about the supposed murders committed by the military construction workers and the alleged outbursts of an anti-Soviet nature imparted a certain moral meaning to what had essentially been vulgar mass hooliganism. Consequently, more or less respectable onlookers in the streets found themselves pulled into these events. Local residents began to gather at the dormitory. Several thousand people came, many of whom were drunk. In contrast to the initiators of the confrontation, for whom hooligan activities were to a certain degree self-satisfying, the crowd that was forming needed additional reasons for aggression. There had to be at least an illusory rationalization for what was taking place. It was necessary to assign some kind of higher meaning to the destruction of the enemy and to their own cruelty. Cries rang out: "Beat up the Chuchmeki; they are for Beria."* The name of Beria by this time had been transformed by the efforts of Khrushchevian propaganda into the most loathsome form of political abuse and the supreme manifestation of forces dangerous to the people. Therefore, associating the military construction workers with Beria completely liberated the destructive instincts of the crowd.

Taking advantage of the moral and physical support of local residents, hooligans boldly attacked the police who were guarding the entrance to the dormitory. The rioters broke the glass in the windows, burst into the building, and carried out reprisals against those military workers who had ended up there (several persons were ill and lay on cots). Escaping the attack, construction workers, without offering any opposition, took shelter and barricaded themselves in the attic.

Over several hours the crowd, seized by a mania of murder, repeatedly broke into the dormitory. When they found workers who had been unable to hide, they beat them with shovels, hammers, stools, and rocks, displaying extraordinary cruelty in the process. Six former construction battalion soldiers were attacked and then thrown from the second floor down to the street, where they were beaten to death. Military construction workers from other

---

*Lavrenty Pavlovich Beria (1899–1953) served under Stalin as the head of the NKVD, the secret police. A master of intrigue, Beria was universally feared, and after Stalin's death, Khrushchev and other leaders conspired to have him arrested and put on trial. Charged with a range of crimes against the state, including acting as a British spy, Beria was shot in 1953.—E.M.

dormitories soon got involved in the disturbances. It took additional military units (up to 450 people) to clear the building and push the crowd back. Eleven construction workers died as a result of the battle and three people were seriously wounded. The attackers had smashed all of the glass in the dormitory as well as the window frames, torn down the doors, destroyed tables, beds, and stools, and broken into suitcases, plundering the personal items contained within.[51]

Two other May 1 episodes were much more modest in scale and in destructiveness, but even they were accompanied by confrontations with authorities. In the village of Sokolniki, a fight broke out between a group of local youth and former soldiers during a dance. The fracas ended in the deaths of two military construction workers. Authorities had to employ military patrols of seventy people and two operative police squads to prevent further confrontations.[52] The second conflict, in the town of Ekibastuz, was ethnic in nature. A confrontation of military construction workers with Chechen special settlers was accompanied by an attack on the police department and the murder of three Chechens.[53]

The regular report of Procurator-General Rudenko on these and the March events of 1955 pointed out the acute problems of using militarized labor in industry and on construction sites as well as the need to clarify the legal status of such "demobilized mobilized persons." But it had no impact, and officials continued to improvise with the use of mobilized workers. One of these improvisations ended in scandal. In September 1955, the most significant of all of the known conflicts involving the use of militarized labor in the coal industry occurred in the town of Kemerovo.

The Strike at Kemerovo (September 1955)

This time the disturbances represented a socially conscious protest against an unjust decision of the state. In terms of the scenario, it was very similar to the spontaneous workers' strike of prerevolutionary times. However, the workers had to confront a specific property owner—the state—which predetermined the character of the conflict. They also had to deal with the particular sensitivity of the Moscow bosses toward the demands of the participants in the disorders.

The investigation revealed that in Kemerovo the standard factors exacerbated the already heightened aggression of mobilized workers: many violations of labor discipline, truancy, abolition of the right to a day off, lengthening of the work day in cases of emergency labor, delays in payment of wages and illegal holding back of wages, and difficult working conditions. In some dormitories it was damp and cold. The dining halls and stores were dirty and the personnel often cheated the workers.[54]

Typical symptoms of the Virgin Lands–new-construction-sites syndrome thus existed: a high crime rate, mass hooliganism, the appearance of criminalized subgroups, confrontations between these subgroups, terrorizing of the local populace, and, in extreme cases, conflicts with the police, pogroms, and mass disturbances. The majority of these disorders did not grow to the level of socially conscious actions. At the top of the formulated demands was an insistence that the bad bosses be punished and that comrades detained by the police be freed. Sometimes these comrades were genuine hooligans. Yet sometimes they were simply people who had been on the scene either by mistake or as a result of a misunderstanding.

In the course of the Kemerovo strike, however, the typical volatility of militarized workers came to be ennobled by a conscious struggle for rights against the tyranny of the state. This view imparted obvious political significance to the mass disorders in Kemerovo and graphically demonstrated the limits on the power of Moscow oligarches, who, as it turned out, were not able "to do everything that they desired." The people had their own capacity to provide a popular corrective to Moscow politics, though it was usually hidden behind the cruelty and irrationality of mass uprisings and riots. Moreover, without putting forth any kind of special political demands, a conflictive group achieved a concession and a correction of the line by sacrificing its own spontaneous leaders to the regime: Instigators of these disorders were usually subject to the harshest provisions of the criminal code.

The conflict that broke out in Kemerovo in September 1955 arose from the following events. On July 18, 1955, the Council of Ministers issued a secret decree extending by six months (until April 1, 1956) the term of service for soldiers who had been demobilized from military construction battalions and transferred to build two factories and the Novokemerov Chemical Plant. This decree contradicted the previous promises of the state to allow the demobilized personnel to return home along with their age cohort when they had completed their mandatory service in the regular army. Furthermore, the demobilized construction workers were told nothing about the decree. The construction bosses were thus trying to resolve their problem at someone else's expense, and resorted to unseemly subterfuges.[55]

On September 6, 1955, the newspapers published an order of the minister of defense, Marshal G.K. Zhukov, concerning the discharge to the military reserve of those who had completed their required term of service. The mobilized construction workers, who remained ignorant of the bureaucratic games going on behind the scenes, expected to be returning home soon. The authorities, however, remained silent. Finally, on the morning of September 10, already three days after the publication of the Zhukov order, a large group of mobilized workers in the construction battalions demanded their discharge and payment. In response, the management informed them about the order of the Council of Ministers from July 18, 1955.

Upon learning that, for reasons not fully understood and in spite of promises given earlier, their term of work had been extended for six months, the workers were outraged. What happened next was described in detail by the manager of the enterprise, Stepanenko, to the KGB:

> Question: Will you reconstruct the picture of the mass disorders which occurred in Trust No. 96?

> Answer: At ten o'clock in the morning, a large group came from dormitory 606, where people of different nationalities live . . . and we began to talk with them. Everything was peaceful. As soon as it was read out . . . , that the government had decided to temporarily detain them at the construction site until April 1, 1956, nothing could be discussed. Everyone began speaking at once. Enraged, they broke things and cried out: "So, go ahead and revoke the order of Marshal Zhukov." One stood up, took a pen and ink, and gave it to me to sign! Each man was holding a newspaper. "Sign that you are canceling the order of Zhukov, and stamp it." I said, "I am not Marshal Zhukov and I am not the government, I do not have the right to sign any documents." Then they began to show their own documents which they had received from the Ministry of Defense.[56]

Judging by this account, the crowd at this time was still open to a dialogue with the authorities. Taking the manager of the trust with them, the workers headed for the regional military commissariat. But the military commissar declared that the matter had nothing to do with him, that "these soldiers are not under my jurisdiction, they are demobilized, I do not have any connection with them. Take them away, take them anywhere you wish."[57] The workers dispersed after this altercation, but promised to return on Monday.

Stepanenko then went to the offices of the regional party committee, where the regional procurator and the head of the party committee's administrative department were meeting. The procurator, like the military commissar, tried to shirk all responsibility: "This is not a resolution from the Council of Ministers, but an order, and thus this matter requires an edict about the extension of service, for they have served out their time." They phoned Moscow and reached all the way to the deputy minister of construction. Yet nothing could be resolved there either, and it was decided to phone the head of the construction department of the Central Committee. But at six o'clock in the evening, no one was in the office.[58]

On September 11 (a Sunday), it seemed that everything was peaceful. In the garden, the construction workers had organized an outing. Workers went up to Stepanenko, listened to his promises, and dispersed peacefully. Members of the Communist Party went to the dormitory to try to convince people to go to work on Monday and cease their dawdling. There were no disturbances that day, and the bosses breathed a slight sigh of relief. Subsequently, the bureau of the Kemerovo city party committee in its investigation of events pointed out that the deputy head of the local KGB Main Board "showed a lack of concern and did not know what was going on among the workers on the eve of the mass unrest."[59]

While the authorities consoled themselves with the hope that a peaceful settlement was possible, among the workers informal leaders had already emerged who were busy preparing for a strike. One of them, a foreman, was a native of Tadzhikistan. Uzbek by nationality, he had, at most, two years of education. He first went to his friends among the former soldiers of the construction battalion and then returned to the dormitory. He reported that on September 12, the mobilized construction workers were not going to work, but instead were going to the administration offices to demand a discharge. He called on the civilian workers to support their comrades and not report to work.[60]

During the morning of September 12, someone posted on the doors of one of the dormitories an anonymous, half-literate proclamation: Do not go to work, go to the administration building to resolve the issue of demobilization with the "highest boss from the Ministry of Construction."[61] Stepanenko described events of the day:

> On Monday they came to the office, they beat on the table, on the decanter . . . crying out: "When will you let us go.." . . . I began to say that this was a government decision, and I offered to record for them the number of the order, but I could not give this to them because it was secret. I then said that there is such a resolution in the regional military committee. . . . There the military commissar said to me: "Why have you brought them to me?" I told him: "I am not leading them, they are leading me." He again said that these were not his soldiers, and he had no connection with them, and that we did not have any right to bring them there, they were my employees and I could do with them what I wanted. Then, when they began to force their way in, he started to phone the garrison to send in troops. I told him: do not do this, after all this was not 500, not 200, this was already 1,500 men. I said: I will go to them, I am not afraid.
>
> Question: Where did he [the military commissar] speak with them?
>
> Answer: He spoke with them from the window of the second floor. I went out into the courtyard and said: "Let's go to the club." At this point cries

rang out: "We want the general!" I said that I could not give orders to the general. All of us, over 1,000 people, went directly to the club. I telephoned the plant management office, our party organizer Semenov came to us, as well as the head of the political department, a colonel. They began to converse, and I explained that I had reported to Moscow, that people had come from headquarters, so why don't we all disperse and go to work. Tomorrow cars will be necessary, I will provide them . . . and there will be some kind of clarification. . . . They did not want to listen, but they did disperse.[62]

During the evening of that same day, the head of the Main Board of Construction for Siberia under the Ministry of Construction *(Sibstroi)* flew in from Moscow. On September 13, the workers, numbering around 2,000 people, assembled. Present at the meeting were representatives from the regional and city party committees, the regional procurator, the military commissar, the deputy head of the regional Main Board of the KGB, the boss of Sibstroi, and Stepanenko. They tried to explain the government's order. At first the workers listened calmly, but when, despite their expectations, the leader of Sibstroi again repeated that their term had been extended till April 1, they erupted in anger. At this moment, the bosses simply lost control of the situation. The workers began to go up to the tribunal and read "guarantee letters" that had promised demobilization together with their peers of the same age. Further promises failed to pacify them. The official meeting was disrupted. Stepanenko recalled:

> Everyone threw themselves at me and began to curse: "So, you must dismiss us." One pushed, then another pushed, and then they all encircled me and said that bloodshed was needed. Then they shoved me. I got up and they hit me in the head, then in the side, then on the legs. Then they searched me, thinking that I had the government's resolution in my pocket. All I had was my party card. They examined it and put it in the pocket of my cloak. Then they said: "Where is the decision?" I said: "I have it in my office," and they led me there. While they were taking me, I recall that one dark-skinned man stood near me and defended me, saying, "It's not necessary to kill him." A young guy with a knife came up to me, and to the man who defended me; he also was struck. They took me to the management office. I sat down and felt that I was losing consciousness. There they cried: "Give us the order." I said: "This order will not have any meaning. I cannot overturn government decrees. . . ." Then they all pounced on me, and I felt that the end had come. I said: "The military commissar will not release you." "Well, then we will rip open the general's potbellied stomach." When I signed the order, they said: "Well, the boss is a good man after all, bring some wine, we will treat you to a drink. . . ."

Question: Do you recall the statements, the declarations addressed by the crowd to you and in general?

Answer: I heard shouts from the crowd that this demonstration would be famous in America, that "there is no force capable of opposing those who are armed with an idea." The police were not allowed to approach. When someone came up to me in civilian clothes, they said: "He is a spy, get all these spies away from us." They pushed him away. Basically they demanded that blood had to be spilled, then a decision would come rapidly from Moscow. In any case, they demanded one thing—murder.[63]

In the end, Stepanenko lost consciousness and was taken to the hospital. The crowd, having received their "order," gradually calmed down. In comparison with typical episodes of unrest, the events in Kemerovo were distinguished by a rather high level of self-discipline among participants. In the crowd there were clearly forces for restraint that prevented senseless bloodspilling and human victims, in spite of the provocation. Participants in the disturbances did not engage in the vandalism and looting typical for such situations. The material damage was strikingly minor for such a large number of participants.

Those on strike had their own homespun ideology, based on collective solidarity and on confidence in the force of people united behind a just idea. At the same time, an idea was present in the strikers' motives that had been familiar to Russian authorities since the 1861 abolition of serfdom—the motif of a forged document and negligent bureaucrats who have distorted the will of higher authorities, in this case, Marshal Zhukov. The KGB, in spite of all its efforts, was not able to find in the actions of the participants even the slightest hint of "anti-Soviet agitation." Participants in the Kemerovo disturbances were content to wait rather patiently for the arrival from Moscow of the "correct paper." Cries about how these proceedings would become famous in America were a subconscious attempt to embarrass the state: What will the imperialists think about us? The Moscow leadership, for its part, decided in this case to reach a compromise with the people and support the reputation of the good and just Central Committee. The three hundred party workers sent to the trust "to conduct political work" repeated tirelessly: "There is a decree of the government about their demobilization beginning December 1, 1955."[64] The rebels had won a whole three months from the bosses!

A month later reverberations from the Kemerovo events reached Kiselevsk, a small town in the same Kemerovo Oblast. Ivan Trofimovich Zhukov, deputy head of the Kiselevsk city department of the MVD, who was a CPSU member and a decorated veteran of World War II, agonized over "incorrect communism" and the injustices of the state. Influenced by events in Kemerovo, this honest Soviet citizen wrote several leaflets, which he sent to the Central Committee and posted all over the town:

> Comrade miners, workers! The workers of Kemerovo went on strike in September. Why did they go on strike? They struck against illegal actions and the tyranny of the Soviet bourgeoisie, and not against Soviet power.
>
> The basic law of Soviet power is that everything is for the good of the people. So they say in lectures and write in the newspapers. What does this mean in reality? The reality is quite different. The riches in life are enjoyed by a small clique of people—the Soviet bourgeoisie and their toadies. . . .
>
> Workers do not have flour, or there is one bag for 1,000 people, but for the city party committee there is a closed distribution of goods. Here is the so-called free trade. . . .
>
> Comrades, criticism at meetings will not help. Read our leaflets and relay their contents to your comrades. Expose the Soviet bourgeoisie, their arbitrariness toward you and write leaflets. Reach out and contact us.
>
> For Soviet power without the bourgeoisie. Signed, "The Union of the Just"[65]

These thoughts, which the Kemerovo crowd shared but did not know how to express, about "incorrect" and unjust officials and about the Soviet bourgeoisie who distorted the correct line of Soviet power, were in fact pronounced—in another place and at another time, but for the same reason. Thus, supporters of the regime experienced their first disappointment in the communist utopia. The Soviet bourgeoisie had robbed the people of their "heaven on earth."

Chapter 3

Violent Ethnic Conflicts in the Virgin Lands

The Geography of Violent Ethnic Conflicts

The main centers of violent ethnic conflict in the 1950s were the Virgin Lands, the new industrial construction projects, and the Northern Caucasus. Of the twenty-four known confrontations that had ethnic overtones, twenty occurred in these locations. Outside of this designated conflict zone, ethnic tension either found other, nonviolent forms of expression, bore a political character (the organized nationalist underground in western Ukraine and in the Baltic republics, which engaged in a secret war against the "imperial" state), or existed in a latent, smoldering form that was not visible to authorities. Exceptions would include two gang fights in Kalmykia, in which participants cried out "Beat up the Russians!" and "Beat up the Kalmyks!";[1] an attack by a group of Estonian youth on Russians in 1957;[2] a spontaneous demonstration of Estonian students in Tartu in November 1957, the suppression of which required military intervention;[3] and, in addition, eleven other episodes where ethnicity potentially played a role. But these conflicts were not interpreted by authorities as ethnic, and they hardly alter the general picture.

Out of the twenty-four episodes that are known to have occurred between 1953 and 1960 involving conflict between different ethnic groups, thirteen involved Chechens and Ingush against Russians and three involved Chechens and Ingush against Ossetians and Avars. These make up almost 70 percent of all the documented violent ethnic conflicts. Only Russians engaged in such conflicts more often than did the Chechens and the Ingush (there were sixteen documented episodes involving Chechens and Ingush against nineteen episodes involving Russians).

The Chechens were more involved in violent conflicts than the Ingush were. From time to time during the period of their exile to Kazakhstan and other areas in Central Asia, arguments arose between these two related ethnic groups, *(Vainakhi)** particularly over who had been more guilty in causing the deportation. In August 1946, the minister of internal affairs, S.N. Kruglov, reported that some Ingush special settlers who had once occupied high posts in the party-state hierarchy "suggested in conversations that the Ingush would not have been exiled if they had not been united with the Chechens." Such conversations, Kruglov wrote, had sown "antagonism between the Chechens and the Ingush. The latter consider that the Chechens were the first to organize bands and help the Germans in occupying the Northern Caucasus."[4]

In 1944, the majority of the Vainakhi (335,000) had been deported to Kazakhstan. A smaller number, about 77,000, went to Kirgizia. During the term of exile, while the so-called "restriction of special settlement" functioned, limits existed on mobility—the freedom to relocate was prohibited, and there were systematic identity checks, along with other harsh methods of police control. Such measures were to ensure that the "punished peoples" did not present any special problems for the government.

Understanding their own weakness before the cruel government machine and its "all-seeing eye," the NKVD, the Chechens and the Ingush, like the other deported nationalities, were externally submissive and appeared to have reconciled themselves with their fate. They began to create a new life in their places of exile. Keeping a watchful eye on the special settlers, the Moscow party leadership in August 1945 received soothing news from the MVD chief Kruglov: "The majority of the Chechen and Ingush accepted the decree abolishing the Chechen-Ingush Autonomous Soviet Socialist Republic (ASSR) as a measure that decisively excluded any hope for their return to their homeland. Correspondingly, they have decided to establish a permanent home in the area of their new settlement."[5]

To a certain degree, the peaceful statements of the Vainakhi, many of which Kruglov quoted in his report, were purposefully tactful, uttered with the recognition that words of humility would go straight to the bosses. In their own circles, among trustworthy people, the Chechens spoke in a much different tone. They did not lose hope, which was nurtured by extremely

---

*The Chechens and Ingush (related groups collectively known as *Vainakhi*) had been among those nationalities exiled from their homelands to Kazakhstan and Siberia during World War II. They were accused by the Stalinist government of having collaborated with the German occupiers, but were mainly being punished for earlier resistance to Soviet rule.—E.M.

improbable rumors: allegedly the United States, England, and France at an upcoming international conference would demand from the Soviet government that the special settlers be returned to the place of their former residence, and so on.[6]

In general, after deportation the police state sought both to utilize old mechanisms of control over "dangerous" nationalities as well as to create new ones. For example, the national elites, although exiled along with everyone else, nonetheless preserved their membership in the Communist Party. This membership provided certain privileges (subsequently party members were the first to be freed from the "restrictions of special settlement"), but morally it disarmed these elites, rendering them incapable of leading any active resistance or having any influence on public opinion.

Having thereby neutralized the Soviet ethnic elite and intelligentsia, the secret police focused on religious authorities, who always seem to be found in a natural opposition to the unbelievers. In 1946, the Kazakh Ministry of Internal Affairs successfully conducted the "dispersal of several anti-Soviet groupings, which consisted of Islamic clergy." But in addition to carrying out repression against irreconcilable elements, the organs of state security quite widely and sometimes successfully used the more loyal part of the Islamic clergy to control the behavior of the "dangerous" peoples. Minister of Internal Affairs Kruglov, for example, developed a facile myth of the loyal Islamic mullah, whose teachings helped to improve labor discipline and even doubled labor productivity.[7]

The Chechens and the Ingush: Between Exile and Repatriation

Until 1954, the deported peoples, who, according to Stalin's intentions, were to remain in the places of their exile forever, did not cause any special worries for authorities (the use of harsh measures stopped any flights of freedom-loving Vainakhi to their homelands). But in 1954, an indecisive and contradictory process of rehabilitation and the return of civil rights began. In the course of 1954, 1955, and the first half of 1956, all Germans, Crimean Tatars, Kalmyks, and Balkars were no longer to be registered as special settlers, but did not yet receive the right to return to their former homelands.

The Karachaevtsy, Chechens, and Ingush remained under suspicion from the state for a longer time than did the others, although, in truth, some allowances were made even for them. On July 5, 1954, administrative limitations on children up to sixteen years of age were lifted, thereby allowing at least the youth to breathe more freely. On March 9, 1955, the Central Committee Presidium liquidated all restrictions on special settlers who were party members, and on the next day, the Chechens, Ingush, and Karachaevtsy received the right to have a passport along with all the other exiled peoples.[8]

All of these principled and somewhat cautious political actions coincided with a massive flood of new peoples into the Virgin Lands. Within this already seething cauldron of social passions and group conflicts, there arose new potential conflictive groups—the repressed peoples who were now freed from police control but were still deprived until 1957 of the right to return to their homeland. Today it is possible only to speculate where the line of conflict would have developed in the Virgin Lands if the restoration of civil rights had not quickly been followed by another decision restoring the autonomy of the majority of the deported peoples (except for the Volga Germans and the Crimean Tatars), thereby relieving tensions at least temporarily.

The fate of Chechen-Ingush autonomy for some time hung by a thread. At first, the Chechens and Ingush faced returning not to their old home as they remembered it, but to land that had been occupied after their deportation by new settlers from central Russia and from areas in the Northern Caucasus that were lacking in arable land. But the chief of police—the minister of internal affairs, N.P. Dudorov*—advised against the restoration of Chechen-Ingush autonomy in the Northern Caucasus, citing the potentially high activism of these ethnic groups and the possibility of excessive violence in the region. Instead he proposed a purely bureaucratic solution—create an autonomous oblast (not even a republic) for the Chechens and Ingush in the territory of Kazakhstan or Kirgizia.[9] Without even realizing it, the Soviet minister had repeated the same cautious logic and arguments of the tsarist government. In response to the "anti-imperial" attitude of the Chechens and Ingush, who had never accepted the legitimacy of the "white tsar," the tsarist regime had dreamed about the complete deportation of these "disturbers of the peace."

The moral side of this issue is obvious. But from a purely utilitarian police point of view, to leave the Chechens and Ingush in the Virgin Lands was potentially explosive. Both peoples had made themselves at home and had adapted to their new situation. The majority worked on collective and state farms, and also in enterprises of nonferrous metallurgy, in coal and other local industries. For twelve years, many had built their own homes with private plots or lived in communal apartments. No matter how much the Chechens and Ingush thirsted for their homeland (and among them in the mid-1950s the desire to return was especially strong), they had come to con-

---

*N.P. Dudorov, a Central Committee functionary, replaced Kruglov as head of the MVD on the eve of the Twentieth Party Congress in 1956.—E.M.

sider themselves to be local inhabitants. As such, they had even experienced the powerful pressure of new waves of migration, as well as the delights of the Virgin Lands–new-construction-site syndrome. Certainly they were capable of making their own contribution to the riots and disorders of these areas.

Violent Conflicts Involving the Chechens and Ingush in the Virgin Lands

These ethnic groups possessed a high degree of internal self-organization. Even in exile the Vainakhi preserved the traditions of the Murids, a hierarchical Muslim religious brotherhood dating back to a nineteenth-century Sufi movement fanatically opposed to Russian imperial expansion (according to NKVD estimates, this movement numbered about 20,000 people in the Chechen-Ingush ASSR before World War II).[10] Thus, when they faced a new migration of settlers from Russia to Kazakhstan, after having just experienced the stress of deportation and exile, the Chechens and Ingush were capable of responding with corresponding aggression, and in a number of cases did so. In their structure, these violent conflicts differed little from the collective fights, mass hooliganism, and confrontations among competing youth groups that were typical of the Virgin Lands and new construction site districts. In a number of cases, the Chechens and Ingush were obvious victims of aggression from newcomers, while in other cases the Vainakhi were the instigators of conflict. But usually the situation in the Kazakh Virgin Lands did not reach the point of serious ethnic riots and disorders.

In the first known conflicts involving Russians against the Chechens and Ingush, the latter were still acting in their capacity as special settlers (December 1954). For example, in the village of Elizavetinka in the Kazakh SSR, an additional mobilizing factor for the Russian participants in a collective fight were political accusations levied at the Chechens. Students at a vocational school taunted the latter as "betrayers and traitors of the Motherland."[11] Other such cases involving political motives for Russian participation in ethnic conflicts in Kazakhstan have not been discovered. There were certainly none in the criminal activities of the laborers mobilized for work in the coal industry as described in the previous chapter. In May 1955, a fight broke out between one such worker in the coal industry and a Chechen special settler in the Kazakh city of Ekibastuz. The confrontation ended in a drunken pogrom against Chechens, which then grew into an attack of Russian hooligans on police headquarters, where the Chechens had run for protection.[12]

On July 16, 1956, the Presidium of the USSR Supreme Soviet abolished administrative restrictions over the Chechens, Ingush, Karachaevtsy, and members of their families who had been exiled during World War II. Although they no longer had to regularly check in at special offices, they did not receive the right to have property that had been confiscated during their exile restored or remunerated, nor were they allowed to move back to their homeland. Nonetheless, the Chechens and Ingush were eager to regain their former homes, and under various pretexts, began to return on their own to the Northern Caucasus. Only force could stop this movement. But political considerations prohibited the Soviet leadership from using such means. Khrushchev had just delivered his secret speech at the Twentieth Party Congress, where he had exposed the crimes of Stalin, including the violent deportation of non-Russian nationalities. Through careful police measures, assurances, and promises of rapid restoration of autonomy, the state was able for a brief period to stop the wave of unauthorized returns to the Northern Caucasus.

Restoration of Chechen-Ingush Autonomy and the Mass Repatriation of the Chechen and Ingush Peoples

On January 9, 1957, the Presidiums of the USSR and RSFSR Supreme Soviets restored Chechen-Ingush autonomy and defined its territorial structure. The ban on the return of the Vainakhi to their homeland was lifted. The state created a special Organizational Committee to organize the repatriation, which until the elections to the Supreme Soviet of the newly restored autonomous republic, was to occupy itself with "economic and cultural construction on the territory of the republic."[13]

After this political decision, ethnic conflicts in the Virgin Lands involving Chechens and Ingush basically ended, at least until the summer of 1958. Yet tensions remained and even strengthened. With the onset of spring, a mass spontaneous exodus of Chechens and Ingush to the Chechen-Ingush and North Ossetian ASSR began in 1957. People were afraid that they were going to miss the spring agricultural work. But police cordons stopped them on the road. A large number of impatient and unsettled people gathered in towns and temporary settlements.[14] MVD agents reported that all the Chechens and Ingush were prepared to leave for their former homes in May and June.[15] Authorities considered mass disorders a definite possibility. Near the building of the Karaganda regional party committee, large crowds of Chechens and Ingush gathered every day, stopping cars of the party secretaries and demanding that they be allowed to pass through freely.[16]

There were no laws or general legal decisions that could have prevented an immediate exodus. Driven by their own fears, MVD organs detained the Chechens and Ingush at railroad stations and took them off the trains. This was nothing other than blatant arbitrariness, without any legal basis. The Soviet leadership, which was preoccupied with purely police problems, seemingly did not even notice that, instead of the usual spontaneous disorders and violent conflicts, it faced an even more significant phenomenon. The spring events of 1957 not only reanimated the centuries-old conflict between empire and ethnicity, but also infused it with new meaning and strengthened it with new resentments.

The Ministry of Internal Affairs, despite its arbitrary administrative decisions, nonetheless managed to get local party authorities to provide temporary housing and work for those Chechen and Ingush settlers who had been detained while making their way back to their homeland.[17] At the same time, the MVD requested from the Central Committee additional restrictions limiting the freedom of movement for Chechens and Ingush (refusing to sell them train tickets, not removing them from Communist Party and Komsomol registration in their place of exile, and so on).[18] All of this was typical police improvisation which the Central Committee, nonetheless, fully supported.

Finding itself caught between a rock and a hard place, the Moscow leadership temporarily halted the return of the Chechens and Ingush to their homeland during the summer of 1957. The Chechens and Ingush, who had sold their homes and part of their belongings, quit their jobs, and were living out of suitcases in the volatile Virgin Land zone, represented a potentially destabilizing force. However, in the Northern Caucasus a tense situation was also taking shape, for the mass, spontaneous return of the Vainakhi to their homeland had caught the authorities by surprise. The center of ethnic conflicts began to shift to the Chechen districts in the Northern Caucasus, where conflicts erupted increasingly, often between the Vainakhi and those settlers who had occupied Chechen lands and homes after 1944. Again authorities basically improvised. The choice was made between two evils. They decided to detain the Chechens and Ingush in the Virgin Lands, where a police-secured "organized resettlement" had already been imposed.

April 1957: Roadblocks

In order to stop the spontaneous flow of the "returnees," authorities instituted a wide-scale operation. On April 8, 1957, Minister of Internal Affairs Dudorov reported to the Central Committee secretary, N.I. Beliaev:

. . . measures have been taken to bring an immediate end to this unautho-rized movement, to detain those leaving without permission of the Organi-zational Committee, and to return them to the areas of their former resettlement. As a result of the measures taken by the railroad police de-partments with the help of internal affairs territorial institutions, by the morning of April 8 the unorganized migration of Chechens and Ingush on the railroads was halted.

According to the report of the Kazakh minister of internal affairs, a large number of Chechens and Ingush had already been congregating in the re-gional centers of the republic; they had "been discharged from work, had sold their possessions and were insistent upon leaving for their former place of residence."[19]

The Organizing Committee was supposed to establish administrative con-trol over this spontaneous migration homeward, but serious corruption and abuses marred its effectiveness.[20] Those guilty did receive party reprimands, but rumors had exaggerated the abuses, and the Vainakhi had already lost confidence in the committee. As a result, it was not able to control the situa-tion. Among the Chechens and Ingush, the opinion was widespread that sev-eral members of the Organizing Committee, who were former leaders of the Chechen-Ingush ASSR, had been coparticipants in the deportation. Even the attempts of the committee to rely on authoritative elders and on the families of sheiks did not work.

The mass flight of the Vainakhi continued. Even attempts to fortify police arbitrariness with mass propaganda and economic stimuli—the right to re-ceive generous loans to construct homes, acquire horned cattle, etc.—did not halt the exodus. Such benefits would only accrue to those former special settlers who returned "in an organized manner."[21] Up to six months after the spring events of 1957, the MVD organs were still continuing to catch and detain the fugitives.

In 1958, during the summer (the traditional time for an outflow of tempo-rary workers to the Virgin Lands to gather the harvest and engage in agricul-tural work, as well as for incidental gang fights and mass hooliganism), conflicts in Kazakhstan involving Chechen and Ingush youth again erupted.[22] But these conflicts were small in number (only three episodes are docu-mented), and there was nothing in them that distinguished them from the usual Virgin Lands confrontations between locals and newcomers.

By the spring of 1959, the majority of the Vainakhi had departed.[23] Yet some had decided to remain. Included among those who stayed were future victims of a cruel Ingush pogrom and mass disorders in the city of Dzhetygara, Kustanaisk Oblast, Kazakh SSR.

July 1960: The Ingush Pogrom in Dzhetygara

The Wealthy Sagadaevs

The events of July 31, 1960, began as a typical Virgin Lands confrontation among local (meaning permanent residents of the city) Ingush and newcomers. However, subsequent events proved to be unusual. Other local residents (the non-Ingush) not only did not repulse the newcomers, but they joined with them against the local Ingush, bringing appalling brutality to the conflict.

The Ingush family known as the Sagadaevs (the family name has been changed by the author to protect the privacy of the victims) was traditional in structure, with fourteen children and three generations united under one roof. The head of the family, a retiree on a pension, was fifty-eight years old. Two sons worked as dentists, with one employed in a hospital and the other practicing at home. Two other sons were truck drivers, work that in provincial areas always brought opportunities for reliable profits and extra earnings "under the table." The family was well provided for and quite comfortable. It was even able to buy two new cars, although just buying one in this time period would be sufficient to gain a reputation as being wealthy. In the house there were many expensive fabrics, textiles, a large quantity of wheat, and other necessities that were being rationed, such as 138 sheets of roofing iron. It was impossible simply to buy such items. Rather, one had to "acquire," "to know how to live," which in popular consciousness was associated usually with slyness and resourcefulness, as well as with a certain degree of dishonesty. On the eve of these events in Dzhetygara, one of the brothers was suspected of having stolen 2,800 kilograms of grain through artless intrigues. In the excitement of the unrest, the criminal matter was dropped, insofar as the suspect was brutally murdered during the disorders.[24] Information about the alleged theft even ended up in the formal indictment of one of the murderers, as if to justify indirectly the suspect's murder.[25] All of the remaining suspicions were never substantiated.[26]

The family, judging by all the evidence, lived in seclusion. The sons, however, if one believes the police reports, acted as though they were "masters of life": "They behaved aggressively toward others, and there were cases of hooliganism connected with them."[27] Such aggressive self-assertiveness was typical in the Virgin Lands and new construction sites, representing a paradoxical form of adaptation to an alien environment under the conditions of deep cultural stress. The unique aspect of the given situation, which was inflamed by ethnic competition, lay only in the fact that the group in conflict was not an accidental or fluid association of people, but constituted a solid single family unit. It was precisely this family unit that engendered the envy and irritation of the residents of Dzhetygara. The indictment especially emphasized that "one of the reasons for the mass disorders and the mob trial of Ingush people was the fact that the victims . . . engaged in a suspicious (criminal) way of life."[28]

The Crowd and the Demobilized Sailors

According to different sources, from 500 to 1,000 residents of Dzhetygara took part in the disorders. The investigation asserted that "the active participation in the violence of morally degenerate persons with prior convictions, the majority of whom were drunk, encouraged the involvement of residents of Dzhetygara in the group fight."[29] The majority of those tried, however, did not have prior convictions, and there is nothing remarkable in their biographies. In general, the local inhabitants appear in the materials of the case as an amorphous and faceless mob—a crowd practically deprived of individuality, but whose collective ferocity inspired the active participants in the conflict. Certain nameless persons flash by continually in the unfolding drama: teenagers who brought their parents' weapons and gave these to participants in the attack, those who plundered the pilfered possessions, and those who spread rumors through the crowd that gathered at the home of the Sagadaevs. Nothing more is known about them, as if they rose only momentarily from dormancy and then disappeared again into the general mass of people. The common thread for all was envy of the "dishonest, wealthy Sagadaevs." "Dishonest" could have been forgiven, but it was impossible to forgive "wealth." The materials of the case reveal only one person who tried to calm down the attackers, a man named N.G. Ershov, but for this he received a blow to the face.[30]

The prelude to the mass disorders and pogrom was a confrontation between demobilized sailors and a member of the Sagadaev family, who was accompanied by a friend. The sailors represented a rather typical, potentially volatile virgin lands–new construction-site group. They were outsiders who had arrived in the city less than a month earlier. Studying to be drivers, they lived eight kilometers from the city. Receiving only a very small stipend, the sailors, it seems, were not very satisfied with their lives. There was little in the way of entertainment, and the club at the motor depot did not have a movie theater, a record player, or even a single chessboard.

In the aggressive actions of the sailors, there was no indication of ethnic hostility, nor any kind of particular social envy toward the Sagadaevs. The sailors simply did not know the city and the people well enough. Shortly after the events, former sailors of the Baltic fleet sent a complaint to the Communist Party leadership in which they talked about one motive quite standard for conflicts—competition with other groups. Not long prior to these events, the Ingush had cursed and beaten up one of the demobilized sailors at a dance.[31]

On July 31, 1960, after a drinking bout celebrating the Soviet holiday devoted to the Navy (the Day of the Soviet Navy), the demobilized sailors wandered drunkenly through the city. At approximately three o'clock in the afternoon, three of the sailors ended up in the center of the city, where they encountered the elder Sagadaev and his Tatar friend, both of whom were also drunk. All of the participants in the conflict recalled previous grievances and acted aggressively and provocatively. One of the sailors hit the Tatar, and in response the latter joined with Sagadaev to bloody the sailor's nose. Three people passing by (judging by their names, they were Ingush or Tatar) stepped in and separated the two sides, thereby preventing the fight from expanding.

Sagadaev and his friend left, but the remaining sailors picked a fight with new antagonists. The police then arrived at the scene and sent the wounded man with the broken nose to the hospital. His comrades, about fifteen to twenty in number, learned about the fight and set out to find the ill-fated trio who had intervened in the original confrontation. The search failed, so the soldiers instead sought out the home of the Sagadaevs. The police, sensing trouble, tried to terminate the conflict by detaining Sagadaev and his friend "for questioning," but they were too late. The police arrived at the home almost at the same time as the group of determined sailors.[32]

When the police brought out the Sagadaevs from the house, a large group of the sailors approached and began to physically attack the family members. With the help of the police, the Sagadaevs broke loose and ran back into their home. By this time, a large crowd of 500 to 1,000 local residents had gathered. Some called for settling accounts with the Sagadaevs; others called for disobeying the police. The agitated crowd began to storm the house, flinging rocks and sticks at the windows.

The family prepared to defend itself. In the house there were two small-caliber rifles and three hunting rifles, for which the Sagadaevs had official licenses—obviously the future victims had felt uncomfortable in the city and had prepared in advance to defend themselves and all that they held dear. In the end, the six men who were inside the house responded to the crowd's aggression by firing shots. They seem to have been aiming directly at the sailors, who were distinguished from the rest of the crowd by their uniforms.[33] One bullet accidentally hit a policeman. The official investigation reported that he had arrived on the scene, saw several persons wounded by the Sagadaevs, received a light head wound, and then "opened fire on the house with his pistol."[34]

The police acted quite ambivalently. On the one hand, they tried to stop the unrest and defend the Sagadaevs. On the other hand, however, after the shots were fired, they basically joined in storming the house with the crowd. The investigation later made note of the "absence of requisite organization" in the actions of the police and of the troops that were brought to the scene—twenty unarmed soldiers from the antiaircraft defense battalion. In reality, the "absence of requisite organization" meant the use by the military of chlorine cartridges, the random firing by police into the house, and the like.[35] As a result, a large part of the crowd simply did not comprehend what was going on. It was not clear whether they were storming the house of the "wealthy ones" at their own risk and peril or whether they were helping the police storm the house, or whether the police and soldiers were trying to save the Ingush from reprisals. The fighting grew more brutal when the shots from the house wounded fifteen local residents (one of whom subsequently died) and sailors.

Those who were attacking the Sagadaev home acquired weapons and began to fire in response. A dump truck came up to the house, and the attackers were able to use it as a shield to get closer to the fence. Someone climbed up onto the roof of the house and began to throw rocks from there. One of the defendants in his subsequent appeal described the course of events as such:

> From the side of the house, not far from the crowd, shots rang out. The people demanded that we help to disarm the Ingush, who had killed several sailors. I asked, "But where are the police, and why are they allowing these disturbances?" . . . I was told: "The police are afraid and have run away." I was not able to make further inquiries, since at this time I saw three Ingush men running out onto the street with weapons in their hands, and one of them had two small-caliber guns and began to fire at the crowd. In front of my eyes a shot felled a sailor who had been standing at the edge of the roof. Some civilians took his body down from the roof and carried him away. . . . All around people were crying that these sailors had been beaten to death. Everyone was shouting that it was necessary to immediately disarm the Ingush. I looked around, hoping to see the police, but there was not a single one present. People were making a stir all around, fussing that you could not disarm the Ingush with your bare hands, it was necessary to bring in some weapons and intimidate them, so that they would stop killing people and hand over their guns. At this time several young people about fifteen years old came up to me and said that in their home there was a weapon, and they could give it to me, so I went off together with these guys. At their home they gave me a gun and some cartridges. I decided to take the weapon in order to help disarm the Ingush, and to intimidate them. . . . I then set off for the place where shots continued to be heard.

On the road back a woman came up to me and said: "Do not go to that house, young man, you might get killed there. The Ingush have already killed many of your sailors."[36]

By this time the crowd had brutally murdered the elder Sagadaev as revenge for the sailors wounded and killed during the storming of the house. Those defenders of the Sagadaev house who were still alive prepared to escape by car.[37]

The agitated crowd, though, was not satisfied even with the murders that had already been committed. Someone set the house on fire, and while it was burning, part of the attackers began to plunder. Others were consumed with thirst for senseless destruction, caring nothing for personal gain but simply seizing items taken from the home and throwing them into the fire. They also burned one of the Sagadaev automobiles and a motorcycle that belonged to a guest from the Northern Caucasus.[38] In the indictment these illogical actions were described by one of the participants in the events: "When the fire began, I repeatedly went into the burning house and brought out various things and threw them into the fire I smashed the radio and the wall clocks. In addition, along with others I took part in burning grain, which was stored in bags lying in the yard."[39]

The firemen could not even get through to put out the fire. They received threats, which appeared convincing given the blood already shed. Then, during the first attempt to douse the fire, the fire truck was put out of service. Subsequently the house and all of the belongings of the Sagadaevs burned to ashes.

While a large portion of the crowd was destroying the home and possessions of the Sagadaevs, the family members who had escaped from the house in a car left the city in an attempt to hide themselves. An organized pursuit commenced as a group of sailors and local residents in three trucks began to follow the Ingush. Once again an inexplicable situation emerged for all participants in the events. A group of police and civilian police volunteers, headed by the district police chief, went off in the same direction in two police cars. Once again the situation appeared as though the rioters and the police were acting together—to catch criminals (the Ingush).[40]

The Ingush, having realized that they were being pursued, turned back toward the city and tried to barricade themselves in the police building. A crowd of four to five hundred people quickly gathered at the building and began to beat on the windows, break down doors, and demand that the Sagadaevs be handed over. The latter, for their own part, again opened fire. According to eyewitnesses, shots rang out continuously and wounded several persons. Attempts by the police to defend the Ingush from the mob immediately made the police the target of aggression. Part of the crowd went into police headquarters, where they cut telephone lines (probably out of fear that the police would call for help and interfere in the reprisals), disarmed the policemen assigned to guard the preliminary detention cell, and beat up the duty officer. Participants in the attack threatened violence against the district police chief and forced him to open up the detention cell and other service rooms.[41]

Complete turmoil reigned within the police building and all around it. Someone unsuccessfully tried to calm the crowd. Others threw themselves on the police chief and tried to disarm him, and a third group stopped the attackers.[42] The majority went looking for the Ingush. Having found the latter in the office of the police chief, the mob brutally murdered them. The crowd threw stones at its victims, stomped on them, threw their bodies under the wheels of a car, and so on.[43]

What Happened in Dzhetygara?

The unrest in Dzhetygara more closely resembled prerevolutionary Jewish pogroms than the typical virgin lands–new-construction-site disturbances. Behind the guise of ethnic conflict, however, was hidden an even uglier egalitarian reaction of post-Stalinist mass consciousness to a new social phenomenon, which at the end of the 1950s was called "dacha capitalism" (this phrase was used to criticize those who were violating the egalitarian values of early Bolshevism in their drive to acquire such capitalist attributes as property, summer homes, etc.—V.K.). Postwar Soviet society had just crawled up out of the abyss of Stalinist purges and social leveling. It had faced and overcome the destruction of war and postwar famines. Consequently, the scorn and even boundless hatred and cruelty of "honest folk" toward "those who know how to live" became a "distorted class consciousness" that the regime itself cultivated. This primitive consciousness perceived the reality with feelings of surprise and disappointment. Social envy and traditional Russian hatred for the rich were reborn. Unconscious egalitarianism, which had already turned into disappointment in "hackneyed" Soviet bosses, targeted those persons who did not live by the rules, or whose well-being, either as it seemed or as it was in reality, was based on suspicious foundations.

In a word, the events in Dzhetygara, in an obscure, extremely distorted, and slurred form, hinted at certain substantial transformations in everyday life, which had great significance for the fate of Soviet communism. The ideology, which used the semantics of West European Marxism but in truth was primitive, "peasantized," and vulgar, thus revealed the first signs of degradation—disappointment in the "incorrect socialism" that had triumphed in the Soviet Union. The time of passion and enthusiasm for supporters of the regime had passed. It was replaced by something new and inexplicable. The pro-Soviet and pro-Communist mass consciousness had lost its former guideposts and consequently it grew embittered.

The state faced a dilemma. Its representatives had to defend the rich and the "politically suspicious" Ingush from its own people—the volunteers in the Virgin Lands and the demobilized sailors. It was not accidental that in the official correspondence that arose in the course of the investigation and preparation for the trial, one question was exaggerated: Where did the wealth come from? It was as if the authorities were trying to explain and justify subconsciously the pathological cruelty of the crowd, which had consisted of the "simple Soviet people." Despite the fact that only one of the suspicions about the Sagadaevs, the theft of grain from the local state farm warehouse, was more or less verified, the conclusion about the "suspicious [read criminal] way of life" of the Sagadaevs nonetheless was drawn and even found its way into the indictment. In the end, the inexplicable behavior of the Soviet people was ascribed to certain "dark forces," allegations that also were not substantiated by the materials of the judicial investigation.

Maybe the truly guilty ones were not found?

Chapter 4

The Return of the Deported Nations to the Northern Caucasus: The 1958 Riots in Grozny

The "Syndrome of Return"

In the mid-1950s, national autonomy was restored to the Kalmyks, Chechens, Ingush, Karachaevtsy, and Balkars, all of whom had been deported during World War II. Over several years, they returned to their homelands from exile. On the whole, the repatriation went rather smoothly, with only eight documented cases of violent conflicts. Two gang fights between Russian and Kalmyk youth[1] occurred in Eliste, the capital of Kalmykiia, in 1957 and 1959, while the rest occurred on the territory of Chechnia, Ingushetiia, and the bordering districts of North Ossetia and Dagestan. But one episode stands out as one of the largest and most enigmatic of all of the mass disorders of the 1950s—the Grozny disturbances, which included riots, a Chechen pogrom, a two-day-long protest meeting, the distribution of leaflets and collective petitions, strikes, and attacks on the offices of the regional party committee, the MVD, and the KGB.

The first signs of a "syndrome" connected with repatriation to Chechnia and Ingushetiia emerged in 1955, when the restrictions on the deported peoples were lifted from party members, but without allowing them to go back to their homeland. Taking advantage of their relative freedom, some Chechens and Ingush (Vainakhi), including nonparty members, decided to risk returning to the North Caucasus. The few who were able to break through the roadblocks to Chechnia, Ingushetiia, Northern Ossetiia, Dagestan, and Kabarda tried to find work. They also asked the state to return to them their homes that had been given away to new settlers who had come into the region after the 1944 deportation of the Vainakhi. Rumors circulated, exaggerated as always, about threatening nighttime visits from the former proprietors, and this caused the frightened settlers from central Russia to consider returning to their own original homelands.

In particular, the party leadership in Grozny Oblast feared either possible counteraggression from the Russian settlers or an uncontrollable exodus of Russians from the Northern Caucasus. Thus, at first it sought to control the situation by detaining those Chechens and Ingush who had forced their way through the roadblocks. They were then returned to their legal place of residence, that is, their places of exile.

In 1956, however, this spontaneous return to the homeland accelerated as the Chechens and Ingush continued to pine for the Northern Caucasus. They did not want to wait patiently for their fate to be resolved, nor did they wish to be settled in those areas prescribed for them by the bureaucratic bosses. They wanted to regain their native homes, which the state had taken from them in 1944. But now these homes were occupied, and the people who were living in them could not, even if they desired, give up their household overnight. Tense competition for resources and living space arose.

In December 1956, the situation in the Northern Caucasus became violent. An Ingush man who had returned from exile showed up with his family at the house of a resident living in the settlement of Novyi Ardon, Kosta-Khetagurov district. The Ingush returnee announced that this house had belonged to him before the deportation, and his family intended to live in it once again. The Ossetian resident declared that only the village council could resolve the matter. A fight broke out when a group of drunken collective farmers interfered in the argument. One Ingush was killed and ten were wounded, three of whom were Ossetian.[2] The first alarm bell had sounded.

In January 1957, the Presidium of the USSR Supreme Soviet finally restored Chechen-Ingush autonomy. This act not only renamed Grozny Oblast the Chechen-Ingush ASSR, but restored autonomy practically to the prewar borders, with an exception being made for the Prigorod district, which remained part of the North Ossetian ASSR. The restored autonomous republic received territory from the Dagestan ASSR and from the North Ossetian ASSR, as well as the northern part of the Dushet district of the Georgian SSR.[3]

The newly recarved borders presupposed an orderly, planned resettlement of some of the postwar settlers to other territories, but bureaucratic dreams of a painless process collided with the mass, partially planned, partially spontaneous, return of Chechens and Ingush to their homelands. Police measures and propagandistic efforts of party and soviet organs failed to substantially slow down this fast-flowing repatriation. According to the plan, 17,000 families were to return in 1957 to Chechnia-Ingushetiia, but in reality, twice this number, 34,635 families, had already returned by September 1, 1957.[4]

Many Chechens and Ingush insisted that they be allowed to return to the land of their ancestors—"to those villages and even to those homes, in which they had lived before their deportation."[5] As discussed earlier, this natural desire collided with the reality that their native homeland was now occupied by new settlers from other districts of the Caucasus and from central Russia. For these people who had been living in Chechnia-Ingushetiia since 1944, the return of the Vainakhi was a great shock. The authorities planned to send the Dagestan population[6] and the Ossetians who had settled there back to their respective homelands in order to relieve the growing tension, but this process clearly lagged behind the mass return of the Vainakhi to Chechnia-Ingushetiia.

An acute conflict of interests thus emerged with little hope for compromise. In the settlement of Moksob, thirty-two Chechen families were housed temporarily in the village club, under terribly crowded conditions. All efforts to convince local residents, who were Avars, to voluntarily share their homes with Chechen families were unsuccessful. Even an attempt to place one of the Chechens in an empty home angered the Avars. About a hundred people immediately gathered near the house and tried to beat up the Chechen, and they would have killed him if the police had not intervened. After this, the crowd of Avars, armed with sticks, headed to the club demanding the removal of the Chechens. Fearing the conflict would expand, the authorities conceded and took the Chechens out of the settlement.[7] The roles of victim and aggressor varied in each case. In the Novoselsk district, for example, it was the Chechens who went into the recreation center, used foul language, refused to allow anyone into the building, waved knives, and "let out cries of a nationalist character."[8]

The history of ethnic opposition in the first months of 1957 is filled with these unpleasant episodes. Rumors further strengthened their popular impact. Consequently, the Chechens were a mobilized ethnic group ready to defend their interests aggressively, and this made them ultimate victors in the war of nerves taking place in the Chechen-Ingush territory and in the border districts of neighboring republics.

Ethnic Competition and the "Strategy for Survival"

The success of the Chechens was determined by the systematic squeezing out of ethnic competitors. Preferring to avoid violent confrontations, the

Chechens obviously sensed subconsciously that a strategy of small steps would be most effective. Perhaps Chechen elders and religious authorities consciously restrained the youth, or an instinct of self-preservation prevailed, since open conflicts and mass disorders could provoke a reaction from the state. Regardless of the reason, despite continual ethnic tension in the rural districts of the republic, mass confrontations were rare, and only one was truly serious. On July 17, 1957, in the village of Shali, four soldiers of the local MVD guard garrison went to the river, where two decided to bathe. A young Chechen approached them and "cursing the soldiers, forbid them to bathe." A fight broke out and the Chechen called for help from his relatives. Several men and women armed with hoes, sticks, axes, and a gun attacked the soldiers, three of whom were wounded.

When he heard about this incident, the commander of the MVD unit went to the river with an armed detachment. They disarmed the Chechen attackers and took six to the Shali police department. The daughter of one of the Chechens involved in the fight later appeared on the streets of Shali crying out that during the fracas, the soldiers had drowned her nursing baby in the river, though in reality she had given the baby over to a relative. Subsequently about two hundred men and women gathered around the police department, demanding immediate punishment for the soldiers and the removal of the military. After an explanation from police, the protesters gradually dispersed.[9]

Despite the rarity of open conflict, the ever growing pressure from the returning Vainakhi distressed the settlers who had moved to the Northern Caucasus after 1944. Consequently, those desiring to leave the rural districts of Chechnia-Ingushetiia turned out to be several times larger in number than the authorities had originally planned. The current settlers in the Northern Caucasus flooded Moscow with collective appeals rejecting any possible compromise or even joint habitation in the same territory with the repatriated Chechens and Ingush. In addition, they described the tactics being used by the Vainakhi to regain their homes and lands. In April 1957, the farmers of the Lenin Collective Farm, Malgobek district, wrote to the Soviet leaders N.S. Khrushchev and N.A. Bulganin:* "Everywhere you hear about outrages, insults, fights, thieving, intimidation—there is hatred and national hostility between Chechens and Ingush on the one side and Russians, Ossetians, and Kumyki on the other." For example, the collective farmers

---

*The letters would be addressed to Bulganin and Khrushchev because they were the two most visible leaders at this time. Nikita Sergeevich Khrushchev (1894–1971) was first secretary of the Central Committee and Marshal Nikolai Aleksandrovich Bulganin (1895–1975) was prime minister (chairman of the Council of Ministers).—E.M.

complained that a Chechen tractor operator had plowed up a Russian-Ossetian Orthodox cemetery, which compelled people to seek burial sites outside the borders of the Chechen-Ingush republic. The authors of the letter closed with the announcement that "All of this is forcing us to leave," and requested that they be resettled in the more peaceful North Ossetian ASSR.[10]

These same complaints resounded in a statement from April 1957 made by the party organization, the executive committee of the village council, and the management of the M. Dakhadaev Collective Farm, which was addressed to Bulganin. The local representatives complained: "We, Avars, who were resettled to this same territory, have had to face former proprietors demanding and even impertinently seizing houses and land, talking as if it all belongs to them. If you can visualize the situation created here, it should become clear that dissension between Chechens and Avars is being sown and with each day grows more intense."[11]

Attempts to Politicize Ethnic Conflicts

The problems connected with the repatriation of the Vainakhi involved not only aggression but a definite incompatibility of cultures and values. Their ethnic competitors in a number of cases tried to exaggerate these cultural differences in order to gain state support. The complaint of the residents of the village of Bukovka, Novoselsk district, from April 24, 1957, was written in the "name of the Russian people" and blamed ethnic conflict on the Chechens' rejection of Soviet political values. The authors of the complaint clearly wanted Moscow to recognize that the residents were on the correct side in the conflict:

> The Chechens and Ingush are telling Russians that their exile from the Caucasus was illegal. Stalin and Beria were the ones guilty of this, and therefore they demand that the Russians give back their homes and everything else that had earlier belonged to them. They claim that during the deportation they left everything here. Now they are forcing the Russians to flee. With a ribald sneer, they gibe about how their people will soon be sitting in power and you [Russians] will be digging bathrooms for us. . . . The land is ours [they say], the Russians do not belong here, the Russians are interfering with our lives. We can manage our own republic, and now we will uphold our old law of the Caucasus. Both young and old have begun to pray to God. They have chosen a mullah, and under the leadership of the mullah they are working wonders that are sickening to hear about. Russian women and children fear their glance, because each day brings new incidents. . . .

In general this nation has awoken to fight for goals they themselves do not fully understand. For the fortieth anniversary of the Great October Revolution, they [the Chechens and Ingush] want to restore private property, make the republic independent from Russians, Dagestans, and others. Kazakhstan did not educate them, but on the contrary, embittered them against Russians and the Soviet state. Without any shame they tell the people: We cannot live together with Russians and Dagestans, just as two wolves cannot live in the same den and they either must remove us, or they must remove the Russians and the Tavlin* from this territory.[12]

The authors of the letter, along with others at this time, were trying to politicize ethnic conflict by equating personal enmity with political opposition. Clearly exaggerating the "anti Soviet" character of the Chechens, they tried to drag the state into the conflict through such denunciations to state organs.[13] Yet, behind these accusations a certain degree of reality lay hidden. The Chechen economic structure did contradict the collective farms, particularly the collective farm communalism of Russian settlers. The majority of Chechen and Ingush collective farms that had been established in the republic before the war were basically touched-up facades hiding traditional economic structures and activities. Such a description appeared in *A Short Historical Handbook on the Economic and Political Condition of the Former Chechen-Ingush ASSR During the Period 1937–1944* completed in August 1956. But even if one rejects this conclusion as an ideological cliche, it is true that the economic traditions of the Chechens and Ingush survived even into the 1930s. In truth, the leaders of the Miurids, who practiced a special form of militant Islam, had amassed a striking amount of wealth even under Stalin, and they helped preserve the unique value system of the Chechen people during their exile.[14] Nonetheless, attempts to stretch commonplace, everyday ethnic conflicts to the level of high politics and to enlist the support of the bosses did not get any response in Moscow. But ethnic tension in Chechnia-Ingushetiia, complaints about the ambiguous and explosive situation, and requests from the Dagestan, Ossetian, and Russian settlers for help in getting out of Chechnia forced the Soviet leadership to make the seemingly obvious decision. On April 12, 1957, three whole months after the restoration of Chechen-Ingush autonomy, the RSFSR Council of Ministers accepted a special resolution about evacuation from the territories of Chechnia and Ingushetiia. Because

---

*It is not clear from the source who the Tavlin are. The *tavlintsy* are a population of the Northern Dagestan mountains, mainly Avars. But according to the 1901 *Entsiklopedicheskii Slovar'*, this was not an ethnic term and it was not in common use by the people of the region.—E.M.

many more wished to leave than the authorities originally planned,[15] it was economically possible to settle them in Dagestan, but not in the places where people preferred to return. This difficulty laid the foundation for ethnic strife in Dagestan.[16]

The situation was aggravated by the fact that, parallel with the unexpected flood of settlers back to Dagestan, both a planned and unplanned return of Chechens was also taking place. Before the exile in 1944, 4,700 Chechen families had lived in the Dagestan ASSR, and many now sought to return there. Some of the repatriated Chechens voluntarily settled in the city of Khasaviurt, or in the Kazbekov, Novolak, and Kiziliurtov districts of the republic. The majority, like the returning Dagestan peoples, suffered difficult living conditions, with some lacking jobs and housing.[17] It is not surprising that local authorities asked that the return of the remaining Chechens be postponed for an indefinite period.

In the majority of cases, Moscow leaders tried not to show support for any one particular side in ethnic conflict. But in reality, they shrank even from their habitual role as supreme arbiter and the personification of higher justice. They simply continued to shuffle ethnicities into the volatile districts of the Northern Caucasus, relying above all on police measures for control. As a result, the state fell into its own kind of vicious cycle. In order to stop the massive, partially spontaneous, and poorly organized return of Chechens and Ingush, and to hold them in their places of exile or along the course of their return journey, authorities created additional sources of potential conflict. But to liberalize police control, meaning to allow the unregulated return of the Vainakhi to their homeland, was no less dangerous. Ethnic tension in the Northern Caucasus thus reached an extraordinarily high level.

In the end, the problem did acquire political significance, but as in the past, authorities turned to police measures for resolution. On June 10, 1957, the Central Committee Presidium examined the question "On the Voluntary Transfer of Chechen-Ingush families to the city of Grozny and the surrounding region." The MVD subsequently issued directives to the ministries of internal affairs of the Russian, Kazakh, Kirgiz, Uzbek, and Turkmen republics that noted the rise of disturbances on the railroads, where vast numbers of people by this time were congregating. Authorities posted police detachments at all of the large railroad stations along the path of repatriation. Fortunately, MVD personnel and police were ordered to avoid measures that could elicit aggressive responses. Some even managed to convince people to return to their place of settlement and "await an organized departure for the Caucasus."[18]

The authorities hoped to succeed before passions reached a critical point. The ethnic competitors of the Chechens and Ingush, and above all the representatives of the imperial people, the Russians, tried to push the bosses to take action. In August 1958, tensions peaked in the explosion of violence that rocked the capital of the reestablished Chechen-Ingush Autonomous Republic, the city of Grozny.

Mass Disorders in Grozny, August 26–28, 1958

Grozny on the Eve of the Unrest

Prior to the riots in Grozny, the police had been monitoring the volatile situation in the rural districts of Chechnia-Ingushetiia, where a struggle over resources among different ethnic groups was unfolding and where the squeezing out of settlers from other districts of the country had run into resistance, either secret or open. In contrast, Grozny, the capital of the republic and a rather large multiethnic industrial city, seemed more peaceful, though even there tension could be felt. Rumors had spread among the residents about conflict in rural localities, and the city also experienced a steady stream of the post-1944 Russian settlers leaving the region to return to their homelands.

In rural areas, the Chechens had history on their side. The other nationalities that had settled in the region after 1944 in accordance with state directives were in a psychologically difficult situation. It was they who had come and inhabited someone else's land. It was different, though, in Grozny. Empire, after all, had built the city. It had been founded by Russians as a military outpost at the beginning of the nineteenth century. During the 1920s, with the creation of the Chechen-Ingush Autonomous Republic, there was some discussion about the need to give Grozny special status as an independent administrative unit, a step strongly supported by the leaders of the local oil industry. In the 1930s, due to the efforts of Soviet authorities to "civilize" the Vainakhi, the city became the political and cultural center of the republic, though its economic life was, as in the past, connected with the oil industry.

Furthermore, if the deportation in 1944 had emptied rural districts, then in Grozny, which became the center of a new oblast, the situation was different. In the 1950s, the greater part of the population consisted of workers of different nationalities who were employed in the oil industry. Here their historical longevity could at least compete with that of the Chechens, who at this time were not employed in the oil industry. Psychologically the non-Chechens also felt more secure. Yes, the city did stand on Chechen territory, but in Grozny a multinational community, which spoke Russian to a significant degree, had already existed for an entire century. The Chechens were not, generally speaking, in a position to squeeze out this community, or at least not in the near future. In other words, the Chechens were not dominant in Grozny. But the multinational populace of the capital city, like people throughout the Caucasus, had a heightened ethnic consciousness.

Consequently, aggrieved citizens, when complaining about crime and street hooliganism, without even looking at statistics, were inclined everywhere to see the "Chechen footprint" and blame ethnicity for whatever displeased them. In and of itself, such primitive psychology was rather typical in multiethnic communities. Scapegoats can always be found and inserted into a primitive system of symbols and ethnic stereotypes. For those who cannot trouble themselves with a more complex understanding of the social environment—and such, generally speaking, are the majority—ethnic symbols often provide orientation in the world of people and objects. When the situation is normal and peaceful, with effectively functioning police services and rational central and local policies, these psychological constructions simply slumber and, despite their moral dubiousness, do not spawn social conflict.

In the capital of the newly restored Chechen-Ingush ASSR, however, there was neither a normal situation nor an effectively functioning police force. Furthermore, even the reasonableness and foresight of central and local authorities were questionable. The symptoms of potential ethnic conflict were visible in Grozny even before the mass return of the Chechens. For example, early in 1955, a conflict occurred between authorities and young people of the Stalin district of Grozny. On December 25, 1954, a student by the name of Lisovskii at Vocational School No. 2 decided "to settle personal scores" and picked an argument with a student at the truck-driving school, G.S. Agabekov. The latter was returning home late in the evening from the local recreational center along with S.A. Akbulatov, a student at the mechanics school. A friend of Lisovskii's ran to the vocational students' dormitory with the cry "They are beating up one of our guys." A crowd began to hurl stones at Agabekov and Akbulatov, who then jumped onto a passing streetcar. But the vocational students stopped the streetcar, pulled their opponents out onto the street, and began to beat them. Other students from the vocational school joined in the fracas. A police detachment had great difficulty getting the victims away from the raging crowd of young people. The police detained two hooligans and were taking them to the station when a group of about two hundred young people armed with stones accosted them and demanded that the two prisoners be set free. The mob dispersed only after their comrades were released.[19] Although memoranda from the Ministry of Internal Affairs concerning these disturbances contained no references to the ethnic underpinning of the events, the names of the participants in the conflict—Lisovskii (Russian), Agabekov and Akbulatov (Chechen)—reveal its ethnic dimension.

Further evidence of preexisting tension in Grozny can be found in statements made by a person identified in the sources as S., a forty-six-year-old father of two children and a decorated veteran. In 1958 he was employed in the oil industry. A braggart, dissatisfied with life and his own fate, S. was angry at the state and especially at Khrushchev. He loved to write anti-Khrushchev inscriptions on the walls and fences of public toilets. Witnesses testified that when S. had been drinking, he would say "that if war came, then he would immediately get himself captured and not fight."[20] This migrant from the Kursk countryside had been raised on commonplace chauvinism. While riding on the bus, S. was heard to say: "Who sent the Chechens here to us in Grozny? You are parasites, bandits, we should slits your throats. You would rather have the Turks come here."[21]

From 1956 to 1957, amid growing tensions compounded by the mass return of Chechens and Ingush to the restored autonomous republic, the law enforcement agencies of Grozny functioned ineffectively, failing to adjust to the new situation. More than 50 percent of all crimes reported in the republic were committed in Grozny, and there was widespread fighting.[22] One of these fights ended in a murder, which unnerved the entire city and set off "an avalanche of unrest."

August 23, 1958. Murder of the Worker Stepashin

The Grozny events began with an "international" drinking binge involving three Chechens and a Russian. An argument broke out, and the Russian received a slight stomach wound. He ran back to his dormitory and lay down in bed while the others continued to drink. Soon one of the Chechens, Veziev, went to check on the wounded man. The other two also declared that they would join him, but upon seeing the injured Russian, they attacked him with a knife. Vesiev not only defended the victim, but himself received a knife wound in the arm.

The now vexed and aggressive hooligans headed to a dance at the cultural center, where they met up with E. Stepashin, a young Russian worker at a chemical factory, and his friend, A. Riabov, a sailor in the Soviet navy who had come from Sevastopol on leave to see his parents. The two drunken Chechens started an argument over a young woman, and the conflict ended with a large group of young Chechens attacking Riabov and Stepashin. Riabov was able to run away and hide behind the building, but Stepashin stumbled and fell. His pursuers beat him and then knifed him five times. The young worker died at the scene. The two Chechens were arrested and taken to a preliminary detention cell pending investigation and trial.

The brutal murder received wide publicity. Rumors spread through the city and people began to engage in anti-Chechen conversations. The psychological soil and moral justification for harsh anti-Chechen pronouncements appeared, though it is extremely difficult to discern the true meaning behind standard police phrases about "provocative rumors" and "inflammatory conversations." But as the city began to speculate about the murder, in the home of the slain Stepashin, the family prepared for a funeral.

Fearing potential unrest, the director of the chemical factory tried to turn the funeral of Stepashin into an official function, which suited the friends of the slain man. They had requested from the factory's official funeral commission that the body be laid out for viewing at the factory club. The factory bosses, however, got tangled up in bureaucracy, and caused the irritated and disappointed friends of Stepashin to take everything upon themselves at great personal risk. As a result, the authorities lost the initiative.

During the afternoon of August 25, the body of Stepashin was taken out of the morgue. "Against the directives of the city party committee," his friends set up his coffin in front of the home of Stepashin's fiance in the village of Chernoreche, where most of the chemical factory workers lived. The coffin was too large to put in the Stepashin family home. But no one wanted to put it in the local reading and recreation center, which is where the party committee had given permission to have the viewing. On their own, a group of young people decided to turn the viewing into a protest meeting, declaring that "it is necessary to bring an end to these actions by the Chechens and therefore it would be good to conduct a meeting on the issue of Stepashin's murder . . . and demand the expulsion of Chechens from Grozny."

Announcements about the meeting were posted in obvious places in the village and at the chemical factory. The bosses took down the announcements, but preparations continued nonetheless: "We have decided on our own to conduct a meeting, in spite of the fact that it has been prohibited." The shock of the murder was too strong, and the prohibition seemed too unjust. People wanted to demand publicly that the authorities defend them, but the latter, concerned over ethnic tensions, simply brushed aside the frustrations of these workers. It was already impossible, however, to prohibit the meeting.

The viewing of Stepashin's body now became a platform for spontaneous speeches by individuals who were normally obedient, respected, and fully law-abiding citizens. One such individual was L.I. Miakinin, who had known the deceased as a friend of his son. That evening Miakinin had come with Riabov, the second victim of the Chechen attack who had successfully run away, and Riabov's father. Miakinin was a Civil War veteran and an invalid, having lost both legs in 1951. He was a longtime employee of the oil industry and in 1955, for his many years of irreproachable work, had been awarded the Order of Lenin.

Miakinin, supported by Riabov and several others, spoke as he stood by Stepashin's coffin:

> Chechens are killing Russians, they do not want to live in peace. It is necessary to write a collective letter in the name of the Russian people, to gather signatures, and to designate a person to carry the letter to Moscow with a request for a commission to be sent to Grozny, and if the commission is not formed, then let comrade Khrushchev himself come in order to investigate on the spot.[23]

Already during the nightly vigil at the coffin, close friends and acquaintances of Stepashin had decided among themselves that if the funeral meeting in Chernoreche were to be canceled, they would then carry the coffin on their shoulders to the regional party committee offices and conduct the meeting there. Toward morning, the participants in the nighttime conversations told Stepashin's mother about their decision, and she agreed to it as well.

During the morning of August 26, the inhabitants of Chernoreche and workers of the chemical factory continued to organize and prepare petitions to the authorities. The author of one of these documents, Galina Korchagina, an invalid who walked with the aid of crutches, described the murder of Stepashin and brought forth even more accusations against the Chechens. She stood next to the coffin and read aloud her appeal, asking those who had gathered to sign her document and collect money so that it could be taken to Moscow by a trustworthy person. Those who were present signed the appeal and threw money into the coffin. According to the later investigation, unidentified persons wrote two more petitions, which were addressed to Voroshilov* in the name of the workers of the chemical and oil-refining factories. They put forth a harsh demand to expel the Chechens from the city. Several days later, Korchagina burned all three letters, which residents and workers had signed, and gave the money that had been collected to the mother of Stepashin.

In the early afternoon local party bosses including the secretary of the regional party committee and four officials in the party apparatus, accompanied by fifteen policemen, appeared in the village of Chernoreche. The majority of the police were disguised in civilian clothing, and undoubtedly there were also KGB personnel among them, but the available sources say nothing about this. The secretary prohibited public speeches during the funeral pro-

---

*A former ally of Stalin, Marshal Kliment Efremovich Voroshilov (1881–1969) was chairman of the Presidium of the Supreme Soviet, which made him the head of state.—E.M.

cession. Those assembled then recalled the nighttime plan of Stepashin's friends and began to talk about going to the regional party committee building and conducting a meeting there. Facilitating this step was the fact that Stepashin's mother had decided to bury her son in the Grozny city cemetery, and the road leading there from Chernoreche, which lay on the outskirts of the city, passed close to the central square where the regional party building was located.

About 1,000 residents of Chernoreche gathered for the carrying out of the slain man's coffin. Approximately two hundred people set off for the cemetery, embarking on what would be a long journey, but the organizers and participants in the funeral firmly intended to make a stop at the regional party building and conduct a meeting. Friends of the slain worker carried his coffin on their shoulders, as every participant in the procession had categorically rejected all proposals by the factory's funeral commission and the police to transport the body by car. The procession expanded as new people joined its ranks, gradually growing into an anti-Chechen demonstration. An elderly woman, a member of the Communist Party since 1927, was the most active, continually calling for the procession to go to the regional party building. But the authorities tried to steer it away from the center of Grozny by blocking access to the central square. Several participants in the procession cried out angrily: "Why are you not allowing us to carry the body to where it should be!" Finally, a group of about fifty women broke through the police blockade and, shouting loudly, led the crowd onto the street leading to the center. Now numbering up to three hundred, the women prevented the police from closing off this street. One woman began to call people for a meeting.

By late afternoon, the funeral procession, which already numbered around eight hundred, approached the regional party committee headquarters. The square was overflowing with people, with anywhere from 4,000 to 7,000 gathered there,[24] including many drunks as well as paupers, hooligans, and thieves who had latched onto the funeral procession. Various rumors passed through the crowd, including one that claimed Stepashin's mother had died from her overwhelming grief, though in truth she had only fainted. Calls for reprisals against the Chechens rang out continually.

Finally giving in to the entreaties of the authorities, the residents of Chernoreche moved away from the building of the regional party committee to Ordzhonikidze Square and from there headed for the cemetery in the official company cars of the chemical factory. One of the regional party secretaries was present at the burial ceremony, and everything went peacefully. Probably even the participants in the funeral themselves had been frightened by the actions of the crowd. They were driven back in cars to Chernoreche, where tables were set up in the streets and food was laid out for the funeral repast. The residents of Chernoreche took no part whatsoever in the ensuing mass disorders, nor was there anything criminal in their actions during the funeral. The prehistory of the Grozny events ends at this point.

August 26. A Spontaneous Meeting in the Central Square

The funeral procession had withdrawn to the cemetery. But a large number of onlookers, largely drunks, hooligans, and paupers who lacked any connection at all with the funeral, remained on the square by the regional party building. There were also many teenagers and students from the vocational institute, who were well known in the city for their hooligan escapades.[25] The crowd demanded that the secretary of the regional party committee open the meeting and make a speech. In the end, the meeting developed spontaneously. Not only anti-Chechen, but even anti-Soviet statements resounded, including dissatisfaction with Khrushchev and his policies as well as cries for a strike.

Purely by accident, one of the first roles in the drama belonged to a Russian, Viktor Egorovich Isaev, who had a secondary education and three grown children. From 1922 to 1923, Isaev had been a fighter in the Special Duty Troops.* He was a Komsomol member from 1922 on, and then in 1927, he had joined the Communist Party, which he subsequently quit.[26] He fought in the war from 1941 to 1943, and at the beginning of the 1950s became the director of the Krasnodar district bookstore. But then he was convicted of abusing his official position and lost his job. In 1958, he was unemployed; he could not find work because his record had a blemish and therefore he was not considered suitable for leadership positions. Isaev spent his days at home and generally felt himself ill-used. On August 26, he had spent the whole day busy with household matters, and then drank two glasses of wine and a mug of beer. In the early evening, he went out to a department store, where he heard that Chechens had killed a worker, and that the people were gathering near the statue of Lenin.[27] Isaev gave his basket for the store to his wife and ran to the square. Isaev later recounted:

> A large crowd gathered there and many were speaking. After one of the speeches, someone shouted: "Let's go on strike." I also was riled up and said to those around me that I was going to speak.
>
> They supported me, raising me up on their arms, and I began to speak.
> In my speech to the crowd I recounted the outrages of the Chechens, the

---

*Known by the acronym ChON, the Special Duty Troops were created to fight against "counterrevolution and banditry."—E.M.

murders . . . and I demanded that the leaders of the Central Committee come. Besides this, I spoke about false Communists and also demanded reprisals against them. After the speech, I headed toward the Lenin Bridge and began to weep. One citizen came up to me and said that he had been a Communist since 1941, and that I should beat him up, since I had accused all Communists of being dishonest. I responded that I had not been talking about all Communists. . . . I continued to cry while I headed home, and a woman approached me and tried to calm me down. I told her that I do not have a job, I have a great work record and everything was getting to me, especially the fact that no one would hire me.[28]

Witnesses later described Isaev as being drunk. An employee of the district party committee testified: "He said that the time had come when it was possible for him to say, 'Down with false Communists.' He demanded that the Central Committee come and that the Chechens be expelled. . . . At this moment the crowd lifted another man up and either he or Isaev said, 'Down with Soviet Power.' " The witness T. reported that Isaev "asked people not to disperse and to support his speech. . . . He said that when he had fought against the White Army Cossacks, there had not been any regional party officials around. Now in the regional party committee there were false Communists. He also demanded expulsion of the Chechens." Another person, Kh., added to the picture. According to his testimony, Isaev said: "Great Russia [Rus] is waking up," having in mind the gathering crowd, and added: "The chemical factory is on strike and if you will support the Red Hammer Factory and others, then much can be done."

Isaev was one of the first to call for reaching Moscow by telephone or telegraph in order to demand that the Central Committee send representatives. It seems that the crowd reacted positively to his words, but when talk of a strike commenced, many grew frightened: "They stopped listening and even threw up their hands." Many in the square, however, were already repeating the now familiar theme of "incorrect Communists," protection from whom could only be found in Moscow. Communist abundance and justice could only come to the citizens of Grozny from Moscow, and only Khrushchev and the Central Committee could save them from the "evil Chechens." Isaev called for a strike primarily to gain Moscow's attention. He was fighting against "false Communists" at whose hands he had suffered, who had kept him from being hired. It was for this reason that he cried out, "Let us raise high the Leninist banner."[29]

At first the crowd that had assembled for the spontaneous funeral meeting was inclined to talk with authorities and even to make conscious political demands. Close to nightfall, however, as the more healthy-minded people headed for their homes, the aggressive and non-law-abiding part of the crowd left the meeting to storm the offices of the regional party committee. The seventy police who had been brought in to help guard the building responded sluggishly, and fortunately did not shoot at the crowd. The rioters succeeded in breaking into the building, where they "committed outrages, opened up offices, and tried to find the secretary of the regional party committee." By midnight the police and a subdivision of 120 MVD soldiers and officers had cleared the premises. But fired up by alcohol, a crowd of the more inveterate rioters did not disperse. During the early hours of the morning, a wave of attackers, mainly young people headed by the vocational students notorious for their hooliganism, broke through the police cordon and rushed into the building. They swung their belt buckles in the air as they raced wildly through the corridors and offices, hardly giving any thought as to why they were doing this.

The police and the KGB again cleared the building of hooligans. Within an hour, the now weary crowd was finally dispersed and "small groups were scattered." The police detained twenty inebriated participants, all of whom were later set free. The police chief, assuming that public order had finally been restored, breathed a sigh of relief.

During the morning hours of August 27 in Grozny, leaflets addressed to workers appeared in the streets. Apparently the authorities were never able to explain who, during the brief reprieve from three to eight o'clock in the morning, was able to type and make copies of these leaflets. According to the available information, a morning meeting took place at the chemical factory between a carpenter employed at the plant and an unidentified young man, who had in his hands a whole bundle of machine-printed leaflets. He handed one to the worker:

> Leaflet.
>
> On August 26, 1958, our comrades passed by the regional party building carrying a coffin with the body of a man slain by Chechens. The police, instead of taking measures to punish the murderers, **DETAINED FIFTY OF OUR OWN WORKERS**. So at 11:00 A.M. let us stop working and go to the regional party offices to demand their liberation [The words 'detained fifty of our own workers' were typed in boldface].[30]

As he handed over the leaflets, the unidentified man said that cars had been specially apportioned for the trip to the regional party building and were parked near the garage of the chemical factory. The carpenter showed the leaflet to the foreman of his crew, who then ordered a work stoppage, and the crew members went off with other workers to the meeting in the central square.

This is one of the most inexplicable episodes in the history of the Grozny disturbances. How was it that there were cars already standing ready? Who was able to organize the collective convoy of workers to the meeting, and when did they do this? Is it possible to suspect the authors of this literately written leaflet, which was even typed, of being the same hooligans who had stormed the regional party building during the night, rushing senselessly around the building and waving their belt buckles? The alternative supposition that comes to mind is shocking. Did one of the local Russian bosses or someone from the local KGB office try to take advantage of the disorder for purposes of provocation? Was this done to push the Central Committee to take a strong stand to resolve the Chechen issue, or to revive the repressive spirit of the Stalinist period as well as the special status of the police forces? From other sources we know, for example, that at this time in the city there were several former NKVD employees who had been guilty of illegal (even by Stalinist standards) shootings of peaceful Chechens back in 1943. Eyewitnesses to the reprisals had demanded they be punished, and they had been forced out under fire.[31]

Furthermore, there are still some gaps in the MVD sources. What happened to an unidentified worker from the canning factory who went out to Chernoreche and who, according to the police data, played the "most active role in inflaming national hostility and instigating the workers to become disorderly"? The KGB was following this man, but there are no traces of an investigation or trial. If there was no official investigation, then why not? Was he a KGB provocateur? Why did the authorities allow the case of the Stepashin funeral organizers to be closed so readily? Is it really because they did not wish to agitate the populace? Nothing could be found either about the nine organizers of the funeral who were investigated by the KGB. There was almost an entire organization that was functioning and printing leaflets, yet there is no information about them! Why are there no traces of the KGB investigation?

Also inexplicable is the lack of action by the secret police, who knew about the plan for turning the funeral into a protest meeting but did not take any preemptive measures. What has been said in no way casts doubt on the spontaneous character of the disorders in Grozny and the self-organization of the rioters. But it is impossible to get rid of the thought that someone, "for a reason known only to himself," as is written in police protocols, helped the disturbances to reach full force. Furthermore, how could this person, this "someone," as well as the reasons for his actions, not be known to the KGB?

In the early morning, people began to reassemble at the square in front of regional party headquarters, demanding that representatives from Moscow be called to the scene. Two hours later, some of those present broke into the regional party building, dragged out the regional party secretary, Shepelev, and forced him to speak. But when Shepelev finally began, "wild cries and whistles" interrupted him. The fickle crowd no longer wanted to listen to him.

This morning attack on the regional party offices petered out as the rioters were pushed out of the building. But the crowd did not disperse, instead making ready for a new assault. By noon, more than 1,000 people had congregated on the square. A young woman stood on the bed of a truck and spoke through a microphone, calling for a delegation to be sent to area factories and plants. She also called for a work stoppage until the fifty people who had been arrested during the night were freed, and announced that the chemical factory and the Red Hammer Factory had already gone on strike, though in reality they were still operating. An unidentified man echoed her demands and also called for the expulsion of the Chechens and Ingush.

Within an hour, a large group of hooligans renewed the assault on the regional party committee and soon occupied the entire building. Repeated attempts to clear the building failed. The hooligans noisily destroyed furniture, broke windows, shattered glasses and carafes, poured out ink, tore up desk calendars, and threw official papers out onto the street. In the dining hall of the building, they turned on all the faucets as well as the gas burners. Fortunately, the state gas company, Gorgaz, had stopped the flow of gas to the building. On the roof, paper was set on fire.

Several participants called for beating up Chechens and for removing local government and party leaders. The rioters tried to use the local radio broadcasting network to transmit speeches to the crowd, but one of the Communists had succeeded in dismantling the transmitter. In addition, the rioters searched the building for weapons, but they had fortunately been transferred to a safe place. Frightened party personnel had requested arms for self-defense, but the regional party first secretary had not given his permission.

Officials attempted to negotiate, but the mob attacked the bosses, beating them up and tearing their clothing. Some of the regional party and government officials hid in the basement offices, while others were able to get out through emergency exits. At the same time, various groups of rioters began stopping automobiles in the streets of Grozny and searching for Chechens. Fearing personal reprisals, the "leadership cadre and a significant portion of the MVD personnel, along with district police departments, took off their official uniforms." About 400 Communists, sent by the Stalin and Lenin district party committees, tried to reason with the crowd but to no avail.

In the late afternoon, a group of hooligans attacked the deputy minister of internal affairs for the Chechen-Ingush ASSR, Shadrin, and demanded the release of those arrested on August 26. The hooligans refused to believe the assurances given that all persons detained had already been released that morning. Undercover police personnel failed to free their boss, who was dragged by force to the MVD, where, in spite of the guard's resistance, the entire crowd broke into the building. At the same time, another group of rioters attacked the KGB building, but the details of this episode are missing in the available sources.

The MVD personnel did not use weapons, and instead tried to negotiate. But the crowd refused to listen and began looking for the detained prisoners. Around 250 people penetrated the courtyard and then made their way into the preliminary detention cell where the murderers of the worker Stepashin were being held. For some reason, however, the attackers paid no attention to them, although it would seem that there ought to have been some kind of reaction to the Chechens. But the mob was interested only in the hooligans detained during the previous night, and it took the assurances of prisoners sitting in the cells to convince them finally that all had been set free. Even then the rioters demanded that the supervisor of the preliminary detention cell provide the addresses of those who had been freed and left thirty minutes after receiving this information. In parting, they broke the telephone, tore off the supervisor's shoulder strap, stole a police car, and then sent several persons to verify the liberation of the detained workers.

The remaining rioters returned to the square and to the regional party headquarters, where several party officials were being forced to speak to the crowd. Two fire trucks arrived on the scene, supposedly to put out a fire. The crowd turned over one of the trucks and in the other damaged the electrical wiring and let out all the air from the tires.

The Evening of August 27. Georgii Shvaiuk and His "Draft Resolution"

Later that evening, Georgii Shvaiuk entered the captured party building with a draft resolution he had written. Shvaiuk had been born in the Northern Caucasus in 1914 to a family of white-collar workers. He had higher education and worked as a senior engineer–hydro technician at the Gudermes State Farm in the Chechen-Ingush ASSR. On August 27, he had left Gudermes to come to Grozny, where he had an apartment. Shvaiuk said in court:

> On the bus, I overheard a conversation. People were talking about a meeting that was being set up on account of the brutal murder of a worker at the chemical factory. . . . In an outburst of anger over what I had heard, when I arrived home I wrote a draft resolution for the meeting and then went out to the central square. Upon arrival, I went to the regional party offices, where I gave this draft resolution to two Komsomol members.[32]

In just a short period of time, the author of this draft became the ideologue for the disorders, striving to ennoble the actions of the rioters with conscious political demands. In court Shvaiuk argued that he was innocent, declaring: "I do not deny my actions and I do not consider them criminal," and then adding, "The purpose of my draft was not to inflame ethnic hostility." The draft resolution read as follows:

> Due to the savage treatment by the Chechen-Ingush population of other na-
> tionalities, expressed in butchery, murder, rape, and insults, the laborers of
> the city of Grozny in the name of the majority of the population propose:
>
> 1. To rename, beginning on August 27, the Chechen-Ingush ASSR either
>   Grozny Oblast or a multinational Soviet socialist republic.
> 2. The Chechen-Ingush population in Grozny Oblast must not be more
>   than 10 percent of the general population.
> 3. All privileges of the Chechen-Ingush population relative to other na-
>   tionalities must be revoked.[33]

This chauvinistic draft was immediately duplicated on typewriters and publicized by participants in the disorders. It was found several hours later in the building of the regional party committee together with copies printed on official letterhead paper.[34]

That same evening, the crowd, sensing a power vacuum and finally convinced that those detained the previous night were at liberty, put forth a new goal: to seek the truth from the supreme arbiter—the Central Committee. The rioters thereupon headed for the city radio station under a red banner that had been acquired from the regional party offices. This banner had obvious symbolic meaning for the rioters, transforming their actions from a criminal act into the "word and deed of the ruler."

Heading this group that was demanding to speak with Moscow was a man about fifty years old and wearing a straw hat. He cried out that he was a resident of Chernoreche and that "he was sick and tired of having to put up with the outrages of Chechens, who made it too dangerous to walk outside on the streets at night." More questions now arise. What was this man doing in Grozny, when the whole village was celebrating the funeral repast for the deceased Stepashin? Why did the investigation emphatically assert that the residents of Chernoreche did not take part in the disorders? Finally, who was this strange leader of the rioters with his straw hat? These are still more mysteries of the Grozny history.

The authorities set up a guard of three soldiers at the station and barricaded the entrance. Repulsed, the rioters left peacefully, having decided to try to find satisfaction at the local telephone station, where calls could be made to other cities. This time the crowd acted more aggressively, but the guards used weapons and wounded three people, one of whom later died in the hospital. The crowd sought revenge, but the soldiers succeeded in hiding inside the building. The rioters broke into the telephone station and insisted that they be allowed to call Moscow. One young woman "with insolent persistence demanded immediate connection with Moscow." But "the conversation with the government" did not take place at this time, for the telephone station employees claimed that the lines were damaged.

Only on the third attempt, at the city post office, did participants in the unrest finally get through to Moscow by telephone. According to the court, Shvaiuk, the author of the draft resolution, was the "initiator of the conversation over the telephone with the receptionist of the Central Committee Secretariat." As Shvaiuk himself recounted:

> [The telephone operator] connected us with Moscow, but since no one would talk, they handed the phone to me. I began to converse with Moscow, with the receptionist of the Central Committee first secretary. I asked him: "Do you know what is happening in Grozny, that the people await representatives from Moscow, that it is necessary to put an end to beastly murders, that the matter has come to the point that some have demanded the return of Grozny Oblast and the expulsion of the Chechens. . ."[35]

What Shvaiuk heard in response was probably a promise "to look into the matter," but with whom he really spoke is not known.

While participants in the disorders were establishing contact with Moscow, a strange episode took place on the square at the regional party offices. During the night a bus arrived, and its driver climbed up on the roof to announce that he had transported murdered corpses and that the blood of the slain had stained the whole interior of the bus. Someone sought to detain the driver, but the crowd defended him and he soon left. The identity of the driver was established and the KGB handled his case, but mysteriously, there is no documentary evidence that it ever came to trial.

Meanwhile, about three hundred people, still marching under the same red banner, headed directly from the post office to the city railway station. Thirty minutes earlier, the police detachment at the station had received a warning from the MVD, but failed to successfully prepare for the encounter. For almost two hours the crowd held up the departure of the passenger train from Rostov to Baku. A large group thronged near the engine, raising anti-Chechen cries and writing "provocative inscriptions" on the cars. Some tried to persuade the passengers to join them, while others found two Chechens and attacked them. One person persisted in the attempt to reach the Central Committee, this time by telegram. But the police detachment confiscated the telegram, thereby perpetuating the common myth about evil local bosses hiding the truth from the righteous Central Committee.

At midnight troops entered Grozny and in twenty minutes were at the railway station. The crowd resisted, throwing rocks at the soldiers and the railway workers. The soldiers leveled their rifles but did not fire them and quickly suppressed the resistance. The graffiti markings were removed from the railroad cars, and extraneous objects that had been thrown onto the tracks were cleared. In less than an hour, the train was able to set off for its destination. The military intervention thus brought an end to the disorders and put the city under a curfew. Until August 30, army divisions guarded the most important points in the city and patrolled the streets.

Tension in the city, however, did not immediately abate. On August 29 in the city market, a drunken, unemployed man by the name of Kovalev "said something improper about Khrushchev and the government, calling them parasites living at the expense of the laborers"; he also swore at Chechens, yelled out, "Down with Chechnia-Ingushetia!," and even said that he was going to go to the factories and call for an uprising.[36] A man with shattered nerves who was frustrated with life and constantly ready for alcohol-induced aggression, Kovalev hated the Chechens and Khrushchev equally, and basically resented the whole world. It was precisely people of this psychological type, "marketplace hooligans," who gave the actions of the crowd a vicious, violent character, and who then dissolved anonymously into the urban masses. They remained a potential source for ethnic tension and politically based violence.

As a result of the disorders, thirty-two people were wounded, including four MVD employees and police officers. Two civilians died and ten were hospitalized. Many official personages were among those injured, including the secretary of the regional party committee, the deputy minister of internal affairs for the republic, the deputy head of the district police department, two operative police agents, the lecturer of the Grozny city party committee, as well as two representatives of the Oil Institute, a Chechen driver, and others. In the list of the injured, there were few people with Chechen last names, further proof of how the unrest, which had begun under anti-Chechen slogans, clearly grew beyond the limits of an ethnic pogrom and turned into an uprising against state power. This is why the MVD concluded that the disorders in Grozny "by their own character were anti-Soviet actions."[37]

After these events, MVD organs carefully screened the city. Many agents and officers came from Moscow and from other autonomous republics and regions to help in the effort. A special investigative group carried out the inquiry and the "exposure of the main organizers and instigators of the disorders." All employees of MVD organs were mobilized to "identify participants in the disorders and those who tried to provoke city inhabitants, and

arrest those who were uncovered." Divisional police agents kept watch over identified instigators. By September 15, 273 participants in the Grozny mass disorders had been recorded. Ninety-three people had been detained by this point, out of which 57 were arrested, and 7 lost their right to leave the area. Nine persons were transferred to the KGB, and 2 to the office of the local procurator. The KGB organs arrested 19 organizers and active participants. The police instituted 58 criminal proceedings against 64 people, among whom 8 were younger than eighteen, 27 were from ages nineteen to twenty-five, and 29 were older than twenty-five. Among those arrested were 31 workers and 26 unemployed. Fourteen had prior convictions, and 29 had taken part in disorders in two or even more places.[38] Thus far, however, in the materials of the Procuracy's Department of Surveillance no traces have been found of these wide-scale arrests and investigations, for only materials dealing with several minor, peripheral, and accidental cases are preserved. Where the rest are is not known.

The crimes of people arrested by the MVD could qualify, for example, as malicious hooliganism and not fall under control of the Department of Surveillance. But what happened to those arrested by the KGB? Was there really not a single participant in the mass disorders in Grozny subject to surveillance procedures? Did no one appeal a sentence or request a pardon? The impression emerges that the surveillance cases either were removed from general correspondence or did not get to court. Meanwhile, an analogous gap exists in the surveillance proceedings over another ambiguous event of the 1950s, the mass uprisings in Tbilisi in support of Stalin in 1956 (see Chapter 5).

Authorities not only screened the population of the city, but also purged it. In order to "resolve questions of removal from Grozny," they identified "persons who are not engaged in socially useful labor, who lead parasitic ways of life and who are inclined to carry out criminal acts." On September 15, 1958, there were 365 such people, including 167 with prior convictions, 172 unemployed, 22 prostitutes, and 32 indigent.[39]

On September 15 and 16, Stepashin's murderers were tried, with one sentenced to be shot, and the other to ten years in prison and five years "disenfranchisement." No signs of antigovernment activity among the populace of Grozny were recorded during the time of the trial.

After Grozny

Participants in the Grozny disturbances achieved one thing. The situation in the city and in the republic became a subject of discussion at the Central Committee plenum in September 1958. This is the one case known to us of a party plenum discussing mass uprisings. Yet there was not a discussion as such, for the draft resolution prepared in advance was not actually put on the agenda. There was only a short informational report delivered at a special session of secretaries from republic-level Communist Party central committees, district party committees, and regional party committees, which took place after the plenum. The report itself, given by N.G. Ignatov,* who had gone to Grozny for the trial, identified serious problems in the local party's ability to respond to extreme situations and criticized the party bureaucracy's lack of political qualities that had belonged to early Bolshevism.

In the evaluation of Ignatov, one of the main reasons for the unrest in Grozny was the "major mistakes in the work of the bureau of the regional party committee, the city party committee, and the republican Council of Ministers," for between them the "necessary unity" did not exist. As a result, during the course of events "the secretaries and members of the bureau made decisions unilaterally." In other words, the principle of collective leadership proclaimed by Khrushchev had proved dysfunctional in an extreme situation. Ignatov stated a fact that was deplorable to the state: On August 26 and 27, the party committees and the Council of Ministers were not only paralyzed, but did not even try to seize the initiative and appeal to the "party activists and to the workers."[40] Clearly there was no mutual understanding between the new party oligarchs and the masses. The bureaucrats did not know how and were basically afraid to "[talk] with the people" (this had been done superbly by their predecessors in the years of revolution and civil war). In an extreme situation they turned to violence, rather than seek the support of social groups whose interests they were supposed to voice. The schism between the state and the people began to take the shape of a chronic disease, although as subsequent meetings of party and worker activists showed, there were still sufficient social forces ready to support the restoration of order in Grozny. But the bureaucracy clearly could not rely on them, for it had lost the initiative and in the end was forced to use the army. The Moscow party leaders thus were unable to make a serious political analysis of the events, which had definitely gone beyond the limits of an isolated episode. In the center of a relatively small city, a crowd numbering up to 10,000 people had risen up in rebellion. Yet authorities dealt with the situation with purely police measures and typical ideological twaddle.

It is not surprising that in spite of all the efforts of the authorities, ethnic tension remained as high in Grozny as in the entire autonomous republic. In October 1958, an argument broke out between Russian and Chechen voca-

---

*Nikaolai Grigorievich Ignatov (1901–1966) was a Central Committee secretary at this time.—E.M.

tional students in the cafeteria of the Red Hammer Factory. The argument grew into a fight. Forty Chechens heard news of the fight and, armed with sticks, began to attack the Russians. Three people were severely beaten.[41] One year after the disturbances in Grozny, almost on the anniversary of the events—August 22, 1959—a gang fight broke out during the night in another ethnically volatile city, Gudermes, between Russians on one side and Chechen and Ingush[42] youth on the other. About a hundred people took part, with ten injured, two seriously. The conflict was stopped only with the intervention of the local military garrison.[43]

On September 6 in the same area of Gudermes, a Russian youth killed a Chechen. The next day about eighty Chechens demanded that the district police chief be fired. The chairman of the Council of Ministers and the minister of internal affairs of the Chechen-Ingush ASSR came out to the scene of events. They were able to convince the Chechens to disperse only with great difficulty.[44] Somewhat earlier, on August 29, 1959, in a Grozny Park of Culture, an unidentified criminal knifed a Russian driver, who subsequently died in the hospital. During the funeral, speakers made harsh statements aimed at Chechens.[45]

Although conflict continued to smoulder, it did not again reach the point of serious public disturbances.

Chapter 5

Political Disturbances in Georgia After the CPSU Twentieth Party Congress

---

March 5: The First Demonstration

On February 25, 1956, at a closed session of the CPSU Twentieth Party Congress, First Secretary Nikita S. Khrushchev delivered the "secret speech" about the "cult of personality of Stalin" and the crimes of the Stalinist regime. Rumors that the great and infallible Stalin himself had been virtually declared an "enemy of the people" quickly spread throughout the country. At first no one knew the details, and Khrushchev's speech itself remained unpublished in Russia until Gorbachev's *glasnost*. The speech, however, shocked even old Communists who were used to anything and everything, though many could not understand or accept the truth about Stalin simply at the command of a new leader. After all, the notion of "The Leader" was the foundation for the entire system of symbols in early Soviet communism. Treating "The Leader" as a simple "enemy of the people" could not help but unsettle people, for the very idea of a higher truth and justice, which was manifested in "The Leader," was collapsing.

In Georgia, the scandalous disclosures wounded national feelings and the popular tradition of reverence for the dead.[1] In March 1956, the residents of Tbilisi protested the national insult inflicted by Moscow. After all, the previous year had seen spontaneous meetings, speeches, and the laying of wreaths on statues and monuments of Stalin, and the memory of such events was particularly powerful. The authorities had not opposed these activities and in fact had actively participated in them.[2]

Historical myth and popular memory connect the beginning of the unrest in Georgia with the spontaneous impulse of the Pioneers* and the schoolchildren of Tbilisi to honor Stalin on March 8, 1956. Yet, according to the special report of V. Dzhandzhgava, Georgian SSR minister of internal affairs, and O. Museridze, the head of the Main Board of the Georgian MVD, the unrest had already begun on March 4, 1956. A crowd of people, many of whom were drunk, had gathered that day near the monument of Stalin, and some of them, according to the police, behaved "provocatively." N.I. Parastishvili, a CPSU member who lived in the countryside, "climbed up on the pedestal of the monument and yelled obscenities. Finishing off a bottle of wine and then breaking it, he said: 'Let us smash the enemies of Stalin just as I have smashed this bottle.'" One of those who had organized the laying of wreaths on the Stalin monument, a correspondence student at the Georgian Polytechnical Institute and resident of the city of Kutais, Z. Devradiani, crudely demanded that a certain unidentified major of the Soviet army set up an honor guard. When the major refused, Devradiani tried to knife him, but was detained by the police. On the way to the city police department, a large crowd of up to three hundred persons liberated Devradiani.[3] At the Stalin monument, a spontaneous meeting went on until midnight under the watch of a large police brigade, half in civilian clothing, that had been stationed in the area earlier in the day.[4]

S. Statnikov, an eyewitness who worked as a correspondent for the central trade union newspaper *Trud* (Labor), described the events of the next day, March 5. At midmorning there arose in the center of the city a shrill chorus of car horns continuously honking. In the middle of the street a procession of students, about 120 to 150 persons, soon appeared. Those in the front carried a portrait of Stalin while organizers of the procession commanded spectators to take off their hats in homage to the leader. From time to time someone demanded that car drivers honk their horns. In all there were several processions, each of which headed to the Stalin monument, where they placed memorial wreaths.[5]

It was quite simple to organize a mourning procession such as this, given the favorable attitude of authorities, for the highest Georgian bosses kept silent and did not prohibit these activities. The standard ritual for such measures was already worked out to the last detail. In each school and institute, in every enterprise and establishment, beginning with the

---

*The All-Union Pioneers, founded in 1922, was the official Communist Party organization for children age ten to fifteen. The main purpose of the Pioneers was the rudimentary political indoctrination of Soviet youth, although many of the activities were recreational in nature.—E.M.

Central Committee of the party and ending with the shabbiest communal offices, there were the necessary prerequisites: banners, posters, portraits of the leaders, etc. Thus, the funeral processions that began on March 5 had all the appearance and obligatory attributes of an official state function. In the beginning, probably very few of the eyewitnesses understood that they were taking place without permission from above. Spontaneous self-organization, along with informal leaders oriented toward different and often contradictory political and ideological goals, filled the emerging organizational vacuum. In general, young people and students were the driving force behind the events. A marginal group of unemployed young people—those who had finished an institute but did not want to go to their assigned jobs in rural districts—played a particularly active role.

March 6–7. Rumors About the "Closed Letter" of the Central Committee. The Growth of Tensions

The following day saw the continuation of demonstrations. But now they became more organized and more numerous, especially in the middle of the day, when classes ended at the institutes. Portraits of Lenin were added to the portraits of Stalin, and flags appeared with mourning ribbons.[6] In the afternoon, the Central Committee of the Georgian Communist Party held a session in which about seventy to eighty heads of the ministries, newspapers, and journals took part. The first secretary of the Central Committee, V.P. Mzhavanadze, opened the session, but then quickly left. A closed letter of the CPSU Central Committee, "On the Cult of Personality," was read aloud, along with a proposal to acquaint all Communists and Komsomol members with this document.[7] Rumors quickly spread about this throughout the city. Instead of mourning Stalin, the deceased great leader, authorities were inflicting a new insult on him, which wounded the nationalist feelings of the Georgians. No one had consciously sought to do this, but as often occurs in Russia, "it just happened."

In this situation, no one could have come up with anything more absurd and ill-considered than to blindly carry out commands from Moscow and immediately read this "closed letter." Political clumsiness definitely contributed to the unrest. Georgian officials did not dare disobey the party leaders in Moscow, but they nonetheless found ways to express their dissatisfaction. They watched the pro-Stalinist hysteria flaring up around them with poorly hidden, though cautious, sympathy. They may even have wanted to make use of the mass demonstrations as an argument to force the Moscow leadership "to correct the general line." Furthermore, if even experienced

Communist bosses were confused and disoriented by the exposure of Stalin's crimes, then the rank-and-file city residents, many of whom were convinced Stalinists brainwashed over many years by myths of the great "Leader," certainly could not switch gears overnight. Their former conception of the world was disintegrating. An entire cosmos of familiar myths, images, and ideas had been shattered, and many did not want to believe that this was possible. For example, the wife of one of the persons convicted for the mass disorders in Tbilisi explained the actions of her husband in an appeal dated August 25, 1956, and addressed to Khrushchev: "He could not conceive, he simply did not have it in his consciousness that one could distinguish between Lenin and Stalin. He did not know and could not know that Stalin was a mere human being and that he could make mistakes."[8] Many ordinary participants in the events found themselves in a similar situation at the beginning of March 1956. They could not believe that their idol had committed crimes.

During the morning of March 7, the students at Stalin State University went out onto the streets instead of attending classes, where they were joined by students from other educational institutions. Schoolchildren also took part in the demonstration. Sometimes, according to the journalist Statnikov, the older students forced the younger pupils to get involved by disrupting classes and threatening school directors. The demonstrators went down the main street, Rustaveli Prospect, to Lenin Square, stopping at the Government Building to shout "Hooray for the Great Stalin," accompanied by the sound of car horns continuously honking. The next stop was the city council building located in Lenin Square, where several people recited verses about Stalin and a chorus sang songs in his honor.[9]

The police tried unsuccessfully to stop the demonstration or at least change its route.[10] At the Stalin monument, a spontaneous meeting began anew with speakers cursing those who were "blackening the name of Stalin."[11] The crowd was in an aggressive mood. The police had to save one man from attack who was suspected of taking pictures of the speakers for KGB records, as well as a retired army major who had said to those around her: "Why are these idlers and fools standing around here, do they really have nothing better to do." Despite police efforts, she had to be carried off in an ambulance.[12] For courageously defending a woman, the crowd beat a police colonel to the point of unconsciousness.[13] By the end of the day, the number of demonstrators reached 70,000 persons.[14] The MVD leadership in Moscow had underestimated the significance of the demonstrations that began on March 7, and information based on the report of Dzhandzhgava, Georgian minister of internal affairs, was only sent to the Central Committee late on the day of March 8.[15]

March 8. The Meeting at Lenin Square and at the Stalin Monument. Escalation of Violence and the Organization of the "Center"

Toward morning on March 8, in the sector of the city where student dormitories were located, an unidentified person announced that wreaths were being removed from the Stalin monument. In response, a large group of up to 1,000 students gathered at the monument. The city practically ceased functioning. Some people simply did not go to work, while others went, but in the course of the day left to go out on the streets. In the Georgian Supreme Court, all scheduled hearings were canceled, and the defendants were left in prison.[16] Obviously, there was a fear of violence in the streets.

Trucks were driving through the city filled with people waving flags and portraits of Lenin and Stalin while shouting "Lenin-Stalin," "Long Live Stalin!" The journalist Statnikov was certain that no one had designated these trucks for this purpose. The crowd had simply confiscated them and forced the drivers either by patriotic slogans or by threats to carry out their orders. This seizure of cars and buses had begun after one of the speakers at the meeting in Lenin Square proclaimed from the tribunal that everything belonged to the people, including transportation.[17] The demonstrators threw one of the truck drivers who had refused to comply off the bridge into the Kura River and beat up several others who were uncooperative. According to F. Baazova, an eyewitness, the demonstrators "directed traffic and in several cases even stopped it."[18] Some clashes broke out between participants and policemen.

During the meeting at the Stalin monument, when the police detained a driver who had stolen a car, the crowd divided into groups of seven to eight hundred and began to beat up traffic cops. They then encircled the police department and demanded liberation of all prisoners, including the driver of the purloined car. The demonstrators resisted the demands of police personnel who were trying to halt the confiscation of automobiles, and usually such skirmishes ended in the crowd's favor. For example, in the course of the day on March 9, the police succeeded in detaining only eighty vehicles. With some of them, the police had to dismantle essential parts in order to "temporarily prohibit use."[19]

The demonstrations became massive in scale. One column of approximately 3,000 people[20] gathered in Lenin Square across from the building of the Central Committee of the Georgian Communist Party. A second column of up to 4,000 gathered at the Stalin monument on the shore of the river, holding up portraits of Lenin, Stalin, and Molotov* and shouting such slo-

---

*Viacheslav Mikhailovich Molotov (1890–1986) was a loyal Stalinist who served as foreign minister from 1939 to 1949 and again from 1953 to 1957. He led the so-called Antiparty Group, which in July 1957 attempted to oust Khrushchev. He was expelled from the CPSU in 1964.—E.M.

gans as "With Lenin and Stalin Onward to the Victory of Communism," "We Will Not Forget Stalin."[21] Pictures of Lenin, which increased in number every hour, psychologically disarmed authorities. It was as if the meeting were demonstrating its Soviet loyalty and using the name of Lenin as a "shield, guarding the inviolability of Stalin's greatness."[22]

The demonstrators demanded a speech from First Secretary Mzhavanadze "about the decisions of the CPSU Twentieth Party Congress."[23] According to F. Baazova, "an elected delegation went to the office and conveyed the demand of the demonstrators to bring forth the first secretary of the Central Committee, Vasilii Pavlovich Mzhavanadze." "At this time," Baazova explained, "the mausoleum in Red Square where Stalin lay next to Lenin had been closed. Rumors were circulating that Stalin had been intentionally embalmed in such a way that he had immediately turned black. Allegedly Mao Zedong had demanded that Stalin's remains be delivered to Chinese specialists who could 'restore' him." Now the demonstrators supposedly "demanded insistently that Mzhavanadze support the efforts of Mao to restore the remains and the honor of Stalin."[24]

At noon on March 8, Mzhavandze did actually speak to the crowd and promised to defend Stalin.[25] But after the speech of the first secretary, the demonstrators presented the authorities with the following demands:

March 9 to be declared a day of mourning with all work canceled.

All local newspapers will publish articles dedicated to the life and work of I.V. Stalin.

The movie theaters will show the films *The Fall of Berlin* and *Unforgettable 1919*.*

The representative of the People's Republic of China, Zhu De, will be invited to the meeting.

The hymn of the Georgian Republic will be performed in full text [i.e., without the exclusion of Stalin's name from it].[26]

After the speech of Mzhavandadze, the crowd wanted to hear Zhu De, a marshal of the People's Republic of China who was visiting Georgia following his participation in the Twentieth Party Congress. Immediately a delegation was prepared. The figure of the Chinese marshal would play an important role in the emerging mythology of the demonstration as confirmation of Stalin's international significance.

---

*Both films glorified Stalin's role as a military leader. The first dealt with World War II and the second with the Russian Civil War.—E.M.

The meeting of the demonstrators with Zhu De actually did take place. An enormous crowd numbering around 5,000 people began moving in the confiscated vehicles toward Krtsanisi, where the marshal was staying in a government-owned *dacha*.* A small number of police tried unsuccessfully to stop the demonstrators. Armed with sticks, however, the demonstrators "broke through the police detachments and burst onto the property of the dacha, where they behaved wantonly and insolently." Now the disorders were spreading beyond the city limits.

At the request of republican leaders, Zhu De greeted the demonstrators twice, but the crowd still did not disperse. People demanded that its representatives be officially received. Five students, according to the information of the Georgian MVD, met face-to-face with Zhu De, but failed to convince him to visit the Stalin monument in Tbilisi. Someone from the Chinese delegation, however, actually did speak at a meeting there.[27]

The journalist Statnikov at this time was at Lenin Square. Someone cried out: Why are there no mourning flags hanging in the city? Should not the panel with portraits of Marx, Engels, Lenin, and Stalin be hanging from the Tbilisi City Council building as was the custom on such occasions? People in the square began to hoot and holler with approval and immediately voted yes in agreement with the speaker. Several dozen people forthwith located the supervisor of the building, and the portraits were soon hanging in their habitual ceremonial spot. This same scenario was repeated at the Transcaucasus Military District headquarters. After an attempt to storm the building, two young people were able to climb up on the drainpipe to the balcony, where they hung two funeral flags. Then the military authorities apparantly gave an order and a large canvas appeared with portraits of Lenin and Stalin.

The police reacted quite sluggishly to these events. They seemed psychologically paralyzed by the demonstrators' appeal to the patriotic feelings of Georgians, who still maintained respect for Stalin and his celestial grandeur, as well as by the communist loyalties and sincere enthusiasm of the crowd. As a result, the authorities completely lost the initiative. Georgian Minister of Internal Affairs Dzhandzhgava was later unable to respond intelligibly to the question of the USSR Ministry of Internal Affairs: why at the very beginning of the disorders were the necessary preventive measures not taken?[28] The MVD accused the Georgian leader of cowardice.[29] It was completely clear, however, that the passivity of the police was due to the lack of clear

---

A *dacha* is a country home or cottage usually allotted to individuals through their workplace or through membership in a public organization. Dachas ranged in size from a simple shed on a small plot of land to elaborate villas.—E.M.

directions from the political leadership of the republic. The Georgian Central Committee, which was demoralized by the closed letter from the CPSU Central Committee, decided not to act against their own people and against the myth of the great Stalin.

People continued to make speeches in Lenin Square throughout the day. New motifs appeared as several orators shifted from Stalinism to nationalism and alluded to foreign enemies, threatening "Them" with bloodshed. Those who overcame the general crowd psychosis and offered a critical perspective on what was occurring were beaten or hissed off the stage. Someone who claimed to be a Russian, although he spoke with a Georgian accent, read a falsified letter from Moscow students in support of the "matter which has begun here." A woman followed this with the appeal: "Listen, fellow Georgians! We have support in Moscow. Right now meetings are taking place not only in Georgia, but in Stalingrad, Leningrad, and other cities. We will struggle for the cause of Stalin, we swear on our honor!" Several representatives of the creative intelligentsia took part. Greeted with a roar of approval, a young poet by the name of Noneishvili read verses about Stalin and finished with the words: "I also stand with you."[30]

At the wreath-covered Stalin monument, a meeting also took place. According to the testimony of one of the participants, "I gave a speech near the monument of Stalin by my own free will. I said that I had thrown many bombs at the front in the name of Stalin at the enemies of Stalin."[31] Into the editorial offices of the newspapers *Kommunist* (The Communist) and *Zaria Vostoka* (Sunrise of the East) "there burst an unknown person who threatened that if they did not publish memorial issues honoring Stalin published, then the building would be destroyed. After this incident a guard was posted in the editorial offices of both newspapers."[32]

Interestingly, the Communist journalist Statnikov, and the future political émigré from the USSR, Faina Baazova, both sensed in the coordinated actions of the demonstrators evidence of some kind of organizational center. Statnikov writes about this quite directly: "An organizing hand was clearly present, and someone worked out in detail a plan of action."[33] Who precisely? It is not clear. Maybe, "chauvinists surfaced and began to function actively," but Statnikov did not rule out "the possible existence of a spy center."[34] Baazova, although she was not specifically discussing the question of instigators, recalled the alarm that came over her on March 8: "Gradually the feeling arose, that somewhere in an inexplicable form, some kind of 'headquarters' had emerged, which was regulating the situation and sending columns of people into different parts of the city."[35]

March 9 and 10. Political Demands. Storming of the Communications Building. The Introduction of Troops and the Shooting of Demonstrators

During the morning of March 9, the authorities finally tried to take back the initiative and introduce memorial manifestos under official auspices. Newspapers came out with lead articles "The Third Anniversary of the Death of I.V. Stalin" and displayed photographs of Lenin and Stalin from 1922. It was announced that at 1:00 P.M. there would be memorial meetings in all enterprises, institutes, and higher educational establishments. All this activity represented a concession by local authorities to the people who already had been independently holding memorial meetings. It is ironic that at this time, all over the country, local party authorities were reading aloud for selected Communist audiences the Central Committee letter criticizing the cult of personality of Stalin.

But the belated attempts of authorities to retake the initiative by holding official memorial meetings failed. "Fanaticism," recalled Statnikov, "was heating up to a maximum level. It was not only young people who were rampaging in the streets, but also adults. The majority of shops were closed. Employees of small enterprises quit work and went out on the streets. Many people in the food and light industries did not even go to work." The city transportation system shut down. Dozens of trucks, overflowing with people, drove the entire day through Tbilisi displaying flags and portraits. People sang songs and cried out "Lenin–Stalin," "Long Live Stalin." Some cursed Khrushchev and, for effect, brandished knives and daggers.[36] During the morning of March 9, there were handwritten broadsides circulating all over the city "which called on workers and employees to stop working and take part in the processions and gatherings."[37]

The official meetings did take place in Tbilisi. They represented a strange hybrid, blending ritualistic Communist Party oratory (speeches of the bosses repeated in leading morning newspapers, workers talking about the fulfillment of the plan) with attacks on the state. First Secretary Mzhavanadze took part in the meeting held in Lenin Square. After his short speech, people began to disperse, but then some woman cried out: "Stop! I was called today to the MVD and was forced to sign a statement that I would not speak today. I ask you, why has this been done?"[38] The crowd remained in place and subsequently became much more aggressive, forcing people to praise Stalin. Unidentified persons attacked employees of the internal affairs organs.[39] Similar events took place as well in Gori, Sukhumi, and Kutaisi.[40]

Politics did enter into the disorders. Already during the daily meetings in Tbilisi, persons had demanded "the immediate removal of party and government leaders," and discussed the "need to seize the post office, telegraph, and newspaper offices," "even if it required bloodshed to accomplish this."[41] In addition, the demonstrators accepted some sort of appeal requesting assistance and support from sixteen republics.[42]

During the evening of March 9, at the meeting near the Stalin monument, political demands were read aloud in the presence of several party and government leaders who had been sent to "seize control of the platform." The contents of this petition are known to us through the Procuracy files on the case of Ruben Kipiani, who was tried for having read the demands aloud at the meeting on March 9. The original disappeared without a trace. In court, however, Kipiani and other witnesses related its contents. Kipiani's testimony:

> First, return of the closed letter [on the cult of Stalin] to the CPSU Central Committee; second, removal of Mikoian*, Bulganin, and Khrushchev from their posts; third, creation of a new government; fourth, liberation of Bagirov [former first secretary of the Azerbaijan Central Committee of the Communist Party –V.K.] from prison; fifth, promotion of Mgeladze and Mzhavanadze [presumably to the Central Committee Presidium–V.K.]; sixth, appointment of Stalin's son Vasilii to the Central Committee; seventh, institution of an amnesty.[43]

While the contents of the petition were more or less clear, everything else in this episode is covered in fog. Kipiani claimed that, in general, he was not the author of this document. According to the defendant, he had been standing in line waiting to speak at the tribune for three or four hours, and witnesses confirmed this. The events that followed are less clear, for Kipiani gave conflicting versions in different documents. In court: "On March 9, I drank a lot of vodka and stood in line to speak at the meeting. When my turn came, someone gave me a paper with writing on it and asked me to read it. I took it and read all of its contents."[44] In an appeal from February 4, 1957:

> The chairman signaled and I approached the microphone. Taking a deep breath, I prepared to recite verses. But at this moment three brave "knights" rushed up to the tribune, as if they were heralds who were delivering some important and very timely information. Not only I, but all the leaders of the meeting and the hundreds of people who were standing by the main tribune focused on these heroes and showed understandable interest in the

*Anastas Ivanovich Mikoian (1895–1978) served under Stalin, Khrushchev, and Brezhnev. From 1953 to 1955, he was USSR minister of trade and then became first deputy prime minister from 1955 to 1964.—E.M.

document that they handed to me. I came to my senses when one of them, having given me the paper they had delivered, clearly pronounced: "This is from the Central Committee secretary, comrade Mzhavanadze, immediately make this public." I hurriedly began to read it aloud, without understanding the meaning of the words.[45]

In an appeal from July 22, 1959:

At the Stalin memorial, a meeting was taking place, and I, Kipiani, ended up there along with a crowd of people. I pushed myself to the front, in order to hear what the orators were saying. My entire chest was covered in medals for service in the Great Fatherland War [World War II] Several persons approached me, insistently demanding that I read the text aloud for all with my own eyes, for the crowd knew that I was a Stalinist, and they would trust me. I could not refuse, or the crowd would have torn me apart.[46]

The court trial named Kipiani as the document's author. In all probability, the question about the real authors did not arise in court. Everything was blamed on one person who had ended up where he did purely by chance. The subsequent fate of the petition is a mystery. One of the witnesses claimed that Kipiani had put it in his pocket. Kipiani himself declared at the trial that he had given the paper to a member of the meeting's presidium. In an appeal from February 4, 1957, he added new details.

I heard only the roar of approval and continued to read loudly, distinctly, as drunken people do when they play a role. Under the thunder of applause and exclamations of "Lenin–Stalin," "Lenin-Stalin!" I finished the reading, and this document was torn from my hands by those who had given it to me, declaring that "It is necessary to return this personally to Mzhavanadze."[47]

After the document had been read aloud, disagreements arose in the meeting's so-called "official presidium." One of the members immediately "proposed to declare Kipiani's speech incorrect,"[48] but apparently no one listened to him. Kipiani's own statement in court sounded completely mysterious: "After this Mzhavanadze himself brought me home by car."[49]

The information available does not allow conclusive answers to the questions that inevitably arise concerning the case of Kipiani. The main question is: Did the Georgian leaders, rather than object openly, really try to manipulate the mass disturbances and protests? Did they hope to frighten Moscow with the possibility of analogous protests across the entire country and thereby force a change in the political course? The second question is no less vital: What was the real role of Mzhavanadze, whose name surfaced from time to time in court? Either some sort of experienced provocateurs knew how to use the name of the first secretary of the Georgian Communist Party to their advantage or he very naively offered himself.

Because at present these questions, which are vital for understanding the political significance of the Georgian events, cannot be answered, one is limited here to stating the obvious. Kipiani's trial indirectly confirmed the unanimous impression of eyewitnesses that during the time of the uprisings in Tbilisi, there seemed to be some kind of headquarters operating behind the scenes. In his report on events during the early hours of March 10, the first deputy of the Georgian SSR minister of internal affairs concluded that in Tbilisi there existed "some kind of underground center that was directing all of these disorders."[50] Another police document agreed with the idea that such a "center" existed and that the disorders were planned in advance.[51]

Generally speaking, the comparison of sources suggests that there was not one but at least two headquarters or centers. They may even have competed with each other for influence over the crowd. According to F. Baazova, during the evening of March 9, Kolkhoz Square became still another center of events, and certain unidentified youths were directing the crowd to this area. At the center of this small square, an improvised podium had been set up.

> One after another, a series of young people spoke, but their faces were impossible to make out in the darkness. They yelled very loudly, but the general uproar drowned out their words. Somewhere people were singing a long suppressed Georgian national hymn. Some persons in civilian dress tried to interfere with the singing. The crowd supported the singers and small fights broke out. Unexpectedly in the area of the fighting, unidentified persons with armbands appeared, and the singing of the hymn continued.[52]

Leaflets appeared next. Baazova recalled only one point in the leaflet: a call for Georgia to secede from the Soviet Union. This was a demand not heard previously.

But if some kind of single center was indeed functioning, then the question arises: Why did it so quickly move from pro-Soviet opposition and defense of Stalin (the petition of Kipiani) to separatist slogans? It would seem as though there was a behind-the-scenes, hidden competition among different organizational forces, each of which was pursuing its own specific and complex goals. At Kolkhoz Square, these forces at some moment or another collided directly with each other: "persons in civilian dress" against "unidentified persons in armbands."

The existence of one or more organizational centers, which helped push events clearly beyond the boundaries of standard mass disorders, was indirectly confirmed by several other episodes: an attack on the city's bus depot aimed at seizing a large number of buses that had not gone out on their routes that day; the attempt of a group of young people to send an appeal over the radio to "students in several central cities of the Soviet Union" and finally, the discovery of a radio apparatus at the home of one of those arrested on March 10.[53]

During the evening of March 9, according to the testimony of the head of the border troops of the Transcaucasus Military District, Major-General Bannykh, Tbilisi was essentially "out of control. There was no order. The city was in complete anarchy. Transportation, cars and trucks, taxis, buses, and trolley cars were all in the hands of the mob. The cars were driving around the city incessantly honking their horns. The crowds presented an ultimatum demanding that the local government be replaced. Dissatisfaction with higher authorities was expressed." During the meeting at the Stalin monument, there were even calls for pogroms: "Beat the Armenians," "Drive the Russians out of here!"[54]

According to Major-General Bannykh, at the end of the day developments transpired that imparted an unusual, almost carnival-like atmosphere to these tragic events: 2,000 people came from Gori, the birthplace of Stalin, in trucks. The head vehicle was an armored car. Two individuals dressed as Lenin and Stalin were standing on it, surrounded by people wearing naval uniforms with machine gun cartridge belts slung across their shoulders.[55] The reliability of this information has not been confirmed by other sources. It is known that a group from Gori left late at night, but it could not have arrived in Tbilisi by the end of the day on March 9. Maybe there was another group, but it also possible that Bannykh, who was under pressure to inform Moscow but who had not been able to verify this information immediately, simply trusted the rumors that were spreading through the city. In any case, at the very least, the appearance (real or imagined) among the demonstrators of the "living" Lenin and Stalin imparted to events a certain sacred meaning and consecrated, with the names of these great leaders, the actions of those organizing the demonstrations.

Late in the evening of March 9, USSR Minister of Internal Affairs Dudorov informed A.B. Aristov, member of the CPSU Central Committee Secretariat, about the growing tensions in the city. Aristov in turn ordered that Mikhail Suslov, another Central Committee secretary, be informed. As it turned out, Suslov "knew everything," and "all necessary directives had been issued" to the commander of the troops of the Transcaucasus Military District.[56] Thus, Moscow had already made the decision to bring the army into the matter.

That same evening, a document appeared: "Appeal to Communists, Members of the Komsomol, Workers and Employees, and to all Laborers of Tbilisi!" The appeal stated that the "period from March 5 to March 9 had been days of mourning for the laborers of Tbilisi, marking the sorrowful dates of the death and the funeral of I.V. Stalin." However, "dishonest people had turned up—disrupters and provocateurs." They had "committed outrageous acts, violated the social order with the goal of interfering with the normal work of institutions, enterprises, schools, and the life of the city in general." But the appeal failed to explain why "dishonest people" had felt the need to do this. The short document ended with a call to "restore full order in the city" and "restrain the unruly and the provocateurs." "Those who had been deceived" should "return immediately to their regular occupations."[57] Order No. 14 from the head of the Tbilisi garrison introduced a military patrol beginning at midnight on March 10.[58] Both documents were read aloud over the radio every fifteen to twenty minutes on March 9 and 10 in both the Georgian and Russian languages, and the order was posted in the streets.[59] In some places it was immediately torn down. People sensed an approaching threat, and many participants in the meeting began fleeing from the center of the city.

Earlier, during the meeting at the Stalin monument, where Kipiani's petition had been read, it was decided to send approximately ten persons to the nearby Communications Building in order to send a telegram to Moscow. The delegation entered the building but then was detained for a verification of identity. When news of this delay reached the monument, part of the crowd went to their rescue.

Close to midnight, a bloody confrontation took place. According to Statnikov:

> the entry to the building naturally was under guard. Someone from the rear began to shoot, and one of the soldiers was stabbed. The crowd pressed hard, and had to be beaten off with gun butts. Hooligans made use of everything available: fists, knives, rocks, belts. Warning shots were fired into the air. The crowd returned the fire, and provocateurs continued to press hard. The soldiers had no way out. Their lives were under threat, and defensive measures had to be taken. Only after this did the crowd disperse.[60]

During the storming of the Communications Building, several police officers were beaten severely.

According to the report of Major-General Bannykh, after the first shots at the Communications Building, the mob rushed back from Rustaveli Prospect to the neighboring alley where "outcries and meetings" continued. Later "shots, cries of 'Hoorah,' and automobile horns" rang out again from the

Communications Building. Two barricades built out of trolley cars and buses emerged on Rustavelli Prospect: one was near the Tbilisi Hotel and the other was near the Communications Building.[61]

Simultaneously with the attempt to capture the Communications Building, demonstrators tried unsuccessfully to seize the editorial offices of the newspaper *Kommunist.* Around midnight an agitated crowd numbering around 3,000 people who were returning from the Communications Building besieged the city police department "with the goal of disarming police employees and seizing weapons." Rocks and sticks entered into the picture as rioters broke windows and doors in the duty officer's room and attacked several police personnel. Someone stole four official automobiles. Three were found by morning in the city, and one was sunk in the Kura River.

Tanks dispersed the throngs of people in Lenin Square, causing many to flee to their homes. But about five hundred persons carried on a meeting at the Government Building, which was being guarded by border troops. Among the slogans that could be heard was "Hail to Beria!"[62]

About 5,000 people attended a meeting at the Stalin monument during the early hours of March 10. This gathering lasted longer than the other meetings and was marked by demands from those in attendance for the "removal of the central government." Attacks on Mikoian, Bulganin, and Khrushchev were especially sharp. One of the speakers counterposed Molotov to these "traitors": "Hail the new government to be headed by Comrade Molotov!"

Armored carriers entered the area around the monument.[63] It was more difficult to break up the demonstrators here than in other places, for the monument was located in a park and was surrounded by trees. Cries rang out from the crowd: "Georgians, blood has already been spilled for Stalin, we will continue the fight, not one single Georgian will give in."[64] Troops then surrounded the park and prepared to disperse the meeting. Statnikov described what followed:

> Sneers and insults greeted the soldiers. Their repeated warnings were met with fists and knives. Around three o'clock in the morning, when the soldiers began to drive them back, the hooligans and provocateurs resisted. They attacked the soldiers with guns and wounded some of the troops. Once again the soldiers were forced to use weapons.[65]

Statnikov, an official journalist and a Communist, was inclined to present these events as the "necessary self-defense" of soldiers. This version was supported in the Georgian Ministry of Internal Affairs: When soldiers tried to disperse the crowd, they encountered "strong physical resistance, the soldiers were beaten with rocks, sticks, metal rods, bottles, and other objects," all the while being called fascists, Gestapo thugs, and monsters. According to the Georgian MVD, the soldiers shot into the air without any command from officers but, after a minute, followed orders to cease the shooting. There were casualties, however. A young man trampled by the crowd and a young girl with "a serious head wound from a heavy object" died in the hospital. Two more, a young fellow and a girl, refused to get down from the pedestal of the monument. The girl was knocked off with a blow from a bayonet and died on the spot, and the young man was killed by a pistol shot.[66] One of the eyewitnesses stated a year after the events: "The soldiers opened fire on the demonstrators, and one seriously wounded girl declared to a state official who was approaching her: 'Go away, I hate you.' "[67]

When tanks appeared at the Stalin monument and subsequently opened fire, they pushed the crowd back. Unarmed persons then began to climb up on the military vehicles and throw down portraits and banners. Some painted swastikas on several tanks.[68] As troops sought to disperse the crowd at the Government Building, angry cries rang out: "Why have you come here?"; "The army is not needed here!;" "Russians, get out of the city!"; "Destroy the Russians!"[69] When rumors about the murders spread through the city, the slogan, "Blood for Blood," could be heard.[70]

Unfortunately, information about the number of victims on both sides is not available. Obviously, there was an order issued to shoot, and it is clear that among the killed and wounded there were far more enthusiastic and naive young people than provocateurs and firebrands. According to F. Baazova, after midnight a regiment armed with tanks entered the city, and its soldiers without any warnings began to shoot point-blank at students and schoolchildren.[71] The data of the Georgian MVD states that fifteen persons, including two women, were killed and fifty-four were wounded (seven persons subsequently died) during the fighting at the Communications Building and the Stalin monument alone.[72] According to several witnesses, there were also casualties among the soldiers.[73] In addition, during the several days of disturbances, crowds attacked 146 police personnel.[74]

Overnight in the city, police arrested about two hundred people, mainly young students, and a hundred more the next day. Some of those detained had revolvers or other weapons such as knives and daggers. Those arrested ended up in the KGB internal prison under reinforced guard. Agitated by the night's events, the prisoners behaved quite fearlessly ("insolently," according to police), crying out from time to time: "Today we will be liberated," and "Soon our allies will come and help us."[75]

In their discussions during the morning of March 10 about the nighttime shootings, people on the street blamed the government and Russian soldiers. Meanwhile, the situation grew more tense. A cordon of machine gunners surrounded the monument to Stalin, and authorities also stationed military pickets with machine guns along the main streets, in the crossroads, bridges, and at the highway exits. People tried to gather in groups, especially at the Stalin monument and near the railroad station, but patrols dispersed them. At 11:00 A.M., a group of about 150 young people arrived by train from Gori. They tried to go to the center of the city in an organized fashion, forming a column with red flags raised high, but were stopped by troops. The authorities had been warned by agents in the field that the young people would attempt to liberate those who had been arrested. Around noon, demonstrators gathered at a bridge and then rushed toward the monument, but the soldiers fired warning shots into the air to disperse the crowd.

In the second half of the day, a certain "Organizational Committee" prepared handwritten leaflets aimed at organizing (or provoking?) an act of civil disobedience. "During the night of March 10," it was stated in the leaflets, which for some unknown reason were written in Russian, "our best people were shot, including students. Tomorrow (March 11, a Sunday) a memorial meeting will be held in honor of these victims. The place of the meeting will be Lenin Square, by the Stalin monument."[76] Similar appeals and calls were spread by word of mouth.

The tension continued to build. In the evening, military and police organs received information from the KGB about persons allegedly heading along the streetcar routes from the center of the city toward the Armenian district, Avlabara, intending to carry out violence and looting. The information was not confirmed, but additional security measures were taken. During the course of the day, more than 2,000 people, according to police data, left the city for the countryside. After 11:00 P.M., the streets were empty.

The following day, March 11, police reported normal conditions on the streets. They noted "individual cases, when workers going to their jobs were approached by persons and warned that they should not go to work since today, March 11, there would be a meeting in honor of the slain victims." But the search for those who were accosting workers turned up nothing. At dawn, several more leaflets in Russian were picked up, again announcing the memorial meeting.

Only small groups of persons passed through the cordon surrounding the Stalin monument. In the second half of the day, the military equipment was removed from the streets and the squares, but the patrols continued. Passions did not rise as high on March 11 as on previous days. Yet, the question of victims' funerals emerged, and the failure to resolve this issue remained a strong irritant for the entire population of the city. Relatives of the slain insisted on removal of the bodies, but republic-level party leaders feared the explosion of emotions that such funerals could spur. The wounded were put under police guard in hospitals, with strict regulation of visits from relatives and friends.

Police organs noted the "abundance of various provocative rumors and threats" and raised the possibility of further disturbances in the evening of March 11. However, nothing happened.[77] A secret police agent reported that the memorial meeting slated for March 11 had been "rescheduled by provo cateurs for March 24."[78] Indirectly, this confirms the existence of an organizational center for the disturbances in Georgia. Remarkably, its influence even spread to other cities in the republic, for in Gori, a similar meeting was also rescheduled to March 24. In spite of the cancellation of the memorial meeting, Georgians nonetheless expressed their attitude toward the tragedy. For example, Georgians showed up in the markets of the city of Sochi, Krasnodar Krai, RSFSR, with memorial armbands.[79] Someone expressed disappointment about their lack of weapons, and among the crowd could be heard "great threats against the head of the garrison who had ordered the soldiers to open fire."[80]

The Gori "Conspiracy"

On March 5, 1956, in Gori, Stalin's birthplace, approximately 50,000 people, mainly youths, came to Stalin Square and the little house where "the father of the peoples" had been born. This gathering lasted the entire day, and some even spent the night at the monument. From March 6 to 8, 5,000 to 6,000 people visited the square and domicile of Stalin daily. Someone even organized an honor guard. A spontaneous meeting arose, at which individuals recited poems about Stalin and delivered laudatory speeches. During the morning of March 9, the crowd grew significantly larger in scale. A delegation of residents from different cities and districts of the republic, including Tbilisi, joined with the people of Gori.

At 1:00 P.M., just as in the rest of Georgia, an official meeting took place, and as in Tbilisi, it was "taken over" by informal leaders.[81] Among them, young Makvala Okroperidze, who worked for the local party newspaper *Stalineli* (The Stalinist), distinguished herself with a powerfully passionate defense of Stalin. Subsequently, police confiscated 45 declarations and proposals that had been presented at the meeting. Another active participant in the spontaneous proceedings was a seamstress, Meri Dzhioeva, who also read declarations and appeals from the podium. In all, the police found 323 handwritten documents hidden, in all probability, by Dzhioeva herself amid the wreaths and flowers at the Stalin monument.[82] Those who spoke assured the crowd that they were not alone and that similar meetings were being held in other cities of the USSR as well. They simultaneously cursed Khrushchev and the entire Moscow leadership for having insulted Stalin.[83]

Stalin Square and the neighboring streets were filled with people, up to 70,000 in number. In the evening, a person speaking from the tribune demanded the liberation of two individuals who had been detained by the police during the night of March 9. An estimated 5,000 demonstrators encircled the city police department. "In order to avoid complications and undesirable consequences," according to a special report of the Georgian MVD to the USSR MVD, the detained persons were released. Almost simultaneously, a group of young people, after unsuccessfully trying to enter one of the rail cars of the Tbilisi-Moscow train, threw rocks and broke the windows in dozens of cars, delaying the train's departure by thirty-eight minutes.[84] Several automobiles filled with workers left for Tbilisi, but the majority were stopped on route by military units and police, though some did get through to Tbilisi by morning. Holding wreaths and portraits of Lenin and Stalin, they tried to approach the Stalin monument, but were turned back by threats and by persuasion.[85]

The meeting in Gori continued until the morning hours of March 10, but it gradually lost steam until the organizers themselves suspended it. One of the leaders declared that the demands advanced had to be fulfilled by authorities by March 24 and, if rejected, were to be followed by a general strike. Only after this did troops enter the city, although people had voluntarily left the square, with the exception of a small group of young people, the honor guard. Just after midnight on March 11, authorities demanded that they leave the square. When the youths refused, the police detained them. One of them, who had a prior criminal conviction, tried to disarm a police officer, whose colleagues then fired in response, wounding the attacker in the leg.[86]

But the matter was not limited to this skirmish. After the suppression of the disturbances in Tbilisi, during the late hours of March 11 and the early hours of March 12, a clandestine meeting occurred in Gori. Two active participants in the memorial meeting—the Senior Lieutenant Georgadze and the artist Gongadze—gathered at the apartment of Senior Lieutenant I. Kukhianidze, who worked in the city's military registration and enlistment office. They discussed events in Gori and Tbilisi and the future meeting designated for March 24. Kukhianidze proposed to change its location in order to fool the authorities. They chose Kutaisi, where in the opinion of Kukhianidze, it was possible to "rely on one of the non-Russian national military units." Kukhianidze assured his comrades that it would be possible to get weapons, but, if the police suppressed the mass demonstration, it would be necessary to flee abroad. All three resolved to hide Makvala Okroperidze from possible arrest, and that same night went to her and proposed to conceal her in Kutaisi, Svanetiia, or in Tbilisi. Okropiridze agreed and moved to the apartment of Gongadze, where she stayed until the morning of March 12, 1956.

Most likely the unsuccessful conspirators were arrested on March 12, and their plan for continuing the political disturbances in Georgia was never put into action. Kukhianidze subsequently claimed that everything said by them had been a joke. Even the military tribunal did not find in the actions of Kukhianidze either an attempt to organize an armed uprising or "any particularly serious type of propaganda and agitation."[87] The sentence, nonetheless, was harsh—eight years in prison for anti-Soviet agitation and propaganda.

March 5–9, 1956: Sukhumi and Batumi

Events in Sukhumi, the capital of the autonomous Abkhazian republic within Georgia, unfolded as a mirror image of the unrest in Tbilisi and Gori, although they took a less aggressive form. Once again this provides indirect evidence of possible national-level coordination of the spontaneous meetings, manifestos, and the actions of the leaders. During the morning of March 5, 1956, Georgian schoolchildren carried wreaths and began to gather in Sukhumi's central park near the Stalin memorial. The process continued until March 9. Everyday someone from the meeting bought twenty to thirty liters of wine from a local restaurant, which were then distributed in the park to be poured on the memorial, in accordance with ritual.

With each day, the crowd at the memorial expanded, reaching a height of over 2,000 people. There was an uninterrupted flow of speeches and poetry readings. During the evening of March 6, authorities ordered a Russian worker in a florist shop to remove the flowers and wreaths that had been laid upon the Stalin memorial. But the crowd attacked the woman, and only the intervention of plainclothes policemen on duty in the park saved her. From this moment on, the participants in the spontaneous meeting posted their own guard at the monument. The meeting raged on with unabated force through the following day. On March 8, participants set up searchlights in the park and, for protection from the rain, stretched out two tarpaulin covers. Schoolchildren, university students, and adults recited verses until late in the evening.

On March 9 at 1:00 P.M., in Sukhumi as well as all across Georgia, the authorities conducted an official meeting. But as in Tbilisi, its participants refused to disperse after the official ceremony, and the speeches continued. Breaking away from the crowd, a large group of people began stopping cars and forcing the drivers to honk their horns. Those who refused were beaten.

The rioters also stopped city buses that passed by the park and forced the passengers to get off and kneel in the street.

During the evening, nationalism was a powerful theme as the singing of Georgian national songs resounded through the streets. From time to time, people in the streets and parks kneeled reverently. Party and state functionaries who had been fired from leadership posts after the death of Stalin, such as the former first secretary of the Sukhumi regional committee of the Georgian Communist Party and the former deputy chairman of the Council of Ministers of the Abkhazian ASSR, took an active role in organizing these demonstrations.

One of the groups (again, as in Tbilisi) began a spontaneous meeting at the Abkhazian regional party committee building. A second group organized a meeting at the Government Building, and then headed to the so-called "hill of Stalin." At a meeting there, people heard anti-Soviet speeches. Afterward, the women went home, but the men, as they headed back, threw stones and broke the windows of the pedagogical institute. After stopping for a short meeting at the Transcaucasus Military District recreation center, the group headed for the Sukhumi harbor; there they found the captain of a ship docked there and demanded that he sound his horn in honor of Stalin, but he categorically refused. Then about two hundred young people left the harbor and headed toward the city theater. As the performance ended, those in attendance at the theater found themselves dragged into a new meeting, which went on for forty minutes. In the end, the crowd splintered into small groups and scattered around the city. These groups were, by police definition, truly dispersed only in the early morning hours of March 10.[88]

In the city of Batumi, the situation remained calm. On March 5 by the statue of Stalin, a rather peaceful meeting occurred which involved, as everywhere else in Georgia this day, mainly children and young people. On March 9 at 1:00 P.M., the memorial meeting sanctioned by Georgian authorities took place and continued, even after the official closing, until almost midnight, when the crowd dispersed. According to police information, in Batumi "there were no hooligan acts or unhealthy speeches."[89]

The Political Echo of the Georgian Disorders

Influenced by of the March disturbances, a group of young people, in 1956, formed an underground organization, in which Zviad Gamsakhurdiia, the son of a famous Georgian writer and a future Soviet dissident, took part.*

---

*At the end of the 1980s, Gamsakhurdiia became the leader of the movement for Georgian independence and then won election as the first president of an independent Georgia before being overthrown and murdered.—E.M.

From the materials of the Procuracy concerning the case of Z.K. Gamsakhurdiia, A.A. Mikadze, T.T. Gundzhua, and V.V. Sikharuladze, it is obvious that, even prior to March 1956, they had been discussing among themselves the creation of an illegal association. But it took the events of March 5 to 9 to galvanize them into action. It was possibly members of this circle who were among the unidentified young people attempting to lead the unrest in the city. Soon after the March shootings, Gamsakhurdiia "again posited the question . . . about engaging in illegal anti-Soviet work," and "noted as a goal" the creation of an independent Georgian state. Thus, these young people may well have authored the leaflets calling for the secession of Georgia from the USSR that were distributed in Kolkhoz Square in Tbilisi. This group gathered for the first time in July of 1956 in Gamsakhurdiia's apartment. They decided to try to increase the number of participants, "to establish a connection with persons in other illegal circles," and to acquire a typewriter. Late on December 1 and during the early hours of December 2, Gamsakhurdiia's circle distributed a broadside through the streets of Tbilisi. The authors drew attention to past grievances—the March 1956 shootings, the suppression of a Georgian peasant rebellion in 1924, the Stalinist purges, and the introduction of Soviet troops into Hungary—and called for the expulsion of "Russian occupiers" and of "traitors–[defined as] Georgian Communists."[90]

Nothing is known about the existence of other illegal organizations. But several cases have been verified of the distribution (or attempts to distribute) leaflets and anonymous letters that directly or indirectly referred to events in Tbilisi.[91] A case is also known of a spontaneous uprising of young people at the scene of the bloody events in Tbilisi—on Rustaveli Prospekt by the Communications Building. On October 3, 1956, a group of twenty-five students celebrated the award of their stipends by drinking at the Voroshilov Club. After this, they went to the Communications Building, where they stopped at the steps, set up a clay pot of flowers, and sang a song much beloved by Stalin, *Gafrindi shauo metskhalo* (Fly Black Swallow). The deputy police chief ordered the students to disperse, but they refused and instead sang even more loudly. The police detained fifteen persons, while the rest ran away. That evening administrative protocols about the violation of the social order were promulgated, and the young people were allowed to go home in the custody of relatives. The city police chief tried to cover for the students. He did not inform the Georgian MVD about the incident and did not carry the case any further. But when the events at the Communications Building did become known to the republic-level police authorities, they issued an order to "uncover the organizers of the given occurrence."[92] In the end, this case did reach the CPSU Central Committee.[93]

The outburst of Georgian nationalism provoked by the events in Tbilisi frightened other ethnic groups and exacerbated ethnic tensions in Georgia. A month after the disturbances, on April 13, one of the eyewitnesses of the disturbances, presumably an Armenian, sent an anonymous letter complaining about Georgians to the CPSU Central Auditing Commission. Repeating rumors that had spread at this time, the author described a frightening scenario—practically the mass murder of Russians and Armenians, the bodies of whom were thrown into the Kura River. He tried to convince the Moscow leadership that the Georgians were politically unreliable and called for the state, "before it is too late," "to shoot traitors of the Motherland, send their children and relatives to Siberia, and contain them within a closed, forbidden zone."[94] Even while eschewing the names of Stalin and Beria, he was still ready to use their exact same methods to handle ethnic conflict.

Events in Georgia were a diseased reaction of society to the destruction of the great Stalinist myth, and marked a frightening end to a frightening epoch. The denunciation of Stalin psychologically disarmed the more fanatical supporters of the regime, whose irrational loyalty had done as much as violence and terror to sustain the Stalinist system. Their great saint had turned out to have been a great devil. But his debunking had not been constructed according to the proper laws of mythology. This was no fallen angel transformed into Satan. It was not the overthrow of the idol that was so insulting and unbearable to "The Leader's" loyal worshipers; on the contrary, this could still have implied a certain "other worldly–type" greatness. It was the simplicity and commonality of his debunking that proved to be so upsetting. Stalin turned out to be mortal, which meant that the whole messianic preaching of world communism had lost its importance. Consequently, people's sacrifices were rendered meaningless, the cruelty was now unjustified, and life had been lost in vain. Into the place of the great and frightening leader had come a man who was bald and overweight, Nikita Khrushchev. One could relate to him as if he were an equal, curse him and revile him as one would an ordinary man, which was quite different from Stalin's critics cursing him as the anti-Christ himself.

The ideological-psychological crisis that society experienced as a result of the half-hearted denunciation of Stalin, and which culminated in the disorders in Georgia, pricked up the ears of the Communist oligarchs. They understood that a full exposure of the Stalin myth would mean a complete loss of legitimacy for the regime and the devaluation of all of its real and imaginary accomplishments. The reevaluation of Stalin's role and significance had been launched too quickly, confusing not only mass consciousness but even party functionaries accustomed to "oscillating together with the general line." The Tbilisi events were a signal to the state. Even if the regime's ideological foundations had proved capable of sustaining the exposure of Stalinist crimes, the legitimacy of the country's new leader—Khrushchev—clearly was in question.

Khrushchev definitely understood the signal. Until 1961 and the Twenty-second Party Congress, official criticism of Stalin remained remarkably moderate in tone. Many cities, streets, squares, villages, and collective farms were still named after Stalin. Stalin's body remained in the mausoleum next to Lenin, which had indisputable symbolic meaning. It was as if Stalin was being gradually squeezed out of mass consciousness, but it was impossible to imagine any other person in his place. Yet, the time of fanatical faith in communist idols had passed. It was possible to resurrect the rituals and the incantations, but by this point, no one really took them seriously. The myth had died, and the great communist dream had turned out to be a fiction. The system had simply stopped working. Khrushchev's attempts to mobilize the people for "new historical achievements," such as the building of communism in twenty years (the "program for the construction of communism" was accepted simultaneously with Khrushchev's new attack on Stalin in 1961), represented neither a myth nor a great utopia. They were simply a naive deception of the bosses, which the people, who were "living from one day to the next," ignored. There were no fanatical supporters of Khrushchev. His removal in 1964 turned out to be a rather mundane event, which neither upset nor offended anyone, and even gladdened some, to the extent that they again began to write anonymous letters to the top criticizing the deposed "Nikita." The epoch of awesome and frightening leaders had ended.

The spontaneous mobilization of the crowd under the banner of the fallen idol from the past was short-term and cautious. The majority of healthy-minded persons who were sucked into the whirlwind of events in Tbilisi experienced fear and a desire to step back into the shadows. Some sensed that people were trying to manipulate their illusions and political passions either for narrow political goals, to force Khrushchev to "put the brakes on" and thereby preserve the remnants of Communist Party legitimacy, or for nationalist reasons, to switch the "cult of personality" to a "cult of the nation." The appeal to nationalism, which in and of itself transformed Stalin's name from a symbol of communism to a symbol of denigrated national feeling, was a symptom of the future crisis of the Soviet empire, which was comparable in degree to the crisis of Russian communism that had already begun.

The culmination, however, of these crises and their catastrophic denouement were still far in the future.

Chapter 6

A Hooligan's War, or Battles on the Margins: Uprisings of Marginalized Urban Masses

The State versus Hooligans: From Competition to Confrontation

Postwar Hooliganism as a Social Phenomenon

Marginalized elements among the urban population (*marginaly**) consistently participated in practically all of the large-scale disorders known to us. Their criminally organized part–the *blatnye* (thieves)–were indistinguishable in a crowd usually blending right into a rioting mob. Yet they always played their own separate role in the disorders and sought to realize goals that were often far from the aims of the rest of the urban crowd. The blatnye were not, however, the main driving force behind any of the large-scale mass uprisings examined thus far (Temirtau, Kemerovo, Grozny, Tbilisi, even Dzhetygara), although they sometimes imparted a criminal hue to these events. Cruel and aggressive in their actions, the blatnye would provoke participants to confront authorities directly, often by storming the police department. In the majority of small-scale confrontations with authorities, it was precisely these "self-organized half-criminalized elements" who were the instigators and leaders, and they demonstrated a surprising capacity to manipulate the people around them.

---

*This term literally means those persons living on the edge or in the margins, that is, those who exist on the fringes of society without set employment or residence. The author includes in this category the unemployed, idlers, small-scale market peddlers, and hooligans.—E.M.

Special circumstances facilitated this ability. Above all, when human beings are drawn into conflict, they become socially and culturally marginalized. Separated from their normal social environment, people experience deep stress and are more susceptible to primitive forms of self-organization. However, even beyond these particular circumstances, hooligan gangs could cause considerable trouble for authorities, and, in certain situations, even occupied various sectors of a city or entire suburbs. Without the urban riffraff, lone hooligans, and organized hooligan gangs, many smouldering conflicts would never have turned into full-fledged disorders.

During the postwar years, hooliganism* became a serious and progressively expanding social disease. A deep analysis of the reasons for this phenomenon is beyond the scope of this study. But certainly this was a society torn by multiple crises—demographic losses, "modernization," urbanization, and so on. It had lost 30 million people in World War II and now had millions of postwar orphans in need of care. Exhausted from the terror and mass political purges of the 1930s and 1940s, Soviet society was now filled with people who had been in forced labor camps, convicted for insignificant acts on the basis of extraordinary decrees and laws, as well as with millions of "declassed" peasants. There were also an enormous number of people who were still experiencing a personal identity crisis after being forced to leave the stable environment of traditional rural life. They were both socially disoriented and either actually or potentially asocial.

All these marginalized people were products of varying circumstances and life experiences that were connected both with the standard military and social cataclysms suffered by any country as well as with the particularly repressive nature of the Soviet regime. The need for periodic liberalization created confusion and typically ended up in a willful, unbridled "free-for-all." Traditional (family-communal) mechanisms of social control had gradually been destroyed. But there were no internal, modern forms of self-organization among the population to replace them, since the regime considered practically any semblance of such to be a political crime.

In general, a modern industrial society, which the USSR was becoming during the course of the 1950s, has an extremely limited choice of mechanisms for self-regulation. With varying success, the Soviet regime filled this

---

*Hooliganism was a broad category in the Soviet legal system, covering a wide range of actions, from violent robbery, beatings, and rape to bottle throwing and juvenile delinquency.—E.M.

enormous gap with a system of ideological and political controls in addition to periodically strengthening its repressive measures against the populace. When Khrushchev came to power, he not only had to deal with the consequences of the Stalinist mass terror, but he also had to find appropriate responses to both newly emerging social problems and those that were growing more acute. Thus, all social anomalies, which are inevitable in any society, acquired in the post-Stalinist USSR a definite political resonance, as much from the scale of their dissemination as from the archaic means used to treat them.

Soviet society, while trying to accommodate itself to the new realities of industrial, post-Stalinist, and postwar society, suffered heavily from mass hooliganism. In 1946, there was an explosion of criminality, with approximately 70,000 people convicted for hooliganism. But in the following years, the number of those convicted kept increasing and culminated in a sharp rise in 1956 to almost 200,000.[1] But even these convictions were only a drop in the ocean compared with the number arrested for petty hooliganism and those punished by decision of people's courts*—the total was almost 500,000 people in 1957.[2]

Judging from the constant complaints from the populace about the failure to investigate and punish petty hooligans, the scale of the hooligan epidemic was unusual. Along with small-scale misappropriation of "socialist property," hooliganism was the most widespread form of crime. Hooliganism together with assault and battery comprised more than 40 percent of all registered crimes. In addition, in 1957, about 1.4 million people were picked up on the streets for alcohol abuse. A decisive growth in the use of alcohol, which partly stemmed from a certain increase in the material well-being of the population in the 1950s, clearly correlated with this spread of mass hooliganism.

The number of career hooligans kept increasing. If in 1953 the share of repeat offenders for hooliganism was 5 percent, then in 1957 it had increased almost two times to 9.6 percent. More than 10 percent of those convicted of hooliganism had already served time in prison.[3] The number of murders connected with hooliganism, jealousy, arguments, and other everyday domestic incidents also grew.[4]

The majority of those convicted for hooliganism were workers (71.3 percent), followed by collective farmers (16.8 percent) and white-collar

---

*People's courts were the lowest-level courts in the Soviet system with jurisdiction in most civil and criminal cases. The court was presided over by an elected professional judge and two elected lay judges (people's assessors). The latter are similar to juries in the United States.—E.M.

employees (4.1 percent). The "industrial-urbanization" factor in this hooligan crisis is obvious. The percentage of workers among those convicted of hooliganism at the end of the 1950s significantly exceeded the share of this social group in the country's population. Out of the total number of persons convicted for hooliganism, 9.9 percent lacked a definite occupation or had "quit work," that is, they were classic paupers.[5] To understand this situation, one must keep in mind that impoverished persons and tramps, contrary to the assertions of official propaganda, were at this time a rather habitual part of the urban landscape, with the exception of perhaps Moscow and Leningrad. In the first six months of 1957, more than 75,000 such persons were detained by the police, and during the same period of 1958, more than 80,000.[6]

Hooliganism involved both young and old. But the extremely high rate of criminality among the youth had a definite impact on the social volatility of the population as a whole. Young people comprised almost half of those arrested in 1956, and in Kazakhstan, Armenia, Georgia, and Belorussia their share was even higher.[7] The MVD directly connected the heightened criminalization of youth with a social phenomenon fully denied by official propaganda—unemployment. According to incomplete data, even in Moscow Oblast in the mid-1950s there were approximately 20,000 people under the age of twenty-five who did not attend school or hold a job, including more than 8,000 graduates of secondary schools. In many large towns and industrial centers of the country, enterprise managers simply refused to hire young people.[8] Those under the age of eighteen who were not in school, mainly men, experienced particular difficulty in finding employment. As a general rule, they were not hired because employers did not want to lose time and money training workers who in a year or two would have to serve in the army.[9] Thus, tens of thousands of young people ended up outside the jurisdiction of any kind of social institutions except for the police, and instead fell into asocial activities, fights, and hooligan gangs. This type of experience characterized the riots and disorders discussed in earlier chapters involving soldiers, the Virgin Lands, and new construction sites.

In the regions of new construction and the Virgin Lands, the creation of police institutions lagged behind the boom in immigration. In the more stable areas—above all Moscow, Leningrad, the capitals of the union republics, and the majority of the older industrial centers—the situation did not generally develop into the type of mass unrest seen in the Virgin Lands and new construction sites. This stability was achieved through more or less effective attempts at reeducating and finding jobs for unemployed "parasites,"[10] but the main factor was forcibly controlling the movement of the population into large cities through the passport system.*[11] The latter limited spontaneous migration and also pushed paupers and other marginalized elements to the periphery, meaning to towns beyond the range of "101 kilometers" from major cities such as Moscow, although the administrative exile of "parasites" at the end of the 1950s was rarely practiced.[12] The unforeseen explosion in criminality, including hooliganism, also coincided with the mass amnesty of condemned criminals after the death of Stalin, which had been initiated by secret police chief Lavrenty Beria. This amnesty, contrived as a demonstrative political act, was organized poorly and executed too hastily. As a result, a wave of real criminal terror began in certain cities and regions.

By an order of the Supreme Soviet Presidium, 1,195,248 people were liberated from incarceration. Another 25,000 were amnestied and freed from investigation and trial, with the majority already liberated by the beginning of July 1953.[13] But many could not find employment, and even formal job placement still did not mean that real social rehabilitation had occurred.[14] These ex-convicts became an increasingly prominent part of the urban social environment and were a constant source of constant problems for the preservation of law and order.

"The Molotov Syndrome"

This situation is clearly illustrated in the example of Molotov (contemporary Perm) Oblast, which was numbered among those regions particularly troubled by crime. On February 27, 1954, the minister of internal affairs, S.N. Kruglov, and Procurator-General R. Rudenko had to make a special report to top Soviet leaders about the sharp growth in crime in this area.[15] The problem was not simply the criminalization of the city of Molotov. Certainly the influx of amnestied criminals did provoke an outburst of mass street hooliganism and other crimes. But the problem was that the police had to focus on the more dangerous crimes and consequently left hooliganism virtually unpunished. Street violence became so habitual that people simply stopped reporting such incidents to the police, believing themselves to be defenseless victims of total and impunitive criminal terror. All the blame for the crime wave was put on the amnestied prisoners, although in Molotov a significant portion of the most serious crimes were carried out by persons without a prior criminal

---

*In 1932, to combat high levels of job changing and mobility, the Soviet government had revived the tsarist system of internal passports. Each citizen upon reaching the age of sixteen was issued a personal passport containing vital personal information, including the place of permanent residence. To change residence required police permission.—E.M.

record. Frustrated, Molotov residents finally wrote a letter to V.M. Molotov, in whose honor the city of Perm had been renamed, demanding that the authorities restore the death penalty for murder and other particularly dangerous crimes:

> Since the publication of the Decree on Amnesty in the spring of 1953, throughout the entire city, and especially in the area where workers from the Molotov Factory live, acts of robbery, violence, and murder have been committed and continue to increase in number. All of this begins from seven o'clock to eight o'clock in the evening, but theft of money, watches, and clothing from residents often goes on all day.[16]

The letter went on to give examples even more appalling than these.

The Soviet leadership took measures to strengthen punishment for particularly serious crimes, but these were already inadequate for stopping the mass street hooliganism provoked by the amnesty. Entire regions of the country were suffering from "the Molotov syndrome," even Moscow. During the spring of 1955, Khrushchev personally ordered the Moscow city party committee and the Ministry of Internal Affairs to verify the facts about heightened criminal activity taking place directly under the nose of the CPSU Central Committee in Moscow. To battle against street crime and hooliganism, the city had to strengthen patrols during the evening and night hours.[17]

During the summer of 1955, the Central Committee Letters Department gathered and sent to the MVD for review numerous complaints and petitions by the inhabitants of Cherepovets, Engels, Baku, Voronezh, Noginsk (Moscow Oblast), Rovenki (Voroshilovgrad Oblast), and the Piatigorsk State Grain Farm (Akmolinsk Oblast). The letters basically addressed the unprecedented wave of street hooliganism and the rumors of dozens of murders being committed within this context. In order to mollify heightened popular nervousness and normalize the situation in the designated cities and population centers, the MVD had to strengthen the police presence in the more disreputable and dangerous locations, as well as in parks, clubs, and public gardens. In addition, it turned to extraordinary measures, such as increasing the number of MVD troops patrolling the streets.[18]

In the end, the matter went all the way to the highest levels of power. In September 1956, the Central Committee Secretariat accepted a special resolution obliging the law enforcement organs to restore order in the city of Gorky, where criminalization of the district around the Gorky Automobile Factory (GAZ) had reached a critical point. Life for law-abiding citizens had become unbearable, and this time the matter was not simply limited to petty hooliganism. There were murders, rapes, and muggings. In addition, the automobile factory itself experienced massive theft of spare automobile parts. A team of Moscow investigators and operatives arrived and quickly uncovered several notorious crimes. Resorting to intimidation, authorities held public show trials of those arrested for these criminal acts.[19]

The actions of the police to bring order to cities, sometimes rational, but often hurried and superficial, could provoke hooligans to respond with even greater aggression, which put the police in a difficult position. They could not keep pace with the new mutations of this old social disease. Meanwhile hooligans targeted not only the police, but also their more or less voluntary auxiliaries, at first the Brigades for Assisting the Militia [brigadmil'tsy], then the People's Squads.[20]

The increasingly brutal confrontations between authorities and urban mobs or organized hooligan gangs clearly perplexed Moscow. The police, as has been explained, lacked adequate skills for controlling large spontaneous gatherings of people. Officers did not know how to restrain hooligans without violating their legal rights, which clearly contradicted the spirit of the post-Stalinist liberal trends. At the end of August 1953, during a meeting with the deputy minister of internal affairs, Maslennikov, policemen in a reserve regiment asked about their official rights:

> In the detention of persons who violate public order and especially in the conveyance of hooligans and drunks to the police station, police are subjected to insults and often to physical assault.
>
> Without being able to hold these people responsible for their actions, since in many cases citizens who could act as witnesses decline to do so, citing their jobs or their fear that hooligans who go unpunished will seek revenge, police are forced to suffer both verbal and physical insults which are humiliating to the dignity of a human being and a member of the police force.[21]

Participants in the meeting with Maslennikov were frustrated by the fact that "policemen at their posts are completely defenseless in circumstances when there are large gatherings of the public, and certain undisciplined citizens do not obey the legal demands of the police, while others incite the public against the police, insulting and abusing the police in every way possible." The men in the reserve regiment demanded that in the investigation of such cases "the courts have greater trust in police as human beings who are engaged in state service, than in hooligans and rogues."[22]

During the 1950s the police failed to develop an effective strategy for extinguishing such conflicts at the moment of their genesis. Too often MVD personnel, due to their own impotence and clumsiness, had to resort to an extreme method of persuasion—a weapon—and sometimes they themselves became the defenseless victims of hooligan aggression.

The Hooligan "Occupation" of the Town of Ludz

In September 1953, Procurator-General Rudenko received a memorandum from the Latvian procurator, V. Lipin, about hooligan gangs among the students at Vocational School No. 5 in the town of Ludz. There were 201 people enrolled in the school, half of whom were Belorussian youths raised in an orphanage after losing their parents during World War II. There was no discipline or order in the school, and the students had gotten completely out of hand. Older pupils were disrupting classes and attacking the younger students. Thieving and pilfering also flourished. The older pupils not only stole items themselves, but they forced others to do so as well, targeting the yards and gardens of local residents. The teachers handled the students roughly, but this only further angered them. School personnel, feeling helpless, increasingly turned to the police for help. Consequently, an antagonism arose between the youth and the police, which was strengthened by the group dynamics and internal solidarity among the students.

In the end, the criminal activity of these "criminal" juveniles spilled over into the city. In the middle of September, a real "hooligan war" began. Students went on a rampage through the streets of the town, drinking, intimidating residents, and disturbing the peace. On September 17, 1953, the police picked up one of the young persons for some "hooligan acts near the memorial to a deceased lieutenant-colonel in the Soviet Army." Friends of the detained youth went to the district police station to demand his release and, in the case of a refusal, intended to free him by force. The young people dispersed only when they learned that the detained student had already been set free.

During the evening of September 19, a group of vocational students surrounded a policeman and beat him. The next day, the eighth-grade students learned that the dorm superintendent had complained to the school principal about them. They subsequently tried to break into the superintendent's room, but failed to knock down the doors. They then crawled through a broken window, beat and knifed the man, and destroyed his furniture. That same evening the juveniles broke into the dormitory of the younger grades, beat up several pupils, stole their possessions, and swore everyone to silence under threat of reprisals.

During the evening of September 21, a new attack occurred when a group of the vocational students surrounded a policeman and pounded him with a rock. The victim lashed his attackers with a bridle and then hid in the district police department. The youths ran to the dormitory, announced that the police were beating up students, and demanded that everyone immediately go out to fight the police. Through verbal threats and physical force, they gathered a student "militia," which ran to the police department armed with sticks and stones. They threw rocks at the building and broke twenty windows (after the attack on the police headquarters, fifty-five heavy stones, each weighing up to half a kilogram, were discovered). The police panicked and ran away, pursued by hooligans. The latter found a policeman in a classroom at the evening school and beat him.

During the early hours of September 23, the juveniles effectively occupied the city. Armed with sticks and stones, they patrolled the streets until the early hours of the morning. During this same period they also broke down the doors of the dorm cloakroom, stole everything belonging to the other students, and then hid the plundered items in hedges and near the homes of town residents. Frightened by the hooligan terror, the younger pupils at the school stopped attending class. After some left for their homes, the school canceled classes.

It took a special police operation to restore order, resulting in the detention of forty-three of the Belorussian orphans. Seventeen students who had been forced to take part in criminal activities returned on that same day to the school. Fourteen were sent to study in other institutes. Eight students were arrested, and the police proposed sending three or four to a colony for juvenile criminals.[23]

Occupation of the Dance Pavilion in Magnitogorsk

Youth gangs in Magnitogorsk had similar clashes with police during 1956 to 1957. But the scale of the phenomenon, as well as the duration of the confrontation, significantly exceeded the Ludz episode. There were more than 5,000 young people studying various specialities in fifteen vocational and technical schools in Magnitogorsk. All of these schools were filled with "difficult youth" and suffered from inadequate discipline, poor teaching, and hooliganism.

During spring evenings beginning in April, several hundred vocational students, mainly Tatars and Bashkirs, gathered at the edge of town at an improvised dance pavilion. At first they used the lighted asphalt street, but then the police ordered them to move to a dark vacant lot next to a trash dump. The majority of those attending the dances would be inebriated. Sometimes fights and brawls broke out, but the police tried not to intervene, preferring to let the students sort out such matters among themselves. This was a special world, solidly opposed to any encroachment from the outside.

During the evening of April 27, 1955, while the students were dancing, a two-man police patrol intervened in a fight and detained two young men. To verify the youths' identity, they took them to the *krasnyi ugolok* (Red Corner, a special kind of recreation room in various state and public institutions always associated with communist propaganda and agitation tasks—V.K.) of the closest dormitory. Irritated at this interference in their own "internal affairs," students began to break down the doors and demand the liberation of their comrades. A policeman went out on the street and called for the mob to disperse. The response was crude swearing followed by a shower of rocks. In order to calm the enraged young people, the policeman shot his pistol twice into the air. He had hardly returned to the Red Corner when there was a knock on the door and again rocks flew in through the window. This time the policeman, joined by auxiliary police volunteers who had just arrived on the scene, detained one of the drunken hooligans.

The police began to gather their forces at the dormitory. In order to relieve tension, they freed one of the detained youths, but took two others to the police station. One group of policemen went with the detained youths, and a second group went to the vacant lot. On the way there, several hundred youths encountered the police and began to throw rocks. The police fired into the air, but one officer, acting in self-defense, wounded a young firebrand at the very moment he was preparing to throw a rock. Subsequently it was found that the policeman had fired in defense of a colleague, and he received a medal.

Over the course of the spring and early summer, relations between the police and the vocational students continued to worsen. On June 13, 1955, upon encountering a nighttime patrol, an unidentified youth knocked off the hat of one of the policemen. A conflict arose and a large group of about a hundred vocational students began to throw rocks at the policemen. Two shots rang out in response, and one student suffered a slight leg wound.

Having heard the shots and learned about the wounding of their comrade, students from the Factory-Plant School* (FZO), already numbering around three hundred people, rushed to the police station and demanded the release of those being held. Negotiations with the police led nowhere. The students began to throw stones, breaking windows, electric lights, and even the departmental signboard. The duty officer agreed to permit a delegation of three people to enter the premises and then tried to assure them that there were no vocational students being held at the station. But the crowd was beginning to sense its own power. It demanded not only the liberation of the unidentified

---

*Factory-Plant Schools were institutes for training state labor reserves, instituted in 1940.—E.M.

"hero," the one who had knocked off the policeman's hat, but even insisted that the policeman who had been involved in the confrontation be delivered to them for reprisal. The crowd began to throw rocks at the duty officer, who had gone out on the front landing. In response, the police fired twelve shots in the air. But it took the arrival of military troops, who fired automatic weapons into the air, for people to disperse. The court later found that the mass disorders had been provoked by the wounding of the FZO student.

Consequently, the vocational students were resentful, and thus the police prepared themselves for new confrontations. Ominously, the conflict had ceased being impersonal, and both sides were in a state of acute psychological tension. But hooligan terror did not end and the authorities did not know what to do. During the fall of 1956, a new confrontation with the police occurred. At the same dance pavilion, a vocational student was detained on suspicion of having beaten up an unidentified youth. Subsequently about forty students from the FZO attacked the police with rocks, demanding the liberation of the detained man. Driven back by their opponents, the police fired into the air without any hesitation. Nevertheless, the detained youth succeeded in getting away from the police, who then replaced him with one of the participants in the "liberation." At this point, about a hundred students gathered and demanded anew the release of the man being held by the police. Again they threw rocks, this time at the police department windows and into the apartments of peaceful bystanders, and again they broke down the police department signboard. The police were able to disperse the crowd and detain several participants in the attack only with the help of personnel from other police departments. In all, the police fired 117 shots into the air.

The Communist Party leadership in the city had stumbled. Something clearly was wrong with the administration of the FZO school and with the police. One director of the FZO was fired and two others received party reprimands. The head of the much beleaguered Seventh Division of the Police received a severe reprimand "for failing to take measures to prevent hooligan activities among students and for aimless shooting by police employees." But the claim of the students about being beaten by police during the identity verification process was not substantiated.

News of the Magnitogorsk scandal made its way to Moscow. The Komsomol Central Committee and the Procuracy intervened in the case. The investigation showed that the city had literally been occupied by hooligans. From 1954 to 1956, the number of cases involving hooliganism had almost doubled. The Moscow inspectors concluded that one of the reasons for the ongoing confrontations was the "incorrect behavior of individual police personnel." In fact, during 1955 and 1956, five policemen in Magnitogorsk had been held criminally responsible for exceeding their authority.[24]

The Signal from Kherson

From 1953 to 1955, mass hooliganism increasingly spread across the country. Even more troubling was the fact that hooligans were able to pull other marginalized groups into their own aggressive actions. They were even able to attract peaceful bystanders in the cities of the European part of the USSR, where the tranquility of the inhabitants had special political significance. The areas where hooliganism was now spreading lacked the typical preconditions for unrest seen in such regions as the Virgin Lands and the Northern Caucasus. Nonetheless, as early as 1953, for example, during a market riot in the Ukrainian city of Kherson, townspeople took part in a conflict on the side of hooligans.

During the morning of August 4, 1953, a policeman in Kherson detained a thirteen-year-old youth in the central market for selling corn. Frightened by his detention, the schoolchild began to cry and resisted the officer. The latter, although he knew that the boy was not homeless and that the corn had not been stolen, used physical force in detaining him, which caused the child to faint. Witnesses took the boy from the policeman and went to the nearest drugstore, where they revived him and called for an ambulance.

The police officer's behavior prompted an angry crowd numbering up to five hundred people to gather first at the market police station and then at the regional police department. Some called for mob justice as rumors spread that the boy had been killed. In response the police brought him and his mother to show the crowd, but people cried out, "This is police forgery, this boy is an imposter." Some hooligans insulted and threatened the frightened mother for allegedly "selling herself to the police."

The police called to the scene local school directors and teachers, regional and city party officials, and city council members. Their speeches and threats subdued part of the crowd, some of whom then dispersed. But new people kept arriving and so the demonstration continued until late in the evening. Windows were broken in the market police station and in the regional police department building as anti-Soviet statements rang out. In the end, the policeman who had handled the boy roughly was arrested, and an investigation commenced.[25]

Hooligan "Resistance" 1956–1958

The Growth of Antipolice Attitudes and the "Hooliganization" of the Country

The signal from Kherson had important meaning for authorities. In the majority of cases, hooligan gangs acted as the natural opponents of peaceful citizens. The latter demanded protection from authorities, and were often ready to assist and support them. However, under certain circumstances, the temporary marginalization of law-abiding citizens occurred, and they then joined under the banner of local hooligans. Often this move was connected with police brutality, and with violations of legality by law enforcement personnel. Such acts engendered rumors, and in certain regions policemen already had poor reputations. Antipolice attitudes could easily pull peaceful bystanders into violent conflict with the police, especially if there was a rumor circulating about appalling injustices having been permitted by authorities. In this way, fertile soil developed both for a coalition between the crowd and local hooligans and for local hooligan aggression to grow into mass disorders.

Certainly there were definite foundations for antipolice attitudes, and hence for the involvement of law-abiding bystanders in mass disturbances, all of which seriously alarmed higher party and state officials. The police had been too slow to detach themselves from the ugly practices of the Stalinist period, which had greatly harmed their reputation. Truthfully, cases of serious criminal acts, as well as corruption and bribery, were actually very rare at this time among police personnel. But hooliganism and the lack of discipline, along with disrespect for the law, from which all of Soviet society suffered, were widespread police vices. When crimes were committed by police, analysis shows that in the majority of cases excessive drinking was a factor. In other words, the situation in the police force was a mirror image of the general situation in Soviet society.[26]

The spark for many confrontations was the detention of persons who were disturbing public order and their subsequent mistreatment by the police. Among the most widespread abuses were illegal arrests and the beating of detained prisoners. But the factor that often deepened the conflict was the use of weapons by the authorities. The illegal use of weapons occurred most often during the detention and interrogation of prisoners, as well as when police were defending themselves against attack. In 1955 alone, 345 people suffered police brutality and related abuses, including 78 who were killed and 89 wounded. Such cases, exaggerated by rumors many times over, created fertile soil for confrontations between the police and ordinary citizens.

The more troubled regions of the Russian Republic, which were distinguished by a very high level of police criminality, were also the areas marked by heightened social volatility and the spread of mass hooliganism (for example, the Kemerov, Kamensk, and Molotov Oblasts). Undoubtedly there were concrete linkages between police criminality and the hooliganization of the region, making a unique vicious circle. Hooligan activity and "wars" with authorities could be provoked by police brutality, the illegal use of weapons, and so on. Such actions of the police, however, could also be the product of hooligan encroachment upon the territory entrusted to police "care" and the personalization of relations with local hooligans, as well as individual grievances.

Among the police, there also existed a unique form of group solidarity, which reached in a number of cases to the level of "mutual responsibility" [krugovaia poruka]. Some police chiefs, after having fiercely beaten back the attack of hooligans, were inclined at the very least to overlook certain abuses by their subordinates.[27] Such examples of police "liberalism" could not help but irritate the populace, and thus it transpired that frequently during mass conflicts and disorders the crowd demanded that the "bad policeman" be handed over for mob reprisals.

Thus, the MVD failed to control the activity of law enforcement personnel who provoked the populace into conflicts and riots. Attempts to rein in police behavior in 1955 and early 1956 proved to be inadequate as murder and mistreatment of citizens continued, fueled by drunkenness and irresponsibility.[28] In 1956, in cities that had previously been relatively prosperous, hooligan aggression now tended to grow into broad mass disturbances, thanks to the illegalities and abuses of policemen themselves.

Hooligan Uprisings in 1956

On January 10, 1956, the Ministry of Internal Affairs informed the Central Committee and the Council of Ministers about hooliganism among youth gangs in the city of Novorossiisk, RSFSR. During the evening of January 9, on one of the main streets, a group of about fifteen to eighteen drunken youth harassed women and blocked people from entering the road. One of the hooligans, an unemployed youth by the name of Ch., resisted detention and repeatedly struck the on-duty policeman. The friends of Ch. tried to free him and were joined by several patrons from a neighboring movie theater.

A large crowd gathered and threw stones at the police station, then broke into the premises and attacked the employees, some of whom hid in the State Bank building. The mob also rushed there, hurling sticks and stones in the process. In self-defense, the police used weapons and killed one of the young attackers, who was armed with a dagger. An elderly police officer hiding in the bank building suffered a heart attack and subsequently died. Simultaneously with the assault on the State Bank, about 1,000 people, armed with sticks and stones, tried to break into the police station and the post office. This same crowd attacked a policeman on post duty. Only the assistance of border troops and a military patrol enabled the police to restore order. Through joint efforts and the use of weapons, the police and the military were able to halt the hooligan actions and detain fifteen hooligans. As a result of the disorders, three police workers and two Soviet army officers were wounded.[29]

Two weeks after these events in Novorossiisk, a market riot flared up in the Lithuanian city of Klaiped. Curiously, police identified the incident as one involving "dawdling," although there is no such concept in the criminal code. Obviously, they were at a loss to find some way to define or classify what had occurred as criminal. In the Klaiped market shortly before noon on January 21, 1956, a police detachment received a report from a civilian police volunteer about a woman selling herring without official permission. When the civilian policeman tried to detain the perpetrator, her husband, D., began pounding him with his fists. Subsequently the police volunteer grabbed the husband and took him to the police station in the market.

The man, D., kept struggling while being detained by the volunteer and again at the police station. But then he began to experience an epileptic attack. As he lay on the floor writhing in convulsions, his wife began to shout that the police had killed her husband. Upon hearing her cries, the people in the market came running. Altogether about five hundred people took part in the disorders. Someone began to call out: "Attack the police." Those assembled refused to accept assurances from the police that the man, D., was ill and had been taken to the hospital, and that no one had beaten him. The crowd attacked the police with the cry: "Why did you kill this man?" Rocks and bricks flew into the police station.

Several police officers were able to get away from the besieged station and headed to the municipal police department located at the edge of the market. The hooligans rushed there as well and threw stones. Six police officers and four KGB agents were seriously wounded in the confrontation. It took fifty people, including border troops and local prison wardens, to end the unrest, but no one used weapons. Fifteen active participants in the disorders were detained, seven of whom were unemployed, and four of whom had been repeatedly arrested for speculation (selling without state permission) in the market.[30]

During the summer a bloody skirmish took place in the Ukrainian city of Enakievo. On the evening of June 17, 1956, a group of thirty young people attacked the patrons of a dance pavilion in the city park, beating them with iron rods and sticks. When the police tried to stop the violence, the hooligans resisted and began to throw rocks. The police shot three times into the air as a warning, and then the mob fired back in response, wounding an officer. The police detained several participants in the attack. An hour later, about five hundred meters from the park the body of one of the attackers was found, but this murder was never solved, though the populace, of course, suspected that the police were involved.[31]

In October 1956, mass disorders exploded in Slaviansk, producing a scenario that almost literally repeated the events in Novorossiisk. During the early evening on October 28, 1956, certain citizens brought into the city police department a metal worker named B., who was extremely drunk and had cursed passengers on the bus. Subsequently an unidentified man came into the duty officer's room and demanded B.'s release. Upon being refused, the unknown person went out onto the street and began yelling that the police were beating prisoners.

Patrons who had just left the movie theater began to assemble at the city police department, forming a large throng of five to six hundred people. The unidentified person who had demanded B.'s liberation broke into the police station accompanied by a group of hooligans. He then led B. onto the street and again began to cry out about police brutality. The crowd refused to believe police protestations and threatened violence against them. Hooligans took advantage of the large accumulation of people and began to throw rocks at the police building. They also tried to break into the preliminary detention cell, but were stopped by warning shots from an automatic weapon. Lasting four hours, the unrest ended only with the assistance of police from neighboring cities and delegates from the Slaviansk Communist Party conference, which was in session at this time.

Rioters broke the windows of the city police department building and assaulted prominent local officials, including the secretary of the Slaviansk city party committee, the secretary of the Komsomol city committee, an investigator in the procurator's office, a number of police officers, and several others who were not named in the police report. The investigation identified four active participants in the disorders. One, the unidentified man who had demanded B.'s release, turned out to be a worker with a prior conviction for petty theft. A second was a person with similar criminal experience. The third participant was charged with violation of public order and the fourth was the man, B.[32]

The Toughening of Police Measures

The spread of the "hooligan" disease, along with its new mutations, forced authorities to act more decisively, and therefore on October 25, 1956, the Council of Ministers and the CPSU Central Committee accepted the secret resolution "On Measures to Improve the Work of the USSR MVD." The republic-level Supreme Soviet presidiums in turn strengthened penalties for petty hooliganism. The number of hooligans and drunks removed from the streets sharply increased. In the first six months of 1957, police detained almost two times more drunks than for the same period in 1956.[33]

As a result of this toughening of police work, as well as measures for restoring order in the police force itself, mass unrest subsided and hooliganism returned to its more habitual forms. But already in September 1958 in Riga, capital of the Latvian SSR, hooligans attacked police officers and civilians who had tried to help them. The police had provoked the attack by encroaching upon the right usurped by local riffraff to drink alcohol directly on the street. During the evening of September 7, 1958, a group of local drunks had made themselves comfortable with bottles in an open square close to the streetcar terminal. Most probably, they were cursing loudly at the top of their voices and in general behaving provocatively. After failing to respond to the reprimands of the on-duty policeman, the drunks argued with him, and after repeated warnings to "stop imbibing alcoholic drinks," they began to pound him with their fists. They also beat up a worker who had come to the officer's assistance. Digging himself out from the mound of bodies, the policeman tried to run away, but one of the hooligans broke off a slab of wood from a fence and pursued the officer. After a warning, the policeman shot and killed his pursuer, then called an ambulance and began to phone the district police department from the pavilion of the streetcar terminal. A crowd that had gathered by this time, incited by friends of the slain man, broke out the pavilion's windows and doors and severely beat the policeman and a fellow officer who had tried to help him.[34] After these events, the Latvian Communist Party Central Committee Bureau ruled in favor of establishing a forty-kilometer zone around Riga with special passport requirements, which would give authorities the right to refuse passage to individuals with passport limitations, such as persons with convictions for dangerous crimes, etc.[35]

In May 1959, in the city of Gorky a gang of hooligans attacked members of the People's Squad. Two drunk men encountered the volunteer policemen and, recalling that they had at some point in the past detained them for hooliganism, decided to seek revenge. Five or six of their acquaintances turned out to be nearby, and they joined the two drunks in assaulting the volunteers. One of the latter, a student at the Engineering-Construction Institute, against whom the hooligans bore a grudge, received seven knife wounds.[36]

In this and other cases similar to it, hooligans either did not know how to organize the crowd for mass riots or simply did not succeed in doing so. Yet the problems internal to the police, which had created fertile soil for the hooligan-citizen coalition, were far from being resolved. Therefore, hooligans' appeal to a sense of injustice (phenomenon of the "innocent victim," for example) could fully mobilize a crowd and turn a confrontation between hooligans and the police into a violent conflict between the people and the state. Additional measures would be required to restore order in the Ministry of Internal Affairs itself.

On January 29, 1958, the Central Committee adopted the resolution "On the Facts of the Violation of Legality in the Police." On February 24, Procurator-General R. Rudenko ordered that the Procuracy's powers of surveillance over the police be strengthened, that the Procuracy more actively institute criminal proceedings against the falsification of interrogations, that it verify citizens' complaints and the validity of MVD decisions, and that it identify those who were guilty of illegal detention and incarceration of citizens, and so on.[37]

Nonetheless, "crude violations of legality" remained a chronic disease of MVD organs. Procurator-General Rudenko wrote, for example, in July 1960 that "individual police officers in their inquiries and also in their investigative work, turn to illegal methods even to the point of using physical means to influence witnesses and suspects. They directly falsify charges and use agents against innocent citizens in a provocative manner."[38] The risk factor thus remained, and even the social background was preserved for confrontations between the police and not only hooligans but also law-abiding citizens.

The "Ideology" of Marginalized Masses, or What Was the Crowd Shouting About?

In the documents that describe the urban riots and disorders during the early Khrushchev period, from time to time there is mention of certain "anti-Soviet outbursts" that came from the agitated crowd. The source usually fails to explain the content of these statements. But undoubtedly the irritated, aggrieved, and often drunk persons on these occasions did not cry out anything exceptional or distinctive from the usual verbal banter against authority.

It is fully possible to reconstruct statements made in the crowds. It is sufficient to turn to cases of those sentenced according to Article 58–10 of the RSFSR Criminal Code (anti-Soviet agitation and propaganda) and analogous articles of the criminal codes for other union republics. In all, 4,676 people were sentenced under this article from 1956 to 1960. The majority of them (3,380 or 72.3 percent) were victims in the wave of political repressions that occurred in 1957 to 1958.[39] It is the more simplistic episodes that are most relative to this study, such as indecent and "bathroom" graffiti, abusive comments and letters addressed to Soviet leaders, tattoos that were widespread in prisons and labor camps, and so on.

The hooligans, drunks, and thieves, as well as the more hardened criminals, all of whom had suffered at the hands of the state and its harsh laws and procedures, certainly did not accept official Soviet goals and values. Furthermore, they insulted and scorned the symbols and attributes, the ideological and political sacred cows of the state. But it is hardly possible to attach any special political significance to these "anti-Sovietisms" and thereby repeat in reverse the mistake of the anarchist Mikhail Bakunin, who considered the criminal to be an "embryonic revolutionary." Criminals, drunks, and juvenile deliquents were no more embryonic revolutionaries than they were anticommunists. They were rebels and rioters and remained such, capable only of senseless, ruthless aggression. If there was an ideology in their outbursts and statements, then it was above all antistatist, and they would have rejected with the same level of passion the principles and attributes of any state, whether capitalist or communist.

The Soviet situation, however, was nonetheless unique. It was not only the natural opponents of the state who felt wronged by it, but millions of other people as well who had suffered from the unyielding and unjust sentences of the Stalinist period, when a person could receive a long prison term simply for being late to work, for loafing, or for any insignificant pilfering of state property. The Soviet state had cruelly torn many people from their normal lives and transformed them into the refuse of society. In this sense, the abuse levied at the state was more than deserved. Consequently, it was not only persons with a criminal past, thieves, or malicious hooligans under the influence of alcohol who let loose a tirade of anti-Soviet verbiage. From time to time, most often while inebriated, people who previously had no record of anything like this suddenly burst out into embittered cursing, profaning the state and its official Communist saints and even poking the eyes out from official portraits of the leaders.

There were, therefore, a multiplicity of hues and gradations in hooligan anti-Sovietism, ranging from principled criminal opposition to an uncontrollable, spontaneous hatred or outbursts of justified resentment against a regime that for no reason had ground down someone's life on its millstones. Among the marginalized layers of the urban population were people who were simply lacking in any restraint, and whose spontaneity turned them into a special kind of anti-Soviet loudspeaker. One example was the invalid L., who had never completed higher education and had a prior conviction for hooliganism. In November 1956, after drinking heavily, L. ended up at the city police department, and there he began to "curse conditions of life in the USSR." Several days later, L. tore down portraits of Voroshilov and Mikoian and then defaced them with anti-Soviet inscriptions. L. even cursed at length the Soviet intervention in Hungary.[40] Remarkably, all of this was done completely uninhibitedly and in the open. If L. had ended up near some kind of antipolice confrontation, he might have become an instigator of unrest.

Vodka loosened tongues of both thieves and hooligans. Bars and snack bars, which during the 1950s were still many in number and relatively inexpensive, from time to time turned into political clubs in which citizens who were fully law-abiding but, temporarily emancipated by alcohol, stood up and made speeches. On November 9, 1956, a man by the name of D., who was an assistant to the captain of a local fishing boat, recited verses at a Georgian restaurant. He read aloud Lermontov's *Proshchai nemytaia Rossiia* (Farewell Unwashed Russia) and Nekrasov's *Komu na Rusi zhit'khorosho* (Who Then Is Happy in Russia), and *Neszhataia polosa* (Freedom).* Then, as if connecting nineteenth-century critical realism with the present, he pronounced in a loud voice, "Down with the Gentlemen-Communists." He continued in this same spirit: "We have now not only fields but entire hectares that are being sold," and "It is time to finish with the Communists and the Soviet government, it is time for the working class to take weapons in their hands and achieve their own freedom, for our government does not care about the people." He added the following concerning Hungary: "Let us join with the West and break with the Communists."[41] In the criminal and half-criminal milieu, it was common to hear the promise to construct a "second Hungary" or a "second Budapest," as well as other widely spread anti-Soviet cliches.[42]

Demonstrative anti-Sovietism was generally characteristic of hardened criminals. It was considered the height of fashion to imprint your own organic hostility to the state in the form of tattoos. Many cases are known of anti-Soviet inscriptions on the body. A man by the name of Zh., with two convictions, one for murder and the other for escaping from prison, inscribed a tattoo on his stomach "with a call to overthrow one of the Soviet leaders and to exalt Truman."[43] The prisoner G., with four convictions, made a similar inscription on his body. At the same time, he and a fellow prisoner also wrote in their own blood on the walls of the cell "calls for overthrowing Soviet power."[44]

Criminals often made tattoos of Lenin and Stalin and used them as "visual agitation."** Some would point to the tattooed portrait of Lenin and say: "It is because of him that we are suffering in these prisons."[45] Others, while raising an uproar in a public place, would open their shirts to reveal Lenin and Stalin and then cry out, "I bear these (calling them something obscene) on my chest."[46] Such tattoos sometimes covered nearly the entire body. In one case, a man identified as Ts. was convicted for drawing tattoos

*Mikhail Lermontov (1814–1841) and Nikolai Nekrasov (1821–1877) were both nineteenth-century poets whose work was distinguished by strong nationalistic feeling for the people and the landscape of Russia. But they were also sharply critical of the social and political order.—E.M.

**In the Soviet system, agitation encompassed political education and propaganda work conducted by Communist Party members and officials.—E.M.

on a cellmate: He inscribed on the neck, "victim of the CPSU"; on the cheeks, "slave of Lenin" and "death to the CPSU"; on the back of the head, "Lenin is a cannibal"; and on the top of the head, "Down with Lenin" and "Lenin is a butcher."[47] The three-time convicted thief known as N. even drew on his body a certain "tattoo of welcome to the U.S.A."[48]

A certain notion of the far away "Amerika," a land hostile to the Soviet bosses, and its remarkable President Truman, who would one day begin a war against the Soviet Union and then liberate the prisoners, generally occupied an important position in criminal mythology at the beginning of the 1950s. This mythology employed the principle "the enemy of my enemy is my friend." The half-folklorish personage "Truman the Liberator" and then "Eisenhower the Liberator" enjoyed exceptional popularity among condemned criminals and thieves. The brothers K., convicted for robbery and assault in 1955, declared during their trial that war with America was inevitable. They claimed that soon Eisenhower would come and liberate them, then they would struggle against Soviet power and "kill officials in the party and state apparatus from the bottom to the top."[49] A man identified as I., who was twenty-two years old with three convictions, cried out during the reading of his sentence: "Down with Soviet power, Long live Eisenhower!" In the cell he said that if he had been given a machine gun, he would have shot down all Communists, first of all Khrushchev and Bulganin.[50]

The prisoner O., convicted of theft, systematically spread rumors in the forced labor camp about the inevitability of war with America, the impending defeat of the USSR, and even about the need to prepare people to cross over to the side of the Americans.[51] Another prisoner, by the name of Z., repeatedly wrote slogans in the corridor of the prison and in the penal isolator cell: "The end is coming soon to Soviet power, Long live the capitalist order in America," "Down with Bulganin and Khrushchev, Long live Eisenhower and Chiang Kai-shek," and "Down with Soviet Power and its government, Long live the United States of America."[52]

The four-time convicted prisoner T. composed similar slogans, but in a more elaborate fashion. On October 20, 1957, he threw out two leaflets from the window of his cell: "Down with Bolshevik power. It is time for the Soviets to take that piece of rotting Leninist meat out of the mausoleum before it decomposes. Long live and prosper Eisenhower, Dulles, and the United States of Capitalist Countries"; "Down with Soviet power. Long live Eisenhower and Dulles and the United States of America. Down with Socialism and Communism. Long live Capitalism." On October 25 and November 18, 1957, T. drew a fascist swastika on the wall of his cell and wrote: "Down with Soviet Power!," "Death to Communism," "Turn the rotting body of Stalin over to Dulles!"[53]

D., a war invalid who was unemployed and homeless, with three convictions for hooliganism, tried unsuccessfully to get payment of his pension from the state. He then found, perhaps, a more refined way to demonstratively protest the situation. He went to the USSR Ministry of Social Security with a broadside containing a "call to overthrow Soviet power and to exalt Eisenhower" fastened to his clothing.[54]

One could replace the mythical "Amerika" (or conjoin it) with the mythical Hitler or any other of yesterday's or today's state enemies. The prisoner Zh., homeless and unemployed with two convictions and one escape from exile, got drunk and went to the movie theater to watch *Urok istorii* (Lessons of History), which depicted the Leipzig trial against Georgy Dmitrov.* During the film, and then also later at the police station, he cursed the Communist Party, Lenin, Stalin, and Dmitrov, but he also cried out: "Long live Hitler! Long live fascism! Long live America!"[55]

In general, the confused merger of the two enemies of the Soviet regime—past (Nazi Germany) and present (the United States)—was quite typical for persons with poorly developed political consciousness. The author of this book, myself a former victim of Cold War propaganda, acutely remembers how in 1955 at age five, I depicted a battle between "Us" and American fighter pilots, and, for some reason, I drew a swastika on the wings of the American airplanes. Enemy No. 1 of the present was somehow associated with the most horrific enemy of the recent past, with absolute evil, that is, with fascism. The swastika practically became a symbol of hooligan anti-Sovietism, and during my childhood was inscribed all over fences and on the walls of buildings by the local riffraff and the young boys who mimicked them.

"Amerika" was not the only alternative image that was widespread. The very goals proclaimed by communism itself could also be posited as an alternative. In this context, the theme of treason resounded ("they are not really Communists, they are traitors"),[56] slightly tinted with primitive egalitarianism. This was an important new accent in the "agitation" of hooligans and other marginalized elements. It brought this agitation closer to serious anti-Sovietism and, just as if it were ennobling primitive curse words, raised it almost to the level of social protest, counterposing to the unjust state its own values, myths, and utopias.

For example, in July 1957, the man A., who was a repeat offender, unem-

---

*Georgy Dmitrov (1882–1949) was a Bulgarian Communist who faithfully served Stalin as head of the Comintern from 1935 until its dissolution in 1943. He was put on trial in Leipzig for the burning of the German Reichstag in 1933 and became famous for his stirring speeches against Nazi leaders such as Goebbels. He was acquitted and became a Soviet citizen.—E.M.

ployed, and homeless, went beyond cursing Khrushchev and Bulganin while riding on the passenger ship *Usievich* from Moscow to Gorky. He called Communists "Soviet bourgeoisie," and said that they did not care about the masses—they receive enormous salaries, they have large apartments and summer homes, and it was simply inconvenient for them to think about the people's needs.[57] A metal worker in a Moscow factory by the name of Ch. said in June 1957 at the Kazan Station in Moscow that in the USSR, "the restoration of capitalism was taking place, the working class had a poor standard of living, and Khrushchev and Bulganin had debased Lenin's ideals and betrayed Russia."[58] The worker F. with two earlier convictions, while attending a lecture on the international situation at a club in Belogorsk, called the talk dull chatter and said that Khrushchev had arranged it "where they could squander the working man's kopek." The following day F. was called into the office of the local party secretary, but he repeated the same words and added that Khrushchev and Bulganin had taken part in the Stalinist repressions. During the summer of 1958, he cursed Khrushchev and called his speeches nonsense—"they had caused division between our Chinese and Korean brothers. Before helping them, it is necessary to create normal living standards in the Soviet Union."[59]

Whether joined with the myth of "Amerika" or not, the use of values, utopias, and ritual oaths of the regime itself to criticize and condemn it represents a much more complex ideological construction than the usual lamentation about "my whole life being taken away"[60] or indignant anti-Soviet cursing. The difference between hooligan and ideological opposition to the regime lies in the fact that the Soviet paraphrase of the old Russian myth about the "good tsar" and his "evil servants" was more deeply rooted and resounded significantly stronger among marginalized layers of the population. Police who used force against one or another hooligan could be perceived as unjust government servants who had arbitrarily counteracted the wise will of higher authority, of the infallible leaders. But in this capacity, it was usually the leaders of yesterday who were exalted—the dead Stalin, the executed Beria, the former Prime Minister Bulganin, and the members of the "antiparty group" of Molotov and Malenkov, who had been expelled by Khrushchev from the higher party leadership.*

A leader who had lost his post acquired all conceivable and inconceivable features of an ideal. It was as if he were "good" and a comrade in misfortune precisely because he no longer had power. In one case, after being amnestied

---

*The antiparty group consisted of hard-line Stalinists such as Molotov, Malenkov, and Kaganovich, who tried in 1957 to oust Khrushchev, but were outmaneuvered and subsequently expelled from the CPSU Central Committee by Khrushchev and his supporters.—E.M.

from prison, the man P. came to his former employer, raised an uproar in the boss's office, and then tussled with police, calling them fascists, traitors, and reptiles. At the same time, he accused them of having "poisoned Stalin."[61]

A prisoner wrote to his mother:

> The question arises why Molotov, Malenkov, and Kaganovich were expelled from the Central Committee, despite the fact that Malenkov had begun to improve conditions for workers and peasants.* Khrushchev did not like this, he found it necessary to slander our old revolutionaries who had built socialism, and they have been found to be enemies of the people.[62]

Those who possessed this mindset were capable (due to their peculiar Manichean "white-black" comprehension of reality) of staunch resistance. Sometimes a conscious enemy of the regime did emerge from their midst. The very author of this letter, who was tried not as a criminal but as a political prisoner, stated in court: "It is useless for me to defend myself. I will defend myself against you only when I have a gun. I wrote such letters and will continue to write them. There are many of us. We must unite for a general struggle."[63]

As we have seen, the widespread myth about "Malenkov and Molotov having allowed the people to live better" nurtured more than just criminal opposition to the state. It contained a fundamental lack of faith in the state as a potential source of well-being. Therefore, everyone who tried to "help people live well" could not remain in power. The evil manifested in the state would immediately dispense with such people.

The disappearance of a leader from the political arena immediately turned him into a symbol of protest. The worse the official propaganda presented the deposed idol, the more saintly he became. For example, the twice-convicted worker I., who had finished the tenth grade in school, and the unemployed A. continually listened to the broadcasts of the Voice of America and the BBC. The two condemned the suppression of the revolution in Hungary and told anti-Soviet anecdotes, acting as if they were transmitting conscious anti-Soviet propaganda. But they also cried out on the streets in hooligan fashion, "Kill the Communists" and were confident that if the so-called "agent of imperialism" Beria had carried out a coup, then everything would have been better.[64] Thus, even the bloody Beria, who had been destroyed and it would seem fully discredited by his own rivals, in mythological consciousness could receive the laurels of a positive hero.

------

*As prime minister from 1953 to 1955, G.M. Malenkov had placed less emphasis on heavy industry in favor of light and consumer industries, which brought him into conflict with Khrushchev, who forced him to resign in 1955.—E.M.

In the pantheon of abased and insulted leaders, it was even possible to run across the name of Leon Trotsky. One K., convicted previously for hooliganism, had "exalted the enemy of the people Trotsky."[65] But K. had been born in 1919 and consequently could not have had any personal memories of the revolutionary exploits of Trotsky, one of the main Bolshevik leaders in the first years of Soviet power. The logic K. used was that if Soviet propaganda reviled Trotsky, this meant precisely that he had been for the people. Thriving leaders of today, on the contrary, were evil by definition.[66]

Interestingly, praise of former Communist leaders was sometimes combined in a remarkable way with depictions of that same swastika and other fully anticommunist symbolism.[67] This again proves that deposed leaders, for a particular type of mindset, were not an alternative good communism to bad communism, but a convincing confirmation that a good person could not survive long among the Soviet bosses. This psychology of the marginalized urban population was essentially different from the psychology of many ideological anti-Soviet elements of the 1950s, who were convinced that good communism could be achieved.

The deposed leader could also act the part of the devil. By combining the offenders, such as police and prison guards, with the absolute personification of evil, a person could seemingly reject the right of his personal enemies to represent the state and to take advantage of it for defense. Aggression thereby acquired a certain moral motivation. For example, the prisoner S., thirty years of age with two convictions, cried out in the penal isolator cell, "Beat those with the red epaulets [krasnopogonniki]!* Down with Soviet power. Bring in Eisenhower. Let Truman come here!" He called the prison personnel "Beria's men."[68] The prisoner T., who considered himself to be unjustly convicted, called Communists "bloodsuckers" and "Bulganin's men," adding that when Malenkov came to power, he (T.) would hang the chairman of the Supreme Soviet Presidium.[69]

The consciousness of marginalized persons, especially those who were drunk, could interpret reality as a myth and thereby combine irreconcilable elements. A man known as K., with a prior conviction and no place of employment, got drunk and went on a rampage of hooliganism and fighting. When he promised to beat up the chairman of the local city council, he not only cursed the Soviet leadership but also Jews, Ukrainians, and Georgians. Yet, at the same time he "exalted the enemy of the people Beria" (obviously

---

*The prisoner was referring to the Internal Troops of the MVD who wore red shoulder straps or epaulets on their uniforms. They joined with the police to control crowds in large cities and guard large-scale industrial enterprises, railroad stations, and communication centers.—V.K.

for the famous amnesty), who, in keeping with the laws of mythology, was seemingly no longer Georgian.[70]

In the drunken cries of "forced criminals," though, such as the man P., who was turned into a criminal by his six convictions for truancy and for leaving work without permission under Stalin, there was nonetheless an attempt to establish a connection between the leaders and their nationality. P., insulted by the refusal of a Georgian soldier to drink with him in a railroad snack bar in Krasnoiarsk, sought to amplify the offensive sound of his words by not only cursing the soldier but Stalin as well. Indeed, Stalin, also a Georgian, was his main opponent, and now P. seemed to ascribe his bad qualities to the soldier, his current nemesis. At the same time, P. was essentially attaching all of his past troubles to the present insult.[71]

The theme of the hostile "Others"—the Communists, the bosses, representatives of other nationalities, and so on—who do not let "Us" live well and who are responsible for all of the evil in this world, sometimes sounded antiquated and emitted a poisonous odor of anti-Semitism. Completely pathological anti-Semites were found among criminals and urban riffraff (though not only among them). They built their own picture of the world in opposition to "pernicious Jews," and offered a program for salvation that was a sadly well-known cliche of prerevolutionary participants in pogroms: "Kill the Jews! Save Russia!" It was precisely this phrase that the filing clerk Z. repeatedly cried out while in a drunken state. Z. was a war veteran decorated with medals who had been expelled from the Communist Party and convicted in 1945.[72] He had found his own explanation for his personal troubles.

"Hooligan anti-Sovietism" was highly emotional and spontaneously aggressive. It was closest to the anti-Soviet outcries heard during mass disorders. People who were capable of more complex and civilized forms of protest—from writing anonymous essays and letters to creating underground circles, groups, and organizations—had more rational motives, a different logic of argumentation, were more articulate, and did not usually participate in urban riots. Yet in the 1950s, typical urban bystanders, those who were normal and more or less satisfied with their lives, could nonetheless be drawn into such disorders. They still believed, though, in communist myths, the action of which was strengthened by extensive exposure to propaganda. Therefore, it took either a blatant political mistake or an obvious abuse of power to pull such people in to mass urban riots and even support hooligans against the police. The romantic dreams preserved among the peoples of the USSR about the bright communist future and present had once created the psychological basis for regime stability, but now they had become a motive for aggression. Moreover, the sense of violated justice (whether real or imaginary has no meaning in the given case) turned urban bystanders into either a passively empathetic crowd of onlookers or an aroused mob following the lead of hooligans and thieves. In this sense, no matter how paradoxical, the pragmatic cynicism and degradation of the communist dream in the 1970s and 1980s actually created far fewer possibilities for drawing urban bystanders into disorders. By then people had accommodated themselves to the state and its injustices, for they knew the real price of its myths and were not at all ready to risk their lives for legends about "real communism."

Chapter 7

Orthodoxy in Revolt: Uprisings Among Religious Believers

Religious Holidays as Potential Catalysts for Conflict

Religious holidays in the Soviet Union always contained the potential for mass disturbances, since in addition to devout believers, the crowds that gathered around churches always included, criminals, drifters, drunks, and hooligans. Fights that broke out during religious holidays due to excessive drinking often led to serious consequences. Sometimes even party and Komsomol activists, as well as collective farm chairmen, took part in these drinking bouts and brawls.[1]

Conflicts occurring during religious holidays had political significance only in the outlying regions of the USSR. Taking the form of "confessional hooliganism," or the defacement of churches, aggression in these areas reflected a negative attitude toward Russians and their religious symbols, which were equated with concepts of empire, "invaders," "occupiers," and so on. This was particularly true in the Baltic republics, where there were documented cases of hooligan attacks on Orthodox cathedrals during religious holidays. For example, in Riga on the Orthodox Easter in 1960, a group of hooligans tried to break into a church, while in Tallin a similar incident occurred on the same day.[2]

It must be emphasized, however, that the actual celebration of religious holidays, despite all of their potential volatility, did not spawn any disorders that were rooted in religious concerns, or at least no such cases are documented. It is another matter that, in the "godless" Soviet state, mere participation in a religious holiday was, if not a form of political protest, then at minimum a demonstration of nonconformist attitudes. At least that is how

Soviet authorities regarded it, regardless of the reasons people participated in these events or whether or not they were even conscious of how nonconformist their actions were.

In certain situations, veiled protest of this nature (participation in a religious holiday) could develop into events very similar to political demonstrations. This was most clearly evident in Lithuania on All Souls' Day, when typically the Lithuanian KGB would send agents to the cemeteries, since it was alleged that "hostile elements take advantage of mass gatherings of believers for their own subversive work." In November 1956, the usual tension of All Souls' Day was heightened by the sympathy of many Lithuanians for the anticommunist uprising in Hungary. In Kaunas, people gathered and sang the hymn *Lithuania Our Homeland* and the song *Lithuania, You Are My Beautiful Motherland*. Cries rang out from the crowd: "Long Live Hungary," "Down with Moscow," "Hooray for the Independence of Lithuania," and "Freedom and Independence."[3]

In Russia, at least one incident is also known (though at a much later date, in 1970) of an underground group taking advantage of a religious gathering during the Easter holidays in Sverdlovsk to distribute leaflets.[4] But neither this nor similar episodes can be equated to or even linked with disorders arising from religious concerns. Believers tried to coexist peacefully with the state. Even in potentially volatile situations they themselves controlled crowd behavior, unless authorities blundered in their handling of the unrest. There are only a few known cases in which Moscow's religious policy, with its typical "tightening of the screws," combined with the bureaucratic feeble-mindedness of local officials to provoke spontaneous riots involving religious believers.

State Restrictions on the Orthodox Church as a Factor in Mass Uprisings of Religious Believers

In the second half of the 1950s, the period of the "new religious policy" ended. According to the church historian, Vadislav Tsybin, this period had lasted about fifteen years, dating from the end of World War II.[5] In January 1960, G.G. Karpov, the chairman of the Council on Matters of the Russian Orthodox Church under the USSR Council of Ministers, reported to Khrushchev that a "basic increase in the number of churches took place during the war due to the mass, unrestricted opening of churches on occupied territory." After the end of the war, the growth in the number of Orthodox churches had continued. From 1944 to 1947 in the Russian Republic, 1,270 new churches opened. Three thousand new Orthodox churches were established as a result of the unification of Greek-Catholic (Uniate) churches with

Orthodox churches in the five western regions of Ukraine, though with a simultaneous reduction in Uniate churches. In total, by January 1, 1948, there were 14,320 churches in the USSR. But from this time on, the number of Orthodox churches began to decline due to the conscious policy of Soviet authorities.

For the last twelve years, Karpov claimed, "we have refrained from attacking [the Orthodox Church], and ignored all of the announcements about the opening of churches and prayer houses." Yet, at the same time, churches had been closed, especially in the Ukraine.[6] In truth, an attack on the Orthodox Church began in 1948 involving a series of substantial limitations on the activity of the clergy. From 1948 on, there was in operation "an order of the patriarch forbidding any kind of social prayer service to be conducted in fields or generally anywhere outside the church, including services in the case of drought. The bishops and clergy could not make trips through districts and villages during working hours, and in general could not travel with a large retinue." Organizing religious concerts in churches outside of the public worship service was forbidden. The explanation given for these restrictions was that the sermon explains only the gospel and must not interfere in politics or social life. From 1949 on, the blessing of water in rivers and other reservoirs was forbidden, and additionally, religious rites could not be conducted outside the church without invitations or requests from individual believers. From 1950 on, the taking of monastic vows was possible only with permission of the patriarch.[7]

Yet, in spite of all the efforts of Soviet authorities, Orthodoxy had absolutely no intentions of disappearing. For example, according to church records, in Kirov Oblast 56 percent of the infants born in 1959 were baptized and 75 percent of the people who died had a religious funeral service. In Vladimir Oblast, these numbers were 39 percent and 46 percent respectively, and in Kursk Oblast, 48 percent and 35 percent.[8]

Khrushchev, seeking to reanimate the faded enthusiasm of the first postrevolutionary decades, encouraged intensification of the struggle with "religious remnants." The residual religiosity of a significant portion of the country's population seemed to contradict the propagandistic thesis about the "complete and final victory of socialism in the USSR." According to the testimony of G. Karpov, in 1959 "the greatest number of restrictive measures were enacted," provoking a sharp reaction from the church and the clergy.[9] Even the aged and complaisant Patriarch Aleksii was outraged.[10] Nevertheless, pressured by the Council on Matters of the Russian Orthodox Church, Aleksii had to agree to new restrictions on the activity of the church. Russian Orthodoxy also experienced a serious financial blow—an increase in the tax from 1.5 to 70 million rubles a year for candle production. Candle-making had previously provided a large portion, up to 70 percent,[11] of all profits to the church.[12]

The antireligious wave of 1958 to 1959 was fully in the spirit of the notorious Khrushchevian "voluntarism"*—the attack on the rights of the church and of believers could not be stopped, delayed, or even slowed. The Communist bosses were ready to believe that reality was completely pliable to their orders and resolutions, and that they had jurisdiction over the everyday life of the people. The Christian submissiveness of the Orthodox hierarchy, which demonstrated a readiness to sacrifice much for the sake of compromise with the state, backfired, for it only inspired Communist leaders in the central cities and in the provinces to take new steps against religion. In the final account, it was more the spontaneous protests of believers themselves than the organized opposition of Orthodox leaders that brought an end to the official attack on the rights of the church. The last straws were the decision to reduce sharply the number of monasteries and the zealous efforts of Moldavian and Ukrainian authorities to carry out these policies.

Spontaneous Protests of Religious Believers Against the Closing of Monasteries and Churches During 1959 and 1960

On October 16, 1958, the Council of Ministers adopted the resolution "On Monasteries in the USSR." To fulfill this decree, the Council on Matters of the Russian Orthodox Church proposed in 1959 to 1960 to reduce by consolidation the number of monasteries and *skity*** located within the USSR from sixty-three to twenty-nine. The authorities did not foresee any special difficulties, since in 1946, the "reduction through mergers" of monasteries had occurred without any problems.[13] From 1947 to 1957, thirty-eight more monasteries had been closed. The meekness of the church had only inspired bureaucrats to be even more ruthless in their "reduction." This time, however, believers demonstrated to authorities a growing readiness to defend their rights and put limits on "administrative enthusiasm" and bureaucratic high-handedness.

On June 5, 1959, the Council of Ministers of the Moldavian SSR resolved to reduce the number of Orthodox monasteries in the republic from fourteen

---

*Meaning to act in an impulsive, unrealistic fashion, ignoring reason and existing circumstances, this was the critical label officially applied from 1964 on to describe Khrushchev's approach to policy-making, thereby justifying his ouster and the subsequent dismantling of his reforms.—E.M.

**Skity* were a type of small monastery, often located in a secluded place. Usually a *skit* was attached to a larger monastery, and it provided a place for quiet meditation and contemplation for small numbers of monks.—E.M.

to eight. Within a month, four monasteries had been immediately closed, according to telephone reports to Moscow from Moldavia.[14] During the liquidation of the fifth, the Rechulsk Convent (with 225 nuns), "a serious incident occurred." According to the careful words of G. Karpov, local authorities acted in haste and "began to close the church without considering the special nature of this monastery." Believers were prohibited from preserving the monastery chapel as a parish church, although such a possibility had indeed been stipulated in the recommendations of the Council on Matters of the Russian Orthodox Church.

On June 23, 1959, the nuns of the Rechulsk Convent appealed to their relatives and friends in the surrounding villages: "We are being pushed out of the convent and there is a rumor spreading that all nuns are to be deported to the north." Subsequently, 150 to 200 residents from the surrounding villages rushed to the convent, where they organized a twenty-four-hour guard, armed with sticks, stones, and pitchforks. Every time local authorities tried to close the church, the voluntary guard rang the bell, gathered people from the fields, and did not allow anyone near the chapel. The nuns gave shelter for the night to those who had gathered to defend them, and provided food and wine.

On July 1 a group of Soviet and party activists tried to "establish contact with the people who were in the convent," but were beaten back with sticks and stones. The police lieutenant, who had also became a victim of the crowd's aggression, shot his pistol twice and wounded two of the attackers, one of whom died from his injuries.[15] The incident ended with the arrest of eleven people.

Local authorities in Ukraine also tried to liquidate the monasteries hurriedly, in one fell swoop, and similarly, their actions spurred mass protests among believers. On June 18 and 19, 1959, the Ternopol Oblast Council, along with local authorities from the town of Krements, announced to the nuns of the Krements Convent that their cloister was to be closed. The nuns did not obey the order, and, according to some reports, believers established a guard in order to prevent the monastery's liquidation. The lady superior sent a telegram to Khrushchev with a request that the cloister be preserved. In addition, the archbishop for Lvov and Ternopol asked the patriarch to seek an immediate compromise with authorities and postpone the closing of the monastery for at least one year, when "everything will have calmed down." Aleksii sent the archbishop's report to G. Karpov, having added to it his own commentary: "What can be done about this report? In any case we, that is the church authority, are powerless to assist if civil authorities refuse to help resolve this issue, which has led to such incidents."[16] The authorities temporarily relented.[17]

In Zakarpatsk Oblast of the Ukrainian SSR, the republic-level Council of Ministers proposed to close one large convent and two smaller skity. The bishop of Mukachev, along with the official regional council, negotiated with the nuns of the Uspenskii Convent in the village of Chervenevo, Mukachev district. But the nuns remained firm: "We will die rather than leave the convent. The Catholics in Hungary squeezed us, then the Uniates, and now you are chasing us out, and we do not understand why this is happening."[18] In the city of Lokhvitsa, Poltava Oblast, "during the closing of churches authorities were coarse in their methods, they rudely opened doors and removed crosses, threw out implements and consequently ignited a mass protest."[19]

The excesses continued in 1960 and took place in the Russian Republic as well. In March in the town of Zlatoust, Cheliabinsk Oblast, the representative for the Council on Matters of the Russian Orthodox Church took part in the demolition of a church building, which was to be replaced by a movie theater. In the subsequent chaos, religious objects were confiscated, which angered believers and caused panic to spread. The liquidation had been done in military style, completed in the course of an hour, yet believers had not received any warning. Rumors about these events in Zlatoust reached Cheliabinsk, where practically at the same time clergy were being stripped of their registration documents and services in the local church terminated. As a result, over the course of ten days, three delegations of believers traveled from Cheliabinsk to Moscow to petition the Council on Matters of the Russian Orthodox Church. At this point, the authorities made partial concessions and restored services in the cathedral.

In June 1960, a group of volunteer civilian police, regular police officers, the head of the local district party committee, and the deputy chairman of the district executive committee arrived at the Ukrainian village of Paskovshchin, Zgurov district, Kiev Oblast, where they removed the lock from the door of the church and began to pack up religious objects. Although it was early in the morning, about two hundred believers gathered. Angered by this cavalier intrusion into the church, they drove the local authorities from the village and damaged the bosses' automobile. Tensions grew when seven policemen were dispatched to "restore order." A fight broke out between the policemen and the local residents, who had camped around the church. These events were the subject of discussion for the top leaders of the Kiev regional party committee of the Ukrainian Communist Party.[20]

One of the last known incidents erupted in July of 1962 in the Ukrainian village of Dupliska, Ternopol Oblast. On July 5, "local organs of authority had organized the removal of crosses and cupolas from a closed church." A group of residents began ringing the bell to summon their fellow villagers. When three activists—the chairman of the village soviet, the instructor for the district Komsomol committee, and a local worker—tried to arbitrate the conflict, the villagers assaulted them. Four of the most active participants in the events were arrested under Article 71 of the Ukrainian SSR Criminal Code (the provision on mass disorders) and in October 1962 were sentenced to prison terms of four to six years.[21]

These disturbances involving religious believers, although they did not discourage Khrushchev and his bureaucrats from wanting to abolish "religious intoxication" in record time, did exercise a certain disciplinary influence over the state. In a number of cases, they succeeded not only in stopping the execution of a policy, but achieved its revocation. Even the typically complaisant church hierarchy tried to use the spontaneous uprisings of believers to put pressure on Khrushchev and his officials. In 1958, Patriarch Aleksii had agreed to the reduction of monasteries, but requested that this be done over a period of two to three years.[22] Subsequently, when he saw the government's haste and the popular reaction, he repudiated his earlier agreement.[23] Aleksii did not have any other choice, however, for to be identified with the stupidity of the anti-Church persecutions of 1959 would have lowered the prestige of the patriarchy to an unacceptably low level.

Furthermore, after each incident, local bosses had to report personally to the higher levels. Standing in the offices of their superiors, they faced reprimands and charges of "excessive administrativeness." Although it was difficult for believers to defend their rights, they at least won greater administrative restraint from the political leadership. Such conflicts facilitated the unity of religious believers and gave the church hierarchy additional leverage in its interactions with state authorities.

PART II

THE CRISIS OF "LIBERAL COMMUNISM" "ANTI-KHRUSHCHEV" URBAN UPRISINGS AND DISORDERS, 1961–1964

Chapter 8

The Early 1960s: Symptoms of a Social-Political Crisis

On July 19, 1962, the Central Committee Presidium discussed a draft resolution of the Council of Ministers concerning a proposed statute on passports. A number of cities in southern Russia were added to the list of localities that were off-limits to persons who had been in prison or exile for committing particularly dangerous crimes. Some of the cities on the prohibited list were health resorts in the Northern Caucasus, where the party-state elite loved to vacation, while the rest represented a zone of heightened social conflict. In particular, Krasnodar, Grozny, Novocherkassk, and Shakhty had already experienced mass disturbances or could potentially experience them in the future.[1]

Among the documents gathered by the Central Committee apparatus for the Presidium session was a KGB report that directly discussed symptoms of a social-political crisis in the USSR. The 1962 order of the KGB chairman "On Strengthening the Struggle of the Organs of State Security Against Hostile Actions of Anti-Soviet Elements" stated:

> During recent years in several cities of the country, mass disorders have occurred, accompanied by the looting of administrative buildings, the destruction of public property, attacks on representatives of the state, and other such outrages. The instigators of these disorders as a rule have been criminal-hooligan elements; however, in the course of the disorders, hostile-minded people have surfaced and shown heightened activity, including former members of German punitive squads and their accomplices, and clergymen and religious sectarians, who in a number of cases have by their own actions sought to push spontaneously arising events in a counter-revolutionary direction.[2]

Authorities clearly feared that anti-Soviet groups and organizations might link up with spontaneous mass disorders, and thereby turn asocial urban riots into anti-Soviet uprisings. Earlier, the "Hungarian syndrome"* and the development of increasingly autonomous, that is, not organized and controlled by the CPSU, political activism among various groups after the revelations of the Twentieth Party Congress had spurred a crackdown on dissidents. But this had been accompanied by substantial concessions to workers aimed at lowering their potential volatility. It was not without reason that at the end of 1956, a Central Committee plenum adopted a decision to lower work norms, which in reality meant an increase in wages.**[3]

Eliminating to a significant degree the potentially dangerous union between worker dissatisfaction and intellectual dissidence, this heavy blow against "everyday anti-Sovietism" allowed authorities to overcome the first crisis in state-society relations after the death of Stalin.

At the beginning of the 1960s, however, what had earlier been merely an implied, phantom threat now began to acquire a more distinct outline. The Soviet leadership by its own sweeping actions provoked conflict and opened the door to this union of popular dissatisfaction with the ideology of political protest. In a short time, practically simultaneously, the regime carried out the currency reform of 1961 to 1962, raising prices for basic food products, and it increased work norms, thereby lowering earnings. These developments, combined with growing problems of social justice and mass egalitarian criticism of new "Soviet barons" and "dacha capitalism," raised popular unrest. As a KGB report to the CPSU Central Committee on July 25, 1962, noted, "After a long break, anonymous documents praising participants in the Antiparty Group have again begun to be distributed. There are significantly more letters containing terrorist intentions toward leaders of the Communist Party and the state."[4]

The number of so-called "hostile phenomena" during the first half of 1962 exceeded the level of 1961 by two to three times.[5] Among the authors of anti-Soviet letters and leaflets, about one-third were workers, almost half were younger than thirty years old, and 40 percent had secondary or higher education. During the period 1960 to 1962, more than 34,600 anonymous anti-Soviet writings were distributed in the territories of the Soviet Union, including 23,213 leaflets.[6] At the beginning of the 1960s, underground anti-

---

*The author is referring to protests against the Soviet invasion of Hungary in 1956 that crushed the uprising that had begun there in October.—E.M.

**Work norms were the target output quotas Soviet workers were expected to fulfill. Traditionally work norms were kept low so that workers could easily overfulfill plan targets and gain bonuses, a tactic designed to protect overall earnings and stem discontent.—E.M.

Soviet groups grew in number. In just the first six months of 1962, the organs of state security uncovered sixty such groups, while for the whole of 1961 there had been only forty-seven such cases.[7]

In a certain sense, the Soviet state at the end of the 1950s and the beginning of the 1960s fell into a vicious cycle. The imbalance between wages and prices for consumer goods, especially food products, which was partly caused by concessions to workers in the second half of the 1950s, exacerbated the traditional (Soviet) problem of shortages. With low prices for agricultural products and the relative growth of wages, the deficit became catastrophic and caused outbursts of dissatisfaction. Yet the solution to these economic problems would inevitably make people indignant, create the preconditions for the growth of oppositionist attitudes, and provoke unfavorable comparisons between declared communist goals and dismal reality.

Six months prior to the 1962 price increases, during the early hours of December 31, 1961, leaflets were uncovered in the city of Chita that reflected the growing indignation: "The domestic policy of Khrushchev is rotten!" "Down with the dictator Khrushchev!" "Khrushchev you windbag, where is the abundance you promise?"[8] Popular expectations clearly conflicted with economic demands. The writing on ballots dropped into urns on March 10, 1962, for the USSR Supreme Soviet elections called for equalizing or raising wages and lowering prices for food, shoes, and clothing: "Why are many products, chiefly sugar, candy, and consumer goods, not being sold at the prewar prices?" "You are a good guy. And it would be good if you would give us a little more money." Popular consciousness recalled nostalgically the "positive experience" of Khrushchev's predecessor, that is, Stalin's habitual lowering of prices: "Comrade Khrushchev! Since the time you entered into your post you have not lowered prices even once. It is time to lower prices and improve the material situation of the laborers." "As we eliminate the cult of personality of Stalin, we must move jointly toward a new decrease in prices."[9]

Soon after these elections, in the summer of 1962, the popular reputation of the "good guy" was threatened as Khrushchev fell into a unique political conundrum: The preservation of the status quo in price policy would cause increased dissatisfaction from the shortage of goods. But the economically correct measure—raising purchase and retail prices—signified a break with the populist policy of systematically lowering prices, which had brought Stalin no small political dividends in large cities. Few grasped the artificial, countereconomic character of this Stalinist policy; meanwhile Soviet citizens expected "new manifestations of the concern of the party and state" for the people. When the "concern" turned into dashed hopes, then a natural outburst of indignation followed.

Key symptoms of the crisis in Khrushchev's personal reputation at the beginning of the 1960s were the plots against his life unearthed from time to time by the organs of state security. The potential assassins did not do anything serious to carry out their goals, but the very appearance of terrorist themes among the standard collection of "anti-Soviet phenomena" was significant in and of itself. Among those arrested by the KGB for terrorism were two young men from Tbilisi—Shota Mekvabishvili and Albert Meladze. According to KGB information, they had prepared at the end of 1960 to assassinate Khrushchev during his scheduled visit to Georgia. The young men apparently hoped that a terrorist act would bring in its wake a "change in the external and internal policy of the Soviet state." The conspirators discussed at length the possible scenario for the assassination: where to store the weapons, how to prepare the bomb, and so on. But fortunately for them and for Khrushchev, nothing practical ever came of these plans.[10]

Still another terrorist was arrested by the KGB in Dushanbe, Tadzhik SSR. On October 1, 1962, during Khrushchev's visit to the republic, Stanislav Vorobev took an enormous cobblestone weighing over a kilogram, covered it with flowers, and prepared to hurl it at the official procession as it passed down the street. Thirty minutes before the festive event, police detained Vorobev, who had impulsively resolved to carry out the attempt on Khrushchev's life in a moment of emotional crisis. During the trial he said that "he did not read newspapers, he did not attend political education classes, his personal life had turned out to be a failure, and consequently he drank a lot, the collective did not interest him, and all of this had led to the actions for which he had been arrested."[11]

In a certain sense, Vorobev, who was sentenced to twelve years in prison, was a typical participant in the mass disorders and uprisings at the beginning of the 1960s. He may not have taken part in a riot in a market or on a city square, and only lost his inhibitions at the moment of Khrushchev's visit, but what he said in court was a commonplace theme in many anti-Soviet documents, statements, and everyday conversations, and was directly or indirectly present in the attitudes of many Soviet instigators of mass disorders:

> I wanted to kill Khrushchev for his incorrect policy. After conquering Germany, is it really possible to be on friendly terms with it[?]. Germany killed my father, and now, how can it be my friend? I do not agree that we should be friendly with Poland and Czechoslovakia. We have sent equipment and bread there, but who sends us anything? From China come goods at one price, but then we buy them at a price two times higher. In order to buy a suit, it is necessary to work for an entire month.[12]

Nonetheless, the price increase planned by Khrushchev, no matter how painful, did not generate extensive social protest, for the Soviet system at this time still had a sufficiently large reserve of ideological and political strength. But the country's leaders had permitted a flagrant political miscalculation: Along with the price increase, in a whole series of enterprises there was a reexamination of work norms and piece rates that made them stricter and thereby harder to overfulfill. The Novocherkassk tragedy was only the visible tip of the iceberg—the unseen part was the pent-up grumbling and various "anti-Soviet phenomena" that were occurring all over the country.

After the official announcement on June 1, 1962, about the price increases for meat, and butter, the KGB daily informed the Central Committee about popular attitudes. Reports for June 1 to 4, 1962, which are stored in the Russian Presidential Archive, reveal that protest leaflets appeared even in Moscow: From Gorky Street, "Today there is a price increase, but what awaits us tomorrow?" On Sirenevyi Boulevard, a leaflet called for workers to "struggle for their own rights and for the lowering of prices." In the train station *Pobeda* ("Victory," Kiev railway line), located on the outskirts of Moscow, "an inscription was made with slanderous fabrications about the Soviet state and demands to lower prices for food." On the first day of the price increase there already were reports of various demonstrations of dissatisfaction in Donetsk, Dnepropetrovsk, Pavlov Posad, Zagorsk, Leningrad, Vyborg, Tbilisi, Novosibirsk, and Grozny. Attempts at open protests took place: The worker Karpov from Vyborg pinned to his chest the saying "Down with the new prices" and tried to walk around the city like this.

On June 2, the day after the announced price increases, criticism grew in scope. The meat shortage in the country was declared to be the result of limits put on the supplemental livestock kept by collective farmers: "The number of individual cows has been cut, calves are not being raised. Where are we going to get meat from? A mistake is being made here."[13] Doubts about the effectiveness of the system itself appeared: "Everything bad is blamed on Stalin, they say that his policy destroyed agriculture. But why has it been impossible to revitalize agriculture during the period since his death? No, there are deeper roots for its decay, about which, obviously, nothing can be said."[14] Numerous calls for strikes resounded. Some people referred to the experience of struggle among Western workers: "If workers were to follow the example of the West and strike, then they would immediately revoke the price increase."[15]

According to the fragmentary data available, already in 1961 the first signs of a spontaneous strike movement had appeared. Its beginning was not connected with the growth of prices, but with labor and wage policies. For example, each of the three documented cases of collective walkouts by workers in the enterprises of Primorskii Krai in 1961 was connected either with increased work norms or with delays in the payment of wages.[16] On December 7, 1961, workers at a textile mill in Gori (Georgian SSR) stopped the machines after the introduction of new work norms. Work resumed only on the following day.[17]

Growing social tension in 1961 and during the first half of 1962 culminated in an explosion of oppositionist attitudes and actions that reached its height in the June 1962 riots in Novocherkassk. The circumstances seem to suggest a logical chain of cause and effect connections. The economic troubles of the regime, particularly the worsening of shortages, attempts to overcome them through stricter labor and wage policies, and finally the uneven increase in purchase and retail prices for agricultural goods spurred a growth in autonomous political activism among the population. This movement resulted in the strikes and uprisings in Novocherkassk. But there were other disorders extending over many days and involving thousands of people that do not fully fit into this temptingly logical framework, particularly since they occurred even before the price increases. In this sense, 1961 was even more disruptive than 1962. Spontaneous uprisings in Krasnodar, Murom, Aleksandrov, and Biisk (see chapters 9, 10, and 11) had no connection with the price increases.

The social-political crisis of the early 1960s manifested itself in the visible growth of "anti-Soviet phenomena," in nationwide grumbling, and in spontaneous strikes, as well as in less obvious forms—a wave of criminality, the hooliganization of the country, the spread of social pathologies such as parasitism, petty theft, prostitution, alcoholism, and drug abuse. In 1961, there was a noted growth both in certain especially dangerous crimes and in the number of convictions for crimes committed. The number of those tried for crimes rose by more than 50 percent in comparison with 1960, totaling 771,238 people. Convictions for particularly malicious cases of hooliganism[18] almost doubled in comparison with 1960, bringing the number close to the critically high level of the mid-1950s.

The state's campaign against mass forms of criminality at the end of the 1950s and the beginning of the 1960s was perceived by many as a blow against the daily life of the people, for whom, since the time of Stalin, despite the harsh repressions, half-criminal behavior had either been a specific condition for survival or a distorted outlet for relieving social stress. In response to the new social pressures provoked by the regime's sweeping struggle to restore order, a significant layer of marginalized persons carried out a new wave of "hooligan resistance," producing the unprecedented outbreak of uprisings and mass disturbances in 1961 and 1962.

From the second half of the 1950s to the beginning of the 1960s, there were also clear signs of an ideological-psychological crisis, generated by de-

Stalinization and the "assessment of the results of socialist construction." At the end of the 1950s the CPSU announced that socialism had been built "completely and decisively," but this "completely and decisively" constructed socialism was very far from the ideal of the bright future. The regime also engendered this crisis with its inept socioeconomic policy. Against a background of shortages, lower earnings, and increased prices for food, the mind of the "little man," the "man in the crowd," experienced chaos and confusion, forcing him to look everywhere for a way to express his dissatisfaction with reality: in communist fundamentalism, in nationalism, in anarchism, and in anticommunism. Although the crystallization of spontaneous protest as such did not occur at this time, a large number of "little people" were distinguished by a very unstable mindset and acute ideological turmoil due to the sudden bankruptcy of the state's habitual dogmas and fundamental values.

Consequently, there was considerable vacillation and uncertainty. Some tried to find a way to express their dissatisfaction, although many were quick to repent and return to the bosom of communist orthodoxy. Yet, at the same time they could also become "warriors for the truth," who, despite being repudiated by all, unexpectedly found meaning for their existence in rejecting the regime. Selective and impulsive in their expressions of dissatisfaction, such people were likely one day to curse the Jews as the reason for their and the nation's ills, then the next day blame the bosses, and two days later, Khrushchev personally. One day they sought salutary explanations in official ideology and ascribed all sins of the system to remnants of Stalinism, then the next day they saw a panacea in a return to the Stalinist regime with its annual lowering of prices and its fabled "order."

This internal fermentation of critical attitudes and that which is termed "dissatisfaction of the people" became a political factor as a result of the country's worsening socioeconomic situation at the end of the 1950s and the beginning of the 1960s. Although most people tend to remain silent, at such moments the crowd somehow seems able to produce spontaneously its own charismatic leaders who guide it along the road of uprising and protest. With proper direction, it is an exceptionally simple matter to provoke public disorders under such circumstances. All that is needed for people in a crowd to blame the existing political situation for their own personal problems is one or two individuals who are ready to suffer for the people or who possess a weakened instinct of self-preservation, sometimes as the result of drunkenness, or who have a personal interest in disorders, such as liberating a comrade from the police. As a result, from behind the anonymity of the crowd there emerges a readiness to act.

In such situations, the state found that the gullibility of the Soviet populace, its openness to psychological manipulation (the search for enemies, for example), which it had nurtured through systematic ideological processing, could also be turned against it. The state did not have a monopoly on such manipulation, and any demagogue could use these tactics for completely opposite goals. The state was continually surprised by the fact that it was not the only force capable of instigating and organizing mass actions. In extreme circumstances, there were always people of a certain psychological type who could lead a crowd and take advantage of the individual's ability to comprehend reality independently, despite suppression of this capacity by propaganda and by the peculiarities of socialization under a communist regime.

Thus, in the search for ringleaders of antigovernment disorders, the authorities were never able to discover their true ideological opponents. The majority of those convicted in such cases as a rule had ended up accidentally in the whirlpool of unfolding events, and were not guilty in any way of anti-Soviet sins, such as engaging in organized anti-Soviet agitation and propaganda. Everyday problems and situations more often pushed people into protest than a specific ideology or creed, a maxim repeatedly demonstrated in the urban uprisings from 1961 to 1964.

Chapter 9

Krasnodar, RSFSR, January 15–16, 1961

January 15: The Sennoi Market at Noon

The two-day riots in Krasnodar began with an insignificant episode in the Sennoi Market. The main participant in the incident, a soldier by the name of Vasilii Gren, took an unofficial leave of absence in order to sell some military underclothes. At the market, he caught the eye of a military patrol unfortunately at the very moment when the underwear, which he had hidden in his overcoat, fell to the ground. The patrol ordered Gren to go to the military commander's office, but he refused and began to resist. He attracted the attention of people in the market, who were immediately filled with sympathy for the "poor soldier." Gren himself asserted in court that he did not ask for help from the crowd.[1] But when onlookers seized the members of the patrol by the arm, the reckless soldier ran and hid.

A People's Squad of local volunteer police, who knew the market well, quickly found the soldier and helped the military patrol convey the prisoner to the military commander's office. The squad leader was a worker and Komsomol member named Vasadze, who had repeatedly turned over marketplace drunks and hooligans to the police. Among those demanding liberation of the "poor soldier" was Iurii Buianin, the personal enemy and exact opposite of the volunteer Vasadze. A Krasnodar native, Buianin had been convicted in 1956 for robbery and sentenced to fifteen years imprisonment, though in 1959 he received an early parole.[2] Buianin was unemployed, passing his days in idleness and drinking. Vasadze had detained him several times for hooliganism. The opportunity now emerged to settle personal accounts with the People's Squad commander, and Buianin did not let it slip away, becoming for a short time the catalyst for the Krasnodar disturbances.

181

When the military patrol, backed up by reinforcements, tried to carry the detained Gren away from the market by car, the crowd, fired up by cries that the soldier's arms and legs had been broken and that Vasadze had hit a girl, attacked the volunteer commander. Buianin played first violin in this vicious brawl, which sent one of the wounded to the hospital in serious condition.[3] But after settling his personal grievance, Buianin obviously lost interest in what was going on and did not play a significant role in subsequent events.

The beating of Vasadze did not satisfy the mob that assembled at the police station, which was located near the military commander's office. People demanded that the soldier Gren be released and that the military patrol be handed over to them for reprisals.[4] In order to calm the agitated crowd, the head of the patrol released Gren and proposed that he report to the military commander, which he subsequently did.

At this point the role of ringleader passed to Nikolai Ostroukh, a native of the village of Elizavetinsk, located in the greater Krasnodar region.[5] This barely literate person was drunk on the day of these events and later claimed that he remembered nothing. Having fallen, however, into the middle of the unrest, he acted as if he were intuitively directing the actions of the crowd. Ostroukh was one of the first to attack a member of the military patrol, a man named Paishev who had helped to detain Gren. It was also Ostroukh who proposed to "stage a demonstration," and he led Paishev along the streets of the city, followed by an angry mob. They turned onto Red Street, where the headquarters of the army corps and the military commander's offices were located. Nikolai Ostroukh tried every means to attract the attention of residents as he called for hanging the patrol member Paishev from the nearest tree.[6] Ostroukh's actions laid the foundation for the spontaneous self-organization of the crowd, but after this, as the epicenter of events moved to Red Street, Ostroukh, like Buianin, seemed to lose energy and fell from the active nucleus of rebels.[7]

In the afternoon, between 120 and 150 people from the market went to the military commander's office, where they cried out that the soldier Gren had been maimed and that he should be set free. Gren came out repeatedly to assure the crowd that no one had beaten him, but the people refused to believe him and even accused him of being an imposter who could not be trusted. Within a short time, there were around 3,000 people jammed together on Red Street, including many young adults and juveniles. Having been sucked into the funnel of an emerging riot, the crowd now produced entirely new leaders who shaped the physiognomy of events, clamoring for a pogrom and for reprisals against the soldiers who were guarding the military headquarters, against the People's Squad, and against the police. Among these people were not only riffraff and confirmed hooligans, but also bystanders who appear to have been quite prosperous and established citizens.

One of these bystanders was Anatolii Liashenko, a new father who had no prior convictions.[8] He subsequently explained his actions by referring to some kind of "mysterious force" that had awakened inside of him after drinking with friends at the end of the workday.[9] Liashenko had grown up as an orphan and had been forced to begin working at an early age to help support a brother and a sister. During his army service, Anatolii fell ill and returned to civilian life as an invalid.[10] Although he ended up as a "drunken motor" propelling the disorders forward, it does not appear that Liashenko really thought about the meaning of his actions. The thrill of being active in and of itself drove him.

Another "prosperous" participant in the unrest, lathe operator Petr Simonenko, was a Komsomol member with a wife and daughter.[11] In his actions, one can see political consciousness and purpose. Upon turning up at the military commander's office, he called himself "the representative of the people," and according to the indictment, "organized other hooligans and firebrands, and with the intention of getting into the commander's offices, all the while making provocative demands about liberating the prisoners, he incited the crowd with cries: 'We demand to speak with the officers and generals!' "

Simonenko was one of the first to join in the attack on the military offices and also made an anti-Soviet statement, calling for "sweeping away Soviet power and constructing here a second Hungary." The same goals resounded from the mouth of Vladimir Nikulin, who was unemployed and homeless. In his youth, he had fallen into the flywheels of the heartless Stalinist machinery of repression and since that time had not been able to climb out of the abyss of prison and forced labor camps. In 1929, Nikulin had been sentenced to a one-year term for hooliganism, then in 1934 he received three years in exile as a "socially dangerous element." In 1935, he faced three more years in prison for escaping from exile; then, in 1938, he lost his passport and received a month of corrective labor. In 1939, there was a new sentence, this time for malicious hooliganism and anti-Soviet agitation (in 1965, this case was reexamined and closed). In 1946, he was again sentenced to five years' imprisonment for malicious hooliganism. From 1953 to 1960, Nikulin lived alone, without family and friends, in Krasnodar Krai, fully debased and continually drunk; for this he was often fired from jobs. Several times the police detained him for petty hooliganism.[12] This person, who had been broken by the regime, had every reason to hate the state and its representatives.

Nikulin had come to Krasnodar on the day of the events by freight train, arriving in the midafternoon. He drank heavily and later claimed that he did not remember his actions.[13] According to eyewitnesses, Nikulin echoed Simonenko, crying out in front of the military commander's office that "the people are seeking the truth" but receiving only mockery in return. He called for the "destruction of the leaders of the Communist Party and the Soviet state," and promised to "construct a revolt better than what they did in Hungary."[14]

These spontaneously emerging leaders not only inspired the exploits of the crowd, but also provided a personal example. When the attempt to get inside the military commander's offices did not succeed, Simonenko and Liashenko organized an assault on the building, and in the process their ecstatic activism inspired many onlookers to join the riot. In spite of warnings from soldiers, Simonenko and Liashenko smashed the first-floor windows, brandished an iron box (the luggage carrier from a motorcycle), and declared that this "bomb" would blow up the commander's offices. Simonenko and a young boy standing next to him took several metal pieces from the "bomb" and began to hurl them at the second-floor windows. Finally Simonenko broke down the doors to the commander's offices and demanded the liberation of the soldier Gren, but later was arrested by military personnel.

The crowd had lost its chief agitator, but it was still capable of generating a fresh cadre of leaders. When the riots entered into a new stage, a natural change in leadership occurred. For example, during the attack on the commander's office, the rioters had forced their way into the building. Rising to the occasion, the young Anna Polusmak wrote a note calling for the release of prisoners and threw it down to the crowd from the window. Amid the turmoil of the attack, the first warning shots, both blank and live cartridges, rang out. Then a new round of shots greeted the rioters when they tried to get into the room with secret documents, killing a seventeen-year-old student and wounding a fireman. The first blood had flowed, thereby giving the crowd a justification for continuing the riots—vengeance for the dead.

The body of the slain youth, whose name was Savalev, was taken to the hospital, where the doctors pronounced him dead on arrival. The crowd now produced new leaders, Iurii Pokrovskii and Aleksandr Kapasov, each of whom bore a grudge against the state. Pokrovskii was a Krasnodar native from a working-class background who in 1956 was accused of hooliganism in the city of Sovetskaia Gavan, Khabarovsk Krai. He hid and remained concealed until 1958, when he received an amnesty and the police stopped searching for him.[15] Kapasov was all of nineteen years old, but already he had some criminal experience with hooliganism and petty theft.[16]

The evening of January 15, 1961, became the finest hour in the lives of these people. For the first time, their anger at the state expressed itself in real social activism, and the senselessness of their personal existence for a short time acquired political significance. It was Iurii Pokrovskii who had the idea to continue the unrest. He called for carrying the body of the slain youth to the CPSU regional party committee, and screamed some kind of "slanderous comments addressed to Communists."[17]

Eight people carried Savalev's body to the regional party committee offices, accompanied by a large crowd. Pokrovskii and Kapasov headed the highly organized and solemn funeral procession. Kapasov sang the song *Vikhri vrazhdebnye* (Hostile Winds), which revolutionaries traditionally sang in Soviet films during the most difficult moments of their struggle. This widely recognized revolutionary hymn became the leitmotif of the funeral procession, transforming a mundane popular disturbance into a struggle for truth and justice. The revolutionary pathos of restoring justice transformed the asocial model of behavior typical for such disturbances into something much more conscious. It was not accidental that Kapasov, who in classical hooligan tradition had just threatened to assault the doctors,[18] suddenly took it upon himself to lead the "movement of the crowd and called people to march in orderly ranks. . . . He ordered those citizens who were standing on the sidewalks to take off their hats." Nonetheless, the most persuasive technique Kapasov had was to knock in the head those who did not react quickly enough to his demands.[19] As the mourners proceeded, Pokrovskii cried out various slogans and appeals, first from the roof of a car that had been confiscated and then from a nearby tree. From time to time, Kapasov fired up the crowd with accusations that the military commander had killed the youth Savalev.[20]

As the procession approached the building of the regional party headquarters, Kapasov continued to lead the crowd and pointed out the spot where the body should be placed so that more people could see it. Blood and death always impart to violence and looting an aura of holy retribution, thereby liberating all involved from any sense of guilt. In the presence of death, the feeling of security and impunity typical for a person who has dissolved anonymously into a crowd strengthens. The rioter's agitated conscience begins to believe that seeking vengeance for an innocent victim will bring no retribution, for the state would not dare to challenge popular justice. It is precisely these psychological mechanisms that energized Kapasov when, continuing to follow the revolutionary scenario, he raised the slain youth's bloody coat over his head and showed it to those who had gathered, saying: "Look here, these are the brains of a worker." He then encouraged people in the crowd to seek satisfaction of their own demands and announced his intention to telephone Moscow.[21]

By early evening, around 2,000 people had gathered at the party offices, where a spontaneous meeting began by the entrance and then moved to the vestibule of the building.[22] Both old and new leaders took part in the meeting, one of whom, Nikolai Malyshev, stood out for his heroic past, having been awarded various military awards. A major in the reserves and a party member, after his release from the army Malyshev had worked as an unskilled laborer in a cafeteria.

Malyshev's speech was not that of a hooligan, but was almost political in nature. The major called the arrest of the soldier in the market and the murder of the young student acts of violence and arbitrariness. Exclaiming to the crowd, "How long will we endure this tyranny?" Malyshev demanded a commission be appointed to investigate the murders and punish the guilty.[23] After this, as rioters stormed the building housing the regional party offices, Malyshev, who had stayed behind, spoke out even more verbosely: "The Soviet state has transferred the reins of power to police organs and civilian police volunteers. They say that we have freedom of speech, the press, and assembly. Where are all of these rights? We do not see them!" Then Malyshev further announced: "We are supposed to have a people's state, but it is the people whom they are shooting."[24]

In the speeches of the novice leaders, there were several other topical political themes. Viktor Bozhanov, a successful young man who had completed high school and was preparing to enter an institute for postsecondary studies, had ended up on Red Street accidentally—he had gone to the movies with a girlfriend.[25] He called for the crowd to seek an increase in wages and even "expressed doubt in the building of communism."[26] Another speaker was Ivan Belenkov, a poorly educated elderly man with no prior convictions who had been unemployed since 1953. He began his speech, which he delivered on the landing inside the building, by recalling personal grievances, such as when the police had twisted his arms back for selling three fish at the market, and finished with a call "for a change in the existing government."[27]

But typical calls for looting and inspirational speeches soon replaced political slogans.[28] Several eyewitnesses who called for the restoration of order were beaten. The leaders of the disturbances used threats and physical force to coerce the Communist Metelkin, who had inadvertently ended up in the wrong place at the wrong time, to voice public approval of their actions.[29] Attempts by party personnel to quiet the crowd were blocked by angry cries and curses.[30]

One of the most significant episodes for understanding the disturbances in Krasnodar was the attempt by a group of rebels to make contact with Moscow, which suggests that the protest of these spontaneous leaders was strongly localized. They still saw Moscow as the supreme arbiter capable of restoring order and justice. The traditional social-psychological dichotomy, "the unjust officials–the just supreme authority," worked effectively to localize the conflict, transforming the riots from a blow against the regime into a specific "warning from the provinces."

It was Aleksandr Kapasov, as mentioned above, who initiated the phone call to Moscow. He had gone up to the second floor of the regional party building at the head of a small group of rioters, broke into one of the offices, called the city's telephone station, and demanded that an operator connect him with Moscow. In doing this, Kapasov identified himself as a representative of the people and announced to the operator that he intended to inform Moscow that the workers had carried out an uprising in the city. Kapasov ordered the others to shout into the telephone receiver in order to portray the noise of the crowd, but he failed to get through to Moscow. After announcing this to the crowd from an open window, Kapasov left the building and shouted words reminiscent of a quote from a revolutionary film, "Everyone follow me to the telegraph office!"[31] But again Kapasov was not able to make any contact with Moscow.

The rebels were pushed out of the building, most probably after Kapasov's group had headed off for the telegraph office. Viktor Bozhanov, however, spoke again to the crowd, claiming that the police had detained several persons in the building. His plea for their liberation inspired the crowd to break into the party offices a second time. Meanwhile, outside the building there were outbreaks of hooliganism. That same Bozhanov who had tried to keep passions kindled high cried out, "They are detaining me," and thereby provoked an assault on a person who had called for ending the disorders.[32]

It took until 11:00 P.M. for the police, KGB officials, troops from the local garrison, and local party activists to finally disperse the crowd. Participants in the unrest parted until morning.

The Morning of January 16: Leaflets at the Machine Repair Factory

In the morning a crowd began to gather anew at the military commander's building, but people remained calm.[33] At noon, however, during an ordinary lunch break, several leaflets were found at the Machine Repair Factory. The workers there tore down one of them while two others were immediately taken to the factory's party committee. Attempts at agitation had flopped, and, frightened by their own activism, members of the underground group responsible for the leaflets actually halted their activities after the Krasnodar disturbances.

The author of the leaflets and the leader of this underground group was Vladimir Gorlopanov. Life for this father of two had not worked out very well. He had served fourteen years in the army from 1943 to 1957. In 1957, however, he was inexplicably court-martialed and dismissed from the army "for moral and social degradation." Gorlopanov considered this decision to be unjust and had barely survived his personal ordeal. After demobilization he suffered a series of failures in finding employment and an apartment. He fell ill and became an invalid.[34] An aggrieved and unsettled former officer, as he himself put it, "he could not find the necessary paths of readjustment and assimilation into civilian life."[35]

Gorlopanov's group emerged shortly before the mass disorders in Krasnodar. At the end of December 1960, several weeks before the unrest, Gorlopanov was visiting a man by the name of Reshetov, who subsequently escaped punishment as a "passive participant in the crimes" chiefly on account of his peasant background and his irreproachable past record. During a drinking bout, an open conversation took place among Gorlopanov, Reshetov, and Lunev, who was a metalworker with two children. According to the investigation and the trial, all three were dissatisfied with the "material conditions of life in the USSR" and discussed among themselves the "joint distribution of anti-Soviet materials."[36] In general the conversation was casual and did not go beyond the habitual grumbling about the state: "They talked about the market, the distribution of apartments, the lowering of wages, and said that Khrushchev gave nice speeches but did not show any results." Gorlopanov talked about his meetings with the bosses and described their callous attitude toward his fate. Lunev, judging from testimony in the investigation and trial, had been influenced by numerous conversations among workers ("wages are not increasing but are going down, and conditions are worsening") and thought that "the workers of the factory should unite and seek an end to the lowering of [piece] rates."[37]

Gorlopanov composed the text of the leaflets, finishing in early January. He read the draft to Lunev, who advised adding criticism of Khrushchev to the text. Thus, the final variant emerged and was distributed on January 16, 1961, in one of the shops of Machine Repair Factory No. 4.

An Appeal
To all workers, peasants, soldiers, officers, and laboring intelligentsia.

Dear comrades! Remember that the situation of our Motherland is critical. Only you can save the situation; there is no one else who can do it. You must select honest, steadfast comrades, who can unite you into a firm shock force to struggle with Soviet capitalism. After the October Revolution and especially after the death of Stalin, a number of mistakes were committed. Sons and daughters of the old Russian bourgeoisie, who had wormed their way into the ranks of the party and into leadership posts, enjoyed full freedom of action. . . . These bribetakers among you serve as a breeding ground for trouble. You yourselves see all this clearly and talk much about the circumstances that have been forming, that is, the conditions under which you live at present. Many of you have already heard more than once about the struggle in the Soviet Union to improve living conditions and the subsistence wage. There are strikes in Moscow, Leningrad, Grozny, Gorky, Donbass, etc. You have heard about the uprising in Angarstroe at the Bratsk State Electric Power Station, where thousands of workers were shot, and about the strikes in our region: the Worsted-Cloth Plant, the sugar factor in Guiaguinskaia.

Dear Comrades! The fate of the revolution, the salvation of the revolution is in your hands. . . !
Onward to the Struggle, Comrades! We have no other path!
The organizational group.
Distribute this with caution to your comrades.[38]

Once again criticism of the regime was based upon its own ideological values, actively using ideas of "betrayal" and "bourgeois degeneration," themes popular since the early 1920s. In other words, for Gorlopanov, the system was bad not because it was communist, but because it lacked enough real communism and had degenerated into "Soviet capitalism." In light of this, he appealed to the myth of the correct Stalinist communism, while relating the mistakes to the time of Khrushchev, which is when the author of the appeal had begun to experience a string of failures. All around him there was a sense of declining living standards and heightened exploitation of workers due to the reexamination of work and pay norms. The document is based on themes that are typical of many anti-Soviet letters and leaflets of the later Khrushchev era—egalitarianism and revolutionary bluffing based on rumors and fictitious information about mass protests in different cities of the USSR. In the document there were also revolutionary allusions and appeals to the legacy of the October Revolution.

Thus, Gorlopanov represents a typical "underground Marxist," who was unable to break out of his ideological cage, and in his search for methods of struggle relied entirely on Bolshevik experience. "I have struggled for that very same truth," Gorlopanov himself said, "for which Lenin had struggled."[39] It is understandable that Gorlopanov viewed the mass riots in Krasnodar with caution and a certain squeamish contempt: "Riots do not lead to anything." He considered a strike to be the only effective method of struggle for the rights of workers.[40]

Gorlopanov, the chief ideologue, was not involved in distributing the leaflets at the factory on January 16. Lunev was the one who, acting on his own initiative and under the influence of the developing events, scattered them about at great personal risk, "after which he set himself up to observe the reaction of the workers." But no reaction of any kind ensued.

The second day of the disturbances also brought at least several attempts to renew the riots. Among the particularly active agitators was Gavriil Aleksandrov, a native of Ukraine who was relatively well educated but had been broken by fate and had a bad reputation. Aleksandrov had two convictions. In 1944 he had been sentenced to seven years in the camps, for complicity with the German occupiers and after that his life went downhill.[41]

On January 16, Aleksandrov moved from group to group, everywhere leading "unhealthy conversations." His statements set a new tone for the events and pushed the memory of the innocent victims into the background. Aleksandrov said that in the market there were no goods and that food had become more expensive, thereby raising more substantive but also more mundane themes. He also called for looting.[42]

During the afternoon and evening, when the crowd reached a total of 1,000 people, the situation froze in an uncertain equilibrium. Again cries and threats rang out, but remembering the bloodshed and the shooting, those who had gathered did not dare take further action. Party leaders tried to push the scale to the advantage of the authorities. The regional party first secretary, G.I. Vorobev, and Commander Pliev of the troops of the Northern Caucasus Military District spoke to the crowd and called for it to disperse. Some left, but the majority remained in place.[43] At this critical moment, Gavriil Aleksandrov again tried to intervene in the course of events. In the words of witnesses, "he was vicious and was foaming at the mouth,"[44] saying that "the authorities had taken for themselves the best apartments, while the simple people huddled together in hovels." He castigated "pot-bellied" leaders: "You rake in the money, and you oppress the people."[45] During the speeches of Vorobev and Pliev, Aleksandrov whistled, swore coarsely, made his own demands, and called upon the crowd not to trust the Communists, but "to struggle for the truth." Finally, he and others began stopping cars that were traveling along Red Street. When several workers tried to interfere, Aleksandrov pointed at one of them and cried out: "There is the secretary of the party organization; the Communists are surrounding us."

A man by the name of Aleksei Chernenko joined in as all of these events reached full swing. Chernenko had a higher technical education and had spent the last six to seven years systematically drinking, often missing work as a consequence. Sooner or later he was fired from every job he had, and in 1958 was twice accused of petty hooliganism. On January 16, Chernenko was drunk. In the late afternoon, he stopped a truck on Red Street, took the keys from the driver, climbed up onto the vehicle's footboard, and addressed the crowd with a call to turn Krasnodar into a "city holding a general strike."[46] He resisted arrest and kicked a policeman in the chest.

Despite the efforts of Aleksandrov and Chernenko, the disturbances had passed their peak. According to the Krasnodar regional procurator, I.A. Baranov, local officials invited and received help from "workers in area enterprises who dispersed the crowd,"[47] which suggests that authorities still had sufficient supporters and allies. There was no need to open fire one more time to frighten the people.

V. Nikulin made one last attempt to stir the crowd. First on the Street of Peace and then in the square by the railroad station, he continued to cry out: "We must crush Soviet power, it will not allow us to live peacefully."[48] Nikulin himself claimed in the investigation and trial that he was extremely drunk and could not remember anything. With this, the disturbances in Krasnodar came to an end, and the arrests of the instigators began.

The Investigation and Trial

Frightened by these events, the police and the KGB arrested active participants without separating the guilty from the innocent. Therefore, from the thirty-two people detained, thirteen were released almost immediately and the preliminary inquest concluded that they had not played an active role in the disorders.[49] The KGB conducted the investigation and already by February 14, the case of the mass disorders in Krasnodar for ten defendants was concluded with an inquest. The materials on one more person were put into a separate case.

The evidence shows clearly that the investigation was done in a hurry, and this affected its quality. Certain doubtful details in the definition of the crime attracted the attention of the USSR Procuracy. In a letter from A. Mishutin, the deputy procurator-general, to I.A. Baranov dated February 18, 1961, Mishutin proposed that "attention be paid to the issue of whether or not it was necessary or expedient to bring into this matter a broad circle of people and how correct it was to define their actions by Article 16 of the Law on Criminal Responsibility for State Crimes."[50]

Altogether fifteen people were held criminally responsible for participating in the mass disorders in Krasnodar. In addition, seven participants were arrested for hooliganism under Article 206, Part 2 of the Russian Federation Criminal Code.[51] Two cases were tried in regional courts and the rest in district courts.

From March 14 to March 20, 1961, the regional court tried the first case. Three workers were selected for the role of public prosecutors. Every day in the hall of the court, up to three hundred loyal spectators, all of whom had been selected in advance by authorities, attended. The trial was held in the heat of political passion, without any regard for the legal basis of the charges. An unidentified Procuracy employee immediately noted in a report about the trial: "The general sentence for all is fifteen years, although the guilt of each is variable."[52]

From March 22 to March 24, the regional court tried five people in the second case. This time the sentences were somewhat lighter and much more differentiated.[53] Within two months, the RSFSR Supreme Court had already reduced several sentences. One defendant even had his sentence commuted to probation.[54] Khrushchevian jurisprudence had finally demonstrated a capacity for at least minimal flexibility and a desire to keep within the framework of "socialist legality," even when the cases under review had obvious political overtones.

Chapter 10

101 Kilometers from Moscow: Disorders in Murom and Aleksandrov, RSFSR

Funerals Murom-Style, June 1961

June 26–27: Death in a Prison Cell

The city of Murom, located in Vladimir Oblast, belongs to that category of small provincial towns whose social status is defined by the phrase "101 kilometers from Moscow." People who ended up in these places, "101 kilometers away," included those who did not have the right to live in large cities: people classified as spongers or parasites who had been expelled from Moscow during campaigns aimed at "deporting" those who could not or did not want to work, and certain categories of persons returning from imprisonment. In Soviet political culture, the phrase "101 kilometers" had multiple meanings, all basically negative, and in certain contexts implied "second-rate quality." It should be added that in the majority of such places, the supply of consumer goods and food products was significantly worse than in the capital and in large industrial cities, while, the concentration of potentially volatile groups was somewhat higher. This produced considerable anxiety, not only for law-abiding citizens, but also for the powers that be. Authorities in such provincial towns were quick to recognize a crisis situation, yet the police and KGB were less able to control the course of the conflict than in large cities. Consequently, in a small town, where social relations are not so anonymous and impersonal as in the capital cities, conflict between the individual and the state could easily become personalized.

People knew their antagonists and nursed their grievances over long periods of time.

The unrest in Murom began with an unfortunate accident. On June 26, 1961, a senior foreman at the Ordzhonikidze Factory, Iu. Kostikov, got drunk and tried to climb into the cab of a moving truck. When the truck rounded a curve, Kostikov fell out, hitting the asphalt and cracking his head. The city police chief happened to witness this "violation of order." Acting in the true tradition of a Gogolian town prefect [*gorodnichii*],* the police chief, instead of dispatching the injured Kostikov to the hospital, ordered him to be removed from the street and taken to the police station. There Kostikov, without any medical examination, was placed in a cell designated for drunks, where he spent the entire night. By morning, the guards found him near death and called an ambulance, but it was already too late. Without regaining consciousness, Kostikov died in the hospital from a brain hemorrhage.[1]

News of this tragic and absurd death passed quickly through the town along with rumors that the police had beaten Kostikov. The KGB representative informed the city party committee "about the incorrect attitudes of the workers." On June 29, the city procurator instituted a criminal investigation into the death of Kostikov, but apparently did not find or did not want to find evidence of any police brutality. A party activist conducted a session at the victim's factory, during which the procurator and a specialist in forensic medicine reported on the "genuine causes of the death of Kostikov."[2] The circumstances in the city, however, remained tense. It was clear to everyone that, instead of sending a person with a severe head trauma to the hospital, the police had taken him to jail.

The efforts of local party officials to control the situation ran up against a spontaneously emerging conspiracy headed by a man named Mikhail Panibratsev. By the standards of today, this person was a typical victim of Stalinist tyranny, although in the eyes of authorities in 1961, he was, above all, a former state prisoner and potentially an "anti-Soviet element." At the time of these events, Panibratsev was married with a three-year-old child and worked as a painter-artist in the very same factory shop as Kostikov. Mikhail had a black spot on his record—one prior conviction. The newspaper *Muromskii rabochii* (The Murom Worker) in its article "Banditam vozdano po zaslugam" (The Bandits Got What They Deserve) later claimed that Panibratsev had once been convicted "for provocative fabrications, to ten

---

*In tsarist Russia, the prefect was the main authority in a town, a combination of chief magistrate and chief constable. The author is referring to the conniving and corrupt town prefect in writer Nikolai Gogol's comic nineteenth-century play, *The Inspector*, who shows poor judgment and in the end suffers duly for his many follies and indiscretions.—E.M.

years in prison."[3] In reality, this was a vulgar propagandistic charade. He had actually been convicted in 1941 at the age of twenty-five under Article 19-58-8 and 16-58-7 of the RSFSR Criminal Code. Translated into human terms, this means that a person has been convicted for an attempted act of terrorism (19-58-8) and for some unknown action, insofar as Article 16 stipulates conviction for actions that are not covered directly in the criminal code. In such a case, the closest article is used.

Consequently, the cursory Stalinist justice system arrested Panibratsev under Article 58-8 for disrupting state industry, transportation, trade, and finance, as well as for subverting state enterprises and institutions for "counterrevolutionary purposes." It can be stated with confidence, however, that Panibratsev was not guilty of anything against the regime. Yet for no particular reason, the regime "soldered" a sentence of ten years in the camps to him. Thus, it is understandable that such a person would hate the regime. After having spent eight years in the camps for no reason, Panibratsev was ready to believe in any crime committed by the state, and particularly, such a trifle as beating a drunk in the police station. The post-Stalinist liberalization had not impressed him, since under Khrushchev he had not even been rehabilitated, but simply had his crime reexamined. In a single word, the state had broken this young man's life, and then did not even consider it necessary to apologize and erase the stigma of criminality from him.

On June 29, Mikhail went to the morgue with several other angry workers and met with the specialist in forensic medicine. The workers did not believe the official conclusion about the causes of Kostikov's death and decided that "it was necessary to seek revenge." Panibratsev told his colleagues at work that they needed to write down the slogan "Death to Murderers" and go with him to the police. He himself had prepared a poster with an inscription declaring that the Murom police chief was a sadist and a murderer. According to witnesses, Panibratsev said at his home that evening: "Tomorrow during the funeral we will break all of the windows in the police station," and in response to doubts in the guilt of the police, he said, "All the same, we have no choice."[4]

From a Funeral to an Uprising, June 30

On June 30, the factory directorate and social organizations arranged Kostikov's funeral. According to the bosses' plan, the funeral procession was to keep clear of the city police station, but the informal leaders among the workers had other plans, including raising Panibratsev's poster over the heads of the crowd.[5] The factory bosses managed to confiscate the poster, but were not able to redirect the procession away from the city police station. Mikhail Panibratsev jumped out of the column of marchers and was one of the first to yell, "Attack the dirty bastards," as he hurled two rocks at the windows in the police station. After this, according to witnesses, "a shower of stones poured forth."[6]

Panibratsev, though, did not participate in the subsequent events. The indictment says nothing about his role in the looting of the police station, and this suggests that he left the scene of the events with the funeral procession. Soon after the beginning of the disturbances, the procession had moved on to the cemetery.[7] Just as during the unrest in Grozny and in Krasnodar, the initiator of the Murom protest was not involved in the ensuing uprising. From the drunken crowd that remained at the police station, new leaders emerged who had not participated in the preparations for the funeral and who had not even known the deceased. But they had personal reasons for hating the police.

During the evening, a spontaneous demonstration raged near the police station. According to the testimony of one of the participants in the disorders, "There were many people, and everyone was shouting something different at the police. The windows were all broken, but stones continued to fly. At the entrance door lay an overturned automobile, and various people turned it into a speaker's platform."[8] But there were practically no conscious speeches, only angry outbursts and calls for looting.

The Murom city executive committee chairman, A.K. Sorokin, crawled up onto the overturned automobile and called the crowd to order, but heard in response only cries of outrage: "The police killed the man!" Sorokin promised to uncover the whole truth and punish the guilty, but a soldier who had personal experience in dealing with the city's chief executive exclaimed that he did not trust Sorokin.[9] The crowd's animosity reached a critical point.

After the soldier's outburst, a man by the name of Sergei Denisov climbed up onto the overturned automobile and gave a speech that triggered an explosion of violence and looting. This migrant from the countryside, who labored as a sewage worker at the plant *Krasnyi Luch* (Red Beam), was poorly educated and had two prior convictions for insignificant crimes. He was married and was raising two children.[10] At the beginning of the events in Murom, Denisov was serving fifteen days in jail for having gotten into a fight with his father and brother. In the early evening on June 30, the arrested man heard a noise on the street and slyly escaped from the jail cell onto Moscow Street, where he cried out to the crowd: "Attack the fascists, attack the scum! Liberate the prisoners!"[11] The call fell on fertile soil—in the crowd there were friends of several persons who had been arrested for hooliganism.[12]

According to eyewitness testimony, Denisov declared that "the police beat those who are arrested, throw them into cells, and in the camps they generally murder them." He claimed that he personally saw the police beat Kostikov and that the police had also beaten Denisov. To substantiate his words, he pulled up his shirt and showed the scars of beatings on his left side. The chairman Sorokin, when he met Denisov on the street several days later, asked him about the person who had beaten him. Denisov then admitted that the scars were from a fight with his brother.[13]

After Denisov's speech, "attacks began on police, volunteer police, and other official persons who were trying to bring order."[14] But Denisov was far from being the only orator taking part in the spontaneous meeting at the police station. Stepan Martynov, an illiterate Bessarabian gypsy whose father had been killed at the front in 1943 and whose mother died from hunger that same year, also played an active role among the speakers. Until 1956, Martynov had lived with his cousin and wandered as a nomad, but that year he moved to Murom, settled down, married a woman with two children, and found work as a manual laborer in a brick factory. After this he changed jobs several times in search of higher wages, since he was supporting four dependents.

Stepan had personal reasons for hating the police, for in 1959 he had been arrested for petty hooliganism.[15] According to the testimony of Martynov, the only topic of conversation in the city was Kostikov's death. He had heard about it first at the market, then in conversations with women around his home, and, finally, on the way to the movie theater. The remarks of Denisov, who had related his personal grievances to the crowd, made a strong impression on the drunken Martynov. As a result, Stepan also climbed up to the tribunal to call for a pogrom against the police.[16]

The meeting continued, now against a backdrop of violence, as though it were bolstering the rioters' moral legitimacy and enflamed passions. Orators shouted out challenges, and then they themselves fulfilled them. Among them was a tinsmith by the name of Maksim Usov, a father of three children between the ages of sixteen and twenty-six. Of rural origin and poorly educated, he had been repeatedly detained by the police for public drunkenness and for petty hooliganism.[17] On June 30, Usov was drunk and according to some witnesses, cried out: "Attack the police! They insult us and beat us, and you just watch this! Beat them, rout them some more." Other witnesses reported hearing "Let us burn them, let us destroy them! There is nothing to regret! Let the station burn!"[18]

Such cries also came from the surrounding crowd. Lukin, one of those convicted in the Murom case, called out: "It is necessary to attack the police and to destroy them," and accompanied his statements with drunken oaths. When a witness turned to him with the words, "Why are you yelling, why are you provoking people?" Lukin responded: "Look at you, you too have a red card [the party card of a member of the CPSU—V.K.], you belong with them, you rat."[19] The mob reacted aggressively in this way to all appeals to calm down and be reasonable. For example, for such words a drunken hooligan smashed the head of the witness Chekalov and drew blood.[20]

Between 6:00 P.M. and 7:00 P.M., activists from the crowd broke into the police department and the local KGB offices, where they chopped up furniture with an axe, threw a safe with secret KGB documents out on to the street, and destroyed police papers. Someone set a police car on fire. Rioters beat up several police officers and tried to tear off their uniforms and push them out on the street to be tried by the "People's Court." In self-defense, the police shot at their attackers, wounding one of them. Crying out against the "bastard" and "fascist" police, the crowd broke down the brick wall enclosing the cells, liberated some of the prisoners, and stole a significant amount of live ammunition. After the wounding of their comrade, the angered rioters cried out that "they are killing the people," and tried to draw nearby loiterers into the disturbances. Firemen who had arrived at the scene were not allowed to work, and the water hoses were cut off.

The majority of the active rioters appeared at the scene of the events specifically to participate in the disorders and, as has already been stated above, had personal reasons for hating the police. At the same time, they were all under the inflammatory influence of alcohol. Yet, they seemed to express the instinct of the crowd, which imparted an appearance of logic and purpose to its spontaneous actions. Later, several could barely remember their own behavior: "I could not until this time remember what pushed me."[21] In this statement there was, in all probability, more truth than deception.

A deep resentment against the state, exacerbated by the effect of alcohol, turned into a collective mob psychosis and overcame the restraining influence normally exercised by the fear of punishment. The righteousness of one's actions was sanctified by ideas of retribution for the "innocent victim," which always impart a certain higher meaning to looting. Yet hardly any of the activists thought that, dissolved within the anonymous crowd, they were carrying out something more serious than their typical hooliganism. As soon as such a thought came to mind, they switched off from the looting and disappeared from the scene of the events.

Aleksei Polikarpov, who was one of the first to break into the city police station, where "he used physical violence against police workers, trying to force them out onto the street for reprisals,"[22] described his own participation in the disorders in an appeal to the Procurator-General from August 3, 1962:

I approached the building at several minutes before 7:00 P.M. I was drunk, I believed everyone and stupidly joined in, poking my nose into other people's affairs. I went upstairs and began to argue with employees of the building. I heard shots above me, they were shooting below in another sector, and after the shots, cries could be heard: "Murderers, why are you shooting at the people, you have killed yet another." I began to say to them: "What are you doing, you are attacking people," and I called them beasts, "You are not worthy of wearing this uniform and carrying this weapon." I did nothing more in the building and went out the door. . . . I did not hit anyone, and I did not have any idea of this in my mind, for as far as I can remember, in my entire life I have never fought with anyone. . . . While passing by a window, where persons accused of petty hooliganism were being held, . . . I said to them: "You guys need to get away, they are killing people here." But, after thinking "this is none of my business," I went out through an open gateway to Moscow Street. . . . My mother saw me and exclaimed: "Your wife is here with the children" and then my wife, upon seeing me asked: "Why are you not at the public bath?" and I explained to her what had happened. We went home, and on the way I went into the bathhouse, while she went home with the children.[23]

Konstantin Lukin also played an important role in the attack on the police department. He had lost his childhood to the war and at age seventeen was convicted for theft of personal property. But after his imprisonment Lukin, using the language of those years, "steadfastly entered onto the path of correction": He got a job, married, and had two children. The old resentment, however, stayed fresh in his memory. On July 30, Lukin was drunk and became agitated by the rumors about the police murdering Kostikov. He cried out from the crowd: "It is necessary to attack the police and destroy them."[24] Armed with an axe, Lukin broke furniture and threw police uniforms and other clothing out onto the street, as well as documents.[25]

The trial later identified Valentin Romanenkov as one of the organizers of the assault on the police building. He was distinguished from other instigators of the disorders by the fact that he had started though not completed higher education. Like many of them, though, he led a sordid way of life. He was married but did not live with his wife, and he had one conviction for malicious hooliganism in April 1959. He did not work anywhere, and the police had twice warned him about the need to find employment. A year before the Murom events, he was held on suspicion of being a pickpocket, and during the attack on the police station, he sought to destroy documents concerning this distasteful event. Taking an active part in liberating the prisoners, Romanenkov broke down the door leading to the jail. He cried out: "You bastards, you can kill one or two but you cannot shoot down everyone," and demanded that the police "throw up the white flag" and hand over their weapons. The rest burst in after him. Romanenkov then used a crowbar to break into a cell and let out the prisoners, among whom was a friend of his.[26]

Among those storming the police station were two women, both of whom were single mothers with prior convictions for insignificant crimes. Neither knew how to endure the "burdens of life" and were hardened by the struggle for existence. The state procurator characterized one of them as a "morally degenerate personality," and in the indictment claimed that the other "behaved indecently, drank systematically, and led a debauched way of life."[27] The actions of these unhappy, degraded women in the course of the riot were characterized by strong animosity and vulgar cursing. Like the majority of the rioters, they were drunk, they threw rocks at windows, they cried out "attack the police," and so on. Both brought a sense of hysteria into the disturbances, as if they were venting their own personal grievances and pain on the victims of the assault.

The riots continued about five hours. As a result, all of the windows and doors of the city police department and the KGB offices were broken, telephones lines were cut, safes were broken into, and about sixty barrels of weapons and a large quantity of ammunition were stolen. Twenty-six prisoners who had been arrested for criminal acts were freed, along with twenty-two who had been arrested for petty hooliganism. The interior of the building was set on fire, and many police papers and particularly KGB documents were stolen or burned. Five employees of the police and the procurator's office were beaten. Weapons were used to suppress the disorders, and two of the attackers received bullet wounds.[28] The distinguishing characteristic of the uprising was the almost exclusive focus on the police. In this sense, the Murom disorders were one of the culminating moments of the "hooligan war" that had begun in the 1950s. Hooligans and urban rabble seized the initiative of protest from the workers and turned a funeral demonstration into a bloody assault against the police.

The "Show" Trial

To investigate the events in Murom, authorities formed a group consisting of eight agents from the KGB, headed by a senior investigator. Eight people were subsequently arrested for participation in the mass disorders and eleven people for "acts of hooliganism."[29] In all, there were two trials. The first was held with special fanfare. The preliminary investigation was concluded on August 3, and on that same day the regional procurator approved the indictment. The location selected for the trial was a club for construction workers that seated over three hundred people. Tickets were printed in advance inviting "representatives of the public" for each day of the trial, which the city party committee directly distributed to workers in local enterprises and institutions. Some of the defendants had their own way of preparing for trial: Various witnesses complained at the time of the preliminary investigation that they were afraid of "reprisals from hooligan elements" if they testified.[30]

The trial lasted three days. The hall was full and the outcome was predetermined. The public chosen by party officials was ready to "react correctly." When the state procurator demanded the death sentence for three of the defendants, the hall rang with applause, and the speeches of the public prosecutors all met with applause. The audience gave a standing ovation following the pronouncement of the sentences. Under such circumstances, the lawyers for the defendants could not even try to mount a serious defense. But they did ask the court to lighten the punishment based on various grounds including family situation, past activity, and confession of guilt.[31]

On August 11, the day that the sentences were announced, special sessions were held in all of the city's enterprises. Workers spoke who had been present at the trial. Participants in the meetings and assemblies, of course, angrily and unanimously "condemned the criminal activity of the defendants and other bandits and hooligans, expressed their satisfaction with the sentences given, and demanded that they be carried out."[32]

The Case of Strunnikov or "We Will Avenge the People of Murom"

The trial ended on Friday, August 11, 1961. On Sunday, August 13, the regional Vladimir newspaper *Prizyv* (The Appeal) and the city newspaper *Muromskii rabochii* (The Murom Worker) printed the article "The Bandits Got What They Deserved," which was written by P. Ivanov. This officially sanctioned article emphasized the criminal past of three of the defendants, whom the author called "hardened bandits," a phrase borrowed from the newspaper slang of the Stalinist epoch and, to say the least, very far from reality. Information about the conviction of Panibratsev, a victim of political terror, was distorted, as discussed earlier. The goal of the fabrications and the unfair scrambling of facts was clear—to depict the active participants in the riots as renegades and social pariahs who did not have anything in common with the Soviet people. The laborers themselves, according to the information of these same newspapers, "unanimously approved the just sentence of the bandit-hooligan elements."[33] On August 17, a short piece, "A Just Punishment," appeared in all republic-level newspapers, particularly in *Sovetskaia Rossiia* (Soviet Russia),[34] and in regional newspapers of the USSR. The tone of this article was more moderate and informative, implying that party authorities had decided that information about the three death sentences in and of itself would have the necessary effect.

In reality, however, there was no "unanimity of the laborers" in the evaluation of the events in Murom. Moreover, during the public discussion organized by the authorities in the enterprises of Murom, an incident occurred that not a single newspaper covered. Vladimir Strunnikov, a father of two children with five years of education and a prior conviction, dared to publicly express his disagreement with the sentence and called for the workers of his shop to go on strike. As Strunnikov subsequently stated:

> The workers kept silent, and in protest I quit work and left the shop. Upon arriving home, I changed my clothes and went to the city in order to speak to young people in the Oksk Garden and call on them to join my protest. I came to Moscow Street and went into a restaurant, where I drank 300 grams of vodka, and then, having grabbed a bottle of wine, I went to the Park of Culture and Rest. Passing through a veranda where about fifty young people had gathered, I went into the middle and called upon them to join my protest against the sentence of the court. . . . After this I was taken to the police station.[35]

Strunnikov offered no resistance to the civilian police volunteers who detained him. He conducted himself very honorably and said that, in his opinion, the Murom insurgents "had acted correctly" and he was outraged at their "illegal arrest."[36] The cursory Khrushchevian judicial process did not even begin to investigate the finer points of the matter, but immediately organized among Strunnikov's fellow workers "an angry condemnation" of his actions and a falsified request from workers in his sector for the KGB to arrest Strunnikov.

Strunnikov was hastily and falsely convicted of calling for mass disorders and sentenced to seven years in prison, although the case did not even amount to to the level of petty hooliganism. In May of 1963, the Procuracy already prepared a protest, proposing that the definition of Strunnikov's crime be recategorized under an article for hooliganism and that the punishment be reduced to three years' imprisonment. In the end, after Khrushchev's fall, Vladimir Strunnikov was rehabilitated by a resolution of the Russian Federation Supreme Court.

Still one other hitch in the propaganda campaign was the appearance of graffiti on August 25 in the city of Kovrov in Vladimir Oblast: "We will avenge the people of Murom." On that same day in that same city, someone wrote on a wall, "Down with the Communist regime. The Young Guard."[37] Events in Murom had thus acquired a special political nuance. The attempts by authorities to frighten potential organizers of such phenomena with the death penalty, to a certain degree, had the opposite effect. The state's harshness shocked many and even outraged some.

"Kill the Bastards! They Took Away Half of My Life from Me": Mass Disturbances in Aleksandrov, July 23–24, 1961

Events in Murom had a domino effect. Graffiti on buildings in Kovrov calling for revenge was the first sign, but unrest in Aleksandrov, another city in Vladimir Oblast, was a more serious symptom. Here the disturbances occurred spontaneously, under the influence of a standard conflict—aggrieved soldiers. However, the instigators were unarguably inspired by a desire to "emulate Murom," for different variations of this phrase were heard repeatedly in the course of the uprising.[38] In spite of such references to the Murom experience, however, the disorders in Aleksandrov were primarily a drunken revolt of urban riffraff in which there were almost no politics and no "anti-Sovietism."

Altogether, nineteen people were convicted for participating in the disturbances in Aleksandrov. Of these, twelve had a prior conviction or had been detained for hooliganism and petty theft, which meant, at a minimum, they had spent fifteen days under arrest in the police jail. Four had been previously sentenced to long prison terms for serious crimes or had repeated convictions. Only seven on the list did not have a criminal or hooligan past or, in any case, had not been detained by the police. One of them was a candidate for membership in the CPSU, while another was a war hero decorated with medals for personal bravery. All seven had a reputation for being morally unstable, and they were all drunk at the time of the unrest. Thus, they easily fell under the influence of collective crowd psychosis and afterward could not easily remember their actions.

The leitmotif for the events in Aleksandrov was the usual desire of aggrieved persons for public revenge and reprisals against the hated police. This desire was reflected in the cries, "Kill the bastards! They took away half of my life from me,"[39] "They are far too arrogant," and so on.

The Conflict at Soviet Square. The Soldiers Grezdov and Krylov

On Sunday, July 23, 1961, two soldiers by the name of V. Grezdov and A. Krylov came to Aleksandrov from Zagorsk for entertainment. By evening they were drunk, and it was an ill wind that carried them to the city's center, Soviet Square, where the police department was located. There they caught the eye of a police officer by the name of Kuznetsov. The latter was in civilian dress, and the soldiers did not take seriously his "invitation" to come to the station, which then led to an altercation. In the end, the violators of the peace were tied up and dragged by force to the police department. The duty officer immediately sent news of this to the local garrison commander, Lieutenant-Colonel Chereiskii.

The conflict between the police and the unlucky soldiers, who were subsequently convicted of hooliganism, attracted the attention of several soft-hearted women. Aggrieved "poor little drunkards" often produce an irrational pity in Russian women, and so it was this time. Moreover, several women who witnessed these occurrences were also drunk, and their outcries drew a crowd. Since this was a day off from work, there were many who were drunk. Among those calling for reprisals against the police were an automobile locksmith, Leonid Loginov, who had been detained several times for petty hooliganism, was divorced from his wife, and had to pay alimony for three children; an engineer's assistant, Vladimir Fedotov, who had three convictions for theft of state property and was the father of a small daughter; a stableman at a hospital, Aleksandr Kruchinin, who was a one-eyed invalid and the father of two children; and a carpenter, Vladimir Dmitriev, who had no prior convictions and was the father of a ten-year-old son.[40]

Kruchinin authored the slogan "We will create a second Murom!," which directly referred the crowd to the experience of their predecessors. This same theme was present also in Dmitriev's statements. He unconsciously tried to disconnect the hated police from the defense of Soviet myths about the "most just state on earth," and turn them into something detached from and alien to not only the people, but the regime itself. After several hours of violence and looting, Dmitrev exclaimed, with a threatening gesture directed at a prison guard: "Beat him, he is a Gestapo policeman!"[41] This moral equalization, as if the Aleksandrov police had been transformed into Nazi accomplices, spared those lacking criminal experience from feeling guilty before the state. The majority of the instigators, though, did not delve deeply into any labyrinth of morality, but simply shouted the slogans: "Release the soldiers, you bastards" and attacked because they believed the police to be evil.[42]

The Conflict at Soviet Square

During the early evening, fifty to sixty agitated people gathered at the city police station, cursing and demanding the liberation of the detained soldiers.[43] A little later, Lieutenant-Colonel Chereiskii came to the square with four soldiers, followed by the city procurator, a KGB official, and several middle-ranking local party-state leaders, all of whom unsuccessfully tried to quiet down the crowd. The military commander wanted to carry the detained soldiers to his office by car. Amid a storm of angry outbursts about the beaten soldiers, the crowd, now numbering a hundred people, barricaded the military commander's path to the automobile. The conflict spread to the courtyard around the police station, and in the commotion, the mob pushed the guards back and forcibly freed Krylov. He lost himself in the throngs of people and later returned to his own unit in Zagorsk.[44]

The aggression and fervor of the firebrands intensified. Leonid Loginov, for example, prevented the car with the arrested soldier Grezdov from leaving the gates of the police station. He leaned against the bumper, put his legs under the wheel, beat his fists on the hood, unfastened the tarpaulin, opened the doors, and cried out: "Hand him over to me, I am not leaving." "Kill them, but do not let the car leave." Loginov responded to the officers' demands with vulgar cursing and said to one of them: "I will now tear you apart, you scum."[45]

Authorities failed to control the situation from the very beginning. New people joined the crowd, spreading their infectious hysteria. When the car with Chereiskii and Grezdov nonetheless left the station, the rioters tried to break down the entrance door to the police station. Later in the evening, Lieutenant-Colonel Chereiskii returned to the square, hoping to catch Krylov, and this time he had eight more soldiers with him. But the crowd had also grown, now numbering five hundred people, many of whom were drunk. At this time the slogan "We will do as in Murom!" rang out in conjunction with standard outcries for a pogrom: "Let us storm the police station!" "Attack the police!" People surrounded Chereiskii's car and began to rock it in hopes of overturning it.[46] In truth, there was no logical reason to storm the police station. Grezdov had been taken to the military commander's office, and Krylov had run away. Chereiskii tried to explain this to the crowd, as did state officials and the police chief. But all their efforts were fruitless. The lieutenant-colonel caught the worst of it, for he ended up in the hands of the enraged mob, who insulted him, tore his clothing, and beat him.[47]

New activists, almost all of whom were drunk, emerged from the crowd to achieve the first success for the rioters. In the evening, a young sanitation engineer by the name of Evgenii Vachin, who had a reputation in the city for being a "violator of labor discipline and public order," threw himself energetically into the fracas. He tried to stop Chereiskii's car from leaving the police station, demanded the liberation of the arrested soldiers, chased the lieutenant-colonel through the square, and called for reprisals against the police: "It is necessary to slaughter them, those bastards."[48] An hour later, he tried to break into the police building and took part in knocking down the entry door.

The cries of the harness maker Vasili Barabanshchikov, who had four convictions for hooliganism,[49] intensified the militant mood of the crowd. His father had returned from war in 1945 as an invalid and four years later died from his wounds and from poor health. In 1941 a German bomb had mutilated the hands of Vasilii himself. A typical victim of circumstances and a difficult childhood, Vasilii Barabanshchikov fell into bad company, began to drink, and engaged in hooliganism. Consequently, he spent his youth in the labor camps, but fell seriously ill during his imprisonment and was declared unfit for physical labor.[50]

Barabanshchikov demanded the liberation of the arrested soldiers, burst into the police premises, pursued Chereiskii through the square, and shouted out that the police were beating the arrested soldiers. Barabanshchikov spied a volunteer civilian policewoman standing at the entrance way and he cried out: "Drag her away! If not from here, then from her trial, she must not get away alive!"[51] Yet, the testimony of eyewitnesses established that Barabanshchikov saved an onlooker from being beaten and helped the city party committee secretary to get away from the crowd.[52] Obviously, in the conscience of this son of a veteran who had died fighting for Soviet power, standard ideological concepts of the communist epoch were organically entwined with hatred for the "police scum." Above all, the party secretary personified for Barabanshchikov the just state, before which it was necessary only to shout till one was heard, while the police were the personification of the dark force that had broken his life. To a significant degree, the stability of the Soviet regime was rooted in such psychological stereotypes. Even many of its potential antagonists tried to ascribe their alternate behavior to an ideological myth about "individual inadequacies" caused by the actions of concrete "enemy-bureaucrats."

Vasilii Grechikhin, an unemployed invalid with three children and a conviction for petty speculation, along with minor infractions of public order, also joined in beating Lieutenant-Colonel Chereiskii. Turning up at the scene purely by accident, the inebriated Grechikhin was riding on the bus with his wife when the crowd stopped the vehicle at Soviet Square. But Vasilii Grechikhin flowed so naturally into the rioting human mass that it is difficult to believe that he was an invalid with both hands maimed.[53]

Still another "hero" of the pursuit of Chereiskii was the truck driver Pavel Zaitsev, born in 1925, the father of three children, and a decorated war veteran. On the day of the riots, Zaitsev was twice unlucky. He not only got mixed up in the mass disorders, but he himself became a victim of the riot's irrational frenzy. Late in the evening, when the police began to shoot at the people who were storming the police building, a gang of hooligans mistook Zaitsev, who had turned up in one of the offices, for a police employee. Several persons brutally beat him in the legs, and then seized him by the arms and legs and began to throw him on the floor (a typical form of punishment for informants and traitors in the internal criminal conflicts found in Soviet labor camps and colonies—V.K.). Zaitsev ended up in the hospital with severe bruises.[54]

The manual laborer Anatolii Singinov, who had two convictions for robbery and for theft and several arrests for hooliganism, took an active part as well in the pursuit of Chereiskii through the square. Singinov lived in a dormitory, separated from his wife but not officially divorced. Relentlessly calling for an attack against the police department, Singinov, when the crowd began to rock the military vehicle that had come to carry away the detained soldiers, took on the role of coordinator, giving the command, "One, two."[55]

Further leadership came from Konstantin Savaseev, a carpenter who fiercely hated the police.[56] The reasons for such an attitude are understandable, for by the age of thirty-five, Savaseev had a conviction for attempted murder and two arrests for hooliganism. He had grown up in a large family of six children, was seriously ill as a child, and, according to his mother, only began to talk at age seven, due to complications from scarlet fever. His stepfather was frequently drunk and had basically driven the boy out into the streets, forcing him to begin work at age fifteen. In 1953, again according to his mother's testimony, he ran into the man who had murdered his brother, and asked him why he had done this. When the man replied, "A dog deserves a dog's death," Savaseev savagely beat him, which earned him a conviction for attempted murder. The Savaseev family believed that Konstantin had been treated unjustly.[57]

Savaseev actively stood up for his comrades in misfortune—the detained soldiers—and cried out that they were being held illegally and that it was necessary to liberate them by force. In order to prevent the car with the soldiers from leaving the police station, he grabbed the steering wheel out of the driver's hands and then wrenched off the door handle of the car, hurting his own hand in the process. Savaseev showed his bloodied hand to those around him and accused the police of wounding him, which further enraged the crowd.[58]

In the end, Chereiskii was able to hide from his pursuers in the police station. But as events entered their most active phase, people forgot about the "poor little soldiers" and embraced new goals. A group of forty to fifty people raised the cry "Attack, rout the police!" and began to shower the building with rocks and bricks.[59] Armed with sticks and squared beams from a garden fence, hooligans began to beat on the glass and break down the frames and metal lattices in the windows of the police department. While some hurled rocks at the police building, others overturned and burned the police motorcycle, accompanied by Savaseev performing something similar to a ritual dance around the conflagration.[60] Hooligans rolled a police car to the square, turned it over on its side, and then burned it as well, after which they beat up the commander of the fire brigade. The rioters blocked the path of the fire trucks that had arrived at the square and prevented them from getting through to the burning vehicles.[61]

The attackers besieged the police station from three sides and began to force their way through the front door. As a battering ram they used a garden bench and fencing torn from the earth, as well as other materials. At this time there were twelve police personnel in the building. Some who had been guarding the entry door and the guard room on the first floor blockaded themselves with furniture and fired 364 shots into the air, but this failed to stop the onslaught. Late in the evening, the door gave way under the pressure of the attackers. Bolstering themselves by yelling "Do not be afraid, they are only trying to frighten us!," the mob burst into the first floor. They broke into offices and destroyed furniture, then dragged out safes containing official papers and threw them out into the street. It was precisely at this time that P. Zaitsev was viciously beaten in the corridor, when he was mistaken for a police officer who had fired at the attacking mob.

A little later the building's right wing was set on fire, and the blaze quickly spread,[62] forcing the police to transfer the prisoners being held at the police station to the adjacent prison. Less than an hour later, the left wing began to burn. The city procurator, the police chief, and the local representative of the KGB, all of whose offices were on the second floor of the building, telephoned the city party committee, the regional procurator, and the regional MVD and KGB offices to report on the situation. Troops were dispatched to the scene, though the first two companies did not have weapons and were not able to influence the course of events. Several leaders of the crowd tried to conduct propaganda among these soldiers, calling on them to turn their weapons against the police and "come over to the side of the people." The leaders explained that the people were struggling for the "right cause"— revenge for the persecuted soldiers. Only the armed unit commanded by Major-General Korzhenko, which arrived later, was able to bring the situation under control, but even then not immediately.

In the course of this active phase of the disorders, several local authorities, as well as eyewitnesses who had called for the restoration of order, became the victims of mob violence. Among those beaten up near the police department building were the chief of police, Nikiforov; the secretary of the party organization for one of the factories in Aleksandrov, Romanov; an unidentified lieutenant-colonel of the border troops who was in Aleksandrov on leave; a worker in an Aleksandrov factory; a former KGB employee, I. Babashkin; another former KGB employee, V. Byvatov; and the deputy commander of the civilian People's Squad, P. Shilov. The mob knifed the policeman G. Proshman in the chest.[63]

Such was the external canvas of events that unfolded in Soviet Square in and around the police department building during the evening of July 23, 1961. Familiar heroes had turned up among the activists. Grechikhin had given the first signal to break down the door to the police building,[64] and supporting him were Loginov, Barabanshchikov, and Singinov, all of whom have been previously introduced. It was Barabanshchikov, along with a new personality in the drama, the power-shovel operator Aleksandr Sidorov, who figured out how to use the garden bench as a battering ram. Sidorov, who had three convictions for robbery, hooliganism, and "causing bodily injury,"[65] appeared on the scene at the moment when the mob broke into the police station. He helped initiate the idea to burn down the police building: "Those pigs, we must kill them and then burn them!" Sidorov took part as well in beating up the police chief Nikiforov. He later could not remember his own actions, or, relying on his prior criminal experience, preferred not to remember.[66]

Another active arsonist—Aleksei Ziuzin, a rifleman in the railroad paramilitary guard—turned up three times at the center of events: He liberated the prisoners from the drying-out cells (for drunks), threw a bottle with a gas mixture into the police building, and tried to set fire to the prison. The investigation and trial later characterized him as a "morally unworthy personality." By the standards of the regime, however, not only was Ziuzin a law-abiding citizen without any prior convictions or detentions by the police, but his loyalty was affirmed by the fact that he was a candidate for CPSU membership. He got mixed up in the events primarily due to alcohol, for after work he had drunk a half-liter of vodka with his father-in-law.

The circumstances of Ziuzin's participation in the burning of the building are not clear. It is difficult to believe that a drunken man thrust into the whirlwind of a riot had the time and the ability independently to prepare a bottle with a Molotov cocktail. Ziuzin himself wrote in an appeal that two unidentified persons had approached him and began to propose that he take:

> . . . a bottle with gas, but what kind it was, I do not know. I refused and we all began swearing at each other. But then they threatened violence against me and I gave in; they forced me to go with them, one on each side with me in the middle. We went about fifteen to twenty meters in front of the GOM building [the city police department], they forced me to throw the bottle, showing me where to throw it, inside of the building, but I threw it at the outside corner with the exposed side.[67]

Ziusin's story is direct evidence of the typical forces behind the scenes that drive people and events while remaining hidden in the shadows. As a rule, the authorities tried and punished in such cases only the loudest and the flashiest, but not actually the most dangerous elements.

One of the first victims of physical violence from the rioters had been the former KGB official, I. Babashkin, and it was his brutal beating that fully unleashed the bloody instincts of the crowd. The trigger for the attack was the attempt of Babashkin to intervene in the events, and this turned out to be a critical moment in the disturbances. At such times rioters demonstrate heightened aggression, and apply to any who challenge them the single means accessible to them—violence or the threat of violence. After this, as if crossing the Rubicon, joined by their common sin, they become even more aggressive. The criminal hysteria usually accompanying such actions is calculated to intimidate and decisively suppress all appeals for common sense and sobriety. Such it was this time.

Some of the senior leaders of the disorders, such as Grechikhin, took part in beating Babashkin. But it was the hysterical activism of Zinaida Klochkova that played the decisive role at this critical moment. This woman, like so many others, had turned up in the square by accident while walking home from the movies with a friend, yet she behaved as if she had long prepared for this brief moment in the spotlight. In 1961, Klochkova was working as a cook at the medical clinic located in the Krasnoiarsk airport. But she nursed a deep grievance from her youth. In 1947, at age sixteen, she had been sentenced to a one-year term for unarmed attempted robbery. In reality, the incident involved an attempt to swipe a piece of bread from a trader in the market or something similar to this. But the cruel Stalinist regime at that time was conducting its own campaign against crime, and authorities applied the same method of repressive mass terror that was used in politics. The punishment of one year in the forced labor camps was given at that time "just because," "for no reason," so that others would not commit the same transgression. Thus, the wheel of the callous state machine rode roughshod over this young girl's life.

In 1961, Zinaida Klochkova tried to pay back this old debt, and she followed precisely the same pattern as that of the state that had offended her—she acted without sorting out the innocent and the guilty. She lashed out blindly and savagely, building upon the criminal experience she had gained in the camp. When the women present in the square criticized the behavior of Klochkova ("she is a woman, what does she think she is doing"), from the depths of her subconscious a camp phrase surfaced: "Shut up, you bitches, or I will slit your throat" [zamolchite, padly, a to gorlo peregryzu].[68] Klochkova tried in every way possible to neutralize those who were urging the rioters to come to their senses. Using rather typical criminal methods to frighten victims, she threatened the sober-minded with reprisals such as burning down their homes. Later she entreated the soldiers not to interfere in the disorders, but, on the contrary, to join in storming the police building and the prison.[69] At this moment, according to the investigation and trial, Klochkova turned to the crowd with an appeal to take revenge against Communists and to attack the city party committee offices, though the defendant herself denied this charge.[70]

The crowd wavered momentarily when the police fired warning shots at the very beginning of the assault on the police department building. But what tipped the scales toward continuation of the attack were the loud cries of the plasterer Vladimir Gorshkov. He sounded the pro-Soviet myth typical for the majority of riots of this type: Do not be afraid, the authorities will not fire upon the people.[71] Such confidence was particularly present in those people who had turned up accidentally in the crowd and who lacked camp or prison experience. Such a person was Gorshkov, who was quite educated compared to other activists in the pogrom, having completed nine grades in school, and did not have any convictions for hooliganism. He had ended up at Soviet Square late in the evening and was, by his own admission, "drunk and swayed by the influence of the agitated crowd."[72] To a great degree, it was largely thanks to his efforts that the entry door to the police building was broken down. Leading the onslaught, Gorshkov was the first to burst inside the building, crying out, "Brothers, onward!" "Kill the bastards!" "Destroy!"[73] Gorshkov played an important role as well in the attack on the prison (which is discussed below). In the end, after two hours of trying, his wife succeeded in getting her drunken husband away from the scene.

In the episode with the fire trucks, several soloists also stood out from the crowd. One of the first to rush to meet the vehicles was a leader already introduced, Singinov. As a result, the path to the center of the fire was blocked and the trucks had to turn back.[74] The press operator Nikolai Voronov particularly distinguished himself. A decorated veteran and invalid, he had not been able to adapt to civilian life after the war. Twice tried for malicious vandalism, Voronov was fired from his last job for "systematic violations of labor discipline and the theft of cement."[75] The drunken press operator, along with other rioters, rolled the police car away from the building, and when a worker in the passport department tried to interfere, he kicked her in the stomach and demanded that she go away.[76] Then he took part in the storming and burning of the passport department. When the flames appeared, he called for the others to throw something more flammable in the window in order to make the fire stronger. All of this was accompanied by the words: "Everything has been done correctly. This building should have been burned down a long time ago."[77] At the same time as Voronov, a stoker by the name of Anatolii Borisov, who had three arrests for disturbing the peace,[78] also joined in the rampage. Like Voronov, he took part in the episode with the police car and prevented the firemen from getting to the fire, threatening the driver: "What are you doing, you must be tired of living."[79]

All of these firebrands who pushed the rioters forward seem to have played out their roles and then disappeared behind the scene, dissolving into the crowd in order either to go home to sleep, like Gorshkov, or to emerge from the stormy torrent of the riots in another role, in another place, or at another time. In light of this, as was the case with Ziuzin, certain doubts always remain: Are we dealing exclusively with the spontaneous self-organization of the crowd or, apart from the obvious instigators, were there still other ringleaders who were not so obvious, who worked behind the scenes, substituting others in their place? As a rule, the state, in its hurry to carry out reprisals, rarely tried to find answers to this question.

The Attack on the Prison

An independent episode in the riot, which involved a real battle, was the attack on Prison No. 4, adjacent to the city police department. At the time of the attack, there was a total of 169 prisoners there, including 82 especially dangerous criminals.[80] There were 22 guards. The idea to liberate the prisoners occurred simultaneously to several ringleaders of the disorders at the moment when the fire broke out in the police building.[81] Probably the truck driver Aleksei Fedorov played the most important role;[82] his brother was at this time locked up for petty hooliganism.

Fedorov was drunk when he appeared on the scene. In an appeal to the procurator-general, he wrote: "I had been drinking that evening. Citizen procurator, I did all of this recklessly, without thinking things through. I did not go out with the intention of getting involved in a riot. I went out to a dance in the park. I did not have any purpose in mind. I had bad luck, everything happened to me by accident."[83] Nonetheless, Fedorov acted extremely aggressively and, from the very beginning, had taken part in the storming of the police department,[84] even swearing at colleagues who questioned his actions.[85] When the police department building began to burn, Fedorov grew alarmed for his brother: "He cried out that it was necessary to liberate the prisoners who were locked up for petty hooliganism."[86]

According to the police, only thirty or forty people took part in the storming of the prison. The majority of those who were gathered at the square preferred not to get involved in this act. They were afraid! Konstantin Savaseev unsuccessfully tried to inspire militancy: "People, why are you just standing here? If the people advance, they [the police] will not shoot."[87]

When the assault began, the guard fired several warning shots in the air, but to no avail. The attackers pressed against the gate and doors, making liberation of the imprisoned criminals a real possibility. The prison warden's assistant gave the order to shoot on the basis of the "Instructions on the Organization of Security and Surveillance Services in the Prisons of the Ministry of Internal Affairs." But even shots did not deter participants in the attack. Three times these rampaging "warriors" tried to cover the windows of the building and advance to the prison, but the shots penetrated their makeshift shield and drove them back.

At the same time, an attempt was made to roll a police motorcycle that was burning to the gates of the prison and use it to ignite the entire building. One of the participants in this escapade was killed, and the rest retreated. But the offensive spirit raged on, and some were able to seize and burn the prison automobile. This was particularly dangerous because the fire could spread to the office where the personal files of prisoners were kept, and also to several prison rooms. Gunshots succeeded in driving the rioters away from the burning automobile, and then the guards were able to extinguish the fire.[88]

During the attack on the prison, four of the participants were killed and eleven wounded. A schoolgirl was accidentally wounded in the knee. Several people ended up in the hospital with burns received in the fire. The number of wounded, however, was probably higher. In the city there were cases recorded of anonymous requests for medical treatment of light gunshot wounds.[89]

It was not until the early morning hours of July 24 that the military troops sent to Aleksandrov were able to suppress the uprising and the fire brigades could get through to put out the fires. The police department offices by this time had already burned, destroying in the process a large number of official documents, criminal files, passport blanks, and so on.[90]

"The Taking of Measures"

On July 24, a criminal case concerning the disorders in Aleksandrov was instituted under Article 79 of the RSFSR Criminal Code (mass disorders), and a special KGB operative team was sent to Aleksandrov to conduct the investigation.[91] Regional party and state officials, representatives of the MVD, the regional procurator, the head of the investigative division of the regional procuracy, and others came to the scene of the riots. In the city a special meeting was conducted for party activists, and party-Komsomol sessions were held in the enterprises and institutions.

Such cases, though, were never limited to just ideological measures. The authorities thought about police precautions as well, and for several days, the city was under military surveillance. The volunteer police units were strengthened, and their members also patrolled around Aleksandrov.[92] A search ensued for active participants in the disorders. It was not particularly difficult to find them, for in the first days thirteen people had already been arrested.[93]

One month later, from August 22 to 25, an open assizes session of the Vladimir regional court examined the criminal case against nine active participants in the attack on the Aleksandrov police department and on the prison. Passes were distributed among party, trade union, and Komsomol organizations, for only carefully selected persons were allowed to witness the proceedings. According to the usual practice of such "educational" processes, designed to confirm the "renegade nature" of the defendants, so-called public prosecutors (in this case an electrician and a weaver) spoke out in addition to the government prosecutors. Four of the defendants—Savaseev, Gorshkov, Sidorov, and Barabanshchikov—were sentenced to death by shooting, while the remaining five received the maximum term of imprisonment—fifteen years.[94] After the trial, meetings were held in the industrial enterprises of Aleksandrov and the surrounding area "at which the laborers unanimously approved the sentence of the court." The newspaper for Vladimir Oblast, *Prizyv*, as well as all of the district newspapers in the region, reported on the sentence.[95]

A second open trial was held October 5–9, 1961. This time the location was shifted to the city of Vladimir, the regional center, and there were no public prosecutors. No death sentences were given, but all nine defendants received the maximum term of imprisonment—fifteen years.[96] Unlike, for the first one, authorities did not create any special propaganda campaign around this trial.

The mass disorders in Aleksandrov and the trials of the active participants did not raise any political reaction even among "anti-Soviet elements," unlike the Murom riots. Probably the obvious criminal character of these events, which were not ennobled by anything similar to politics, could not inspire potential protesters to express their dissatisfaction or underground dissidents to write leaflets. Yet there definitely was interest among opposition groups in both the Murom and Aleksandrov events. It is known, for example, that a participant in one of the Moscow underground groups, a student at Moscow State University by the name of E.S. Kuznetsov, after hearing of the events in Murom and Aleksandrov, made special trips to these cities in order to uncover "whether or not these disorders had a political character."[97] The details of his trip, unfortunately, are not known to us.

Chapter 11

Biisk—1961 or The Uprising on Market Day, June 25, 1961

The "Drunken Market" in Biisk and Its Clientele

The summer of 1961 reaped a rich harvest of uprisings and disturbances spurred by excessive drinking. Among them, along with Murom and Aleksandrov, were events in Biisk, Altai Krai, RSFSR. In this city the typical Soviet conflict between economics (fulfillment of the plan) and politics (periodic campaigns against alcoholism) ended in a victory for economics. Trade organizations, striving to complete the plan at any cost, ignored the limits on the sale of hard liquor, and on workers' days off sold vodka right out of cars in the Biisk market. The latter consequently became a unique club for all area drunks, for everyone knew that at the market, and especially on Sundays, it was possible to get alcohol without any trouble. Plus, it provided a convenient location for the immediate enjoyment of vodka. The market thus was filled with potentially volatile social material. Not surprisingly, hostile personal relations developed between the police and local hooligans. Yet the obvious solution was ignored. A drunken mob in the market might supply large numbers of detainees for drunkenness and hooliganism to the local jail, yet Biisk authorities in the course of an ordinary campaign against alcoholism did not attempt the obvious—that is, stop the sale of alcohol in the market.

During the morning of June 25, a police unit consisting of District Commissioner Zosim and Officer Leizerzon was occupied with normal business. They composed protocols about the violation of public order and hauled in two drunks to the police station. Market day could easily have ended normally, if only the head of the Trubnikov family from the Biisk State Grain

215

Farm had not gotten it into his head to go off to the city to buy a car or a motorcycle, carrying with him a sum of money quite large for those days—2,580 rubles.

The Trubnikov Family: A Trip to the District Center to Buy a Car

Nikolai Mikhailovich Trubnikov worked as a carpenter. In 1947, at age thirty-eight, he had been arrested and convicted at the height of Stalin's repressive campaign against pilfering of state property. On June 25, 1961, he came to the Biisk market with his wife Mariia, a housewife, and his son-in-law, A. Prilepskii, with the aim of purchasing a used car. But the Trubnikovs did not have any luck, and in the end did not buy a car.* Before leaving, though, they ran into friends, a married couple by the name of Safronov. In the tradition of the Biisk market, they all finished off about two liters of vodka in a nearby garden, though it was chiefly the men who drank. After a pleasant meal celebrating their meeting, the women went off to the bathroom. Mariia Trubnikov gave the bag with the money over to the care of the son-in-law. The men left the market and went to the bus stop. On the way, Trubnikov was cursing quite loudly, which attracted the attention of Zosim and Leizerzon to the merry group. When the police demanded that they "stop their outrageous behavior," Trubnikov let loose a torrent of swearing. When Zosim and Leizerzon tried to take him to the market police station, Nikolai Trubnikov, who possessed great physical strength, began to resist. His son-in-law came to his assistance, but quickly found himself tied up by the officers.

Officer Leizerzon and a volunteer policeman Ognev took the son-in-law Prilepskii (along with the bag of money!) to the police guard room. Let us now look at the situation through the eyes of Trubnikov: Two policemen had taken his son-in-law away, and the latter, along with the money had disappeared into the bowels of the police station. Agitated by alcohol and vexed over not having protected the family savings, Trubnikov remained alone with Zosim. Trubnikov decided to resolve his dilemma by attacking the policeman. The officer on duty at the market police station learned about the fight and sent a car with two coworkers to the scene, who then detained Trubnikov. But already his cries had attracted a crowd of idlers, composed primarily of the habitual drunken patrons of the Biisk market. They clearly sympathized

---

*Buying a car in the USSR at that time was quite complicated. To buy a new car required official permission and putting one's name on a list. It could take years for a person's name to move to the top. Hence, the Trubnikovs hoped to buy a used car for cash directly from someone in the market, but on this day they could not find any that suited them.—E.M. and V.K.

with Nikolai Trubnikov, since they themselves had all been in his situation at some point in the past. Threats to free the prisoner by force rang out. Trubnikov took off running, and Zosim shot his pistol into the air, forcing the crowd to retreat. The escapee was tied up and shoved into the police wagon, but he continued to struggle to break loose, crying out that the police were beating him. He demanded the return of an astronomical sum of money he now alleged had been stolen from him—30,000 rubles. This was actually more than ten times the sum the Trubnikovs had brought with them. Like a snowball, these unfolding events began rolling down the mountain, picking up speed and volume the entire way.

Mariia Trubnikova: "Let My Husband Go and Give Us Our Money Back!"

While Trubnikov was being put in the police wagon, his wife, Mariia Petrovna, appeared on the scene. She understood only one thing: The police were detaining her husband, her son-in-law had disappeared, and she had no idea where the family savings were. Trubnikova exclaimed, "Why are you arresting my husband?" then grabbed Zosim's shirt and tore it. As the crowd pushed Mariia Petrovna into the wagon, she was screaming, "Thieves, parasites, you have taken our money, police like you should be killed," "Thieves, give us our money back." She spit at Zosim and tore his shoulder straps from his uniform. In the end, the angry woman was nonetheless pulled back out of the police wagon. Then Mariia Petrovna climbed up on top of it, as if it were a podium, and cried out: "We earned that money honestly, and these bastard policemen have stolen it."

Mariia Trubnikova was completely focused on the lost savings. Her husband had already informed her that their son-in-law had the money, but the woman was not pacified. After all, the police had taken away the son-in-law. This agitated housewife would not even calm down when one of the policemen assured her that the money had been found, for she needed to see the money with her own eyes. Besides, in all probability, she did not have even a grain of trust in the words of a policeman.

Nikolai Trubnikov then threw fuel on the fire. He escaped from the police wagon and ran down one of the streets adjacent to the market. He stopped an ambulance and announced to all who were listening: "Police officers have beaten me and stolen my money." After the medical personnel bandaged his head and his arm, Trubnikov returned to the market in this militant guise, shouting out, "Now I will get even with those who beat me." Failing to see his wife, he climbed up onto the police wagon, which by this time rioters had overturned. Waving his arms, Trubnikov addressed the public. Witnesses provided several different versions of his short speech, but the common motif was "We must attack Them [the police]."[1]

The confrontation between the Trubnikov family and the police would hardly have turned into a mass riot if new ringleaders had not immediately emerged from the crowd to lead a defense of the "rightful cause." Several persons shaped the physiognomy of the uprising. One of these, Vitalii Lisin, is particularly notable. He was the first to challenge a group of drunken hooligans to seize the police wagon, free the detained man, and "kill the police officers." It was precisely his actions that at a critical moment turned the private conflict between the Trubnikovs and the police into a mass riot.

Lisin belonged to that category of persons for whom World War II had been especially harsh. Few from the generation born in 1924 (the year of Lisin's birth), who encountered the war at age seventeen, even survived. Vitalii Lisin was lucky, for he remained alive, but he lost his leg and became an invalid. During the time of these events in Biisk, he did not work anywhere and had three children under the age of thirteen.[2] Obviously, like several other war invalids, he had been unable to adapt to civilian life and to his own mutilation. Instead, he grew embittered and turned to drink.

Another instigator of the riots was Ivan Liakhov, half-parasite, half-vagrant, angry at life and at the police. From 1953 on, Liakhov did not work anywhere and did not have a permanent place of residence.[3] He himself did not take part in the violence and the beatings, but he did everything he could to incite the crowd's actions, including calling for murder. Trying to act stealthily, Liakhov followed events closely and at specific moments prompted the rioters to act. The disabled veteran, Bairam Kukoev, played an analogous role as instigator.[4] Kukoev, "without using physical force," in the course of several hours inflamed the crowd with his cries: "We must tear them to pieces." "It is necessary to kill them." "This should have been settled a long time ago." "People, attack them."

Mikhail Melnikov, also an invalid, was an old nemesis of Zosim and Leizerzon.[5] Known for his love of drinking, he earned his living at the market as a petty trader of handmade objects. The police had detained him more than once on charges of petty speculation, as well as for petty hooliganism. Significantly, Melnikov was later tried not simply for participation in the unrest, but for "carrying out repeated acts of hooliganism." From the very beginning of the conflict, he clearly rejoiced in the opportunity to settle accounts, and at the moment of the attack of the crowd on Zosim, he shouted: "The bastard has been caught—beat him, so he will not destroy our lives anymore."[6]

The driver Stanislav Kosykh fell among the rioters in a rather banal fashion. He had been out drinking with friends. Upon leaving the market, he saw the noisy crowd and responded to someone's request for him to help "push the [police] car over."[7] In general, Kosykh was a rather common type of rank-and-file participant in mass disorders. Easily swayed, infantile and irresponsible, he quickly submitted to someone's else's will and with maniacal persistence followed the program laid out by others, even showing ingenuity in doing this. It was Kosykh who suggested detaching the front wheels in order to turn over the police car more easily, and who, fully caught up in the spirit of violence, "cursed, smashed the body of the car with a piece of iron, and then while hitting it all along the car, struck Zosim on the temple with one of the blows and knocked him down."[8]

Similar to the psychological type of "yes-man with initiative" was a metal worker by the name of Nikolai Chentsov.[9] After drinking with friends, he joined the rioters at the very beginning of the disorders, when the crowd had liberated Trubnikov from the police wagon. Later he explained his actions as epically simple: "People were making noise, they were throwing rocks, some guy gave me a rock and I also threw it at the car. I took a second rock and threw it at the window. I jumped onto the car, Zosim yelled at me and I spit in his face. Leizerzon ran past me and I knocked him on his back."[10] Chentsov also suggested lifting up the hood and cutting the wire so that the police car could not get away.[11] In the course of events, he became increasingly cruel and aggressive. When Zosim tried to bandage his head with the remnants of his torn shirt, Chentsov tore off this self-made bandage which, was now drenched with the streaming blood of the policeman.[12]

Local Authorities: An Attempt at Negotiations and the Introduction of Troops

With the help of Kosykh and other firebrands, the mob managed to overturn the police car, and then the rampaging hooligans tried to push Zosim out of the overturned vehicle. At this point, before the riot had acquired full strength, local authorities hoped to negotiate with the crowd in good faith. But people simply whistled at the chairman of the city executive committee, a man by the name of Garkavyi, and drove him away from the overturned car, now serving as a temporary podium. The crowd had already achieved that level of riot hysteria when they listen only to their own voices. Even attempts to disperse the crowd with fire-engine hoses did not help, for the hooligans simply cut the hoses, and the fire brigade had to leave the scene ingloriously.

One notable episode stands out amid the attempts of local authorities to negotiate with the rioters. The deputy chief of police, speaking before the crowd, was introduced as a party official, thereby concealing his connection to the police, an act subsequently criticized as indecisive.[13] Yet behind this seemingly insignificant act stands in reality an instinctive understanding by the wise policeman Kliagin that the aggressiveness of participants in disorders is actually selective. He was counting on the greater legitimacy of Communist Party authority, cognizant that the police had already lost all capacity to command obedience. Consequently, belonging to the police deprived one of all chances of communicating rationally with the rioters. The same logic lay behind an order stating that the twenty-eight policemen who were sent to the market should dress in civilian clothing.[14] Although some people were at first ready to separate the "good" policemen, whom one could forgive, from the "bad," whom it was necessary to "kill," just simply belonging to the police during a riot was its own kind of "mark of Cain," which alienated a person from the populace.

In their hostility toward any authority, certain ringleaders of the disorders in Biisk clearly tried to implant a more generalized image of the enemy in the consciousness of the crowd. They sensed that while the city party committee or the city executive committee continued to be distinguished in the minds of the rioters from the "bastard police," participants in the unrest would be potentially willing to negotiate with authorities. Thus, the young metal worker Iurii Chernyshev, who was well known in the city as a hooligan and an old nemesis of the police,[15] during Garkavyi's speech scornfully threw radishes at him, clearly lowering the dignity of the chairman's speech. In the statements of Liakhov, as well, there were several hints at criticism of the regime as a whole ("dissatisfaction with the existing order," "dissatisfaction with Soviet power"). It was specifically Liakhov who uttered one of the most conscious phrases pronounced by participants in the violence: "Thieves, let us have milk, or we will have to beat you and kill you, people are being robbed."[16] The program of the rioters did not rise any higher than Liakhov's "give us milk," though this does not mean that among the five hundred people taking part in the riot, there were not reasons for participating other than a desire for revenge against the police. But the collective subconscious did not raise this concealed dissatisfaction and secret murmuring to the level of conscious protest. The crowd simply raged through blind alleys of coarse swearing and malicious insults.

Official attempts to negotiate ended in a complete failure due to certain social-psychological mechanisms that created full alienation between the two groups of actors. The crowd's ringleaders drew a line sharply between "Us" and "Them." Some activists such as Petr Lukianov, with two prior convictions for theft and for assault,[17] literally hammered into the consciousness of the crowd images of "vile beasts" and "fascists" who were hostile to the people. Finally recognizing the futility of further negotiations, authorities turned for help to the military. They called in troops, but until the salutary arrival of the soldiers, the life of the district commissioner Zosim hung on a thread. All of the unsuccessful negotiations and discussions had taken place against a backdrop of shooting, blood, and brutal violence.

For a long time, the crowd could not reach its own victim—the commissioner Zosim, who with his last bit of strength had beaten off the attacking hooligans, all the while threatening them with his gun. At this moment the mob even hesitated. But then another new activist emerged to intervene in the events, the driver Mikhail Pankin, with repeated arrests for petty hooliganism.[18] On the day of the disorders, Pankin had shown up at the market square happily drunk just at the moment when the authorities were trying to talk the crowd into dispersing. According to eyewitnesses, it was after his interference in the events that the rioters again moved toward the automobile in which Zosim and Leizerzon were sitting.[19] According to the story of Leizerzon, Zosim asked Pankin for help. Upon assuring the policeman, "Sure, I will help you," Pankin jumped into the car, seized Zosim by the arm and then grabbed his throat. Zosim fell, and when Pankin tried to take the pistol from him, it fired a shot.[20]

As he crawled out of the car with the pistol, Pankin confronted the police chief Ovchinnikov, who immediately took the weapon away from him. Pankin himself later claimed that he gave up the gun voluntarily, but the majority of eyewitnesses failed to corroborate this. In reality there were two shots. The first lightly wounded Pankin and the second wounded Z. Sokolov, who had followed Pankin into the car. As a result of his wound, Sokolov died in the hospital without ever regaining consciousness.

The crowd had become fully brutalized. It finally succeeded in pulling Zosim and Leizerzon from the car. A bloody mob trial grew imminent, but at this moment soldiers appeared in the market and helped the police to safeguard Zosim. Many hooligans resisted desperately, and Iurii Chernyshev kicked one of the police officers in the groin. Zosim's rescuers transferred him, badly beaten, to an ambulance, but the invalid Lisin, who climbed up on top and banged the vehicle with his crutch, prevented it from conveying the wounded man immediately from the scene. The angry mob pulled out the medical attendants from the ambulance and then threw Zosim on the ground.[21] Lisin cried out, "Trample him!" and the crowd brutally beat the tormented Zosim. Lisin joined in the attack, and his face, clothes, and boots were smeared with the blood of the victim. Even the soldiers could not stop this hysterical murder, only managing to save Leizerzon from being beaten.[22] Finally, Lisin decided that Zosim was dead and gave the command: "Well, enough is enough, it is done."[23]

Upon achieving its goal, the crowd dispersed. Five hours after the beginning of the conflict, the joint efforts of the police and the military finally ended the bloody rampage.[24]

The Investigation and Trial

An open show trial was held in Biisk, a device that was becoming fashionable in the early 1960s. The results of the investigation and show trial were intended to demonstrate the "renegade character" and "beastly nature" of enemies of the regime, and thereby exert a sobering effect on potential rebels. In reality, this tactic of educating the people through negative examples very quickly revealed its ineffectiveness.

During the 1940s and 1950s, the specific feature of suppressing disorders, riots, and uprisings had been the silence of authorities, accompanied by typically harsh reprisals. No one was to know about the proceedings, and any attempts to spread rumors were cruelly suppressed. Considering the size of the country, simply hushing up events was a sufficiently effective means of localizing the conflict, for it was difficult for news to leak out to other areas. The Soviet regime had created an effective system of control over information. Furthermore, the party leadership always had sufficient time for the "taking of measures." In the majority of cases, the signal to rise up took too long to reach potentially volatile groups interested in revolt or regions that were predisposed for mass unrest. Only rumors could counter the state's control over information. By the early 1960s, however, the spread of radio across the country had made another source of information available— Western radio broadcasts to the Soviet Union. But even these could make use only of rumors. Even if Western voices had tried to aggravate the situation by publicizing news of popular uprising, the regime had an effective system for jamming broadcasts. Furthermore, Western broadcasters had little access to those who were ready to confront the state. All of this inevitably would have cut off any reports about inspirational acts of resistance, and by the time Western radio stations became substantially more accessible, the social and political situation in the country had changed. A symbiosis of the people and the state had emerged, and the predisposition for conflicts reached the lowest possible level.

The new Khrushchevian practice of public trials for participants in public disorders was partially spurred by vague hopes for the educational and deterrent effect of such processes. But this stick had no carrot. Although open trials could intimidate people, they could also have the opposite effect. For many aggrieved persons, knowledge that they were not alone in their hatred for the state could galvanize them into action. Open judicial processes also proved to law-abiding citizens that it was better not to be connected with the authorities and thereby help tighten the noose around the necks of those incriminated. Thus, publicity and openness proved to be problematic for the regime, which in this case did not have any ideological trump cards besides the false "all-national indignation" of official "vanguard–workers." According to the laws of social psychology, open trials of participants in mass disorders could impart to the actions of insurgents and rioters a more serious political meaning than what they had in reality.

Nonetheless, in 1961 the authorities were still pursuing their propagandistic experiments, though the preparation and conduct of the trials actually followed old ideological and political scenarios. The judicial sentences for cases of mass disorders to a great degree were predetermined in high party offices, not in the courtroom. Rather than showing any capacity for being just, the state demonstrated each time that it could be menacingly dangerous and cruel.

At the beginning of September, the first trial of defendants in the Biisk case took place. The investigation strove to fulfill the desire of the top bosses as quickly as possible. To accomplish this, the case was divided into two groups. The first show trial involving seven defendants, including the Trubnikovs, was the main focus. The investigation that prepared the indictment was carried out hurriedly with little concern for quality or truth, preferring to leave certain questions unanswered, such as the fate of the Trubnikovs' money. The trial lasted three days, September 5 to 7, and took place in a club that seated three hundred people, while outside on the street, authorities set up a loudspeaker.[25] One month later, the trial of the second group of defendants took place.

Three instigators of the disorders were sentenced to death, though subsequently the punishment was lightened, and the rest received long terms of twelve to fifteen years imprisonment. Local bosses, whose official violations and negligence had created a situation in Biisk conducive to the rise of mass unrest, escaped for the most part with only a mild scare—party reprimands. Only one person, the deputy head of the city police department, was fired for "displaying indecisiveness in the liquidation of disorders and for failure to struggle against the violators of public order."[26]

Chapter 12

The Phenomenon of Novocherkassk: Part One

The Social and Political Context of the Novocherkassk Uprising

For a long time, the riots in this city in Southern Russia have served as a symbol of popular resistance to the Soviet regime. "Novocherkassk" constitutes a unique hieroglyph that raises in modern Russia a whole complex of negative emotions and images regarding the Soviet past. But over the years the symbolism of Novocherkassk has lost connection with the actual facts of the uprising. The opening of archives and the publication of recently declassified secret documents, along with the appearance of journalistic accounts of the events, have spurred the first steps toward a multifaceted study of this issue. Both Russian and Western scholars are presently conducting research into the Novocherkassk uprising that will yield a whole series of books and articles. This chapter and the one following present only a preliminary reconstruction and analysis of the Novocherkassk events within the general context of urban unrest during the Khrushchev and Brezhnev eras.

The official version of events in Novocherkassk—as laid out by Presidium member F.R. Kozlov* in his speech over Novocherkassk radio on June 3, 1962, and by the subsequent indictments and convictions of participants in the uprising—blamed hooligan and criminal elements, as well as secret and overt anti-Soviet forces, for misleading naive workers and directing them against the regime. But by the 1960s this explanation no longer seemed convincing and ideologically effective. Given how widespread popular indignation over the 1962 price increases had been, these

*See note, page 9.

events in Novocherkassk were large enough in scale that, if the population of the entire country had found out about them, or even the official version of them, then the phenomenon of Novocherkassk could have turned into a chronic disease. News about such large-scale uprisings could encourage people to believe that revolt against the regime was indeed possible, and could thereby provide an inspiring example for those who were dissatisfied. If such dissatisfied people make up the entire country—for no one really likes it when wages are lowered and prices rise—then it is better for the regime to forgo the possible intimidating effect of public trials and harsh convictions of instigators and keep the events a secret. Therefore, despite the open show trials of participants in Novocherkassk, authorities tried to keep information about the events confined within the city limits, beyond which knowledge of the uprising was cloaked in a veil of silence. They intimidated the city's residents enough that they were afraid to openly discuss the results of the trials, especially since everyone knew that disguised KGB agents and police officers had been secretly photographing those involved in the Novocherkassk events.

In the final account, within their own "family" circle, the Communist rulers were satisfied with the rather artless version crafted by their own ideological and juridical servants. But for external purposes, they retained their habitual silence. The leaders were confident, and not without reason: The longer the population remained ignorant of events similar to those in Novocherkassk, the longer the great Soviet myth about the "indissoluble union of party and the people" would continue to operate.

Although the Novocherkassk uprising has long been transformed into a symbol of popular resistance to the Soviet regime, in reality there was nothing exceptional or unique about what occurred in the course of three summer days in 1962. As shown in previous chapters, there were other cases of spontaneous strikes and antigovernment demonstrations, with red flags flying and even with revolutionary songs blaring, to say nothing of pogroms against police departments or CPSU party committee offices, symbolic actions such as the "defilement" of leaders' portraits, or physical violence against state officials and sober-minded residents; nor was there anything special about the anti-Soviet leaflets, slogans, and statements that accompanied the disorders. Even the scale of the riots in Novocherkassk was not unique, for although larger than other urban uprisings in European Russia, they were smaller, for example, than the riots in Georgia in 1956.

Moreover, the extreme brutality of the authorities does not distinguish the Novocherkassk events nor does it define their unique symbolic meaning. Before Novocherkassk there already had been much shooting and bloodshed, as well as vindictive "justice" applied against the ringleaders of urban unrest. Neither does the significance of Novocherkassk lie in the direct purposefulness of the protest, the largely working-class composition of the participants, or the fact that the actions of Novocherkassk residents were more conscious and organized when compared to other such disturbances.

Instead, there are only two circumstances that make the unrest in this southern town exceptional. In the first place, the disturbances unfolded against a backdrop of mass dissatisfaction with the policies of the state and were not, as was usually the case, a response to an isolated situation in one individual city or settlement. With calls for strikes and uprisings ringing out simultaneously throughout the country,[1] Novocherkassk represents the height of the popular dissatisfaction provoked by the decisions of the Khrushchev leadership. Only the timing was specific to Novocherkassk—the beginning of June 1962, immediately after the publication of a CPSU appeal on the price increases. In the second place, for the first and last time the party hierarchy (Presidium members Mikoian and Kozlov) took a direct role in organizing the suppression of the disorders, which meant that the top political leadership, and not local authorities, were fully responsible for the shootings. In Novocherkassk, the regime basically "tripped itself up."

In order to understand the hysterical reaction of authorities to the events in Novocherkassk, it is necessary to consider the negative information inundating the supreme leadership after the announcement of the price increases. Calls for uprisings and strikes at the beginning of June, reports of antigovernment leaflets and statements, as well as insults addressed to Khrushchev personally, were coming in from everywhere. Yet party leaders were genuinely startled by this wave of popular anger. Significantly, it was at this critical moment that their attention was drawn to Novocherkassk, the place where popular passions reached their peak. The party leadership and the KGB, however, refused to admit that there had been any strategic or tactical miscalculation. They rejected as delusions any alarming thoughts that their social-economic policy was incorrect, that there was a crisis of faith in the state, or that problems with food and high prices were the classic cause not only of strikes and rebellions, but also of revolutions.

A report of the deputy KGB chairman dated June 7, 1962, concerning the mass disorders in Novocherkassk noted that in the place where the strike began, the Novocherkassk Budenny Electric Locomotive Construction Works (NEVZ), even prior to the unrest "several workers in the body-assembly shop had come to the factory, but for three days had refused to do any work, demanding from the directors improvement in work conditions." In other words, the Novocherkassk workers had previous experience with strikes, and furthermore they had ample reason for dissatisfaction and even indignation. At the beginning of 1962, work norms had been revamped by the plant administration and "as a result wages for several categories of workers decreased by up to 30 percent." Another key circumstance that helped to ignite the conflict was the personality of the director of NEVZ, B.N. Kurochkin, who in particular aroused the hostility of workers.[2]

The KGB only touched the surface of the events without even beginning to probe the critical minutiae that are essential for understanding the particular predisposition of these NEVZ workers for extreme forms of protest. In his contemporary account of the unrest, I. Mardar has focused attention on these additional aggravating factors. Formally, NEVZ was considered the leading and most successful factory in Novocherkassk, but in reality, it was one of the most technically backward. Heavy physical labor predominated, and everyday conditions were unsatisfactory, with a shortage of restrooms and frequent breakdowns in the water supply. Wages for most workers were low. As a result, there was a high turnover of labor, and the administration readily and indiscriminately accepted anyone for work, including those whom no other employer would hire, particularly criminals released from imprisonment. According to the information of Mardar, among the workers at NEVZ were persons who had come from remote places of exile and who were directly antagonistic to the state, such as depossessed former kulaks and persons forcibly resettled during collectivization and World War II.[3]

Although the government did pay attention to the high concentration of former prisoners in the city, the significance of the criminal component in the unrest should not be exaggerated. Among the ringleaders who were put on trial, there were very few persons who had a serious criminal past. Furthermore, at this time the hooligans, petty thieves, and other such "populist" criminals numbered in the millions, and were more a part of everyday life of the Soviet people than of the criminal world. Even the purely statistical tally of former criminals living in Novocherkassk, who officially numbered 1,586 people on June 1, is clearly not impressive, especially considering the fact that 12,000 people worked at NEVZ alone, and there were several other large factories as well.[4] "A city of criminals" that rose up against the state in the spirit of Bakuninist revolutionary rebelliousness makes a pretty myth, but it has little in common with reality. It is another matter that the high concentration of former criminals in specific places and at specific times, such as the steel foundry shop and the first shift, frequently intensified the conflict in the initial stages of the unrest.

A much more important factor was the food crisis in the city. There was not enough meat in the stores, and one had to wait in line at the market overnight just to get potatoes. Some were even reduced to eating fried potato peelings. At the beginning of May, when the work norms were increased and wages decreased at NEVZ,[5] life became completely unbearable, especially if one had a family, and there were many who did among the ringleaders of the unrest. It had been difficult enough, even without the price increases, to make ends meet. The final straw came on May 31 when, in spite of the price increases anticipated for the following day, which the directors were well aware of, piece rates were lowered for production in the steel foundry shop of NEVZ.[6] This senseless action forged the first link in the chain of circumstances that would lead workers and the state to a tragic mass shooting. But it is only in retrospect that one realizes how each of these circumstances could have been avoided had the administrators been wiser and the workers more patient.

June 1, 1962: A Day of Alarm Sirens

In the Public Garden in Front of the Steel Foundry Shop

Early in the morning of June 1, 1962, the Soviet people learned that retail and wholesale prices for meat and meat products would rise. Understandably, no one expressed any special joy at this announcement. Law-abiding and prudent citizens nonetheless tried to adjust to the new unpleasant reality, thinking that perhaps there would be more meat products in state stores. But it was, to borrow a KGB phrase, "narrow-minded opinion" that predominated in everyday conversations on June 1. At least this is how the KGB described the egalitarian ideas typical for this time period ("the prices should be kept where they are and the wages of higher-salaried persons lowered") as well as the lack of popular support for the universal mission of world communism ("we should stop helping underdeveloped socialist countries").[7] The majority justifiably thought: problems have emerged, let the government resolve them, but not at our expense. If it cannot, then this means that it is a bad government!

Undoubtedly, the eight to ten workers who gathered in the steel foundry shop of NEVZ at 7:30 A.M. on June 1, 1962, to discuss the announcement of the CPSU Central Committee and the Council of Ministers about the price increases spoke in these or similar tones. Considering that on the previous day these workers had learned that their pay rates would be lowered, it is possible to propose that what they actually said was even more inflammatory than what the KGB considered possible to report to the Central Committee. Others soon joined this group of disgruntled workers. The shop foreman called for the twenty to twenty-five people now gathered to return to work, but they sent him away and continued the discussion in the factory garden.[8]

News of the work stoppage reached the NEVZ director Kurochkin, who then went straight to the "troublemakers." The crowd grew as other workers came to the garden when they heard about the director's appearance. People stated their claims clearly and forcefully, but Kurochkin's response only aroused the anger of the workers still more: "So, if you do not have enough money for meat and sausage, then use offal for your meat pies [*esh 'te pirozhki s liverom*]."[9] This phrase soon gained notoriety and outraged the entire factory. Too much bureaucratic, "pot-bellied [*tolstopuzyi*]" haughtiness and contempt lurked behind Kurochkin's cynicism.

In the end, the director managed to get away from the agitated crowd and return to his office. By break time for the first shift, between three to five hundred people had already gathered in the garden. The crowd moved to the square in front of the NEVZ administration offices and demanded the director. The crowd needed an outlet for its resentment, as it was already impossible to relieve the tension simply by yelling and cursing. Various people began spontaneously to seek a specific ideological and organizational form for the protest. A worker by the name of Udovkin ran to the shop and wrote down on paper an inflammatory slogan. A Communist Party member in the crowd tried to take away the seditious appeal, frightening Udovkin, who tore up and burned his creation.[10]

The Compression Station. The Appearance of the Slogan "We Want Meat, Milk, and a Wage Increase"

Having realized in time the potential dangers, Udovkin did not end up as one of the ringleaders of the disorders. Other people, more decisive and daring, advanced instantaneously to the role of leaders in the first hours of the embryonic strike. Among those who had begun to gather around the administration offices were several potential instigators who rallied behind them other agitated and indignant workers. Some distinguished themselves from the crowd by setting off the plant alarm siren. As they explained later, when they learned about the price increases "they decided to express somehow their dissatisfaction to the administration."[11] Simply communicating their protest and indignation was the workers' only purpose in the beginning.

Viacheslav Chernykh helped to drive events forward, though he had turned up at the center of the unfolding strike entirely by accident. This young man, a son of a miner, had completed nine grades of education and was working in the blacksmith shop of NEZV. Lacking any criminal record, he could hardly have had anything in common with hoodlums and paupers who bore grudges against the state. "I dreamed of being a Soviet man and strived to be one,"[12] Chernykh later said. He romantically subscribed to the ideological myths of the Soviet period. Upon completing seven years of school, he had voluntarily gone to the Virgin Lands with the Komsomol. Following his demobilization from the army, Chernykh had come to work in Novocherkassk. In August 1961, he had married and, together with his wife, rented a small room. He also helped his mother with his wages, for she was remodeling her home at this time. The young couple unquestionably had a hard life. The waiting list for a free state apartment was lengthy, and it would be a long time before their names would move to the top. Nonetheless, they retained an optimistic attitude toward all their problems. During the time of the riots in Novocherkassk, the wife was pregnant. After his arrest, Chernykh suffered for her above all, worrying about her health and anxiously awaiting the birth of their child.[13]

What threw Chernykh into the whirlwind of events was above all his spontaneous protest against the injustice of the state. He found inspiration in the images of collective activism created by Soviet propaganda. He modeled himself on the behavior of revolutionary workers depicted in Soviet films who during strikes and walkouts used alarm sirens, slogans, and posters. In addition, he was also responding to the difficulties of his own life:

> In order to buy meat, butter, and meat products it was necessary to go to another city, to Shakhty or Rostov. Of course, automatically the question arose, why was the city so poorly supplied? There was only one answer. The local organs of government were not paying any attention to the needs of the laborers (since then this has been discussed in the press). When the events occurred, I did not understand their meaning and consequences, and under the influence of all of these circumstances I made a mistake.[14]

Chernykh's mistake was that he, "with a group of people numbering around fifteen . . . came to the compression station" and turned on the plant siren to full power. The employees at the station tried to stop the strikers. This conflict between the strikers and "sober-minded" workers would be repeated in various forms throughout the Novocherkassk events, for the workers were not united, although the price increases and lowered wages in one form or another affected them all. Some joined the strike and imparted to it dynamism and aggressiveness, while others, careful and loyal to the state, tried to stop it and bring people to their senses. The factories of Novocherkassk served as an arena of struggle between aggressive critics of the state and those who still trusted it, or who, at the very least, feared being connected with the strike.

Such confrontations between different models of behavior in a stressful situation continually altered the physiognomy of the crowd and the shape of events.

Ultimately, these conflicts were resolved, crudely speaking, by those who shouted louder than the others. Sometimes great courage was required from the moderates in order to oppose the destructive onslaught of the "hooligan-extremists." Paradoxically, though, even these moderates had already contributed to the collective crowd psychosis simply through their presence on the streets.

Viacheslav Chernykh, who activated the alarm siren, attracting workers from other shops and inhabitants of surrounding settlements to the scene, also penned the slogan "We Want Meat, Milk, and a Wage Increase,"[15] which, according to several sources, also included a demand for housing.[16] A painter in the NEVZ foundry shop, V. Koroteev, helped Chernykh write this slogan which, hoisted on a high steel beam and visible from afar, became the rallying cry of the workers' protest. Koroteev, unlike Chernykh, did have a criminal past, having been convicted for apartment theft and hooliganism,[17] and thus had more reason to hate the state. In reality, however, Koroteev simply followed orders from a more active person.[18]

Shortly before noon, a large crowd of people approached the NEVZ administration building, forced their way through the courtyard, and went out into the square. At this time, officials from the city party committee and the NEVZ party committee, as well as KGB personnel, were all present at the plant. But according to the evidence accumulated by Mardar, they seemed paralyzed and failed to make any decisions at this time.[19] The first reports about "a row" at NEVZ had been sent to the police at around 10:00 A.M. One hour later, the army, police, and the KGB were already on alert,[20] but took no actions for a long time.

At the square by the NEVZ administration building, a crowd of three to five hundred people had come together. In groups they angrily discussed the new prices and the lowered wages. Rumors that were now beginning to spread actually represented a potential program of action: workers in another town had gone on strike, stopped a passenger train, and dismantled the rails.[21] Such reports always serve as an inspiration for participants in disturbances, showing them that they are not alone and that they will not be the only ones answerable for what takes place. In the end, such a "program" was fulfilled—a passenger train would in fact be stopped. But meanwhile, the crowd rhythmically chanted its main slogan: "Meat, Butter, and a Raise in Wages."[22] One person whistled and another shouted insults addressed to the NEVZ plant director.

The Stopping of the Passenger Train. The Spontaneous Meeting at the Railroad Tracks

The NEVZ administration building, where already by noon a large crowd had gathered, was located a hundred meters from the railroad tracks.[23] Thus, when people were talking about stopping a passenger train, there was a railroad right at hand. As people began to gather near the pedestrian tunnel that ran under the railroad, many were yelling: "We must stop the train!" Some boys crawled up onto pillars and whistled loudly.[24] At this time, according to the testimony of one of the witnesses, a banner was raised bearing the slogan about meat, butter, and a wage increase.[25]

People began constructing a barricade on the railroad tracks out of broken fencing. When a train appeared, the crowd tried to meet it, led by Komsomol member G. Polunina.[26] With the crowd following behind her, she picked up a red scarf that had fallen on the ground and tied it to a stick.[27] In the end, the red kerchief, now transformed into a flag flying high, ended up on the barricade that had been lain across the tracks. The passenger train from Saratov to Rostov stopped before reaching the barricade, and the crowd climbed up onto the locomotive. Among those who at this time attracted attention to themselves were the same Polunina and a metalworker by the name of F.F. Zakharov, an unmarried first-year correspondence student at the Novocherkassk Polytechnical Institute. Although the identity of the person who set off the alarm whistles from the locomotive is not clear, the investigation and trial accused Zakharov of this. Both of these youthful romantics in the end changed their minds and hurried to get away from the scene of the riots. Sakharov was not identified as a participant in any further disorders, while Polunina was seen only one more time, during the evening of that same day at the railroad tracks.[28]

With the sounding of the alarm whistles, the crowd around the train grew to over 4,000 people as curious onlookers gathered, including workers from other shops and residents of nearby villages and settlements.[29] Drunkards appeared, though from where they came no one knew (they must have been drinking from the morning on!), and from time to time fights broke out among them. As a result, after Zakharov and Polunina helped to stop the train and then disappeared in the crowd, other individuals who were completely different from these students in terms of psychology, age, and lifestyle moved to the forefront.

Two people attracted the attention of eyewitnesses through their heightened activism: a NEVZ worker by the name of Viktor Ukhanov, whose conviction in 1947 for petty theft of collective and state property had brought him ten years' imprisonment, and a worker named F.V. Fetisov, who had been sentenced in 1949 to two years' imprisonment. The rather vague but highly emotional speeches of these people who had bitter grievances against the state were recalled by many, although Ukhanov later wrote persistently in his appeals: "I did not make any kind of statements there."[30]

Viktor Ukhanov was a person with a damaged reputation. At work "he was evaluated positively" and no one bore him any special grudges.[31] But by his own admission, after his divorce, he had begun to drink heavily and behaved "very stupidly and recklessly." During the morning of June 1, Ukhanov had to go to work, but overslept after having gotten drunk the previous day. Deciding to cure his hangover with a drink, he went to a café, where he met a drinking buddy and had a mug of beer with him. Their conversation, of course, covered the increase in prices and the injustice of the authorities. While in the café, the friends heard the alarm whistle and decided to investigate. There on the tracks stood the immobile train, and coming out to greet them were three men yelling, "People are doing what is right, it is necessary for everyone to break ties with the party."

It is not entirely clear, but it is possible that the "comrade with whom he was drinking" was none other than F.V. Fetisov. On June 1, Fetisov had intended to visit his mother, but he never made it there, since he ran into friends and "got drunk."[32] Fetisov, according to the investigation and trial, "climbed up onto the front platform of the interrupted passenger train and, together with Ukhanov, repeatedly addressed the crowd with provocative speeches." Both were extremely drunk, and as Ukhanov said later, "what we said to the people, I do not remember."[33] But Ukhanov and Fetisov could have repeated what everyone around them was saying: "Rostov, Shakhty, Taganrog all support us, everyone is on strike," "They have raised prices for meat, butter, and milk," and so on. Approximately thirty minutes after this, Ukhanov approached his friend and said bitterly: "They may shoot me."[34] Fetisov did not make any kind of special programmatic declarations, but to the crowd's question, "Where are you climbing to, old man?" he answered passionately, "I am striving for my rights."[35] However, in striving for "his rights," Fetisov succeeded in cutting off the braking system of the stopped train, creating a serious danger for those surrounding it.

A spontaneous meeting developed around the immobile train. Someone used chalk to write on the diesel locomotive, "Trade Khrushchev for Meat."[36] Passengers remained inside the stuffy train without water while on the outside hooligans broke the glass in the cars. According to certain sources, those "who spoke out against the disorders were pushed aside and beaten." The crowd also assaulted the chief engineer of NEVZ, N.S. Elkin, who had tried to make his way to the locomotive to stop the whistles. There were "separate fights between drunks, bottles were thrown about, and the crowd rushed from side to side."[37]

In his recent memoirs, one of the participants in the Novocherkassk events, P.P. Siuda, praised highly the courageous behavior of chief engineer Elkin in the course of the riots. In 1962, Siuda was twenty-five years old and worked as a pipe fitter at NEVZ. While describing the inertia of the bosses in the first stage of the disorders, Siuda noted that Elkin did not make any promises or assurances, but continually encouraged the workers to end the uprising and return to work.[38] According to Siuda's memoirs, no one physically attacked the chief engineer, although in the trial Siuda himself had said that "when he came to the Electric Locomotive Construction Works, he saw workers beating up the chief engineer Elkin and he demanded with others that the beating cease."[39]

The stopping of the train, the blasting of its alarm whistles, the cries, and the spontaneous speeches of workers agitated NEVZ and the surrounding settlements. Employees from the second shift also stopped working and now flowed into the maelstrom of events. New ringleaders appeared. On June 1, V.I. Shcherbakov, a young lathe operator, had reported for work on the second shift in the wood shop of NEVZ. But he did not actually begin working, and instead drank vodka and wrote provocative statements which, though barely legible, were politically unambiguous: "Kolia, this is the beginning, the end is coming. Victory will be ours" (on the doors of the boss's office); "Greetings to the Bolsheviks, who have sold Russia out" (on the wall in the corridor).[40]

News of the growing strike spread to the nearby factories. One of those who tried to rally other workers was a lathe operator at NEVZ, S.E. Efremov. Married with two small children, and a CPSU member since 1959, Efremov had no prior convictions. He later stated that after lunch, when everyone had already quit working, he had gone home. On the way, he decided to look in at his old workplace, the instrument shop at the Nikolskii Factory, where he "talked with four workers about events at NEVZ and noted with irony that they lacked consciousness, for they were working, and therefore not supporting the NEVZ strikers. After being in the shop five to seven minutes, he went home, but the Nikolskii workers continued their labors."[41] The workers later recalled speaking with Efremov, and therefore he received a harsh sentence for his relatively innocent conversation. Dozens of other people who spread news of the strike at NEVZ all over town remained, fortunately for their sake, anonymous. But there is no doubt that insulting comments and challenges to join the mutinous NEVZ workers were heard many times that day all over Novocherkassk.

Several very colorful personalities intervened in the course of the events taking place near the immobile train, though they subsequently disappeared from the view of witnesses. The preliminary investigation paid special attention to the truck driver Efim Fedorovich Silchenkov. This man's life had been filled with misfortune, and at age forty-eight, he had four convictions. From 1933 to 1953, with a break only for the war, which he spent from beginning to end in the army, he was in prisons and labor camps. Efim Fedorovich spoke about his own mishaps:

I was born into a poor peasant family in Smolensk Oblast. I finished the village school [three grades.—V.K.]. In 1933 the famine drove me from the countryside to the city, where in my search for work and a piece of bread I was seized by the OGPU* organs (I was wearing bass shoes**) and was given a sentence of three years by default. . . . Exactly eleven days after my term ended, although I had come to the designated place [of exile], I again was seized and convicted by default . . . to a term of five years. In 1941, on June 30, at the end of my term I was sent to the front. . . . I was wounded four times and I have medals. I was demobilized at the rank of sergeant-major. After demobilization . . . not having any place where I could lay my head, and not having enough strength of my own, [feeling] joy over the victory and sorrow over my loneliness, I began to drink with anyone who turned up in public places. The end result was again prison, two years. In 1948, ten years and all the way until 1953. When I was freed by amnesty and my conviction repealed, I was thirty-eight years old. I went out to the gate and made an oath that I would never go back there again. I went to work at the Electric Locomotive Construction Works, where I mastered the specialty of joiner. I married and started a family. I received a nice apartment, and my wife worked in the cafeteria in the same plant. I was happy with life and breathed easy after all that had happened in the past. The spiritual as well as the physical wounds were healing in the recreation center or in the sanitarium. I arranged for a work pension, but the Rostov court overturned it.[42]

Silchenkov's own psychological profile reveals that he in no way longed for the role of instigator, but found himself sucked into the turbulence purely by chance and circumstance. In describing the events at NEVZ, he emphatically disassociated himself from the "scoundrels," the hooligans who were acting "arbitrarily, without any reason or rationale,"[43] and said that he "became a victim in a crowd that lacked social constraints."[44] To Silchenkov's misfortune, many witnesses saw him in this "crowd that lacked social constraints,"[45] and his four prior convictions made him an ideal scapegoat for the biased investigation and trial.

Silchenkov was accused of having induced the crowd to vote on whether or not to allow the train to pass.[46] According to the testimony of Silchenkov

---

*OGPU stands for the Joint State Political Administration, the security police organ from 1923 to 1934, replaced by the People's Commissariat of Internal Affairs (NKVD).—E.M.

**Bass shoes, or lapti, were similar to slippers and woven from the fibers of the linden tree. Since they were typically worn by peasants, they signified to OGPU officers that he had run away from a collective farm (to escape the famine) in defiance of the newly imposed passport system.—E.M.

himself, the matter unfolded as follows. At first, some unknown person demanded that he come down from the embankment, to which he answered: "Why should I come down, I am no different from you. I also defended the Motherland, and its interests are near and dear to me." Silchenkov shared what he had heard, that allegedly at the Khatunok Station the railroad tracks had been dismantled, "no matter what dire consequences there might be." But at this point Efim Fedorovich saw Communist acquaintances from the plant who were trying to let the train pass through the station. "For me it became clear," Silchenkov later stated, "that they knew more than I whether the tracks had been dismantled or not. So I cried out to the crowd: 'Comrades, let the train pass!' Voices rang out, 'Let the train pass!' And the locomotive gave the departure signal, and I then went home with my fellow workers."[47]

M.A. Zaletina, who worked as a cleaning person at NEVZ, also actively intervened in events around the stopped train. This woman, who had only four years of education and was married with three children (one of whom, due to the family's extreme poverty, had been placed in a children's home), poured out her own grievances to the crowd gathered at the train: "I receive thirty rubles, I have two children, and there is nothing to feed them, and my husband is dead." At this moment Zaletina blamed the Communists for her unhappy life: "Those pot-bellied swine; we must attack the Communists."[48] Still another ringleader of the disorders on the railroad tracks was a metal worker and adjuster at NEVZ, I.D. Ivanov. A father of three children, Ivanov, like Zaletina, simply did not know how he was going to feed his family, and he sought an outlet for his frustration. To the request made to the crowd to let the train pass, Ivanov cried out that while the train still stood on the tracks, it would be possible to gather more people.[49]

At some point, the civilian police volunteers and Communists in the crowd finally got control of the situation and proposed that the train be sent along a back route. But this meant that it would have to pass by the Electric Locomotive Construction Works, that is, through a crowd of agitated workers, thereby opening up the possibility of new excesses. Fearing such, V.F. Gladchenko, a machinist in the experimental station at NEVZ and member of the Communist Party, while proposing that it would be better for the train to return to the preceding station, nonetheless impeded the movement of the locomotive. Eventually, later in the day, after the rioters had finally been pushed out of the train and taken down from the roof, the train ended up reversing direction and going back to the preceding station.[50] Authorities, however, subsequently rejected Gladchenko's version of events, and on July 19, 1962, he, like all of the other real and imaginary ringleaders of the disorders in Novocherkassk, was sentenced by the Rostov regional court to an unjustifiably stiff punishment—ten years imprisonment.[51]

The Confusion of the Authorities. Unsuccessful Attempts to Pacify the Crowd

By midafternoon, all the regional and city officials had already gathered at NEVZ, including the first secretary of the CPSU regional party committee, A.V. Basov.[52] The crowd had moved to the NEVZ administration building and was demanding explanations.[53] A split had already occurred among the strikers, as some tried to force their way into the administration building, while others demanded that the strike continue "but without hooliganism."[54] The actions of extremists, as often happens when passions reach their height, made the crowd's behavior appear more like a riot than a strike. But above all, it was the inaction of authorities that provoked a pogrom.[55]

In the final account, the crowd carried out two programs of action—both an extremist and a moderate one. While the moderates were demanding speeches from the authorities, the extremists began to storm the administration building.[56] Accompanying the attack was the symbolic defilement of the leader's (Khrushchev) portrait, which was carried out by a young romantic, a student lathe operator by the name of Anatolii Desiatnikov. Desiatnikov, who had no prior convictions, had wandered into the crowd during the lunch break of the first shift. He climbed up to the balcony of the administration building and, after several attempts, tore down the large portrait of Khrushchev from the facing. He then threw the defiled portrait to the ground, an act that the crowd wildly applauded, thereby expressing its view of the one who, in its opinion, was the main cause of all of the unhappiness in the country.[57]

The storming of the entrance door began next. Helping to lead the way was a young machinist, Gennadii Goncharov. Although "as a worker he had a positive evaluation,"[58] Goncharov had the reputation of being a rowdy troublemaker and was continually being reprimanded in factory meetings for violations of discipline. In January 1962, for example, he was drunk at work, swore coarsely, beat up a fellow worker, and at the same time even tried to thrash the foreman.[59] It was Goncharov who forced open the door to the administration building and punched a shop foreman named Nasonov, who had been trying to block the mob's entry. As they pushed their way into the building, other participants in the storming beat up an engineer and "destroyed furniture, broke glass and telephones, and tore down portraits."[60]

Participants in the attack did not consider their actions to be a pogrom. Few could say clearly why they had broken into the administration building. It was obvious, however, that the motives were neither revenge nor hooliganism, but a stubborn desire to force the bosses finally to hear the protest of the people: "We are not hooligans, we have demands."[61] Later, in one of the offices in the administration building, authorities found an informational bulletin, "Labor and Wages," on which one of the strikers had poured out his own frustrated soul: "You slog away, but do not receive anything for it."[62]

In the end the threatening actions of the extremists compelled the leaders who were blockaded in the building to make a quick decision. At 4:30 P.M., they set up loudspeakers on the balcony. Coming out to face the people were Basov, the first secretary of the CPSU regional party committee; Zametin, the chairman of the Rostov regional executive committee; Loginov, the first secretary of the Novocherkassk CPSU city party committee; and Kurochkin, the NEVZ director. The moderate program demanding speeches from the leaders had momentarily won, and the crowd prepared to listen. Basov, however, could not find anything better to say than to reread the Central Committee appeal concerning the price increases. An outburst of indignation followed: "We can read ourselves," and "You need to tell us how we are going to live when norms are lowered and prices raised." Zametin was not allowed to speak at all, and when the hated Kurochkin appeared (everyone already had heard about his "offal pies" statement), rocks, metal objects, and bottles came flying through the air toward the balcony. The extremists then renewed their attempts to break into the administration building.[63]

At this time, KGB agents who had infiltrated the crowd "uncovered the ringleaders and secretly photographed them."[64] Several undercover policemen were also engaged in such operations, though one of them was unmasked by the crowd and beaten. "They got a hold of my identification card," the victim testified, "and read that I was a police lieutenant, and then some said: 'He should be hanged.'"[65]

But besides photographing the crowd, no special measures were taken to restore order. Within two hours, NEVZ was literally under the control of the strikers. According to Mardar's account, "feeling helpless, A.V. Basov shut himself up in one of the plant offices belonging to the first department and, in this way, became a hostage of the strikers." There is vague evidence that at 7:00 P.M., Basov again tried to calm the striking workers, but the crowd whistled, booed, and chased him from the balcony under a cloud of abuse.[66] It is not likely, however, that Basov made his speech at that time, for it does not correspond to the internal logic of events nor does it fit the KGB's chronology. By this point, police had already gotten involved in the matter, and the crowd was in the process of chasing them from the plant. This was not at all a suitable moment for such a speech.

It was party leader Bazov who, in the opinion of I. Mardar, let slip the chance to negotiate with the strikers. It was also Bazov who probably initiated the order to use troops right after he and other city leaders were blockaded in the administration building. Although the Charter of the Garrison-Guard Service (the 1960 edition) did not foresee the use of these troops to suppress urban unrest, Basov, who was a member of the District Military Council, had the right to issue an order to the commander of the Novocherkassk garrison.[67]

Yet the role of Basov should not be exaggerated. In his memoirs, the former deputy chief of the General Staff of the Northern Caucasus Military District, Major-General A.I. Nazarko, claimed that he urgently reported after 4:00 P.M. to I.A. Pliev, commander of the district, that local authorities were requesting the dispatch of troops to quell the disorders. Pliev listened to the report, but did not issue any orders before departing for Novocherkassk. Three hours later, the USSR minister of defense, Marshal R.Ia. Malinovskii, personally phoned the General Staff of the military district, but did not get Pliev. He then ordered: "Raise a formation. Do not use tanks. Restore order. Give me a report!"

Nazarko did not see any written documentation confirming this oral order, and he believes that probably there was no such document.[68] If the time of Malinovskii's call to the district headquarters given by Nazarko is correct, then it follows that this call came directly after information from Novocherkassk reached the CPSU Presidium. Thus the troops of the local garrison carried out orders from Moscow, not from Basov. Most importantly, Pliev simply could not have obeyed Basov without a directive from the minister of defense. Yet, since the higher party bosses were not yet involved in the resolution of the situation, on the first day of the riots the military authorities did not display any special activism and were certainly not in a hurry to bring in the police. Rather, in the opinion of P. Ivashutin, the deputy chairman of the KGB, the military acted with clear indecision.[69]

Even before the appearance of troops, Basov ordered the police to restore order at the plant, but "the police detachment numbering 200 uniformed cops that arrived was crushed and dispersed, and 3 policemen were beaten."[70] At the railroad tracks, strikers stopped a diesel locomotive, and again alarm whistles sounded. It was around this time that information about the events was sent directly to the Presidium, and only then, around 8.00 P.M., did soldiers appear. They had been dispatched primarily to rescue the hostages from the administration building—the bosses who were locked up and surrounded on all sides, above all the party secretary Basov. But the task of the soldiers did not include using weapons to suppress the disorders, since they did not even have live ammunition.[71]

During the interval between the first (using the police) and the second (using the local garrison) attempts to restore order by force, a meeting went on at the passenger tunnel that ran underneath the railroad near the NEVZ administration building. There a program of action was proclaimed. According to the investigation and trial, it was Ivan Sluzhenko, a poorly educated, nonparty longshoreman with no criminal record, who "provided the sound track" for this program. Sluzhenko was a good worker, but was known to have a volatile, unbalanced character. "He often yells out for no reason at all," a colleague at work later said about him, dubbing him "Ivan the Trouble-maker."

Sluzhenko turned up on the scene around eight o'clock in the evening. According to Ivan Petrovich's own testimony during his interrogation:

> I spoke to the crowd of people who had gathered at the square, calling for them to remain there until morning, and to not go to work. I said that we needed to send a delegation to the electrode factory and other plants, and to the neighboring towns, so that workers there would also stop working. And I proposed that on the next day, that is June 2, 1962, a demonstration be organized in the center of the city.[72]

In his appeal to the crowd not to go to work, Sluzhenko was subconsciously using a strong psychological argument, which immediately transformed the enemies of the strike into the "enemies of the people": "Whoever goes to work is a fascist."[73] Later, during his arrest, which occurred only three hours later, Sluzhenko cried out: "Brothers, help me, they are seizing the working class."[74] Given that Sluzhenko had been drinking all evening, at the meeting he could only repeat what he had heard from others around him, and he clearly was not fit to be one of the conscious agitators. But he certainly was unlucky, for the investigation later fabricated an accusation against him with the help of police witnesses.

The role of ideologue for the strikers belongs much more to Iurii Dementev, a third-year student at the Novocherkassk Polytechnical Institute who had just become the father of a baby girl. The investigation uncovered no criminal record nor any black marks in his past. After military service in Germany, he had worked for two years in Novocherkassk Chemical Factory No. 17. He had then entered the institute, where he found studying after a long interruption to be difficult. Therefore, the single negative factor contained in the prosecutor's file on Dementev was the unsatisfactory progress he had made in his studies.[75]

Dementev came to the NEVZ administration building during the evening on a bicycle from his family's village of Kamenolomnia, a long trip of nearly thirty kilometers. Iurii remained at the plant until nighttime, and then set off for his dormitory, where he did watch duty with other students in accordance with the curfew that had been imposed on the city. Early in the morning, he again rode his bicycle to see his family. But when he passed by the plant, he saw a friend who played on his soccer team, and began to converse with him and several others who came up to them. Interestingly, although at this moment the police were detaining everyone, they were still allowing such discussions after verifying identity.[76]

The main accusation against Dementev was connected with the program of action he proclaimed during the night from the top of the railroad passenger tunnel. Witnesses recalled a light-haired fellow in a checkered short-sleeve shirt who spoke in guttural tones, mispronouncing the letters "r" and "l" (this did describe Iurii Dementev, although another ideologue of the strike, P. Siuda, known as "guttural-speaking [kartavyi] Peter," also fit this description).[77] In his speech, Dementev allegedly urged the following steps: to send a delegation to the electric plant, cut off the gas line from the gas distribution station, post pickets outside the NEVZ administration building, gather the following morning, and go into the city in order to carry out an uprising there. Then seize the bank and the telegraph office and turn to the whole country with an appeal to overthrow the Soviet government. He called for breaking machines and proclaimed: "We are not alone, the workers of the Donbass, the miners of Rostov Oblast, and the workers of Rostov all support us."[78]

Iurii himself denied his guilt in the investigation and trial. He claimed that he had in fact come to NEVZ, but only in order to satisfy his curiosity. The only thing Dementev admitted to was that, after returning to the dormitory from the scene of the disorders, he told his roommates a joke, but presented it as if it were the truth. He told them that on the administration building, hanging in the place of the torn up portrait of Khrushchev, was a dead cat with the inscription: "I lived under Lenin, I pined away under Stalin, but under Nikita [Khrushchev] I died."[79]

Also playing an important role in the development of events on the evening of June 1 was young Sergei Sotnikov. After completing seven grades in school, he had begun work at NEVZ as a lathe operator, where he remained for seven years, with a break only for military service between 1956 and 1959, right up until his arrest for involvement in the Novocherkassk unrest. Sotnikov's father had died at the front in World War II, and his mother worked as a hospital nurse. A fully loyal and serious young man, Sotnikov was a member of the Communist Party and a commander of the shop unit of the volunteer civilian police corps.[80] In the Sotnikov family, which included two small daughters, there was much love and mutual understanding. There was no kind of criminal past weighing down this man's shoulders.[81]

Sotnikov did not go to work during the morning of June 1, but instead went off to fish. There in the traditional fellowship of fishermen, he drank vodka and toasted his comrades. When he returned home he learned immediately about the price increases and about the strike at NEVZ. This "conscious worker" then began to think about simple but vital issues: how he and his wife, who also worked at NEVZ, were going to live; how they were going to feed two young daughters if prices went up and wages fell; what were they going to do without furniture (in the attempt of the KGB investigator to describe the possessions of the family, it came out that "there is no property to describe");[82] and in particular, how there was not even any place for the young family to live, since apartments were not available. Chagrined, he drank still more vodka with a friend—almost two bottles between the two of them. Then, already drunk, he headed for NEVZ.[83] Fully in accordance with an old Russian proverb, everything that the sober Sergei Sotnikov had on his mind, the drunken Sotnikov expressed openly. But this does not mean that Sergei was acting unconsciously. Taking full responsibility for what happened, he continued to defend his view of events even after his arrest. During the inquest on the eve of the trial, it was noted: "Sotnikov conducted himself defiantly, in conversations declaring that in his own actions he supposedly expressed 'the interests of the working class.'"[84]

According to the inquest, it was Sotnikov who proposed that a delegation be sent to the electrical plant and to Factory No. 17 calling upon the workers to join the strike, and that a protest demonstration be organized. In order to guarantee success and probably to shut down the factories, he proposed that the gas lines to the city's enterprises be cut off. Clearly the practical part of Sotnikov's program is very similar to that which the investigation ascribed to Iurii Dementev. Sergei Sotnikov himself commented on this during the investigation, and he identified Dementev in a one-on-one confrontation at the police station [ochnaia stavka].*[85] This shows once more that a model of behavior and action was worked out spontaneously among the strikers at NEVZ on June 1. There was no single author of this program, for a successful idea thrown out by one person was immediately picked up by another and in the process acquired new features. There was no one single leader over the crowd, nor was there even an organizational nucleus taking concerted action. In spite of all of its efforts, the investigation did not uncover any kind of conspiracy or organization. In truth, the coordination of the strikers' actions on June 1 and 2 stemmed from the unanimous mood of the majority, as well as from the connection of events to the regular schedule of factory work. A crowd gathered simply because people were in the habit of coming to work and taking breaks at the customary times. In this "orderliness" of the riots, or at least of certain significant episodes, and in their attachment to the plant whistle, both literally and figuratively, lies the essential

---

*The ochnaia stavka was a standard procedure during the investigation of a suspect. Usually it involved a meeting between an offender and a witness in the presence of investigators.—E.M.

distinctiveness of the Novocherkassk events in contrast with all of the other known mass disorders of the Khrushchev period.

P. Siuda also spoke at the spontaneous meeting with a conscious program of further actions that closely matched those proposed by Iurii Dementev. As noted above, Siuda resembled Iurii Dementev in physical appearance. Hence, the similarity of their programs may have stemmed less from the affiliation of ideas typical within crowds than from a mistake, either accidental or intentional, in the identification of suspects during the investigation. According to the testimony of witnesses, Siuda called for the workers to gather the following day at the NEVZ administration building and then go into the city to demand that wages be paid during the days the plant was not working and that the arrested strikers be liberated.[86] Siuda, who did not have any illusions regarding the readiness of authorities for repression, was obviously certain that there would be such arrests.

Besides the ideologues, many other people also spoke at the meeting at the railroad passenger tunnel. Although the majority of these speeches were limited to brief shouts and appeals,[87] one drunken rebel "got caught up in politics." M.I. Khaustov was a poorly educated Communist loader at the Novocherkassk Milk Factory and the father of two children. On this day, he drank heavily after work and decided that he was curious about what was happening at NEVZ. In the end, Khaustov turned up at the very center of the spontaneous meeting. Upon hearing other orators, he decided that he himself would speak. According to the testimony of witnesses, he called for obtaining "what is ours" and for "redirecting" the Communist Party onto the correct path. The same witnesses nonetheless confirmed that the orator was so terribly drunk that "it was generally impossible to understand much of what he said." The loader himself did not remember the specific statements he made from atop the railroad passenger tunnel.[88] However, the indictment and the trial interpreted the behavior and the statements of these orators fully in the spirit of popular wisdom: "What the sober have on their mind, the drunken have on their tongue." The sentences were harsh.

Khaustov spoke a second time from the hood of a car that had been brought to the scene by one Airapetian, an Armenian driver for Motor Transport Establishment No. 3. An emotional Airapetian later testified that "his car, which had taken a back route carrying a load, was stopped by a crowd of hooligans on the square by the NEVZ administration building, and he, succumbing to the general mood, approved the actions of hooligan elements and called for reprisals against the 'pot-bellied ones,' having in mind the plant directors who did not know how to lead."[89] All of this he yelled from the roof of his own car, and after him there appeared others who also wished to speak from an elevated place. However, the speakers advanced no programmatic declarations from the roof of Airapetian's car, engaging only in "verbal extremism" and commonplace swearing.

The Arrival and the Expulsion of Troops from NEVZ

During the evening, while the spontaneous meeting was raging in full force at the railroad passenger tunnel, five trucks filled with soldiers and three armored carriers arrived at the plant. Their task was not to suppress the disorders by force, but to free the political bosses who had blockaded themselves in the NEVZ administration building.[90] Therefore the actions of the military personnel appear strange in the majority of accounts and even in the information of the KGB: they came, they hung about the gate, they listened to abuse, they turned around, and then they left. But during this time, the troops were fulfilling a basic task: by attracting attention to themselves, they enabled army intelligence officers and KGB agents disguised in civilian dress to liberate the hostages. No one at this time had ordered that weapons be used to disperse the strikers.

Undoubtedly authorities were counting on some kind of psychological effect—the crowd would see the armed soldiers and disperse. But there was no immediate impact, for no one in the crowd of workers believed that "our own Soviet army" would shoot at the Soviet people. For too long such actions had been associated in official propaganda exclusively with the crimes of the tsarist regime (Bloody Sunday in 1905, the Lena massacre in 1912*). No one raised on Soviet mythology, especially young people, could conceive something like this. The conviction that unarmed people could not be shot often placed riot participants directly in the line of fire of soldiers obligated to carry out their orders. The nonaggressive behavior of the army during the evening of June 1 only strengthened this traditional myth and made the shooting of unarmed people on the following day even more unexpected. The crowd at the NEVZ administration building interpreted the distracting maneuvers of the soldiers as a sign of vacillation, merely a chaotic reshuffling of people and equipment, and consequently was filled with confidence in its own forces.

In order to ascribe logic to their own, also quite irrational acts, the strikers continually needed a close and obvious goal. During the first moments of the confrontation with the soldiers, the barricade at the western gates of the plant,

---

*Bloody Sunday was January 9, 1905, when a peaceful procession of demonstrators led by Father Georgi Gapon was fired upon by tsarist troops outside the Winter Palace in St. Petersburg. Hundreds of unarmed workers, including women and children, were slaughtered. The Lena gold field massacre occurred in April 1912. Tsarist police fired upon striking workers, killing and wounding more than a hundred of them.—E.M.

Admission-Control Point No. 7, became a fulcrum. Briefly, thanks to accidental circumstances, a typical "man in the crowd," an electrician by the name of V.A. Matiash, ended up in the role of leader. A family man with no prior convictions, Matiash seemed to emerge from the faceless masses, to personify their will and desire, to sound out their minimal program—do not allow the soldiers into the plant, so that the strike can continue—and then to disappear once more into the crowd. Matiash was one of the first to arrive at Control Point No. 7, where many had rushed upon seeing the troops. With the words "Brothers, just stand here and do not issue any commands, here the people will command you," he pushed away the gun of the guard and began to twist wire around the side of the gate to secure it.

After the strikers had barricaded the gate, several persons climbed up onto the wooden fence, knocked it down, and then ran to the other gates, where they also blocked the troops from entering the road. At the same time, workers began carrying on conversations with soldiers. Some threatened officers with violence. The troops slowly penetrated the territory of NEVZ, distracting the attention of the crowd and becoming for an extended period of time the center of people's resentment. Near the steel foundry shop, fate threw together the worker F.V. Fetisov (he had earlier been involved with Viktor Ukhanov in the events at the railroad tracks) and a colonel who was leading a group of soldiers. Fetisov grabbed the colonel by the belt and shook him, crying out, "Fascist turncoats, take away your thugs," and, having called the colonel to order, cursed a person who had witnessed this exchange.[91] Such scenes occurred wherever the soldiers came into contact with the strikers.

Despite the workers' efforts, the barricade at Control Point No. 7 failed to stop the soldiers and they, accompanied by the appeals and threats of the strikers, simply entered the plant grounds through other gates. According to several memoirs, the armored cars simply made a breach in the wall, and the soldiers passed through it. But the crowd seemed pleased with its attempts to block the soldiers' path once they were inside the plant. The overturned cars and barricades produced the impression that an actual battle had been waged. In reality, the hostages had already been freed from the building. After this the military forces simply abandoned "the field of combat," but not until after the workers had become exuberantly militant, fully intoxicated with confidence in their own forces.

The concluding stage of this confrontation with the troops was described in the following way by the KGB:

> One of the criminals climbed unimpeded onto one of the armored vehicles and called for the riots to continue and for the soldiers to join them. After

this, under the whistles, shouts, and sneers of the crowd, the vehicles with the soldiers turned around and left.

In the square a mob had begun to form. Speakers proposed to continue the work stoppage, to remain assembled, to appoint a delegation to go to the authorities and present demands that prices for meat, meat products, and butter be lowered and that wages be increased.

Disorders continued the entire time. The crowd overturned a military vehicle with a wireless radio that had been sent to the plant to clarify the situation. In the process, one of the soldiers suffered a broken arm.

After some time a reinforced military unit was sent again to the scene of this mob gathering. The crowd surrounded it and then drove it back with whistles and hooligan jeers.

The amassing of people and the outrages around the plant continued. The most active participants in the disorders called for sending a delegation to other factories in the city with an appeal to stop working.[92]

After a break for repelling the troops, the spontaneous meeting at the railroad passenger tunnel continued. The essence of the speeches did not change, and the program of further action was voiced repeatedly. According to oral reminiscences collected by I. Mardar, when darkness fell "people built a large bonfire using the portraits of Khrushchev taken out of NEVZ administration offices. Eyewitnesses of the meeting state that there were many speakers. One man was recalled saying: 'Let me make use of the darkness to say that I do not wish to be in such a party' and then he tore up his own party card."[93] Probably this story about a desecrated CPSU party card is only a pretty legend. No sources have been found that confirm this actually occurred. Defilement of Khrushchev's portraits did continue,[94] but in all probability, this too has been embellished by rumor. For example, it is not entirely certain that in the administration building there were enough portraits of Khrushchev sufficient even for a small bonfire, to say nothing of a large one.

"The March" of Sergei Sotnikov to the Gas Distribution Station and the Electric Plant

The spontaneous meeting at the railroad passenger tunnel inspired attempts to expand the scale of the strike. According to the procurator for the Department of Surveillance over Investigations in the Organs of State Security, Iu. Shubin, "The decision was made to continue the strike, to send a delegation to other factories and during the morning of June 2, to go in organized fashion to the city, and present their demands to the city party committee."[95] But Shubin exaggerated the logic and purposefulness of the strikers' actions. The only truly established fact is that one of the "organizers" of the unrest, Sergei

Sotnikov, not only was able to sound out the spontaneous desires of the crowd and formulate a program to spread the strike, but also strove to fulfill this program by taking part in an "agitational march" of a group of workers to the neighboring factories.[96]

In the indictment for Case No. 22, Sotnikov's actions during the evening of June 1 were described in detail and with much bias:

> Sotnikov organized a group of hooligans [150 people, which no one could have organized in only 30 minutes.—V.K.], and as its leader directed it to the Gas Distribution Station. There they broke into the operations room and demanded under threat of reprisals that the operator Fedorov cut off the supply of gas to the city's industries. In doing this, Sotnikov personally verified that the valves of the gas line had been cut off.[97]

From the distribution station, the group headed off to the electric plant. As one of the witnesses testified, "A group of hooligans ran through the shop whistling and yelling for people to 'stop working.'" They came up to the machines, demanded that work stop, and willfully turned off the electric motors. The insurgents then broke into the pumping and storage station of the electric plant, surrounded the machinist Viunenko, and demanded that he support the strike. The crowd dispersed only after the machinist threatened to blow up the station, themselves included.[98]

Thus, Sotnikov's heroic efforts to rouse the electric plant to strike ran headfirst into the equally heroic resistance of an ideological opponent of the rebels—Viunenko, who alone knew how to master the situation and even to cause the strikers, who were not very confident in their own forces, to take flight. But Viunenko was unique, for the authorities had few such conscious workers on their side who were capable of opposing the strike forces on idealistic grounds. In all probability, the majority of those who spoke out on the side of the state, such as the troops sent to the scene of the riots and the People's Squad, Communist Party, and Komsomol members who tried during the day to dispatch the stopped passenger train, internally recognized the validity of the workers' protest. It is not surprising that, for example, the operator at the Gas Distribution Center, Nikolai Fedorov, never gave testimony against the strikers and stated that to "identify someone from a group of hooligans is difficult to do."[99] Probably people like Fedorov sympathized in the depths of their soul with the workers' protest, although they did not accept the extreme form of its expression.

Sergei Sotnikov's "march" ended in failure, and he paid for his heroic impulse with his life. The harsh sentence of death by shooting imposed by the cursory Khrushchevian justice system was clearly too heavy a penalty for his deed. According to the information of I. Mardar, there were also other groups of agitators who went to the large-scale enterprises in the city. "They were met there in different ways," writes Mardar. "Some joined, while others received the appeals of the NEVZ workers with misgiving and distrust. There were cases when a delegation was simply thrown out of the factory shop."[100] It can be stated unequivocally that the crowd of 150 people that Sergei Sotnikov headed did not at all resemble a delegation, but seemed more like a military group, though there were few if any rudiments of organization within it. As far as the other delegations are concerned, all of their activity took place only on the following day, June 2. On June 1, the agitation consisted of the few episodes described above when individual workers went to other factories and talked with comrades about the strike at NEVZ. Some really did call for support from their comrades, but on the first day, this primitive agitation basically remained the lot of lone enthusiasts.

Tanks Enter the City

According to deputy KGB chairman Ivashutin's report, "The gathering of people at the Electric Locomotive Construction Works continued until late in the night [of June 1], until troops entered the plant grounds. . . . Hooligans attacked the tanks, spoiled the instruments, and threw rocks, as a result of which several members of tank crews were wounded."[101] The investigation, however, failed to reconstruct the full picture of the nighttime events. In the darkness it was difficult for the KGB and police operatives to identify the ringleaders. Potential witnesses, that is, sensible onlookers, preferred to spend the night at home in their beds, and not side by side with tanks and dangerous rebels and hooligans.

Among the people who tried to intervene in the course of events during the night of June 1 was a tractor operator at the electrical plant by the name of Grigorii Katkov. By the modest standards of his fellow workers, this family man with two children was quite rich. Katkov and his wife received a good wage, and together with his brother he owned half of a large stone house, as well as a car, a Moskvich–401, which he was preparing to trade for a new Volga. Yet Grigorii Katkov was somewhat of a grumbler, and loved to complain about life and his own financial situation. Probably his comments slightly irritated his fellow workers, for everyone knew that Katkov, unlike many others, lived well and was not in poverty. But his neighbors respected Katkov as a hard worker and a good family man, one who was always ready to come to their assistance. Following his arrest, two of them were not afraid to write positive character statements for him. His place of work also gave him a positive evaluation, though it consisted of only one phrase, "He has a conscientious attitude toward work, and did not have any reprimands on his record."[102]

The night of June 1 became to a certain degree Grigorii Katkov's finest hour. As military units entered the city, he came out of his house and tried with his bare hands to stop the tanks. Grigorii himself claimed that when he came out on the street, the crowd had already stopped the tanks. But then, looking at the military hardware that had been sent to suppress unarmed persons, Katkov sealed his fate briefly and caustically: "Good God! So this is how they satisfy the requests of the laboring masses!"[103]

For others as well, this period of time was tumultuous. According to the testimony of witnesses, in the crowd at the plant the fitter A.M. Otroshko "shouted a demand for the removal of soldiers, provocatively declared that the tanks were crushing people, and insulted the officers of the Soviet Army, announcing 'We will show you.'"[104] Another incident involved a student at the Novocherkassk School of Mechanized Agriculture, V.D. Shmoilov, who during the early hours of June 2 showed up near his institute and heard that a tank had run over a man. He then took a sledgehammer and began to beat on the turrets and observation slots of the tanks. "I was angered that a Soviet tank could run over a human being," Shmoilov later explained.[105] This young man, even if he was intoxicated, was truly defending the Soviet propaganda myth with each blow of the sledgehammer. He was not at all programmed for violence and looting, and he was not anyone's puppet. It is not surprising that when he heard the cry of some unidentified provocateur, "Attack the soldier," Shmoilov immediately threw away the sledgehammer and got down from the tank.

The nighttime riots spread beyond the factory to the Novocherkassk police department. Included in the crowd were many students and young people. One such person was Vladimir Globa, a Komsomol member and loader at the Novocherkassk Milk Factory. During the evening of June 1, Globa had been drinking. Alcohol erased his fear, and the loader found words and slogans that made a strong impression on the young people.[106] As Globa testified during his interrogation, he considered that "only by organizing could they achieve the abolition of the proclamation that had raised prices for meat and other products, and having said this to the crowd, I went home."[107]

By bringing tanks into a peaceful Soviet city, the authorities provoked a stormy social-psychological reaction. Until this time, the youth had seen such things only in films about war, and then tanks were always associated with hostile fascist forces. Consequently, in Novocherkassk all the achievements of Soviet propaganda were turned against the state itself. In the eyes of the youth, the state had betrayed the highest ideals of social justice and was acting now as an enemy of the people, not as its servant and leader. As a result, the state itself predetermined the social-psychological shape of events on the following day. Many participants in the riots perceived the actions of authorities—first increasing prices, then introducing troops—as a betrayal of the people and the Soviet legacy. Therefore, the appropriate response could only be to come forward with portraits of Lenin held high and red flags flying. Moreover, for the extremist and marginalized segments of the rioters, the appearance of tanks raised in them not fear but rather irritation and a readiness to continue their aggressive behavior. If anything, even the restrained behavior of the troops made everyone certain that the truth was not on the side of the authorities. The soldiers themselves did not seem to believe in the state's course of action.

During the night leaflets appeared in the city, signifying that some participants and witnesses of the disturbances had begun to conceptualize events ideologically. The author of one of these leaflets was a young electrical fitter at NEVZ, A.F. Zharov, who had completed seven years of education. He had one prior conviction but had received an amnesty. The leaflet represented a rather curious ideological construction, and it is worthwhile to reproduce the text in full:

> On False Leninists.
>
> You have criticized Stalin, you have driven some of his supporters to the grave, and the rest you have removed from power, yet they never forgot to lower prices for all products and goods in April. From year to year Khrushchev raises prices in stores, and at the same time lowers workers' wages, which automatically raises a question among us, who is the real enemy of the people [?]. What liars and hypocrites you are, you power-hungry dogs, you oppressors of the people. What are you striving for? Stalin and his supporters moved consistently toward communism and led everyone, without imitating the dirty tricks of capitalism and without pointing fingers as you liars do.[108]

Thus, on the eve of the second day of unrest in Novocherkassk, people were cursing Khrushchev as a traitor to the cause of communism. Some were nostalgically recalling the Stalin period, "when we were moving consistently toward communism." For many workers of Novocherkassk, the continuation of the disturbances and strikes was a struggle for communism against those who were "power hungry" and "oppressors of the people." The regime, which had expended so many efforts on propagandistic brainwashing, fell into the trap of its own demagogy. It had done something that had contradicted its own core values, and the people now thirsted to express their protest against the "false Leninists."

Chapter 13

The Phenomenon of Novocherkassk: Part Two

June 2, 1962: Bearing a Portrait of Lenin, Under a Red Flag

Continuation of the Strike at the Electric Locomotive Construction Works

On the first day of the unrest, events had remained within the framework of a typical local work stoppage. The scenario fully corresponded to the picture of a spontaneous workers' strike at the beginning of the twentieth century or during the period of War Communism and early NEP.* But overnight all of this changed: troops passed through the city, NEVZ had been occupied, and the first group of Moscow leaders of middling rank hurriedly arrived in Novocherkassk, followed by a second group. The workers' response was to continue the strike and conduct a political demonstration in the center of the city. As on the first day, the workers in the steel foundry shop at NEVZ served as a collective motor propelling events forward. During the morning of June 2 they came to the plant, but instead of working, they discussed the previous day's events.

Following their lead, employees in a number of other shops also did not begin work. But again a split was evident at the plant. The instrumental and electrical shops began working the shift, but according to deputy KGB chair-

---

*Basically the period 1918 to 1924, when there was considerable unrest and activism among workers. War Communism was the policy of the Bolsheviks during the Civil War (1918–1921) that involved nationalization of the economy. NEP, the New Economic Policy, lasted from 1921 to 1929 and allowed for a mixed socialist and capitalist economy.—E.M.

man P. Ivashutin, "They were blocked by hooligan elements, who used force to drive the workers out of the shops and coerced them to join the strike."[1] Both the deputy chairman's report and the indictment emphasized the violence and threats used against loyal workers, but more significant were the psychological pressures and the somewhat hysterical atmosphere. Supporters of the strike accused their comrades of treachery and betrayal of the workers' cause. Alternative points of view and all attempts to warn workers against a direct confrontation with authorities were scorned as emotional rhetoric.

As one of the witnesses told it, when he called for fellow brigade members to return to work, he faced the screams of an indignant and disheveled woman who had turned up by accident in the shop: "What, you pot-bellied pig, you are driving people to work, well, we do not want to work. Their [the bosses's] bellies are full, they have roofs over their head, but we have nothing to live on."[2] These were the words of M. Zaletina, the cleaning woman, already familiar to us from the events of June 1.

Undoubtedly, similar scenes occurred in all of the shops, for the aggressive actions of some truly expressed the outrage and bewilderment of the majority. E.I. Mardar, who at the time worked in the blacksmith shop, recalled that during the morning of June 2, he went to work as usual in an overcrowded streetcar. People were heatedly discussing the preceding day's events and trying to predict what would happen next. What workers had witnessed had left a painful impression on them:

> Soldiers were at the checkpoint. By the entrance to the shop there was a whole platoon of them. It was the same thing at the other shops. Work under the muzzle of an automatic gun? Never. In our blacksmith's shop, this is what occurred: Blacksmiths, not actually entering the shop, sat down on the benches. . . . When the officers demanded that they go to work, the blacksmiths answered: "You should work yourselves, since you are occupying the factory!"[3]

Some of the workers, preferring not to be connected with the conflict that was flaring up, went back home. An hour after the beginning of the shift, the smelters moved to a new machine shop, and then to the plant administration building, joined by workers from the blacksmith and other shops. The crowd surged into the square after tearing down the door from the gateway of the building.[4] What happened subsequently was a mirror image of the preceding day. First the strikers stopped the train running from Shakhty to Rostov, then they halted a diesel locomotive that passed by the NEVZ administration building. All movement on the railway ceased and again, as on June 1, alarm whistles blasted through the plant. Several heroes from the first day of the strike played an active role in these events, particularly Fetisov and Zinenko. In general, Fetisov's behavior was almost a cliche. During the morning, he had again intended to visit his mother (the day before he similarly had been diverted from this trip), but for some reason turned up at the plant, and then at the immobilized locomotive. He again tinkered with the braking system, letting out steam by opening a valve, but the motives for such actions are not entirely clear. According to his testimony, it was as if he were trying to "turn over a new leaf": steam had to be released in order to stop the alarm sirens.[5]

A.I. Zinenko, one of those who had built barricades at the plant gates during the evening of June 1, also turned up at the railroad tracks. From the cab of the locomotive, he agitated the crowd, or as he put it, "I conversed with the people." According to a patrolman, someone rebuked Zinenko and in response heard him say: "The working class is here. It understands us."[6] The conflict between the active strikers and those wishing to restore order was not limited to this reproof and Zinenko's rejoinder. In response to someone's call for allowing the locomotive to pass through, condemning voices rang out from the crowd: "How much have they paid you, go away, or else we will give you a sound thrashing." Moderates reproached A.G. Nesterenko, a milling-machine operator who was an active participant in the pandemonium around the diesel locomotive, saying that he had "gotten into a dirty affair." Nesterenko rejected their criticism and responded: "It is none of your business!" and then called out indignantly to the unidentified "voice of morality": "How much have you sold yourself for?"

Through the scandalous and unattractive picture of the flaring disorders, through the coarseness and vulgarity, nonetheless a class motif was emerging: The mobilization of the crowd occurred on the grounds of hatred and hostility to the "pot-bellied ones" and the bosses (or "pot-bellied bosses"); there was psychological pressure applied to the loyal and the neutral through accusations of betrayal and venality; and, finally, appeals were made to the people, to the "working class," who "understand us."

Other Factories Rise to Action

When the sirens of the diesel locomotive spread over the surrounding areas, one group of workers left the crowd and headed to the electric plant, to Factory No. 17, and to the enterprise *Neftemash* (which produced equipment for the petrol and oil industry.—V.K.) in order to spur their employees to join the revolt. The electric plant, however, already had its own organizers, one of whom was the electrician Andrei Korkach. The investigation identified another active organizer of the strike at the electric plant as G.G. Katkov, who had first joined in the disorders the previous night when he had tried to stop the movement of the tanks. Both were middle-aged and in terms of material possessions were quite secure, at least by the standards of that time. Therefore, it is hardly possible to explain their active participation in the Novocherkassk events exclusively as a spontaneous reaction to the increase in prices or as an accidental confluence of circumstances. In the actions of Katkov and especially of Korkach, it is necessary to seek the influence of deeper, possibly ideological motivations.

The investigation categorically declared that "Korkach by nature is self-seeking." Otherwise, why would he, being a secure person, with a wife who managed a store (a sign of unjustified wealth to many in Soviet society), state: "I have waited for forty years to see life improve"? Everything that is known about Korkach's actions, however, in the organization of the strike at the electric plant makes the accusation of self-aggrandizement psychologically questionable. "Self-seekers" prefer not to bring trouble down on their own heads, and if they do show any kind of activism in conflict situations, then they do this stealthily, preferring to worry about their own selfish interests and not at all about workers' solidarity. Moreover, such types do not enjoy any respect among workers. Yet Korkach's fellow workers, even under the pressure of interrogation, were very unwilling to give testimony against him: "They called him by his name and patronymic, and said that he was a respected person in their eyes."[7]

To unravel the psychological enigma of Korkach, it helps to consider the fact that in 1947 he had been convicted by a military tribunal for abuse of his official position, and had received a three-year term of imprisonment. At that time, Andrei Andreevich had been serving as a commander of a Soviet army squadron. In 1946, he showed excessive zeal in punishing a subordinate for stealing a towel. First he beat him, then he hung a tablet around the neck of the young thief with the words: "I stole a towel, I am a rogue, a thief, and a scoundrel." Korkach made him stand by the orderly's table and then led him with the tablet around his neck before the squad, where he verbally abused the young soldier.[8] Though Korkach was undoubtedly under stress at this time, he possessed a rather primitive sense of justice. This particular attitude toward life is what made him appear in the eyes of workers to be a just man, and not simply a pain in the neck. It was precisely this, and not the hypocrisy and double-dealing described in a report on Korkach by Iu. Shubin, the procurator for the Department of Surveillance over Investigations, that explained his reputation as "a man who was concerned about other workers" and who "defended their interests."

Korkach unarguably was a willful and strong personality, whom even the

KGB interrogators could not break. He had successfully coped with the crisis of his 1947 conviction and dismissal from the army, to which Andrei Andreevich had given eleven years of his life. He practically had to begin life anew, and his new life was a worthy one. The investigation was unable to gather any kind of negative information on Korkach from the period after he was freed under an amnesty in 1947 all the way to June of 1962. On the contrary, as the procurator Shubin reluctantly recognized, Andrei Korkach, who from 1955 on worked as an electrician at the electric plant, "had a positive work record."[9] It must be added that for a simple electrician and for a man of his age, Korkach was quite well educated, having completed nine grades, and could formulate his thoughts distinctly. He stated:

> Turning to the workers, I said that they should change their clothes and leave work, in support of the demands of the workers at the Budenny Plant [NEVZ], who had risen up against the increase in prices for meat and butter. In saying this to the workers, I had in mind the goal of organizing a strike, that is, to have the workers leave the factory and thereby protest the government proclamation about the increase in prices for meat and butter, and the use of tanks to restore order in the city, and to express solidarity with the actions of the workers at NEVZ.[10]

After this Korkach's group went to several more shops, calling for a work stoppage and entering into conversations with workers and representatives of the administration. Several conversations were later recalled by Korkach:

> At the graphite shop, I ended up talking with a boss of this shop by the name of Bruk about the gap in wages between workers and the factory management. I declared to him that he, as a Communist, sees many injustices that take place in the factory (I had in mind the size of apartments, the wage gap, the increase in prices, and other things), yet he never talks about this at the meetings.
>
> A worker with whom I was not acquainted turned to someone in our group and said that the increase in prices was a temporary phenomenon, that the time would come when everyone would live well. I said at this point that I had waited forty years for such a day, that while I am waiting for life to improve, life, on the contrary, gets worse.[11]

Not all of the workers supported the strike; far from everyone had lost their faith in the omniscient and "wise Central Committee," which knew everything about the lives of the workers, and in the need only to wait patiently for everything to be fine. Even Andrei Korkach himself, strictly speaking, was a pro-Soviet critic of Central Committee polices, condemning the state while remaining a captive of its ideological dogmas. Thus, in an argument with the Communist foreman Bruk, Korkach cursed him not as a Communist—that is, as the bearer of a specific worldview—but as a poor Communist, as one who sees injustice and yet remains silent. Only rarely in Korkach's statements did anticommunist remarks burst out: "You, Communists, do you see what you have led the working class to?" For the most part, informal leaders such as Korkach chiefly criticized concrete decisions made by authorities, thereby avoiding alienation of the pro-Soviet working masses and even creating a definite psychological unity: We against Them—the bosses, who are the betrayers of the cause of the working class. This is precisely why Korkach was far more dangerous to the authorities than were hooligans and hysterical urban paupers. Behind him stood a Soviet alternative to the "degenerate" state, an alternative that had every chance of being heard and understood by workers.

Korkach's "anti-Soviet" agitation represented a rather typical selection of critical themes: "He condemned the Soviet government, the fact that it allegedly 'feeds' other states but does not provide for its own workers";[12] and he called for a struggle to raise wages. He cried out, "This is not the time for us to shut our mouths."[13] In trying to draw loyal workers into the strike, Korkach appealed to a sense of class shame and class solidarity: "We are risking our lives . . . they can put us in prison, we may suffer, but you . . . you do not wish to support us." He called these workers "traitors."[14] Right in front of everyone, Andrei Korkach was swiftly becoming a type of worker-organizer who spoke "with a firm conviction."[15] He was subtly similar to the leader of the Polish Solidarity movement, Lech Walesa. The workers' strike also dragged the latter, as is known, into politics. Probably it was the fear of an organized workers' strike that prompted the "workers' state" to deal so harshly (with a death sentence) with Andrei Korkach.

Side by side with Korkach in the group of strike leaders going around to the shops of the electric plant was Grigorii Katkov. The investigation had more than enough basis to call him a self-seeker, rather than Korkach. On this day, however, Grigorii Grigorevich did not behave at all like a self-seeker. Either that reputation was false, or Katkov himself turned out to be by nature more passionate and more easily carried away than is possible to expect from one who is self-seeking. As discussed previously, he did have a habit of complaining about his difficult financial circumstances, and in a conversation with the foreman, Bruk, Grigorii Grigorevich did not hold anything back in reproaching him: "Even before we did not eat meat, but now we will not be able to eat anything at all."[16] Katkov did call for striking and for struggling for a better life, but truly no more than other instigators. Therefore, the conclusion of the investigation and trial about the supposed special role of Katkov in the organization of the strike amounted to a virtual fabrication and a juggling of the facts. In any case, it was impossible to put him on the same level as Korkach. Korkach was a leader, while Katkov was "one of those who. . . ," and therefore, luckily for him, he avoided a death sentence.

On the day of the strike, certain supporters of Korkach and Katkov in the electric plant experienced a special emotional lift. A metal worker in the mechanical repair shop, Vladimir Bakholdin, seemed, like Korkach, "to have waited a long time for this day." At age twenty-seven, V.G. Bakholdin was a man with fully Soviet views and convictions, having been raised in a family with revolutionary traditions. In his case, however, as with many others, these views and convictions did not contradict his participation in the strike, but on the contrary predetermined it. Also joining Korkach and Katkov in the group of agitators was Georgii Vasiukov, an electrical fitter at the electric plant. He fell into the category of ringleaders purely at the will of the investigator, and subsequently appealed his conviction on the basis of the latter's bias. Witnesses recalled that for some time G.S.Vasiukov went about the factory with a delegation of workers from NEVZ. He did not do or say anything special, and witnesses attributed the truly active role to Korkach. In essence, Vasiukov's agitation consisted of a question he asked the chief engineer—"Why did prices go up?" (Vasiukov was told to read the newspapers)—and a fully rational appeal for workers to take off their uniforms and cease working.[17]

The Neftemash Plant also conducted its own agitation. Joining a crowd that had surrounded the plant director, a lathe operator by the name of Grigorii Shcherban called for his fellow workers to strike until the proclamation on increased prices was repealed. "He expressed dissatisfaction with the rates given for parts they worked on, and called for the crowd to go to the neighboring Factory No. 17 to stop work there."[18] It was habitual for Grigorii Shcherban to discuss norms and piece rates with the administration, and in the past he had often argued about this with his supervisors.[19]

The investigation and trial connected two female workers with the instigators of the strike at Neftemash, V.T. Kustova and M.F. Gladkova. Each had three children, each had suffered a difficult life, and when prices had risen, each had wailed inconsolably. On June 2, 1962, Kustova came to the plant and saw that no one was working. Overhearing an argument between the director and a worker (Shcherban), her earlier outrage returned. Then the crowd began to chant, "Let us go to Factory No. 17," and, as Kustova explained, "I also cried out with everyone else, to go to Factory No. 17 . . . the crowd went, and I went . . . the crowd cried out and I cried out, why I did so I cannot explain."[20]

The testimony of witnesses paints a clearer picture of Kustova's participation in the unrest. At some moment during these events, she undoubtedly acted in the role of an unconscious ringleader. Passing by the plant administration building, Kustova cried out, "Office scum, come with us." At Factory No. 17, she and Gladkova cried out at the same time, "Stop working and join with us,"[21] "Stop working, come to the city executive committee, demand milk, butter, and sausage."[22]

At a critical moment, therefore, it was specifically the emotional impulse of these two women that directed the course of events at Neftemash. "It is possible," declared one of the witnesses, "that if Kustova had not cried out, then the workers would not have left and would instead have gone to work."[23] Kustova and Gladkova were sentenced to ten years' imprisonment, but in the end even the state was forced to recognize the complete inappropriateness of the punishment to the "crime." After two years in prison, these two mothers were pardoned by the Presidium of the Russian Federation Supreme Soviet.

The Demonstration

Back at the Electric Locomotive Construction Works, the assembled crowd transformed itself into a political demonstration. Bearing a portrait of Lenin and marching under a red flag, the people headed toward the center of Novocherkassk. With many women and children in the crowd, the scene was very reminiscent of the beginning of Bloody Sunday in 1905. But now the workers were not turning to the "Tsar-Father" (after all, the place of this supreme arbiter was now occupied by the "chief perpetrator" of all of the workers' misfortunes, Nikita Khrushchev), but to certain abstract values of early communism, to an ideal of justice that had been profaned by the "pot-bellied ones." Yet, in the final account, the Novocherkassk workers were unable to defend their sacred communist symbols, just as their fathers and grandfathers in 1905 had been powerless to defend the icons, banners, and portraits of Nicholas II, that they had borne. But the very "flight" of the demonstrators under the protection of Lenin and the red flag made the riots in Novocherkassk sufficiently typical of an internal systemic conflict. The people were not attacking the system's ideological foundations, but were only sending a signal to the top of the hierarchy about their own misfortunes. Although there did exist within the crowd a strong current of impulsive and anarchic anticommunism, which produced repeated calls for reprisals against party members, nonetheless not one of the anticommunists objected to Lenin's portrait and the red flag heading the column of workers. The masses had spontaneously chosen the image of their protest and its ideological coloring.

As the large crowd of several thousand people continued to move toward the city, military authorities erected a barrier on the bridge crossing the river Tuzlov and stationed tanks, motor vehicles, and soldiers there. However, "the agitated crowd passed easily across the bridge and continued on toward the city."[24] KGB Deputy Chairman Ivashutin, to whom the quote above belongs, surely exaggerated the "agitated" state of the workers, for the mood of the demonstration is more accurately described as "determined." Even procurator Shubin was forced to recognize that at first "at least on the surface everything seemed to be peaceful."[25]

Anyone who so desired could join the demonstration. The crowd went along the main thoroughfare, Moscow Street, at the end of which stood the city party committee and the city executive committee building. But also on this street, two blocks closer, were the offices of the police department, the KGB, and the State Bank.[26] Students and other city residents joined the march, which was accompanied by cries of "Meat, butter, and a wage increase!" But as time passed, this mobile human mass became less homogenous, for not only students joined, but also drunks and loiterers. As it moved from the plant to the center of the city, the workers' demonstration appreciably changed in composition, and increasingly its more noisy, aggressive, and far less reasonable members determined its focus and direction.

The Capture of the City Party Committee and the Attack on the Police and KGB Building: The Shooting of the Crowd

It is difficult to say at what moment and for what reason the critical mass of extremists changed the original character of the demonstration. All that is clear is that the procession had already lost its former signs of organization when it reached the building of the city party committee and the city executive committee. The approach of the demonstrators greatly frightened the Central Committee Presidium members who were sitting at that moment in party offices: A.I. Mikoian, F.R. Kozlov, along with A.P. Kirilenko, D.S. Polianskii, A.N. Shelepin, V.I. Stepakov, V.I. Snastin, and P. Ivashutin. Having learned that the tanks had not stopped the column on the bridge, the Moscow leaders then beat a hasty retreat to a military settlement, where a temporary headquarters for the government was established. At this point the demonstrators were a hundred meters from the building.[27] In the opinion of I. Mardar, who cited materials of the 1990 review of the USSR military procurator, it was then, as a result of discussions between Kozlov and Khrushchev, that the latter sanctioned the use of firearms against participants in the disorders.

In Ivashutin's terse summary, the events following the appearance of the demonstration in front of the party offices occurred in the following way:

When the crowd approached the building, the more malicious hooligans and hotheads began to throw rocks and sticks at the doors and windows. They broke through the guards and penetrated the building, where they shattered windows, ruined furniture, tore down portraits and destroyed them, and assaulted party and government workers and employees of the KGB who were located on the premises.

Several hooligans made their way to the balcony, and for provocational purposes brought out and hung before the crowd a red banner and a portrait of V.I. Lenin. Active participants in the excesses began making speeches with demands for decreased food prices and wage increases. Several of them spoke two or three times. Their speeches were accompanied by insults and threats addressed to Communists, by abuse of the soldiers, at whom people threw sticks and stones, and by appeals to the soldiers and the officers to join the criminals.[28]

Mardar has added important details to this description. In the building, as it turns out, several officials from the Central Committee apparatus still remained, along with a representative of the city authorities and employees of the KGB. Using a megaphone that had been set up on the balcony, they tried to begin a dialogue with those who had gathered, but the only response from the crowd was a flurry of sticks and stones. Yet had the demonstration really gone to the center of the city with a portrait of Lenin and with red flags flying only to hurl rocks at the bosses? The single possible explanation is that the crowd did not recognize the status of those who had gone out onto the balcony and were preparing to speak. People had made up their minds to see the highest representatives of supreme authority and listen to their declarations and assurances. When these representatives did not appear, the crowd felt cheated and began to demand a speech from Mikoian. Although by this time he had been clever enough to leave the building under military protection, the idea of Mikoian's speech, as often happens in such cases, became an obsession for the crowd. So, after looting the party and government office building, the demonstrators again began to insist "that Mikoian speak, and that he hear out their demands."[29] He, needless to say, did not come out to address the people at this time, and only later, after the shooting of the crowd, did the radio broadcast a speech that he had taped.

The demonstrators had penetrated all of the barriers to reach the center of the city. They had broken into the party offices, but still had not seen any of the chief bosses to whom they could lay out their demands. This produced a typically stressful situation, as a result of which the crowd began to lose its earlier purpose. Talks with the state, which workers had sought on the second day, did not occur. It is not surprising, therefore, that in the speeches at the party and government office building, anticommunist refrains now resounded more strongly. The following episode significantly influenced the mood of those who had gathered. Grigorii Shcherban from Neftemash carried out to the balcony two plates loaded with cheese and sausage, and cried out: "Look and see what they eat, yet we cannot get such food!"[30] though later he denied having said this, claiming that these were the words of some other person.[31]

If earlier the main target of attack had been Khrushchev, now Lenin himself became the focus. For example, Aleksandr Zaitsev publicly expressed "defamatory fabrications addressed to the Soviet government and the founder of the Soviet state." A native of the Saratov countryside, in 1942 Zaitsev had set off at age fifteen for the city of Kemerovo, where he began to study at a Factory-Plant School. But he lost his arm in an accident and did not finish the school. Having returned home, he worked in a tractor brigade. In 1945, by some kind of miracle, he was able to finish an accounting course, but due to his low literacy level he could not work at this specialty, so he returned to the tractor brigade.

In 1948, Zaitsev was almost caught stealing grain from the collective farm. Authorities arrested and convicted his accomplice, but Zaitsev demonstrated for the first time his own daring and resourceful character. Finding himself on the run, he managed to find work without having a passport, and then through clever maneuvering acquired a new one. At the beginning of the 1950s, the sly adventurer succeeded in finding a job in retail trade. But, during this time, he was drinking heavily, and the affair ended in embezzlement. He fled the investigation, and again schemed to receive a new passport. In 1952, he finally stood before a court and, by the decree of the USSR Supreme Soviet from June 4, 1947, "On Criminal Responsibility for the Theft of State and Public Property," was sentenced for his latest trick to ten years' imprisonment. In December 1954, Zaitsev received early parole. For six months he lived as a free man and worked in the invalids' cooperative workshop in Novocherkassk. In August 1956, he was sentenced to two years' imprisonment for hooliganism. He was freed in 1958 and again came to Novocherkassk, where he worked different jobs, and at times did not work at all. He drank heavily and squandered not only his wages, but even clothing, both his roommates' and his own. In the end, Zaitsev left Novocherkassk in March 1962 for Volgograd Oblast, where he found work on a state farm.[32]

On May 31, Zaitsev officially received twenty-eight rubles to be used for purchasing paint for the state farm, and on June 1 he came to Novocherkassk. He drank heavily, squandered the state money he had been given, and, in purely Russian fashion, gave up all as lost and actively joined in the riots. Besides cursing Lenin, Zaitsev called for "reprisals against local leaders and against the military, stopped a motor transport that was passing by and demanded that the drivers cease working. Storming into the party offices, Zaitsev made his way to the balcony, where he called for looting and banditry, and demanded an attack on the military and the seizure of their weapons." When the building was surrounded by soldiers, "Zaitsev insulted them coarsely, calling them 'fascists,' and he provocatively declared that they were killing invalids, mothers, and children. He demanded that the general who was commanding the military divisions guarding the building be surrendered for reprisals, declaring: 'Hand this general over to us . . . we will tear him to pieces.'"[33]

A program calling for looting and violence sounded even more clearly in the speeches at the spontaneous meeting. Its active "arranger" was a metal worker at the electric plant, Mikhail Kuznetsov, who had been raised in a children's home in Kiev, and at the beginning of World War II had been evacuated to Uzbekistan. In 1945, he had run away from the children's home and thereafter lived as a vagrant. The police detained him as a homeless stray but then sent him to an on-site factory training school (FZU).* After six months of study, Mikhail acquired a specialization as a tool and die maker and went to work in Lvov. But in May 1950, he and some fellow workers stole from the factory club a radio set with a record player. They all fell under the same ill-fated and cruel decree "On Criminal Responsibility for the Theft of State and Public Property," which broke the lives of so many people and embittered them against the Soviet state. For stealing the radio, Kuznetsov received eight years' imprisonment. Other persons had received lesser sentences for premeditated murder! Fortunately, in 1953, Mikhail was freed by amnesty, but six years later got mixed up in an apartment theft as a thieves' informant [navodchik].** At this time "social measures of influence" were fashionable, and the shop collective took responsibility for Kuznetsov, provided that he "sincerely admit his guilt."[34] During the same year, 1959, Mikhail also became the father of a baby girl.

On June 2, Kuznetsov, along with everyone else, quit working, got drunk, and found himself in the crowd at the party and government building. According to the official investigation and trial, M.A. Kuznetsov did not simply call for looting and for reprisals against soldiers and officers, but he also employed standard methods of "revolutionary bluffing," usually effective in keeping vacillating supporters under the influence of the leaders. The metal worker repeated insistently that help was coming to Novcherkassk from other

---

*These were industrial training schools set up within factories, beginning in 1920.—E.M.

**This was an informant who would let thieves know whether a criminal act was feasible.—V.K.

cities. According to Mikhail's own confession, his minimum program consisted of the following outbursts: "Let's Move Bravely Onward! We must destroy everything, so that they will know our strength," having in mind, by his own explanation, "leaders both great and small."[35]

In the end, the call for a pogrom was implemented by a woman who worked as a guard for Construction Board No. 31, Ekaterina Levchenko. Barely educated, having completed only three grades, Levchenko was unmarried and apparently had a complex and quarrelsome character. In 1959, she had been sentenced to two years' imprisonment for stealing a jacket. After being released, she was not able to rebuild her life. Levchenko frequently changed jobs and, being a nervous and emotional person, she continually got involved in arguments and scandals and was notorious for spreading rumors.[36]

It was Ekaterina Levchenko who pointed out to the crowd the immediate moral goal of its further actions. From the balcony of the party building, she cried out that on June 1, she had been detained and beaten by the police, though later the indictment denied this. But her main contribution was to call on the crowd to rescue those strikers who had been arrested, despite the fact that at this time there were no workers being held behind bars in the police department.[37] Therefore the speech of Levchenko was provocative in the full sense of the word, and it was followed by cries of "Free the Workers!"[38] A group of thirty to fifty people broke off from the demonstration and moved toward the police building. The majority sincerely believed that they were going to free their brother workers.[39] A crowd of curious onlookers, who had already gathered at the police building, was peaceful, and was not making any preparations to penetrate the building. But Levchenko continued her own agitation, and in the end outraged voices rang out with claims that the police were beating workers inside the building.

Extremists threw themselves into the attack on the police department. It is not surprising that among them could be heard clear anticommunist sentiments. A young cook at Boarding School No. 2 by the name of Vladimir Shuvaev, who was drunk during these events, not only threatened the soldiers and Communists with reprisals, but also formulated unique ideological postulates for the rioters: "It is useless to speak with Communists"; "It is necessary to shoot all of them."[40] In order to take away from Communists the psychological defense of the collective "we," Shuvaev equated them with fascists and murderers and called for soldiers to shoot those "who force you to fire at the people." But the matter was not limited to ideology. Vladimir Shuvaev behaved extremely aggressively and demanded from one of the soldiers, "Give me your gun, I will shoot everyone in sight." He threw stones at the tanks, cursed and used foul language.[41] When Shuvaev was arrested, police found a cutlass in his possession.[42]

In spite of resistance from police and soldiers, the rioters successfully tore down the outer door from the hinges and then used it as a battering ram to break down the inside door. As they burst into the police department, a real battle began, in the course of which the attackers shouted threats and insults, threw rocks, shattered glass, beat the soldiers, and then tried to take their weapons. This unsightly scene is partially brightened by the fact that the rioters continually demanded the liberation of the prisoners, that is, they were seeking, as it seemed to them, the restoration of justice.

A mass psychosis sucked people in and caused them to lose their self-control. As one of the participants in the events testified:

> For some reason some kind of force filled me as well, and I also cried out, "Set them free." Once people began entering the building, I joined them. I had not gone eight meters when shooting began on the premises. I was scared and I ran into a room, where they [the police] locked us in.[43] Until this day, I do not understand how I got into this. What kind of devil was it that asked me to go and forced me to enter into the police department?[44]

Even in this agitated crowd, so bent on violence, there were people who tried, if not to stop the assault, then at least to behave humanely. For example, one of those convicted for participation in the attack on the police department, G.G. Larenkov, tried to stop the beating of a soldier who had been knocked down.[45]

During the storming of the police department, there were attempts to seize firearms. In the course of the fighting, a metal worker by the name of Vladimir Cherpanov tried to tear a gun away from one of the soldiers,[46] but the attempt ended in failure. The attackers did succeed, however, in getting a gun away from another soldier named Repkin. The indictment claimed that the "robbers" tried to use this weapon against the guards, and therefore the "military personnel, acting in accordance with the Statutes of the Sentry and Internal Service, were forced to use weapons against the bandits and thereby stop their attempt to murder people who were taking part in the effort to restore order."[47] One of the attackers was killed by the gunfire.

The first blood had now been spilled, but this did not stop the agitated rioters, nor did it seem even to frighten them. The crowd tried to penetrate the police building from behind, through the courtyard of the Novocherkassk branch of the State Bank. When the senior bank guard demanded that the rioters leave the area adjoining the police department, someone tugged at the guard's shirt and yelled, "Go ahead, shoot me!"[48] This emotional outburst, which betrayed the confidence of the crowd—they will not dare to shoot us—was not the only such incident. There is vague evidence that a child was lifted above the crowd with the cry: "They will not shoot children!"[49]

The restless energy of the crowd at the party building found outlets other than just violence and looting. After the extremists had headed to the police department "to free those who had been arrested," a molding-cutter at the Novocherkassk Machine-Building Factory, Boris Mokrousov, put forward out a new idea to the crowd—select a delegation to demand the removal of troops from the city. Thirty-nine years of age, Mokrousov was in many respects an extraordinary person who had seen much evil in his lifetime. As a young man during World War II, Boris Savelevich Kuzin (the future Mokrousov) ran away to the front but was caught by the police. The youth decided to take the name of Boris Nikolaevich Mokrousov (which he went by for the rest of his life), added two years to his age, and pretended to be a Red Army soldier who had been separated from his unit. He was then accused of desertion, but did not object because he had been told by someone that deserters were sent immediately to the front. Instead, a military tribunal sentenced Mokrousov to ten years' imprisonment. Boris had two additional ten-year terms added on, one for escaping and the other for trying to kill a fellow prisoner with a mining pick. In May 1944, the Military Collegium of the USSR Supreme Court finally investigated the case of the "deserter" Mokrousov and repealed the sentence of the Kzylordinsk Garrison Military Tribunal. But the machinery for carrying out legal decisions was not working, and news of the judgment of the Military Collegium never reached the Bogoslovskii Corrective Labor Camp, where Mokrousov was serving his sentence. So the unlucky fugitive served in the camp, not even suspecting his own partial acquittal, all the way to 1953. But within two years of his release, Mokrousov was again a prisoner, sentenced to seven years in the labor camps for stealing food. Only now did he take charge of his life. In August 1959, he was freed conditionally for good behavior and given three years' probation. He came to Novocherkassk and found work at NEVZ as a castings cutter. There were very few who wanted to do this hard manual labor, and the plant administration willingly hired former criminals. Mokrousov married and began to earn a good wage. Life gradually returned to normal.[50]

Mokrousov had not taken part in the strike on the first day. On June 2 he worked his shift and only then did he head for the city party committee building, where he actively moved from group to group, protesting and expressing his outrage. When Mokrousov proposed to form a delegation, nine people, himself included, volunteered to take part in the negotiations. The delegation was allowed to freely enter the party and government building, where it met with the head of the local garrison. The commander, of course, rejected the demand to remove the troops, claiming to lack the authority to make such decisions. In response Mokrousov declared, "So there is nothing to talk about with him, we need the person who can decide this matter." So the delegation headed to the military settlement where Mikoian and Kozlov were staying. On the way, Mokrousov agitated. He tried to press the officer accompanying them to explain his personal view on the price increases and the lowered pay rates. When the officer tried to keep to himself, Boris explained his reaction very simply: "Why even try to converse with him—He is a Communist."[51]

Mokrousov, fearless and reckless by nature (the indictment called him insolent), in the ensuing discussion with the Moscow leaders, "demanded the removal of the military divisions from the city, maliciously slandered the material condition of the laborers, and levied threats and crude insults at the leaders of the Party and Government."[52] As Mokrousov himself told colleagues from work prior to his arrest on June 4, 1962, he demanded from Mikoian and Kozlov "that they stop putting pressure on the working class," and upon saying this, he hit his fist into his other hand and pointed out, "We are the working class, there are many of us." In general, "I spoke bluntly with them, and I myself do not know why they did not arrest me right then and there."[53]

I. Mardar was able to find one of the eyewitnesses of the meeting—Iu.P. Tupchenko, a former KGB chief in Rostov Oblast—who recalled that F.R. Kozlov himself met with the delegation. Among the latter "there were two or three women. One of the men was pretty drunk. He introduced himself as 'Zhukov'* and spouted obscenities. They discussed the impoverished condition of the workers and of the city's residents." Tupchenko recalled a statement made by members of the delegation: "Among us the only ones living well are Iurka Gagarin** and Manka*** the snack bar waitress." According to Tupchenko, the delegation did not ask the members of the government to speak to the demonstrators. F.R. Kozlov bid farewell to them with these words: "Go to the people, quiet them down, call for them to end the disorders." In the words of I. Mardar, "The meeting ended without any results for the demonstrators, and not one of the 'bigshots' who had come took this delegation seriously." The delegation was allowed to leave in peace and the arrests began only later.[54]

---

*This may have been a reference to Marshal Georgy Konstantinovich Zhukov (1896–1974), the most successful commander during World War II and minister of defense from 1955 to 1957. Despite his critical support of Khrushchev during the 1957 antiparty conspiracy, he was accused of "Bonapartism" and stripped of his post and his Presidium position in October 1957.—E.M.

**Iurii Gagarin (1934–1968) was the much celebrated Soviet astronaut who became in 1961 the first human being to fly into space. Iurka is a nickname for Iurii.—E.M. and V.K.

***Manka—a scornful nickname for Maria, reflecting a common belief that all people who worked in business and trade were dishonest and took unfair advantage of their position and the deficit of goods and food to get more than everyone else.—V.K.

This meeting of the Kremlin oligarchs with "the people" had more symbolic value than practical significance. It helped turn a local conflict between administrators and workers into a confrontation between state power and the entire city of Novocherkassk, with the sides even entering into negotiations. The members of the Central Committee Presidium had to endure harsh demands, rebukes, and accusations from the workers' delegation, criticism the regime had not experienced for forty years! There was definitely something to ponder and to remember, for looming on the horizon was the specter of an organized workers' protest. While these negotiations had been going on, back at the party committee building dramatic events were ensuing that led to the fatal shooting of persons in the crowd. Some of the demonstrators had been inclined to wait for the results of the negotiations, but other rebels acted more aggressively. The authorities first tried to clear the building and secure it with military forces. But the bulk of the attackers had already gone out onto the square, since there was nothing further for them to do in the deserted and ravaged party building. Mardar is justified in observing that in practical terms, it made no sense to post a guard over an empty building, and even less so "to defend it using weapons."[55] Nonetheless, a group of soldiers in an armored carrier tried to wedge themselves into the crowd and drive back the demonstrators. They failed and received an order to retreat. Such odd maneuvers are very reminiscent of typical preparations for a shooting: Our own must not suffer.

By this time a new group of gunmen arrived from the MVD troops under the command of General Oleshko, the head of the Novocherkassk garrison. According to Procuracy papers, Oleshko addressed the crowd from the balcony of the building and demanded that the demonstration cease, but the crowd did not respond. The soldiers who were lined up in front of the building fired a warning shot into the air, "which drove back the crowd of noisy, pressing people." However, at this point, voices cried out: "Do not be afraid, they are shooting blanks." After this the crowd again rushed toward the soldiers positioned in front of the building. A repeat warning shot into the air followed, and immediately afterward there was a burst of single gunshots into the crowd. As a result, ten to thirteen people lay prostrate on the square. Subsequently it was explained that a particularly aggressive participant in the riot had tried to take a weapon from a soldier, forcing the latter to fire. Only after these shootings did panic spread among the demonstrators.[56]

According to Mardar, in the Procuracy's files on the case there are documents testifying to the fact that General Oleshko, as he stood on the balcony, did not give any orders to shoot. On the contrary, exasperated by soldiers' actions, Oleshko even shouted at them to stop firing.[57] According to certain information, it was at this moment that one of the demonstrators, an elderly man, addressed the crowd from the balcony, calling for restraint and organization.[58]

The official version tried to present the shooting of the crowd as an accident or a misunderstanding. Above all, it asserted that it was an act of self-defense—the soldiers were responding to the threat upon their lives posed by the crowd. In order to give this version logic and form, the separate assaults on the police department and the city party committee offices were connected in a single chain of cause and effect: Infuriated by their failures at the police department, the hooligans returned to the square, again tried to take weapons away from soldiers, and the soldiers (without a special order) were forced to open fire. This version, however, has long raised fundamental doubts. For some reason, the identity of the soldier who was allegedly attacked was never established, (although to do this would have been quite easy), nor was the person who tried to take the weapon from him and who threatened his life ever identified. The claim of self-defense contradicts the fact, substantiated by many witnesses, that the soldiers fired into the crowd simultaneously and not by single gunshots. So they were shooting on order and not in random attempts to defend their own lives.

In a word, the episode of the fatal shooting has yet to be fully reconstructed. The truth of the attack on the soldier was not established by the investigation, which had to resort to rather crude tricks in order to prove the unprovable. Mardar writes justifiably that neither in 1962 nor in 1990 did investigators find a single witness of the attack on the soldier. There was not even one person who had seen with his or her own eyes what was key for the official version of events, yet many other, far less significant episodes were reconstructed to the most minute details.[59] Thus, the conclusion is correct that there was an order to shoot for effect, but the crowd failed to respond and only became more aggressive. The repeated use of weapons on June 2, 1962, however, was dictated not by police needs but by political motives. Consequently, even the responsibility for the unjustified use of weapons belongs not to individual soldiers, but to much higher levels of authority.

Mardar has proposed that the members of the Presidium were frightened by the meetings with the strike delegation, which appeared to them as an obvious sign of embryonic self-organization among the insurgents.[60] Undoubtedly, this could have caused the Moscow leaders to take advantage of the sanction already given by Khrushchev to use weapons and, in the process overlook such trifles as the legality of shooting at an unarmed crowd.

The Aftermath of the Shooting: The Speech of the Garbage Collector Zhilkin

News of the shots fired at the demonstrators, who up until the last moment had believed that "they will not shoot at the people," spread quickly all over town. It is possible to judge the first reaction to the event by the testimony of the press operator at NEVZ, P.F. Reshetnikov, who was convicted for participating in the unrest:

> Between two o'clock and three o'clock in the afternoon, workers began coming to the plant and reporting how people were being shot in the city. Everyone was outraged, and Diachenko came up to us saying, "Well, it is right that they are shooting people." In response, I declared to Diachenko, "How dare you talk like this and still tie a red bandana, you should tie a black one." A man standing there, whose name I later found out to be Zavalko, also began to say that it was correct for authorities to be shooting people. After this I hit him in the face. People separated us, and I got on my bicycle and rode to the river. Zavalko had said that the people committing outrageous acts had caused great harm to the government, and I had asked him, are peoples' lives really so worthless? I was upset by his comments and so I hit him in the face.[61]

Eyewitnesses tell the story somewhat differently, but the essence of the conflict is clear: The shooting divided the residents of the city. Some from the very beginning had opposed the strike. They therefore, had to seek moral justification for their cooperation with the same authorities who had issued this cruel order to shoot unarmed persons. Others, who up until this point had been neutral, drew their own critical conclusion, even if they did not express it aloud, as Reshetnikov did.

Outrage at the shootings clashed with the fear instilled in law-abiding residents by the regime, causing moral and psychological stress in many city residents that day. One of those disturbed by these events was N.P. Bredikhin, senior engineer at the Novocherkassk branch of an industrial design institute. Bredikhin was a family man with two children and no criminal record and, by all criteria of political trustworthiness, was a fully "Soviet man." Voluntarily, at the call of the party, as it was then said, he had gone to work in the countryside—at a Machine-Tractor Station and in the Virgin Lands. He had more proposals and inventions than everyone else in the Rationalization Sector of his institute and was preparing to enter graduate studies. A portrait of Bredikhin hung on the "Wall of Honor."[62] The engineer did not take part in the unrest. But after learning what had happened, he could not find within himself the power to play the hypocrite or at the very least could not remain silent. Bredikhin stated:

> I sat down at my workplace and began to draw diagrams. In a little while, I heard noises, which reminded me of the sound of a cart moving along cobblestones. Someone said that this was gunfire. I expressed doubt at this

and continued to work. Around 1:00 P.M., the senior engineer-designer Korshikov came. He was pale and agitated, and he began to say that he had seen with his own eyes the soldiers shooting into the crowd at the square, and that a woman and her child had been killed. Such stories caused the technician Sosedko to become hysterical. She cried out that they might have even killed her own mother. Colleagues became outraged that they were shooting at the crowd. Giving in to this indignation and without investigating events, I got up from my chair, took down Khrushchev's portrait, and threw it out into the courtyard.[63]

These brief "moments of stardom" experienced by the engineer Bredikhin raised in those around him a typically Soviet reaction. They immediately moved away from this "defiler," fearing that they would share responsibility with him for his actions. His colleagues, who had just expressed their horror at the shooting of unarmed people, suddenly fell silent and, as Bredikhin expressed it, began to "condemn him with their glances." Bredikin suddenly felt himself to be a social outcast. Frightened, he lost his head and begged his comrades for advice: "What should I do?" The response was fully Soviet—go give yourself up to the KGB—which Bredikhin promptly did. One of his colleagues picked up the defiled "saint," put glue on it, and rehung it in its former place.[64]

Yet, the shooting on the square, though it frightened residents and sober-minded people, did not cause universal paralysis. The spontaneous protest continued. In the second half of the day on June 2, people were still speaking out in front of the party committee building for achieving the goals of the strike and even for avenging those murdered. Mikhail Kuznetsov, a man involved in earlier events, turned out to be a persistent rebel. During the evening of June 2, he "repeatedly tried to throw rocks at the soldiers, who were passing through in cars, blocked their movement, and yelled out threats against them, declaring in the process, 'Tomorrow at six in the morning we will show you.'"[65]

P.F. Zhilkin, a junk collector, stopped his horse near NEVZ, crawled onto the cart, and delivered an entire speech on the shootings. According to the testimony of an eyewitness, the junk collector spoke incoherently but with great fervor: "What are you doing just standing here. In the city a river of blood is flowing, machine guns and tanks are killing women and children. Go and help them!" Pointing to the third floor of the plant administration building, Zhilkin said: "It is necessary to shoot those bastards." The witness stated that "I approached Zhilkin, and he was a little drunk. I told him to go away, but Zhilkin, looking at my glasses, said: 'Look here, it is necessary to whip such scum.' From the crowd people cried out, 'Get away from here,' and then Zhilkin began again to yell: 'Beat up this four-eyes.'"[66]

Throughout the evening at the party committee offices and at the police department, demonstrators continued to make speeches, especially young people, since their elders had prudently gone home. Simultaneously through the whole square, authorities broadcast a taped speech of A. Mikoian. But the crowd provided their own "accompaniment" to the speech of the Presidium member: They cursed the soldiers and again demanded lowered prices for meat and for butter.[67] Neither Mikoian nor Kozlov appeared that day before the people. After the announcement of a curfew, the troops and the police dispersed the crowd.

In all, twenty-three people were killed during the disorders. Dozens of residents, especially young people, sought medical assistance for wounds. Several KGB personnel were wounded, but there was not a single person killed on the side of the government.

June 3, 1962: Attempts to Continue the Disorders and the Pacification of the City

The curfew, the stationing of troops in the city, and the horror of the shooting on June 2 had a powerful impact, causing many demonstrators and strikers to keep a low profile. The morning of June 3, however, was too soon for anyone to be discussing the final pacification of the city. Certain participants in the disorders continued protest actively. For example, the reckless Aleksandr Zaitsev stirred up trouble in the streets for two more days. According to the indictment, he "committed outrageous acts, threatened military and police personnel with reprisals, and blocked the advance of military vehicles."[68] Another striker who tried to maintain the momentum of the unrest was A.M. Otroshko, a young electrical fitter. He was one of those few participants in the Novocherkassk disorders who, according to KGB data, "even earlier among his circle of acquaintances had expressed anti-Soviet fabrications."[69]

Many rioters did prudently retreat to the background, and on June 3 there were few "hooligan phenomena." But the strikers at the Electric Locomotive Construction Works did not surrender. During the morning they came to work, and then in small groups of two to three again went into the city. On the way, larger groups of ten to fifteen workers joined them, with some riding in cars, but the majority traveling on foot. By 8:00 A.M., a crowd was again gathering at the scene of the previous day's battle—the city police department and the city party committee offices. At first it numbered only 150, but people continued to come. An hour later, a critical moment occurred when a woman cried out hysterically that her son had been killed the day before. The crowd now reached 500 people. Passions peaked as people approached the line of soldiers and again began to demand the liberation of those arrested. Authorities decided to remind people of their existence and tried to deflect the attention of the crowd. In the movie theater *Pobeda* (Victory), loudspeakers were set up and again transmitted Mikoian's speech and the district commander's order for a curfew.

Secret information about a group of motorcycle riders who were heading from Novocherkassk to Shakhty, located about forty kilometers to the north, raised serious concerns among authorities. It looked as if the strikers were sending envoys to get support from neighboring areas. Therefore, police set up roadblocks at the city limits, and in the course of the day detained thirty-two people who were heading in the direction of Shakhty on motorcycles, bicycles, or on foot. Three of those detained appeared suspicious and were arrested for participation in the disturbances, though nothing concrete was known about their plans and intentions.[70] This heightened sensitivity of the bosses, who feared the spread of the disorders, was in and of itself symptomatic and revealing.

By noon, the authorities finally succeeded in organizing party activists, civilian police volunteers, and several loyal workers to conduct mass agitation in the factories and among the citizens. Three hours later, F.R. Kozlov spoke over the radio. This speech, in the view of deputy KGB chairman Ivashutin, became the "turning point in the mood of the people."[71] After this the crowds gradually began to disperse.

Certainly Kozlov's speech was skillfully constructed. It took into consideration the desire of the majority of citizens to find some way out of their hopeless confrontation with the state. Kozlov took advantage of the mass guilt complex experienced by many residents and put full blame for organizing the disorders on certain "hooligan elements," "rabble-rousers," whom he distinguished from the majority of the city's inhabitants. This distinction raised hope in these same residents, who had taken part in varying degrees in the unrest, that they might be able to escape punishment. When he referred to the meeting with the group of strike representatives, which, as we recall, was in reality a very heated, intense exchange, Kozlov claimed that it was the representatives who had "posited the question about restoring order in the city and in the enterprises." In addition, they had asked the Presidium members "to speak over local radio and express their views on the disorders,"[72] though eyewitnesses of the meeting, as Mardar has explained, did not recall anything similar to this. Basically Kozlov was trying to depict the shooting of the crowd on June 2 as having been initiated by the workers' delegation itself, which had demanded the restoration of order, no matter how paradoxical and far-fetched such a claim was.

One unfair juggling of facts led to another. Kozlov claimed that participants in the conversation had then returned to the street and "tried to tell those who had gathered about their meeting with us. However, hooligans did not give them any opportunity to speak."[73] In such a context, the events of June 2 looked like a confrontation between the authorities, whom the majority of honest persons in the city supported, and "hooligan elements," people who were seeking "not the good of the people, but other selfish goals, or people who swallowed the bait of provocateurs."[74] It was as if the majority of citizens who made up the crowd on June 1 and 2 were receiving a promise of indulgence from the CPSU Central Committee, meaning there was hope of avoiding punishment. The argument was persuasive, especially since the state had already demonstrated its own capacity for cruel retribution.

Having divided the residents of Novocherkassk into the pure and the impure, Kozlov alluded to the possibility of concessions, promising to investigate the problems with work norms and the supply of goods, but giving no hope of a repeal of the price increases. Moreover, he even described the Novocherkassk strikers as being in conflict with all Soviet people, who, according to Kozlov, "understand and fully support the price increases."[75] Finally, having falsified the course of events, Kozlov made it seem as though he and Mikoian had supposedly fulfilled the demonstrators' demand for a meeting with the representatives of supreme authority. "Yesterday and today we went out to the enterprises," Kozlov claimed. Simply put, the workers of NEVZ had become social outcasts—the Presidium members supposedly visited only those factories that were "laboring honestly" and "fulfilling the production plan." Following the model of behavior presented in Soviet propaganda for leaders of "genuine popular power," Kozlov even gave assurance that he and Mikoian had "talked with workers" on the streets of the city.[76] In reality, there were no such meetings on June 2, and on June 3 Kozlov and Mikoian met only with trustworthy Communist activists at NEVZ and called on a more or less loyal factory that manufactured synthetic products. Nothing is known for certain about any meetings in the streets.

Kozlov's radio speech, although it signified a turning point in favor of the state, nonetheless did not produce any kind of magical effect on the participants in the unrest. During and after the speech, KGB personnel confirmed hearing "various malicious outcries and threats." The restoration of order in the city after 5:00 P.M. was probably due more to the effectiveness of police measures and the curfew. During the night of June 3 and the early hours of June 4, 240 people were detained,[77] thereby blocking the actions of instigators and extremists and depriving them of their fertile breeding ground—a large crowd.

On that same day, June 3, criminal proceedings were instituted against the active participants in the mass disorders on the basis of Article 79 of the RSFSR Criminal Code. Lieutenant-Colonel D.F. Shchebetenko, the deputy chief of the KGB Department of Investigations, accepted the case and headed a team of 26 investigators.[78] In Novocherkassk and the surrounding cities of Rostov, Shakhtyh, and Taganrog, 140 KGB personnel were sent from Moscow to work under the command of Ivashutin.[79]

On June 4, the life of the city began to return to normal, if, of course, one considers it normal for hundreds of people to be fearing arrest, not knowing precisely whom the secret spies and photographs had identified during the days of the riots. The Electric Locomotive Construction Works returned to work. According to the usual ritual, activists conducted sessions where, as authorized, they condemned participants in the disorders; that is, to a significant measure, they condemned themselves. The night-shift workers brought a symbolic peace offering—they overfulfilled the production plan by 150 percent. On June 9, in an attempt to placate the state, the steel foundry shop workers who had begun the strike presented the administration with written and oral petitions to allow them to labor on Sundays in order to "expiate their guilt for the disorders that had occurred." The workers were praised, but it was explained that the day of rest nonetheless "was to be used according to its designated purpose." Unable to endure the nervous strain, expecting arrest at any time, several strikers and demonstrators gave themselves up to the KGB.

Far from everyone who had risen against "our own Soviet power" was filled with repentance. Among their correspondence, organs of state security discovered an anonymous "First Ultimatum," penned by a certain "Peoples' Committee." In it was a demand to allow relatives to see the wounded and to identify the places where bodies were buried, or else the authors of the document threatened to tell foreigners about the shootings. This represented a sensitive issue for authorities, who had set up in Novocherkassk and in Shakhty five machines of the Radio-Counterespionage Service in case any amateur ham radio operators tried to send reports abroad. Additionally, a protest leaflet authored by a lathe operator, V.M. Bogatyrev, was found in one of the shops at NEVZ, while an anonymous inscription threatening the shop foreman was found on a wall. On Herzen Street in a prominent spot, passersby read the words: "Long live the strike."[80]

"Underground and Real Truth"

The Leaflet of the Worker Baskakov and the Appeal of General Shaposhnikov

The authorities spared no efforts to "lock up" information about the strike and the mass disorders in Novocherkassk, yet news did leak out. Many shared the dissatisfaction of the Novocherkassk mutineers and were enraged by the bloody reprisals against them. But only a few decided to express their protest and engage in "anti-Soviet phenomena."

From June 4 to June 6, anti-Soviet leaflets appeared in the city of Zernograd, Rostov Oblast. Their author turned out to be M.P. Baskakov, a polisher and grinder at a machine factory. In 1962, he and his wife had become parents. Life was hard for the young family: They did not have their own apartment and wages were low. Now, in addition, food prices were rising. By his own admission, the rumors about the events in Novocherkassk, where workers had tried to defend their interests and for this had been shot by authorities, left a deep impression on the young man. In the first leaflet, which he wrote on June 4 and posted during the night on the notice board on Lenin Street, Baskakov did not even mention the events in Novocherkassk. Everything he wrote, however, could have been heard somewhere in the smoking room of NEVZ on the first day of the riots:

> Comrades! Think about how many of us simple honest people are still living in poverty and want. Think about how many people in our city lack an apartment. Is it not time to focus all of our attention, all of our efforts, to eliminate these deficiencies in the next two to three years? Could it be that we do not have the strength for this? Excuse me, everything is within the power of the Russian people, to say nothing of the modern development of science and technology. How incompatible with reality is the conclusion of the present government that it was "forced" to increase prices for such basic products as butter, meat, and oils. What is a person to do if he cannot feed himself well on his monthly wage, he cannot clothe himself well, and this means he cannot even relax well? And a humble person cannot even dream about such items identified by Khrushchev as luxury items, such as radios, televisions, vacuums, refrigerators, and automobiles. Khrushchev says that all this is luxury. Then it comes out that even tractors, combines—machines that lighten human labor—are luxuries according to Khrushchev. So let us hand Mr. Khrushchev a hoe from the Stone Age, let him also live without luxury.[81]

On June 6, in a new leaflet, Baskakov was already referring directly to the experience of Novocherkassk. Without going into details, he talked about the shooting as if it were a fact well known to all in Zernograd. Now the abstract protest against the injustice and cruelty of the state was transformed in Baskakov's second publication into a program of actions and demands:

> Citizens! Comrades! My fathers, my brothers and sisters!

> Things cannot go on any further as they are. We cannot react with calm and a callous spirit to these crude and completely unjustified attempts of the

government to stifle the voice of our people. Only in capitalist countries, and in tsarist Russia, have such measures been used as those our government employed in Novocherkassk . . . they are afraid of their own brave and true Russian people—no less than Tsar Nicholas II feared our fathers and grandfathers. The authorities acted in the same way in Novocherkassk. After all, such an important popular issue should be resolved by the entire Soviet people, yet they [the authorities] resolve it themselves, and moreover, they unleash tanks and weapons on unarmed, peaceful people. Shame and disgrace on our government! A shameful blemish lies on your conscience. You have nothing to wash it away with, and in the end, you will have to answer to all of the people. The radios and newspapers are all silent, but you will not be able to remain silent. . . .

Citizens! Let us all together convene a town meeting of our Zernograd.

We will not go on strike, we demand a general town meeting of our Zernograd, and then of the other towns. . . .[82]

Baskakov's protest was written in the classic style of anti-Soviet agitation of the late 1950s and early 1960s. The author borrowed rhetorical methods from Soviet propaganda, such as the theme of "brothers and sisters" from Stalin's famous announcement about the beginning of World War II. He also used as the basis for his revelations a theme that was highly popular at this time in anti-Soviet documents: Khrushchev had betrayed the cause of Lenin, of the working class, and of socialism. Hence Baskakov referred to laws being copied from "cursed capitalists" and linked the Novocherkassk shootings to the actions of the tsarist government. The essential difference from the majority of such documents, however, was the practical program of actions (the creation of a town public committee) that built creatively upon the failure of the Novocherkassk strikers.

The unique ideological basis of Baskakov's program was an anonymous letter that he wrote criticizing the government. Here he supplemented the criticism with one more traditional anti-Soviet subject: he called for returning to power the overthrown leaders—Bulganin, Shepilov, and Zhukov*— who in the minds of ordinary people always seemed better than the current leaders. Like many other "anti-Soviet Leninists," Baskakov sent his letter directly to the main Soviet media organ, the Central Committee newspaper *Pravda* (Truth), demanding that his opinion "reach the people, if not through your newspaper, then through truth that is underground and real."[83]

If the state had allowed rumors of the Novocherkassk shootings to circu-

---

*Baskakov was referring to the former prime minister N.A. Bulganin, former defense minister Marshal G.K. Zhukov, and D.T. Shepilov, who was expelled from the Central Committee Secretariat in 1957 for his support of the antiparty conspiracy.—E.M.

late more widely, then a significant portion of the pro-Soviet-minded populace in the country might have responded to what had occurred in the same way as Baksakov. This mass reaction could not, of course, have brought on the fall of communism, but it undoubtedly would have prepared the social-psychological soil for the replacement of the "bad leaders" by some kind of "genuine Leninist" standing next in line.

The events in Novocherkassk forced not only ordinary citizens to ponder the nature of the regime, for dissatisfaction existed even among the Soviet elite. On September 7, 1967, the former first deputy commander of the North Caucasus Military Distict, lieutenant-general of the tank forces, Hero of the Soviet Union, party member since 1930, Matvei Kuzmich Shaposhnikov, who had been transferred to the military reserve in 1966, was indicted on criminal charges that in July 1962, he "prepared and preserved in his apartment an anonymous letter-appeal with anti-Soviet contents." In the letter there was a condemnation of the Novocherkassk shootings, along with discussion of the need to create a political organization to be named the "Workers' Party of Bolsheviks" and to create "production committees" in enterprises, state farms, and collective farms. The author called for boycotting candidates promoted by public organizations in the elections for local councils. The letter ended with the words: "We call on you to struggle for political power through peaceful means under the leadership of the Workers' Party (of Bolsheviks). Under current political conditions, we aim to gain political power through non-violent means."[84]

This typed letter was sent by mail on June 30, 1962, to the USSR Union of Writers, to the Georgian SSR Union of Writers, to fourth-year students at the Shakhty branch of the Novocherkassk Polytechnical Institute, and on November 12, 1963, to the Komsomol Committee of Tbilisi State University and the Komsomol Committee of the Kirov Factory in Leningrad. The letters sent from Moscow on June 30, 1962, were signed with the pseudonym "Raging Vissarion" (everyone since their schooldays knew that the famous "revolutionary democrat" and literary critic of the nineteenth century, V. Belinskii, had been called this.—V.K.). Six other letters sharing a single theme were signed with this pseudonym and mailed during 1961 to 1963 to several writers. Copies of all of these letters, including the letter-appeal, were found in the apartment of Lieutenant–General Shaposhnikov during a search. Shaposhnikov admitted having authored the documents found in his apartment with the exception of the letter-appeal. In the latter case he claimed that he had found this letter in his office in the headquarters of the Northern Caucasus Military District in March 1963 and, due to its unique contents, had copied it in the notebook that was subsequently confiscated from him during the search. He had destroyed the typed text of the letter-appeal but without reporting it to the high command and without informing the KGB.[85] To prove Shaposhnikov's guilt, the preliminary investigation relied on the general pseudonym ("Raging Vissarion") used in all of the letters found in the general's home.[86]

Shaposhnikov, who personally despised Khrushchev and had been outraged by the events in Novocherkassk, was in truth supporting sufficiently orthodox Marxist positions. The general did not condemn Soviet power, but its "bad leaders" who were "traitors to the cause of the working class." In his rejection of the Khrushchev regime, Shaposhnikov, judging by the evidence of one of the witnesses, was reacting critically to the decisions of the Twentieth Party Congress and to the exposure of the cult of personality of Stalin, which he believed negatively affected "the authority of the Communist Party of the Soviet Union and the government."[87] From this point of view, Shaposhnikov's stance reflected the "popular Stalinism" that was quite widespread at this time, and represented typical internal criticism that did not challenge the basic foundations of the regime.

The Letter of the Engineer Belik to the Writer Paustovskii (June 6, 1962)

Soon after the removal of Khrushchev from power, I.V. Belik, who was convicted in connection with the Novocherkassk events, sent an appeal to L.I. Brezhnev asking for reexamination of his sentence. Belik claimed that at the beginning of the disorders, he had condemned the strikers and was a loyal supporter of the state, but then, upset by the shootings, he could not restrain his indignation and wrote an incriminating letter. His story reveals an important side of the Novocherkassk phenomenon: the alienation from the state of even those people who were never known for any kind of anti-Soviet thought or deed, and who at first had condemned the rebels.

In the end, the Procuracy, in a protest on the case of Belik (March 1965), recognized:

> It has been established that the letter about the events in Novocherkassk has contents that are incorrect, but not anti-Soviet. As Belik explained, he could not independently examine the reasons for the mass disorders, he was shocked by their consequences and "poured out his soul" in a letter to his favorite Soviet writer, Konstantin Paustovskii.* It has been established

---

*Konstantin Georgievich Paustovskii (1892–1968) was a popular Soviet fiction writer best known for his short stories. Because of his high status, in the 1950s and 1960s Paustovskii was able to act as defender of Soviet writers who had been subjected to official criticism.—E.M.

that no one knew about the letter, and numerous witnesses who knew Belik over the course of many years had never heard him express any anti-Soviet opinions.[88]

The episode with Belik is only one of many examples of the peculiarly Soviet relationship between the people and the state, in which an honest "one of our own people" could appear to the Communist oligarchs to be as dangerous as an ideological opponent of the regime. Among "our own people"—honest citizens like Shaposhnikov or Belik—there was not and could not be "unanimous approval" of a bloody reprisal. Consequently the state lost convinced ideological supporters, that is, precisely those who for long years had secured its stability and strength. In situations such as Novocherkassk, the only supporters the government could have were the cynics, the conformists, and the time-servers, or persons who were subordinate in rank, and therefore compelled to fulfill orders. At the very least, there would be those who were easily impressed and fooled by official propaganda. At a critical moment, though, the support of such persons was not guaranteed, for they might refuse to get involved or they might even become traitors.

Thus, the legitimacy of the state turned out to be in question, though the removal of Khrushchev in 1964 opened up possibilities for overcoming this crisis. He was blamed for the mistakes of the regime, and the Communist oligarchs began to search for new means to renew and strengthen popular loyalty. But Novocherkassk stuck in popular memory, and by remaining silent, the state appeared to be accepting blame for this sin. The ideological supporters of communism were left with the consciousness of the fact that "in our country such bloody crimes are indeed possible."

These last words belong to one Z.N. Tkachev. Immediately after the fall of Khrushchev, he wrote a letter to the procurator-general demanding explanations.[89] But there was no point in Tkachev's waiting for any such explanations. People who had been involved in the shooting were still in power, and there certainly were no volunteers in 1962 to repeat the "mistake of Khrushchev" and expose the Novocherkassk shootings in the same way that the Soviet leader had in 1956 exposed the "cult of personality."

In fact, by laying a blanket of secrecy and silence over the events in Novocherkassk, the Communist oligarchs put themselves into a more advantageous position than did the tsarist government in its own day. Party leaders were thereby able to prolong the life of communist illusions and localize the Novocherkassk conflict. In the final account, the state realized the critical necessity of pacifying the people "with steadfast concern for the material well-being of the laborers," which went on to become one of the major ideological motifs of the Brezhnev era. Gradually the Soviet regime began to degenerate and to decompose ideologically, but no kind of revolutionary alternative to this degradation appeared, although the events in Novocherkassk could have provided such a possibility.

The Preliminary Investigation, Trials, and Sentences

On June 7, 1962, KGB Deputy Chairman Ivashutin reported on the events in Novocherkassk to the Central Committee. Three days later, F.R. Kozlov addressed the Central Committee Presidium.[90] The details of such oral discussions and consultations, as a rule, always remain unknown to historians, although the political result is obvious. The Communist leaders in general, and in particular Khrushchev, who had sanctioned the shooting, were angry and resentful toward their own people, and decided to "throw the book" at the instigators. By demonstrating severity toward the rebels, they hoped to eradicate the breeding ground for resistance in Novocherkassk. They resolved not to publicize the case, but in Novocherkassk, where the notion of keeping the matter hushed up was completely inane, the party leaders decided to hold an open show trial.

Because there had been no real organization in Novocherkassk, the preliminary investigation and trial, having received a very clear political directive, began to fabricate a case. The authorities identified as ringleaders everyone whom they could lay their hands on, especially if the individuals could be molded into the image of hooligans, parasites, renegades, and idlers. The ideal candidates for this role were those with prior convictions, and thus they were the first ones investigators targeted in contriving criminal cases. E.F. Silchenkov wrote in one of his appeals, "I asked the prosecutor Krivoshein in court: 'On what charges are you trying me?' He responded that at some time or another I had been convicted, which meant that I was not satisfied with Soviet power; in other words, I do not fit even one point of the standard codex for being a builder of communism."[91]

The investigation stubbornly clung to any evidence that these chosen scapegoats had organized or facilitated the organization of violence or looting. To do this, investigators employed simple measures. The investigation continually returned to the circumstance considered important to the case: that allegedly in carrying out various actions, such as calling for a strike or demanding lower prices, the defendants already knew about the disorders and riots occurring in other places. Therefore, once they knew that "in essence they were calling for their [the disorders'] activization and spread,"[92] the defendants were in fact acting with premeditation and with evil intent. The harshness of the sentence received by the participants in the Novocherkassk events was largely grounded in this absurd assumption. In addition, there were unlimited stretchings of the truth employed in charging some of the defendants with having organized the riots. "For what crime is a fifteen-year sentence under Article 79 given?" asked the same E.F. Silchenkov. "For an organized armed attack on the state. But who organized this?"[93]

Moreover, in the course of the proceedings, authorities used methods that were fully worthy of the Stalinist epoch. For example, it was known about Gennadii Goncharov that he and his comrades on June 2 "took part in the so-called 'demonstration' and even entered into the building of the city party committee."[94] Yet, at the same time the "actual involvement of Goncharov in this was not established," and these actions do not necessarily incriminate him. Nonetheless, the procurator Shubnikov did not hesitate to propose using this evidence in the trial, if only to paint a negative characterization of Goncharov's personality.

The case of E. Levchenko is also telling. The inquest clearly ignored contradictions in the testimonies of witnesses. No one denied that some woman called from the balcony for liberating the allegedly arrested workers from the police station. In the eyewitness accounts, however, there were clear contradictions: the age (either thirty or forty years) and clothing (either a black jacket with a flowered dress or a black dress, or a reddish-colored jumper with a sweater) One witness said that the speaker was known to her by the name of Galia, but Levchenko's name was Ekaterina.[95] Those who from a short distance saw the woman speaking from the balcony, such as A.M. Mironov, who also spoke from the balcony, and V.D. Cherepanov, who took part with her in the attack on the police department, failed to recognize her as Levchenko. It is possible that there were two women who were different in age and in clothing. Not without reason, Levchenko herself admitted only partial guilt. In any case, the preliminary inquest in its haste disregarded such troubling inconsistencies, resorting, softly speaking, to very strange logic: "From the testimonies of the accused Mironov, it is obvious that in the given case he is speaking about Levchenko, although Mironov did not identify her in the inquest."[96]

Such logic could be considered juridically curious, if it were not raised to the level of a systematic policy. The procurator-general's response from January 1965 concerning the appeal of a defendant by the name of Tulnov, who fully denied his guilt, stated that his active participation in the attack on the police department "was substantiated by the fact of his being one of the first to be detained at the scene of the crime." And that was all! Tulnov claimed that he had looked in out of curiosity, and there were no witnesses who could prove the contrary. Neither the investigation nor the trial troubled itself, naturally, even to search for such witnesses, since, as Tulnov declared, "they were trying to find an enemy in me."[97]

Viacheslav Chernykh directly accused the inquest of falsifying his case:

> Major Vasiliev took advantage of my candid admissions, of my ignorance, and smeared me with mud. It is remarkable how the security organs can conduct an inquest without any mistakes. They had to find organizers, and they were lazy, which is why they accused me of something which I did not do. All the mitigating circumstances, and also those witnesses who spoke in my defense, were not taken into account.[98]

Georgii Vasiukov justifiably complained to the Procuracy about "various tricks of the investigator Demidiuk." He claimed that the court "absolutely refused to heed witnesses who changed their testimony, in spite of the fact that earlier a number of witnesses had testified to the complete opposite."[99] Indeed, there was considerable manipulation of witnesses. The only ones chosen were those deemed convenient or those who could be adequately "prepared." E. Silchenkov, who held out until the end and refused to confess his guilt, wrote that witnesses for the prosecution had stated after the trial: "We did not know, they said, that such long terms would be given, the investigator had instructed us. . . ."[100] In an appeal to the KGB chairman sent on January 10, 1964, Silchenkov tried to focus attention on the technique of the fabrication: The testimonies of uncooperative witnesses were ignored, and there was a pathological trust in convenient witnesses. He complained that people who could have proven his distaste for mass disorders were not allowed to testify.[101] He particularly had in mind an acquaintance, a factory Communist, who on the first day of the unrest had asked him as a stable and more mature person to convince the crowd to let the train pass. This episode not only seemed to prove directly that there were no malicious intentions in the actions of the accused, but it also illuminated his sluggish efforts to help authorities restore order. Yet, the preliminary inquest and trial ignored the testimony of this witness, though at the same time neither the inquest nor the trial disproved it.[102]

V.G. Bakholdin also complained about Demidiuk's bias:

> My investigator, Captain Demidiuk, who conducted my case, only gathered material that exposed me and used only those witnesses who could convict me. But with regard to the witnesses whom I pointed out to the investigator, who could correct these false testimonies, Demidiuk under various pretenses either rejected them or did not bother to find these people, although I identified their names and addresses. . . .[103]

V.A. Ukhanov focused attention on the fact that the preliminary inquiry and trial preferred to use those who had seen his actions from afar, and who basically could not hear what he said, instead of the testimonies of witnesses who had been constantly near him at the moment of the events. He identified persons who were prepared to verify that he had not yelled anything. Ukhanov emphasized that a witness under the pressure of the inquiry had identified him, but then during the trial had retracted his statements. However, the court actually changed the witness's statement. Instead of reading that the defendant's outbursts "were not heard," the sentence read "were heard."[104]

Any unbiased professional would have said that in the case of Ukhanov there were loose ends that did not tie together, just as there were in many other cases, if not all of them. Thus, after one of the Ukhanov's appeals, T.G. Sokolova, the procurator for the Procuracy's Department of Surveillance over Investigations in the Organs of State Security, concluded that the convicted man "has raised arguments worthy of attention" and charged the head of the analogous department in the RSFSR Procuracy, M.N. Rogov, with verifying the validity of the conviction.[105] Rogov's answer is shocking in its complete disregard for elementary logic and common sense. The negative response given to the appeal is very strong and suggests that Rogov did not question the absurd logic of the preliminary inquiry and trial. Rogov wrote: "In the appeal addressed to the Procuracy, Ukhanov points out that the sentence did not correspond to the material of the criminal case, that the witness Trofimov slandered him, and that he was convicted without any grounds." Clearly it was necessary to verify Trofimov's testimony and compare it with the statements of other witnesses, but instead Rogov claimed that "the testimonies of witnesses questioned in the inquest and in the trial, however, expose Ukhanov's incriminating actions." Rogov then provides a single quote, but it is from the statements of the very same Trofimov![106] Subsequently Sokolova decided not to get involved and hence pretended that she was satisfied with Rogov's formal reply.

Another example of a flagrant manipulation of facts is the charge against I.A. Grankin regarding the attack on the police department. Investigators ignored witness testimony that Grankin spent the entire day of June 2 at home, nor did they consider clear inconsistencies in descriptions of his physical appearance and behavior. The slanderous statements of a neighbor who had long hated the defendant helped convict this seriously ill invalid.[107]

A number of witnesses tried to resist the pressure from investigators who were forcing them to give the necessary answers. For example, the operator of the Gas Distribution Center, N.G. Fedorov, as explained earlier, refused to identify any of the participants in the "march" of Sergei Sotnikov, and "did not give statements, in part due to threats from hooligans."[108] Several witnesses also did not recognize Ekaterina Levchenko as the instigator of the attack on the police department on June 2, 1962.[109] In those cases when the investigators failed to find cooperative witnesses from among the city's residents, they turned for help to those who were required to "understand the situation," meaning the police. In order to make life easier for obliging witnesses, the investigation in a number of cases refused to allow the defendants to confront their accusers.

In preparing for the first trial and composing the indictment, procurator Iu. Shubin, even before the formulation of the case, wrote reports on all of the accused, for which he gathered every compromising detail that could be used to blacken the characters of the future defendants. He also formulated supposedly practical recommendations on conducting the trial for A.A. Kruglov, who was the state prosecutor for Case No. 22, and L.N. Smirnov, chairman of the RSFSR Supreme Court, who presided over the trial.[110]

The judicial process, as the convicted defendants proved in numerous appeals, followed completely the same spurious logic and used the same tactics as the inquest and the indictment. To prevent any surprises, it was decided that even the lawyers for the defendants should be "prepared" for the trial. In any case, the attempts of relatives to secure their own lawyers were suppressed. According to Silchenkov, his wife hired a lawyer and paid him a sum of money that was quite large for their family, 140 rubles. The advocate acquainted himself with the case, but he was not even allowed to attend the trial, for authorities transferred the defense to the official state-appointed lawyer. The family had wasted its money, and received only 40 rubles back.

The legal proceedings moved quickly without even trying to ascertain the truth. Those defendants who objected and did not wish to repent were immediately silenced. V. Ukhanov complained:

> The court literally did not allow me to speak. Or rather, it allowed me to talk, but as soon as I began, the judge interrupted me: "Sit down, that is enough, everything is clear to the court." In saying this, he took from the file my old sentence from 1947 and, shaking it, said: "Sit down, your past is well known, we know who you are and what you represent. Everything is clear to the court."[111]

The court carried out the command of the supreme authorities and issued sentences, including the death penalty, that did not in any way correspond to the gravity of the crimes and that were based on falsified evidence. Those who were in the worst position, no matter how paradoxically, were those defendants who had not carried out any kind of physical violence against representatives or supporters of the state. E. Silchenkov wrote:

We are all here together in a strict regime camp. . . . And among us there are persons who committed particularly heinous state crimes. But they were condemned as hooligans [under] Article 206. . . . I understand that if there were no hooligans, it would not be necessary to seek out and invent ringleaders, among whom I innocently fell. These creatures, who are direct criminals, they are trusted, they are already on their way out, an article written on white paper does everything, but no one dares even look into their dark souls.[112]

It is not the task of this book to give a detailed analysis of the legal validity of the inquest, trials, and sentences of those indicted for participation in the Novocherkassk events. The evidence given, however, strongly implies that the state ordered a public reprisal for Novocherkassk in order to frighten and bring to their senses undisciplined citizens who had "gotten out of hand," to discredit politically and morally the participants in the riots, and to form a guilt complex even in those who had not been involved.

The first open trial, and the most important one for the state, took place August 14–20, 1962, in Novocherkassk. The defendants were those whom authorities had decided to designate as the ringleaders—A.F. Zaitsev, M.A. Kuznetsov, V.D. Cherepanov, B.N. Mokrousov, A.A. Korkach, S.S. Sotnikov, V.G. Shuvaev, E.P. Levchenko, V.I. Chernykh, G.A. Goncharov, I.P. Sluzhenko, G.G. Katkov, G.M. Shcherban, and Iu.V. Dementev. Seven were sentenced to be shot, and the rest received long prison sentences ranging from ten to fifteen years. In order to issue death sentences, the preliminary inquiry and trial crudely violated the law. Authorities charged the "seven" with banditry under Article 77 of the RSFSR Criminal Code (1960 edition), which stipulated a death sentence. Article 79 of the Criminal Code (mass disturbances) did not stipulate such a punishment. The authors of document collections on the Novocherkassk events have noted that the application of Article 77 to the participants in the disorders was not legal. The Commentary on the RSFSR Criminal Code states that the required condition for identifying an act as banditry is the use of weapons by the accused, that is, objects intended exclusively for hitting a live target and that require special permission to use, bear, and store. In this same commentary, the identifying sign of banditry was given as the stability of the group—a union of people not only for one act, but for subsequent actions.[113] Yet the investigation failed to uncover anything like this in the conduct of even the most active participants in the unrest. But this could hardly stop anyone in a country where the will of the bosses was always more important than the law and moral conscience.

The judicial process was intended not only to frighten the residents of Novocherkassk, but also to prove to them that it had been correct to send tanks into the city, and that the state had not had any other recourse than to shoot at the crowd of "hooligan elements" and "bloodthirsty bandits." At the same time, the party hierarchy, and above all Khrushchev, tried to convince even themselves that the people were on their side. Thus, throughout the course of the trials, the KGB, the Procuracy, and the CPSU Central Committee Department of Propaganda and Agitation for the RSFSR regularly reported information to the top party leaders. Members and candidate members of the Presidium and the Central Committee Secretariat heard the first report, dated August 16, 1962, of the KGB and the Procuracy. Everything in it had to prove that the decision made was absolutely correct and that the Soviet people fully shared the hatred of the state for rebels and "hooligan elements." According to the report, some defendants themselves repented, while others, those who fully or partially denied their guilt, "were exposed by witnesses as inveterate criminals, self-seekers, and morally corrupted persons."[114] The soothing balm for the bosses had to be the pronouncements of the trial's eyewitnesses, who had been carefully selected by the KGB and were repulsive in their thirst for blood. Each day at the trial there were supposedly in attendance up to 1,000 people representing "the public," though according to other estimates, the numbers ranged from 450 to 500.[115] The report stated:

> Many workers who were present in court expressed the opinion that such criminals should not even be tried, but instead should be shot without an investigation and trial. The workers of the assembly shop at the Electric Locomotive Construction Works, Radchenko and Shiniia, after returning from the trial, spoke in the shop about the real face of the individuals who were on trial. Their story was greeted with outbursts directed at the criminals: "Swine," "Money bags," "What did they really hope to achieve?" The lathe operator in the equipment shop of this factory, Ferapontov, told his colleagues at work: "They are trying inveterate scoundrels, many of them former criminals. There were two parasites who cried out more than everyone about improving life. Yet these same people have their own homes, dachas, one has a car and the other a motorcycle. Such vermin must be isolated from society and punished in the harshest way possible."[116]

The state heard what it wanted to hear: "Why could we not see, why did we go, after all, there were only bandits with three and four convictions and seven marriages."[117] On the whole, the first trial accomplished the task presented to it from above. The authorities could be satisfied. The hall of the courtroom greeted the sentences with "continuous applause," and the KGB and the Procuracy proudly announced: "If earlier part of the people did not understand the events that had occurred, then now the residents of Novocherkassk have examined their meaning and understand that the disorders were provoked by criminal-hooligan elements and with outrage condemn the criminal actions of bandits and hooligans."[118] Nonetheless, the head of the Central Committee Department of Propaganda and Agitation for the RSFSR, V.I. Stepakov, had to force himself to confess through clenched teeth that individual persons had nonetheless expressed "their own sympathy with the accused and considered their actions to have been correct."[119]

The condemned themselves, both those who confessed their guilt as well as those who stoically insisted on their complete innocence, were unanimous in one thing: The penalties were not commensurate with the crime in a single case. The court did not consider either the character of the defendants or the reasons for the Novocherkassk events. All subsequent appeals, both individual and collective, to higher party, state, and judicial organs, fell on deaf ears, evoking the same uniform, stamped answer: "Convicted correctly."

Even among the old hands of the Procuracy's Department of Surveillance over Investigations in the Organs of State Security, who were used to following the prevailing political winds, there was a sense that the sentences for the Novocherkassk strikers were on shaky legal ground. In one of the surveillance files of the Procuracy are preserved handwritten notes criticizing the sentences by one of the staff working on the case of Bakholdin, Vasiukov, and other defendants. Attached to the notes is a request dated February 22, 1964: "I ask you to preserve these notes in a special file, for we will yet return to this case."[120]

The overthrow of Khrushchev raised the hopes of the defendants. After all, if the party bosses themselves had identified Khrushchev as the main person responsible for all conceivable problems, then it would be logical to acquit those who already in 1962 had risen up against his mistaken and impulsive policies. A whole flood of collective and individual appeals followed, asking that the cases be reexamined and, at the very least, sentences reduced. The Procuracy finally filed protests against several Novocherkassk cases that criticized individual sentences, particularly the court's failure to consider the character of the accused and the fact that many had played secondary roles in the strike. As a result of the protests, a number of defendants had their prison terms shortened and some were even pardoned. But no one was declared justified in their actions! Right up until the fall of the Soviet regime, the leadership continued to insist the defendants had been "convicted justifiably," even when revoking part of the prison term.

Chapter 14

Rear-Guard Battles of the Late Khrushchev Era

Conflict Between the State and the People in the Aftermath of Novocherkassk

After the events in Novocherkassk, the wave of mass unrest clearly subsided. Whereas for the eighteen-month period between 1961 and June 1962, there had been five large-scale mass uprisings (Krasnodar, Murom, Aleksandrov, Biisk, and Novocherkassk), over the thirty-month period from July 1962 to 1964, there were only two such events that have been documented. These were more or less comparable with the Krasnodar rebellion, but did not reach the scale of Novocherkassk. The regime extricated itself from the crisis by demonstrating that it still had significant reserves of vitality. Popular disenchantment in romantic communist utopias provided the soil in which the people and the state worked out new "rules of the game." These in turn shaped the social-political physiognomy of the phenomenon that would later be called "stagnation," and made mass uprisings against the regime an extraordinary event. Such an alteration in the relations between the state and the people could not have taken place under Khrushchev, who was chained to the past by his many mistakes. The party elite and the bureaucracy, however, began to seek an exit from the impasse of Khrushchevism even while he was still in power.

The unprecedented wave of "anti-Soviet phenomena" was indeed forced back, though not immediately. In June 1964, the KGB chairman, V.F. Semichastny,* reported, for example, "a significant decrease" in the number

*V.F. Semichastny was KGB chairman from 1961 to 1967.—E.M.

of anonymous oppositionist documents distributed underground. During the first five months of 1964, the KGB uncovered 3,000 leaflets and anonymous letters containing calls for overthrowing Soviet power and expressing "a lack of faith in the construction of communist society" and "dissatisfaction with the material conditions of life." This was almost four times less than in the second half of 1963 (11,000).[1]

In 1961, an incident had occurred in the far eastern region of the Russian Republic known as Primorskii Krai that could have set a dangerous precedent. Nonetheless, although frightened by the events in Novocherkassk, the authorities did not permit the "Primorskii Krai model" to be repeated during the critical year of 1962. This "model" provided for prosecuting the behavior of leaders and participants in collective work stoppages (strikes) as a criminal act, that is, equating strikes with mass uprisings and disturbances. The case took the following shape. On May 31, 1961, all seventy fishermen of the processing ship, the *Chernyshevskii*, which was engaged in crab fishing in the Sea of Okhotsk on the western shore of the Kamchatka Peninsula, refused to go to work and demanded a pay increase. Their protest had been spurred by the lowering of piece rates per job as compared with the previous year.[2]

The investigation showed that the initiators and activists in the strike were two young Communists who were subsequently expelled from the CPSU: Ivan Pukman, assistant to the ship's foreman and a member of the Komsomol committee, and Aleksei Ivlev, a fisherman. Pukman was the first to raise the idea of a strike, and Aleksei Ivlev was the first to support it with such comments as "Tomorrow, like we discussed, we will not go to work. Whoever goes out on the boat will be thrown overboard."[3] Another participant in the conspiracy was Aleksandr Semerenko, who, along with Ivlev, was able to make contact with fellow fishermen on other boats and enlist their support.

On May 31, Pukman told his comrades that the work stoppage had to continue until wages were increased. Interestingly, no one, neither the bosses, nor the organizers, nor the rank-and-file participants in the events even once used the seditious word "strike" in their own conversations. This "unpleasant" word associated Soviet power with capitalism, and very nearly aligned the participants with "anti-Soviet elements" and "enemies of the people." Therefore, consciously avoiding such implications, they replaced "strike" with different euphemisms.

On the day when these events transpired, the administration and party organization conducted a general meeting as well as a session of party members. But the general meeting only poured fuel on the fire. The single speaker at the meeting was the captain-director of the factory, Levchenko, and he did not trouble himself to be diplomatic: "Anyone who does not want to work can give written notice." The outraged workers dispersed amicably, but at subsequent sessions, they spoke up, including Semerenko, and they demanded restoration of the rates from the previous year. Moreover, they made this official by a decision of the ship's trade union committee.[4]

Having failed to overcome the solidarity of the fishermen, the bosses tried a method of individual persuasion that was usually effective in such cases. They turned to Communists and demanded that they fulfill their party duty by immediately returning to work. After long negotiations, Pukman, trying to maintain his party status and position, felt compelled to return to work. But he told other fishermen to ignore his decision and to continue to act according to their conscience. Even Ivlev, who on May 31 had been the most active—repeatedly visiting the fishermen's quarters in order to support the militancy of his comrades and threatening physical violence against those who were wavering—left the ranks of the strikers after the captain-director and the deputy political officer had a talk with him that same evening. He, like Pukman, called for the rest to overlook his own submission. But the organizers had been broken, and this was enough for the rank-and-file strikers, who from the very beginning had felt uncomfortable, to back down from their demands. Only on June 1, when it became known that several of the most prominent strikers had been dismissed from their jobs, did courage return to Pukman. He proposed that all the fishermen resign from the factory ship in protest. But it was already too late, and no one supported Pukman.

There was nothing extraordinary about the strike on the *Chernyshevskii*, but the timing was critical. These events occurred only one day before the beginning of the riots in Novocherkassk, which naturally affected the reaction of the Primorskii Krai bosses. Frightened and perplexed by the Novocherkassk uprising, they turned several of the more active strikers into scapegoats. Venting their wrath, the authorities accused these scapegoats of having organized mass disturbances, which meant that they were charged with a state crime. This was done not on the basis of juridical merit, for participation in a strike is not a crime in the Soviet Criminal Code, but under the direct orders of regional party leaders.[5]

On October 3, 1962, Ivan Pukman and Aleksei Ivlev were convicted of criminal charges and sentenced to three years' imprisonment, Aleksandr Semerenko to two years.[6] The definition of the "crime" was clearly far-fetched. The defendants were accused of having organized mass disturbances on the basis of "the fact that the mass walkout of fishermen took place under specific conditions, during the fishing season, when the fishing ship *Chernyshevskii* was far from any populated areas." But neither the "specific conditions" nor the location of the events were definite indicators of mass disorders, which the experienced lawyers from the USSR Procuracy immediately understood. The procurator in the Department of Surveillance over

Investigations in the Organs of State Security, Stepanov, in his own March 1963 conclusion to the case of Pukman and the others, decided to challenge the incorrect definition of the "crime." In these cases, Stepanov did not see anything unusual in the fishermen's actions either in their scale or in their political direction—this was a local conflict, caused basically "by the lack of organization or the incorrect actions of the administration."[7] Moreover, as Stepanov wrote, regional party leaders had themselves identified "insufficiencies in the organization of payment for workers and had charged the leadership of the Crab Fleet [*Kraboflot*] with restructuring pay scales for the labor of fishermen."[8] Ultimately, the *Chernyshevskii* fishermen achieved their goals, but paid the typical price for this—the broken lives of the three instigators.

The procurator proposed submitting a protest to the RSFSR Supreme Court Presidium "concerning the revocation of the sentence and the cessation of the case against I.Iu. Pukman, A.F. Ivlev, and A.N. Semerenko due to the absence of a crime in their actions, as defined in Article 79 (mass disorders) of the RSFSR Criminal Code." But USSR Procurator-General Rudenko rejected Stepanov's protest.

Fortunately for participants in other collective work stoppages, the "Primorskii precedent" did not signal the beginning, in 1962 and 1963, of mass repressions against workers dissatisfied with their wages. Strikers did not come to be equated with vandals and looters, which in the end served the best interests of the state. Losing the trust of the working class, declared by official doctrine to be the "leading and directing force" in Soviet society, would have been far more dangerous and costly. Equating dissatisfied workers with rioters and vandals would have only strengthened opposition to the regime without pacifying the populace. The state also served its own self-interest by refraining from Stalinist tactics of mass intimidation. The few cases of documented labor conflicts in 1962 and 1963 were, on the whole, resolved peacefully.

By the end of Khrushchev's leadership, the regime already was moving into a stage of maturation and bureaucratic stabilization. The new party, state, and economic elite began to realize its desire for stability, which in the end brought about the removal of Khrushchev. The lessons of the early 1960s pushed party leaders to seek a certain compromise in the state-society conflict. The populace, in its turn, mastered its new political and economic situation, which subsequently turned into stagnation, and also revealed an inclination toward appeasement. As a result, the breeding ground for mass riots and rebellions gradually dissipated. The Procuracy began to focus more attention on violations of "socialist legality" in police organs, which could not help but have a calming influence on the populace.[9] The chronic disease of mass disorders that plagued Khrushchev's last years entered into a cold phase and revealed itself only in several rare, although instructive, relapses.

The Krivoi Rog "Petition" to Khrushchev, June 1963

The town of Krivoi Rog, Dnepropetrovsk Oblast, Ukraine SSR, had first fallen into the Procuracy's "Chronicles of Conflict" in the spring of 1961. Here large-scale industrial construction had been going on, which meant that there was a heavy concentration of volatile human material. On March 26, around 4:00 P.M., senior police officer E. Prudnik tried to detain E. Sobol, who had been selling sunflower seeds at a market located in a settlement of construction workers. Upon seeing the policeman, the peddler ran away. Prudnik then scattered the seeds in a fit of anger. Exasperated by the cavalier manner of this representative of state authority, a young civilian police volunteer who was standing nearby reproved him. Prudnik's response was to propose in a threatening tone that the young man "proceed" to the police department. When the latter refused, the infuriated policeman dragged him off by force. A small group of visitors to the market witnessed the incident and, critical of the policeman, set off after them.

The young volunteer was immediately released at the police department, but his mass escort did not disperse. Patrons from a nearby movie theater joined the growing crowd after the end of the show. As usual, a group of hooligans also turned up, who demanded that Prudnik be handed over for reprisals. The situation grew tense, and the appearance of MVD troops whet the crowd's appetite even more. A group of about fifty persons left the crowd and began to throw rocks at the police building. Having broken through the wall, they then turned over and burned a police car. The only injuries were suffered by two policemen. By 10:00 P.M., order was restored, and four of the participants in the attack were soon arrested. The senior policeman Prudnik was discharged from the police force for having "acted incorrectly."[10]

Mass disturbances recurred in Krivoi Rog on June 16 and 17, 1963, a little over two years after this first incident, the plot of which in some aspects mirrored the spring episode of 1961. In addition, there occurred a variation of the often repeated theme of the "poor little soldier." Late in the evening on June 16, a drunken soldier by the name of Aleksei Taranenko was riding on a streetcar. He smoked, pushed passengers, and cursed obscenely. Fortunately for the passengers, but not so for Taranenko, there was a divisional police agent by the name of Panchenko in the car, who told the hooligan to straighten up. The soldier stopped smoking, but then began cursing the policeman. Panchenko stopped the streetcar and tried to remove the offender from the vehicle. Taranenko resisted, and workers who were riding on the streetcar came to the assistance of the policeman. Once on the street, the soldier tried to hide, and Panchenko chased after him. But now a new group of actors emerged to interfere in these events.

About fifteen young persons ran after the policeman yelling: "Do not touch that soldier." They defended Taranenko and helped him to escape. Meanwhile, one of the workers involved in the scuffle with Taranenko reported what had happened to a police patrol, and two officers subsequently set off to help Panchenko. They stopped the fleeing soldier, but Taranenko tripped one of his pursuers, jumped over his fallen opponent, and darted away. He was eventually caught not far from the district police department. The group of young people who throughout this time had been hurriedly following the chase tried once more to defend the soldier. One of the policemen fired three shots in the air, and then help arrived in time from the district police department. The combined police forces finally succeeded in detaining Taranenko. The young people who had tried to free the soldier disappeared somewhere, but, as it turned out, not for long. Soon about fifteen to twenty youths again congregated around the police building and demanded release of the detained soldier.

The noise attracted a crowd. When the news spread that during his detention, someone had hit Taranenko and cracked his skull, people called for an ambulance. The police, however, did not immediately hand over the wounded man to the doctors. In the end, about two hundred outraged people surrounded the police department building, and the cry, "Attack the police building. Why are you just looking at it?" rang out. When told to disperse, the mob hurled stones, and some began to shove employees who were standing around the building. The on-duty police supervisor prohibited the use of weapons and ordered that persuasion be used to restore order. One of the policemen who had arrived at the scene nonetheless fired in the air, and then more shots followed, about twenty in all.

The rioters immediately scattered. Soon it was clear that the agitated policemen had not been shooting just in the air, for two young persons with gunshot wounds were taken to the hospital. Two more persons from the crowd suffered minor injuries, as did five police workers. Even Taranenko ended up in the hospital with a cracked skull. The police claimed that where and how he had been wounded could not immediately be established, but what the city residents thought about this is understandable.[11]

A worker by the name of Trofimov introduced new nuances into this traditional antipolice riot. Together with other citizens outraged by the brutal actions of the police, Trofimov sent a telegram addressed to Khrushchev. In it he reported about the illegal use of weapons by the police and about the victims, and asked for intervention by the Moscow authorities.[12] The next morning near the Dzherzhinskii district police department, about a hundred persons gathered who were angry over the illegal actions of the police in detaining the soldier and especially over the harsh shootings. All of the city's party and Komsomol activists were roused for duty, and the regional and city party committees convened a session of district party heads. Almost immediately mass explanatory work began. Authorities promised those who had assembled at the police building that the guilty would be punished and that the wounded had received medical attention and were alive. Party and state activists, KGB workers, and police mingled in the crowd throughout the entire day, along with almost four hundred civilian police volunteers.

Nonetheless the crowd, vacillating in size over the course of the day, did not disperse and did not yield to persuasion. From time to time demands rang out to hand over the guilty policemen for mob law and reprisals.[13] By evening, around six hundred persons were blockading the police department. Some insisted that those guilty of the night's events be handed over and that the entire personnel of the district police department be replaced. Attempts to disperse the crowd with the help of fire trucks failed and only served to provoke the protesters further. One group of activists broke into the police building and proceeded to loot the premises. Positioning themselves in the corridor, the police began to shoot randomly. As a result, two persons were fatally wounded (one of them a juvenile), while eight workers of the Krivoi Rog Metallurgical Factory and one police officer received less serious gunshot wounds. Twelve persons, including seven policemen, suffered "various physical wounds."[14] But it was only with the help of soldiers from the troops of the Ukrainian SSR Ministry for the Defense of Public Order (MOOP)* and other military personnel that the mass riots were finally suppressed. Several participants in the disorders were detained; however, information about their fate could not be found in the Procuracy's surveillance records. Though larger in scale than other disturbances, the events in Krivoi Rog were not the single antipolice riot during the sunset of Khrushchev's rule. On April 8, 1964, in the city of Stavropol, a crowd of about seven hundred persons tried to liberate a drunken hooligan who, in the opinion of the mob, had been arrested unjustifiably. The conflict ended in the usual scenario: an attack on the police department, the burning of a police car, a beating of the "guilty" policeman, arrival of fire trucks and soldiers' patrols, and arrests of the ringleaders.[15]

---

*In 1960, the USSR MVD was dissolved, and its functions transferred to the ministries of internal affairs of the union republics. In 1962, the MVD was reconstituted but the name was changed to Ministry for the Defense of Public Order (MOOP).—E.M.

Long Live Stalin! The Uprising in Sumgait,
November 7, 1963

In 1961 at the Twenty-second CPSU Party Congress, after a long period of fluctuation in anti-Stalinist policy, Khrushchev tried anew to settle accounts with the shadow of the great dictator. The body of Stalin was removed from the Lenin-Stalin Mausoleum and interred beside the Kremlin wall. With this symbolic gesture, the ruling group, and above all Khrushchev himself, seemed to be revealing their own attitude toward Stalin. They reluctantly recognized him as an honored revolutionary and buried him accordingly. But they deprived him of the aureole of a "Communist God"—the mausoleum would henceforth display only the embalmed mummy of Lenin. For ordinary opponents of the regime, such a step was very significant. Everyday dissatisfaction with the state and its policy always looked for a positive example, and yesterday's idols dethroned by this state immediately became a banner for the enemies of the regime. If the hated Khrushchev—under whose rule prices rise and wages go down, churches close and personal garden plots shrink, police "behave disgracefully" and taxes grow—attacked Stalin, then this means that Stalin had to be "good," and it is necessary to defend this "better man" from the "bad one." The removal of Stalin from his position as a Communist saint inevitably had to turn him into a possible symbol of protest and a potential participant in the Manichean dichotomy of "the bad present" versus the "good past." To love Stalin meant to hate Khrushchev, and to extol Stalin meant to curse Khrushchev.

The nostalgia for the Stalinist period was based largely on the Stalinist ideological myth of a thriving country headed by true Leninists who were unselfishly devoted to communism, where there was no place for fat bureaucrats, where order ruled and every year prices went down out of concern for the "people of labor." Indeed, such an attitude was a remarkably widespread phenomenon, despite the highly critical impression produced on the intelligentsia by the exposure of the "cult of personality of Stalin." Yet, the generation of the 1970s and early 1980s remembers well the fashion that suddenly exploded among truck drivers of putting a photograph of Stalin on the windshield. This act, in addition to expressing a longing for order, constituted demonstrative criticism of a regime that had, in the eyes of these truck drivers, permitted the corruption and debauchery of bureaucrats.

Popular disillusionment in the high ideals of the state sought suitable ideological material for manifesting discontent. The symbol of Stalin was in this respect even better than Lenin, whom official propaganda had fully expropriated. Appealing to "yesterday's leaders," who were good not in and of themselves but as potential enemies of the current state, since they had been rejected and repudiated by it, allowed the disavowal of the regime's legitimacy through its own myths and values. Those who were dissatisfied, as events in Sumgait showed, were ready to appeal to the shadow of Stalin. Consequently, during the Brezhnev era a rather solid ideological construction would be built on this basis, which the liberal intelligentsia interpreted as the rehabilitation of Stalinism. In reality, though, it turned into a rather subtle game. In the actual practice of the Brezhnev era, there would not be any kind of "return to Stalin," despite views widespread in the West and in contemporary Russian literature. In fact, in terms of the scale of political repressions against dissidents, the Khrushchev period stands much closer to Stalinism than does the Brezhnev regime. Under Khrushchev many thousands of persons were convicted of anti-Soviet agitation and propaganda, while during the Brezhnev era, there were at the most only hundreds. But the regime allowed the image of the deceased dictator to project once more on movie screens and television sets, on the pages of books and newspapers, making him, in somewhat sanitized form, part of the official value system.

Therefore, the history of the events in Sumgait, the last large-scale mass disorder of the Khrushchev era, offers insight into the subtle transformations in mass psychology that prepared the way for the ideological hypocrisy of the Brezhnev period. It also illuminates the reasons that the new regime preferred to absorb Stalin partially into its ideological value system while leaving him in the role of the devil, responsible for mass repressions, abuse of power, destruction of "true Leninists," and so on. In doing so, the regime actually presented Khrushchev's impulsiveness [*voluntarizm*] as a weak form of Stalinism.

The mass disorders in the Azerbaijani city of Sumgait occurred on the "holy day" of the Soviet calendar—November 7, 1963, the forty-sixth anniversary of the October Revolution. At 10:00 A.M., as usually happened everywhere at this date and time in the USSR, an official demonstration of workers and laborers marched through the central city square. From the tribunal, speakers proclaimed slogans and greetings honoring the CPSU and its leader, the "true Leninist," N.S. Khrushchev. The "true Leninist" himself gazed down on this demonstration of his subjects from the enormous portrait hanging on the wall of the Palace of Culture. Everything went according to the expected script, which had been rehearsed and rehashed many times. It had now practically grown into a habit and did not promise anything unusual. This time, however, the official festivities proceeded much differently.

The problem began when, fearing accusations of Stalinism, which after the Twenty-second Congress could quite easily cost one his career and party card, local authorities encroached upon a popular tradition. Even after the

Moscow party bosses had exposed and stigmatized Stalin, the Sumgait workers continued from all pulpits to express their loyalty to the fallen idol. Thus, S. Akperov, the procurator for the Azerbaijan SSR, reported after the events in Sumgait to Procurator-General Rudenko that "in the city of Sumgait this was not the first time that during a demonstration people carried a portrait of Stalin. Such cases had occurred as well during the May First demonstrations in 1962 and 1963, and during the October celebration in 1962."[16] Demonstrators habitually carried even small portraits of Stalin "which no one prevented them from doing."[17]

The longer such clear sedition (disagreement with the official criticism of Stalin) was indulged, the more provocative it became. Losing their nerve, the city authorities resolved in a typical Stalinist way, meaning in the usual arbitrary manner, to struggle against the memory of Stalin.[18] Accordingly, police, civilian police volunteers, and those responsible for the procession of demonstrators "received directives to confiscate portraits of Stalin if such appear."[19]

As the procession of demonstrators approached the end, disturbances arose on the square. Contradictions in the sources suggest that the unrest could have arisen simultaneously in several sections of the demonstration. According to Akperov's report, the cause of the unrest was "the fact that one of the demonstrators had a miniature portrait of Stalin on the lapel of his jacket. The secretary of the party committee for the city's trust, Kerimov Arshad, tried to tear it from the jacket, but participants in the column resisted him." According to the Ministry for the Defense of Public Order, after the end of the demonstration an unidentified young person unexpectedly jumped onto one of the cars leaving from the central square and began waving photographs of Stalin. When civilian police volunteers tried to reprimand the violator, a crowd numbering approximately a hundred persons attacked them. A fight ensued.[20]

This burgeoning confrontation was accompanied by the sound of toasts honoring Stalin as the deceased Supreme High General. Demonstrators threw stones that defaced the portrait of Khrushchev hanging down from the tribunal. From somewhere people had obtained an enormous portrait of Stalin left over from the old times, and they now raised it up over the crowd. A young pipefitter by the name of Mirish Alimirzoev, who had no criminal record and was the father of two children, took an active part in festively destroying a registered timber lorry. From the lorry he took a hammer and knocked down "portraits of Communist Party and government leaders" and Communist Party posters.[21] Helping him was the unemployed and homeless Iashar Makhmudov, who also took part in beating up a police officer and threw stones at Khrushchev's portrait.[22] Further assistance came from a young worker, Nikolai Shevchenko, who not only tried to tear off a shield from the timber lorry, but also participated in beating up a police captain.[23]

When rocks came flying from the crowd at Khrushchev's portrait, the entire city hierarchy left the tribunal and tried unsuccessfully to pacify the enraged residents of Sumgait. The bosses themselves then became the target of attack, and several persons were severely beaten. Two unidentified persons in a stolen bus drove the deputy chief of the city police department, Kildiashvili, to the city police department. On the roof of this same bus, a stonemason by the name of Anver Makhmudov went through the square, shouting out "calls for the overthrow of the leaders of the CPSU Central Committee and the Soviet government."[24]

When the bus approached the city police department, the standard riot situation arose. The crowd decided that the unidentified men who were accompanying Kildiashvili had been detained by the police and began to call for people "to liberate their comrades." No one, naturally, believed the policemen who tried to convince the mob that these persons had already left. Some rioters broke into the police department building and into the jail, where prisoners were being held, including some who had been arrested for murder. Ruffians still out on the street, joined by those who had gotten into the building's courtyard, began to throw rocks and pieces of asphalt. The mob burned two police motorcycles and damaged two other police cars. The police claimed that they only fired into the air, but later, approximately 100 to 150 meters from the police department, twelve-year-old Aivaz Aivazov was picked up with a gunshot wound. Fortunately the boy lived, but the person who wounded him was never identified.

The crowd broke up only after a police brigade from Baku arrived on the scene. By early afternoon, order was fully restored in the city. The pro-Stalinist and anti-Khrushchev psychosis quickly dissipated, and there was no more violence in Sumgait.[25] The Azerbaijan KGB conducted the investigation, but it failed to uncover serious defendants. The disturbances, which had flared up unexpectedly and then ended in an unusually abrupt manner, did not really have any actual ringleaders. In the end, six persons were convicted to prison terms from three to six years.[26]

The Chechen "March" to Dagestan, April 1964

Toward the end of Khrushchev's era, the Soviet regime was increasingly confronting conflicts that were impossible to place under Article 79 (mass disorders). Some of these phenomena, generally speaking, did not have anything in common with riots (strikes, for examples), while others resembled something new for Soviet reality—acts of civil disobedience. "The taking of measures" in these situations became increasingly difficult, for the new rules of the game between the state and the people required observation of "socialist legality." Coping with conflicts in the habitual way through pressure and threats would mean violating this legality. For example, authorities could no longer allow a false definition of the crime in the indictment and sentence.

The problem of categorizing state crimes, including mass disorders, became in this context a litmus test for the regime, which never truly made up its mind whether to try organizers and participants in mass meetings and civil protests under Article 79 of the RSFSR Criminal Code. Such attempts, however, were made by local authorities, who in certain atypical situations were tempted to transform a broad interpretation of mass disturbance into a crippling police cudgel.

During the spring of 1964, the Chechens of the Khasaviurtovsk district, RSFSR, felt the blows of this cudgel. For a long time they had sought unsuccessfully to return to the land of their ancestors—the village of Duchi in the Novolaksk district of the Dagestan ASSR. Either at the end of April or the beginning of May, Moscow received information about certain mass disorders allegedly carried out by the Chechens. Procurator-General Rudenko asked the Dagestan procurator, A. Pakalov, about the circumstances of the matter and obviously expressed his perplexity over the delay in informing Moscow about a state crime. In a memo from May 5, 1964, Pakalov was forced to equivocate and justify himself:

On April 12, 1964 (a Sunday), about 500 persons of Chechen nationality came to the village of Duchi in the Novolaksk district of the Dagestan ASSR. As seen in the materials which you have received, the Chechens threatened violent actions against individual officials and employees of the Novolaksk district division of MOOP. In addition, individuals of Chechen nationality who had arrived in the village of Duchi on April 12, 1964, cut telephone wires that connected this village to the district center.

According to the facts given, the Dagestan KGB instituted criminal proceedings on April 25, 1964, under Article 79 of the RSFSR Criminal Code and is conducting an investigation.

No one has been detained or arrested in this case.

Together with the Dagestan KGB chairman, the Dagestan minister of Public Order [MOOP], and other leading workers of the CPSU and the Dagestan ASSR Communist Party regional committee, I drove out to the place, talked with the representatives of these citizens, and by the evening of that same day, all of the citizens had returned to their own place of permanent residence. There were no fights, no injuries, nor did these people damage any other property besides cutting the telephone lines; therefore, no criminal procedure was instituted at the time.

The arrival of more than five hundred citizens of Chechen nationality in the village of Duchi, Novolaksk district, was explained by their demand to be given permission to live in the village of Duchi, since before their exile they had lived there.

After the aversion of conflict, it was explained in the process of an operative examination that the departure of the above-mentioned citizens in massive disorder to the village of Duchi was arranged in advance in illegal assemblages by individual persons with provocational goals.

Therefore, in the discussion of this question in the regional party committee, it was seen as advisable to institute criminal proceedings and conduct an investigation, which was set in motion by the institution of a criminal case on April 25, 1964.[27]

Thus, the procurator had not found evidence of a crime. But then the regional party authorities, who were alarmed by the periodic return of the Chechens to the locations of their former residence, gave an order, and in the spirit of the good old days, the machinery of intimidation began to operate. As the Chechens complained in a telegram sent to Procurator-General Rudenko and other top officials on May 10, 1964, the Dagestan party leaders had ordered that a falsified case of mass disorders be concocted. Moreover, the Chechens had endured moral pressure and attempts by the state security organs to frighten them.[28]

On June 29, the Dagestan procurator, G. Askarov, reported the results of the investigation to the Department of Surveillance over Investigations in Organs of State Security. Interesting details came out directly connecting this "Chechen march" with ethnic conflicts in the Northern Caucasus during the 1950s, when repressed nationalities were returning to their former homelands after exile.

The report reconstructed the events of the "march." During the evening of April 10, a Chechen by the name of Salikh Saitamulov had come with his wife and three children to the village of Duchi. Saitamulov "attempted an arbitrary seizure of a plot of land, on which, as he claimed, the house of his parents had once stood (before the exile of the Chechens)." Prior to this, Saitamulov had lived in his own home at the Nuradilova State Farm, located thirty-five kilometers from Duchi. Why Saitamulov suddenly, without any rhyme or reason, left his long-occupied home is not clear. Salikh Saitamulov himself asserted that he had negotiated in advance with the chairman of the collective farm in Duchi, who had promised to take him on as a shepherd. The chairman, though, categorically denied this. The relative veracity of these conflicting claims cannot be determined. Nonetheless, the residents of Duchi reacted very harshly to Saitamulov: first they beat him, and then, using force, they took the car with the family and their belongings to the Novolaksk district police department.[29] From there the family was returned to the Nuradilov State Farm as news of the conflict spread throughout the area.

During the following evening, about fifty prominent Chechen leaders, among them Communist Party members, met at Samail Biibulatov's apartment in the city of Khasaviurt. They discussed their resentment at those who were living in the homes that had once belonged to Chechens before their exile in 1944. Many insisted on everyone going together to Duchi, where they would demand to remain at the former home of Saitamulov and punish those who had beaten him. Having learned of the meeting, the Chechen director of the Nuradilov State Farm came and demanded that they all go home and, of course, that no such "march" to Duchi take place. Those assembled reproached the director and even accused him of having been sent by the authorities.

Some of the Chechens set off for Duchi immediately after the meetings, while others went sometime later. They all gathered during the night in a cemetery near Duchi and at dawn on April 12, more than five hundred persons headed to the collective farm administration offices. There during the course of the day "newer and newer crowds of Chechens began to arrive demanding punishment of those who had beaten Saitamulov (some tried themselves to carry out reprisals), permission for Saitamulov and other Chechens to live in Duchi as well as other former Chechen villages, and the return to them of their former homes and plots of land."[30]

The majority of the Chechens tried to remain peaceful, though some made threats. The investigation proposed that in reality what took place was not a spontaneous uprising, but an organized action. "The expulsion of Saitamulov from the village of Duchi on April 10, 1964, was not the reason but only a pretext for organizing a mass demonstrative march of Chechens to the village of Duchi and for the maximal aggravation of circumstances."[31] The following facts attest directly to this: the organized supply of food; the rapid notification of all Chechens who took part in the march; and the cars, the origins of which are unknown, that conveyed the Chechens to the cemetery. The existence of an underground organization was not proven, however, for the Chechens held solid and refused to give any testimonies.[32]

The case was dropped due to the "absence in the actions of persons who took part in the events that occurred on April 12, 1964, of any criminal content as defined in Article 79 of the RSFSR Criminal Code."[33] The nonexistent "Chechen affair" showed that Dagestan authorities confronted a problem that already could not be resolved in the old way. Yet at the same time, they did not know how to use new methods. They could not stop the self-organization of the Chechens along ethnic lines, who sought by a peaceful (or almost peaceful) path to return to their historical homeland. In truth, the conflict, which had deep roots, was not resolved at all. To a certain degree, this helplessness was a sign of new times. As soon as the state began to act according to the very rules it had established, it clearly showed itself to be a weak player. Continually trying to cheat by seeking loopholes in "socialist legality," the state longed for the familiar domain of judicial and extrajudicial tyranny. Nonetheless, the Moscow party bosses did not resort to using "participation in mass disorders" as a threat against organizers of civil disobedience and acts of protest, or as a reason for repressions. The dangerous juridical experiments of the late Khrushchev epoch would be overturned by his successors, who instead searched for other, though no less dubious, paths of preventing social and ethnic conflict.

PART III

"UNRULY" STAGNATION MASS UPRISINGS FROM THE LATE 1960s TO THE MID-1980s

Chapter 15

Social Unrest and Symptoms of Decay in the Brezhnev Years

In 1988, on the instruction of CPSU General Secretary M.S. Gorbachev, KGB Chairman Viktor Chebrikov* prepared a report on mass disturbances during the period 1957 to 1988. The document is incomplete insofar as the first years of Khrushchev's rule were skipped, and a number of large-scale events between 1958 and 1961 did not end up in the summary. But it allows one to evaluate the dynamics of popular riots and compare the Khrushchev and Brezhnev eras in terms of their "unruliness." Under Brezhnev, mass uprisings and disorders occurred approximately once every 2 years, while under Khrushchev, they occurred 2.5 times more often. Moreover, the majority of the uprisings during the Brezhnev period (7 out of 9), judging by Chebrikov's report, took place at the beginning of Brezhnev's rule, 1966–1968. But from 1969 to 1977, the peak of Brezhnevism, or figuratively speaking, the "golden age of stagnation," not a single episode is recorded—there was complete calm! In addition, during the years 1957 to 1964 in 8 out of 11 cases, weapons were used in suppressing the disorders—practically on a regular basis—with 264 persons killed or wounded. But during the Brezhnev era, they were used only in 3 cases out of 9, with 71 killed or wounded. The statistics of those convicted for participation in mass disorders give an analogous picture: an average of 35.1 convictions per year under Khrushchev and 10.3 under Brezhnev.

In 1966, the authorities waged a rather effective attack on the "yeast" of practically all uprisings and riots—mass hooliganism—which had become a

---

*Victor Mikhailovich Chebrikov (born 1923) was KGB Chairman from 1982–1989.—E.M.

chronic disease under Khrushchev and against which he had unsuccessfully struggled in one antihooligan campaign after another. The decree of the Supreme Soviet Presidium from July 26, 1966, "On Strengthening Responsibility for Hooliganism," shortened the time period for investigating petty hooliganism and arresting hooligans, while also broadening the right of the police to exact fines. During the first six months of 1967, in comparison with the previous year, criminally punishable hooliganism dropped by 20.2 percent and petty hooliganism by 24.1 percent.[1]

Administrative decisions to remove a potentially explosive contingent from large cities had a major impact. For example, in a circumvention of the USSR Constitution, a special resolution dated August 16, 1966 of the Council of Ministers on strengthening the passport system in Moscow, Leningrad, and Moscow Oblast could potentially deprive specific categories of the population—the indigent, the homeless, the unemployed, prostitutes, and speculators in foreign goods—of their temporary passport if they took part in religious meetings, festivals, and "other cult ceremonies that violate established laws, as well as in other meetings or street processions that violate public order."[2]

Nonetheless, the state's display of decisiveness and severity during the first years of the Brezhnev era provoked a new outbreak of the hooligan war in 1967. In May and June in the Central Asian towns of Chimkent, Kazakh SSR, and Frunze, the capital of the Kirgiz SSR, the largest mass disorders of the entire Brezhnev era occurred. They had a clear anti-police character, were accompanied by pogroms and by arson, and they carried on the unruly hooligan traditions of the period from the 1950s to the early 1960s. In Frunze, the crowd destroyed and burned the city police department as well as two district departments. In Chimkent, a mob ransacked the building of the city police department, the regional office of the Ministry for the Defense of Public Order, and the investigative isolator cell. The causes of the riots were rumors that the Chimkent police had murdered a driver named Ostroukhov, and in Frunze, rumors that a soldier named Ismailov had been murdered. The Chimkent riots turned out to be the largest-scale disorders of the entire Brezhnev era, with about 1,000 persons taking part in them. Weapons were used to suppress them, with 7 persons killed and 50 persons wounded. Forty-three persons were convicted for participation in the disorders.[3]

In that same year of 1967, several other cities of the USSR suffered similar outbreaks of social unrest. On April 12, 1967, in Tula, the district police agent Iurishchev, while trying to detain a drunk on a streetcar, had to face resistance from a group of hooligans and, in addition, incurred the wrath of a crowd that had gathered at the scene, demanding revenge against the police.[4] In Tiraspol, Moldavian SSR, a group of students from a pedagogical institute (who were basically from the countryside) carried out something similar to an anti-Jewish pogrom. The Moldavian state procurator tried to gloss over the significance of the conflict. His special report described the malicious behavior of the students as being a fight with certain "city fellows," but claimed that the "manifestation of nationalism was not ascertained." Yet one of the workers in the USSR Procuracy wrote in the special report that it had been specifically Jews whom the students had beaten.[5]

Procurator-General Rudenko claimed that one of the main reasons for the mass riots in Chimkent and Frunze was the failure to struggle against hooligans, drunks, and drug addicts. But at the same time, it was clear to him that such an explanation was inadequate, for too many peaceful onlookers were pulled into the events. In truth, they had sufficient cause to get involved. In Chimkent and in Frunze, among the police there were widespread violations of legality, tyranny, and coarseness in the treatment of people. To avoid such mass disorders, it was necessary not only to put pressure on hooligans, but to bring order into the police force itself. On August 23–24, 1967, the expanded Collegium of the Procuracy accepted a special resolution addressing this issue.

Yet it was not so simple to resolve the problem of mass uprisings and disorders that had an ethnic coloring. Here neither a struggle against hooliganism nor reforms within police organs would help. It was impossible to dismiss events similar either to the Grozny or Thilisi riots. Events in Kazakhstan were particularly alarming. A confrontation between Russian and Kazakh youth took place accompanied by cries: "Take revenge upon the Russians for the blood that has been spilled." From time to time, authorities discovered signs in Russian that had been smashed, and nationalist pamphlets, both in Russian and in Kazakh. Among intellectuals and students there was dissatisfaction with the predominance of Russians in the party and state apparatus of the republic, as well as with the widespread use of the Russian language in the educational system and in business.[6]

Potentially disruptive were spontaneous demonstrations and meetings in Armenia in April 1965 and in the Abkhazian ASSR (Georgian SSR) in March and April 1967. The meetings in Erevan were timed to take place on the memorial day for the victims of the Turkish massacre of Armenians (April 24, 1915). The Abkhazian events in 1967 lasted for two weeks and took place under slogans of "legitimation of Abkhazian place-names throughout the whole republic, priority for native Abkhazians in employment and in entry to higher educational institutes, study of the Abkhazian language in all non-Abkhazian schools of the republic," and even the separation of Abkhaziia from the Georgian Republic with the status of a union republic within the USSR. At night someone was painting over Georgian inscriptions on signboards and road signs.[7] Although the spontaneous protests and demonstrations in Armenia and Abkhaziia displayed a high level of self-organization, it was only the restraint and wisdom of local authorities that protected residents of the republic from violent excesses and pogroms, the deployment of troops, and firings into the crowd. After all, marginal and half-criminal elements often try to use such uncontrollable situations for their own purposes.

After 1967, however, a new style of relations between the people and the state emerged. Conflict basically lessened, and even national and ethnic tensions were dormant, in part due to strengthened administrative controls such as a stricter passport regime, "accelerated justice" in cases of hooliganism, and stricter control over the work of the police. More important, authorities created a new course by attempting to resolve a chronic problem in a non-traditional way. The state had to prevent underground political groups and alignments and also individual oppositionists from using mass disorders to conduct anti-Soviet agitation and propaganda, a fear that had deepened under Khrushchev. To deter "anti-Soviet elements," the state turned to *prophylactic* (educational) measures.* According to KGB information sent to the Central Committee in 1967, only 96 persons were tried for anti-Soviet agitation and propaganda, but there were more than 12,000 who had to undergo prophylactic treatment![8] Authorities also sought ways to resolve nonstandard forms of conflict such as workers' strikes, which had accompanied the more conscious uprisings and riots of the 1950s and early 1960s. On January 7, 1970, the Central Committee Secretariat discussed the problem. According to the data available at that time, in 1969 there had been strikes in 20 production collectives. At most, about 1,000 persons took part in them. But the Central Committee leaders took these strikes seriously and did not want to leave the matter solely in the hands of the KGB. After all, the most dangerous mass disorders, such as those in Novocherkassk, shared certain common roots with strikes: mass dissatisfaction with the periodical increase in work norms and the revision of piece rate scales, poor labor conditions, and delayed payment of wages or shortages in the supplies of food products.

Tangible symptoms of popular dissatisfaction along with "unhealthy statements" concerning these problems surfaced once again in 1969. Consequently, authorities turned to basic bribery in their search for a symbiosis with the people. They carried out continual and often economically unfounded

---

*During the mid-1960s the Brezhnev leadership decided to stress education over repression in the fight against crime, particularly with regard to alcoholism. *Profilaktori*, or treatment centers, were to be increased in number. But there was little consensus over the proper approach and in 1966 to 1967, advocates of repressive measures seemed to gain the upper hand with passage of tough anti-hooliganism legislation.—E.M.

increases in wages, pumped money into the consumer sector, permitted the growth of the black market, and redistributed resources to the benefit of national border areas, causing in the end a higher deficit. Through such measures, the state for some time succeeded in distracting people from spontaneous protests and anti-Soviet political activism.

However, particularly with administrative and police measures, and even by bribery, it was impossible to overcome the predisposition of an ailing social consciousness to engage in mass disturbances. The more accustomed Soviet society grew to stagnation, the more noticeable the symptoms of developing social unrest became: from 1966 to 1978 the number of crimes per 100,000 persons grew from 380 to 503, with crime rates rising particularly fast in certain districts of the Urals, Siberia, and the Far East.[10] Cities again came to be occupied by half-criminalized elements, particulary in regions experiencing industrial development and new construction projects. Consequently, residents began sending collective letters and complaints to Moscow with demands for protection from the explosion of crime and hooliganism. In addition, at the end of the 1970s, an epidemic of mass drunkenness gripped the entire country. In comparison with 1960, the consumption of alcohol grew by two times and the number of alcoholics, according to official records, reached two million. In 1978, about nine million drunks were hauled into police departments, and more than six million ended up in sobering stations.[11]

Such depressing statistics on crime, drunkenness, and hooliganism promised a new wave of riots and uprisings. Attempts to restore order through police measures could provoke it, as well as visible signs of weakness on the part of the regime. After the death of Brezhnev but still prior to Gorbachev's election as general secretary, social and ethnic tensions within Soviet society rose. After two rather peaceful years, during the six-month period from the second half of 1984 to the beginning of 1985, two large-scale uprisings occurred. One of them erupted in Dushanbe, capital of the Tadzhik SSR, and was rooted in ethnic soil. In the second half of 1985, there was unrest in the military involving men called up for service in the Soviet army, a type of disturbance not seen since the 1950s.[12]

Unquestionably the era of stagnation was relatively calm in comparison with the pre- and post-stagnation periods. Nonetheless, real or potential conflict seems to have framed Brezhnev's time in power, providing direct evidence of the social frailty of stagnation as a form of rule and a way of life. The country had entered into a new epoch, but it was already sitting on a powder keg with a burning match. Unfulfilled nationalist ambitions and old ethnic grievances, millions of aggrieved drunks who passed their nights in sobering stations or in jail cells on fifteen-day terms, an enormous number of people who every year committed petty embezzlements and, moreover, went unpunished, young people who grew up in alcoholic families—none of this was the best material for constructing the reformist policies of *perestroika* declared by Gorbachev. The country had reached an impasse. Society was disintegrating. But in the search for a way out, marginalized mass consciousness turned out to be as poor an ally for Gorbachev as the "*nomenklatura* capitalism"* of the corrupted Brezhnev bureaucrats.

---

*The term "*nomenklatura* capitalism" refers to the deep involvement of the party elite in corruption and illegal business activity that reached unprecedented heights under Brezhnev. The nomenklatura were the state appointments that required approval by party officials.—E.M.

Conclusion

An American friend who read this book in manuscript form was struck by the cruelty and incomprehensibility of the events described in these pages. He noted sadly: "An unhappy people, who had a government like this, and an unhappy government, which was forced to rule over people like this." Behind this ironic rejoinder hides an old intellectual tradition. The centuries-long "schism" between the people and the state, between the simple folk and the educated elite, often has been interpreted by the West as the *conditio sine qua non* [essential condition] of Russian history. By imparting such universal meaning to this antiquated religious concept, Western intellectuals are heroically trying to describe specific aspects of the relationship between the Russian state and the Russian people that are so alien to contemporary Western society.

In certain chapters of this book when I have referred to a traditional Russian symbiosis of the people and the state, I was inspired by the same desire—to find the correct word to describe the relationship! In truth, the term "schism" *[raskol]* sounds too harsh and categorical to the Russian ear. The inherent meaning implies an almost fathomless abyss through which no one can pass. Meanwhile, research into violent conflicts between the people and the state after the death of Stalin has showed that in the majority of cases, the discussion should not be so much about a schism as about a specific form of cohabitation. The mass disorders themselves, in their very structure and features, were unarguably a direct act against the state or its representatives. But as a rule, they did not reject the existing system of interrelations between the people and the state. Rather, they were a perverse form of reciprocal tie between the Soviet regime and the people, an irrational means for conveying signals of trouble. In the majority of cases, such an interaction through confrontation more accurately is called not a schism, but a social symbiosis.

After all, symbiosis immediately signifies the cohabitation of two organisms of different species. Despite being advantageous to both sides, symbiosis never makes them a single being or, in our case, a united society with common goals and values.

Social symbiosis—that is, a compromise based on a tradition of paternalism, authoritarianism, and violence between the people and the state—favors and accompanies stagnation but, as a rule, endures rapid and dynamic changes poorly. The state then loses its legitimacy, and the people demonstrate a spontaneous predisposition for rebellion. The research that has been done suggests that spontaneous uprisings and rebellions—which under democratic regimes testify to violations of the reciprocal ties between the government and the people, that is, to abnormalities of the state and its administration—under authoritarian-bureaucratic regimes are not a symptom of abnormality, but are part of the supporting foundations for such regimes. Very often there are simply no other outlets for expressing one's attitude toward current politics. Rebellion was often accompanied by more or less purposeful attempts to bring the "Truth" to the Moscow bosses, and the partial success of the riots was paid for by the broken fates and harsh punishment of the ringleaders.

Mass disorders during the epoch of Khrushchev and Brezhnev were a phenomenon quite archaic in nature. Active participants in the riots of the 1950s and 1960s had been raised on such innate myths of "plebeian culture" (an expression of the English historian E. P. Thompson) as faith in the "good tsar and his unjust officials," an egalitarian understanding of justice, the idea of wealth being iniquitous, and the belief that "all truth lies at the top." These hopelessly outdated but extremely enduring ideals were not specific to the Russian tradition of popular protest. For example, the English crowd at the end of the eighteenth and the beginning of the nineteenth century operated according to this same complex of ideas.[1] Innate myths merged in the consciousness of Soviet "troublemakers" with much more contemporary populist interpretations of Communist doctrine. Thus, some participants in mass disorders followed not so much the traditional models of rebellious actions, but rather the propagandistic clichés of Soviet books and films on the revolutionary heroes (the films *Mother* by Vs. Pudovkin, *The Battleship Potemkin* by S. Eisenshtein), and thereby reproduced patterns of behavior of such "warriors for justice" in their interactions with the police and security personnel.

The uprisings and rebellions of the Soviet populace from the second half of the 1950s to the beginning of the 1960s were among the more important symptoms, in terms of practical politics, of the social-political crisis that was engulfing the country. Participants in the disorders were sending numerous signals to the state about the need for respite from the overwhelming stress of forced industrialization and urbanization as well as from police and bureaucratic abuses. Paradoxically, for example, participants in the Novocherkassk events entered into a direct confrontation with the supreme authorities under the state's own ideological slogans. The everyday version of Russian communism, the basis for the regime's ideological legitimacy, allowed participants in the unrest to attack "popular power" without experiencing any guilt in doing this. Acts of protest were perceived to be a struggle against the betrayal of communism by party bureaucrats.

The mask of communist ideals hid from opponents and antagonists, and often even from the rebels themselves, the genuine motives of their actions, and it became an important source for psychological self-justification. Therefore, extreme forms of protest organically coexisted with the ideological conformism characteristic of participants in the rebellions. The efforts of oppositionist consciousness to separate the "bad Communists" from "good Communists" only partially reflected the deep-rootedness, socially and psychologically, of Russian communism. Above all, this tendency represented a principled difference in interpretation by the people and the state of what would seem to be a single complex of ideas, that is, unarguable signs of a schism.

The peak moments of mass uprisings and disorders often coincided in time with the activation of such forms of protest as the distribution of leaflets, appeals, anonymous letters, anti-government slogans on walls and fences, and insults and threats addressed to leaders. It would seem that inevitably a connection had to emerge between sedition (a statement of complaint or criticism by the common people against the state) and subversion (the conscious spread of ideas harmful to authorities). The Moscow leaders seriously feared such connections, which could ennoble spontaneous protests and impart to them a political (anti-Soviet) direction. Mass action could thereby be transformed from a specific means for correcting the system into an instrument of struggle against it. However, the cases of interaction between the crowd and "anti-Soviet elements" in the course of mass unrest were exceptionally rare. On the contrary, the leaders of the uprisings showed signs of distaste for "eggheads" while political oppositionists kept fastidiously aloof from the looting and violent crowds. With few exceptions, the actions of the crowd lacked a conscious principle, and when there were faint signs of its behavior being manipulated, it was more likely to be done by KGB personnel or by self-organized criminals than by underground oppositionist organizations.

My research has established a fact that is substantially important for understanding Soviet forms of popular cohabitation with the bosses. Mass uprisings that were engendered by the deep crisis of postwar Soviet society and that reached their peak at the end of Khrushchev's rule subsided at precisely the same moment when communist ideals were practically squeezed out of mass consciousness by the conformism, consumerism, and individualism of the Brezhnev era. It took people's becoming completely disillusioned in their understanding of communism for the riots and disorders in Russia to come to an end, practically speaking.

It turned out that the spontaneous uprisings of the 1950s and early 1960s against party bosses who had betrayed the "cause of communism" were, no matter how paradoxical it sounds, evidence of the continued ideological stability of the regime and of the still vibrant belief in "real communism." The decline in the wave of mass disorders during the Brezhnev era of stagnation on the contrary, signaled the ideological collapse of the regime and the decay of the entire Soviet system. Without faith, rebelling under old banners did not make any sense. Therefore the state, frightened by the scale of popular unrest under Khrushchev, revealed an unarguable flexibility as it seized back from the "rabble rousers" the banner of popular Stalinism. It entered a path of economically unsound but pleasing handouts to the basic social groups in Soviet society, which made friendship with the state an extraordinarily profitable occupation. Both the representatives of supreme authority and the population of the country sought individual paths to happiness, and used the numerous holes and gaps in the disintegrating system to further their own well being. It was no coincidence that under Brezhnev, the centers of conflict relocated themselves to the outer regions of the USSR, where they relied on nationalist ideas that were much more enduring and primordially confrontational toward Moscow.

At some point in time, the people left agitation and riots behind in favor of the quiet inlets of individual daily existence. In the incubators of Brezhnev stagnation, there grew the fortunate child of modernization and progress— individualism. The traditional communalism of Russian mass consciousness was partially destroyed, and the preconditions for contemporary political forms of protest and self-organization were born. At the same time, in Soviet society the seeds of future conflict were being sown. Social envy intensified, and latent dissatisfaction with the economically ineffective Soviet system grew. In these conditions, any attempt at some kind of dynamic change or reform threatened destruction of the social symbiosis and resurrection of that "discord between people and the state" that old Russian-language dictionaries generally termed *smuta*.[2]

Notes

Translator's Note

1. Alex Pravda also cites a less prominent newspaper, the *New York Herald Tribune*, as an outlet during the early 1960s for reports on unrest in the USSR. See Alex Pravda, "Spontaneous Workers' Activities in the Soviet Union," in Arcadius Kahan and Blair Ruble, eds., *Industrial Labor in the USSR: A Special Study of the Kennan Institute for Advanced Russian Studies*. The Wilson Center No. 1 (New York: 1979), 348–56. In 1977 a group of dissidents headed by Andrei Sakharov described the events at Novocherkassk in an appeal that became known in the West. See Vadim Belotserkovsky, "Workers' Struggles in the USSR in the Early Sixties," *Critique*, nos 10–11 (winter-spring 1978/79): 44–46.

2. There were scholarly treatments of unrest in books on Soviet labor and labor relations, as well as several journal articles and essays. See, for example, Pravda, "Spontaneous Workers' Activities," 333–66; Walter D. Connor, "Workers, Politics, and Class Consciousness," in Kahan and Ruble, *Industrial Labor*, 313–32; Belotserkovsky, "Workers' Struggles in the USSR in the Early Sixties," 37–50; M. Holubenko, "The Soviet Working Class: Dissent and Opposition," *Critique*, no. 4 (spring 1975): 5–21; Charles E. Ziegler, "Worker Participation and Worker Discontent in the Soviet Union," *Political Science Quarterly* 98 (summer 1983): 235–53; M. McAuley, *Labour Disputes in Soviet Russia 1957–65* (Oxford: 1966).

3. There have been several journal articles and essays published on popular unrest, particularly on Novocherkassk. See Ludmilla Alexeyeva and Paul S. Triolo, "Unrest in the Soviet Union," *Washington Quarterly* 13 (winter 1990): 63–77; Olga Nikitina, "Novocherkassk: The Chronicle of a Tragedy," *Russian Social Science Review* 33, no. 5 (September–October 1992): 48–78; Ingo Mannteufel, "Der 'Blutsamstag' in der Sowjetunion. Die Niederschlagung der Proteste in Novocerkassk im Juni 1962," *Osteuropa, Zeitschrift fur Gegenwarsfragen des Ostens*, no. 7 (1998): 724–37.

4. Samuel Baron, *Bloody Saturday in the Soviet Union* (Stanford: 2001).

5. Elena Zubkova, *Russia After the War: Hopes, Illusions, and Disappointments, 1945–1957*, trans. and ed. Hugh Ragsdale (Armonk, NY: 1998). See Iurii Aksiutin,

"Popular Responses to Khrushchev," in *Nikita Khrushchev*, ed. William Taubman, Sergei Khrushchev, and Abbott Gleason (New Haven: 2000), 177–208.

6. For a detailed examination of the Soviet police and criminal justice system, see Louise I. Shelley, *Policing Soviet Society: The Evolution of State Control* (London: 1996).

7. Ibid., pp. 150–68.

Introduction

1. Albert Boiter, "When the Kettle Boils Over," *Problems of Communism*, no. 1 (1964), 33–43.

2. See, for example, Robert Conquest, "Russian Workers' Riots," *Soviet Analyst* (December 13, 1973); Alex Pravda, "Spontaneous Workers' Activities in the Soviet Union" in B. Ruble and A. Kahan, *Industrial Labor in the USSR* (New York, 1979), 333–66.

3. The author is sincerely grateful to Jeffrey Burds for his invaluable assistance with Western historiographical issues and questions.

4. For more about these new phenomena and processes in the historiography and source studies of Soviet society, see V.A. Kozlov, "Rossiiskaia istoriia: obzor idei i kontseptsii (1993–1995)," parts 1 and 2, *Svobodnaia mysl'* nos. 3 and 4 (1996); and V.A. Kozlov and O. Lokteva, "'Arkhivnaia revoliutsiia' v Rossii (1991–1996)," *Svobodnaia mysl'* nos. 1, 3, and 4 (1997). See also the English translation in *Russian Politics and Law*, no. 6 (November-December, 1997).

5. R.G. Pikhoia, *Sovetskii Soiuz: Istoriia vlasti, 1945–1991* (Moscow, 1998); O. Leibovich, *Reform i modernizatsiia v 1953–1964 gg.* (Perm, 1993); E.Iu. Zubkova, *Obshchestvo i reformy. 1945–1964* (Moscow, 1993); *N.S. Khrushchev (1894–1971). Materialy nauchnoi konferentsii, posviashchennoi 100–letiiu so dnia rozhdeniia N.S. Khrushcheva, 18 aprelia 1994 goda* (Moscow, 1994); *Vlast' i oppozitsiia: Rossiiskii politicheskii protsess XX stoletiia* (Moscow, 1995); E. Panovian and A. Panovian, *Uchastie Verkhovnogo Suda SSSR v vyrabotke repressivnoi politiki (1957–1958 gg.)* (Moscow, 1996); A.B. Bezborodov, *Fenomen akademicheskogo dissidentstva v SSSR* (Moscow, 1998); A.B. Bezborodov, M.M. Meier, and E.I. Pivovar, *Materialy po istorii dissidentskogo i pravozashchitnogo dvizheniia v SSSR 50 kh–80kh godov: Uchebnoe posobie* (Moscow, 1994). Obshchestvo "Memorial" Fond imeni Genrikh a Bellia, *Korni travy* (Moscow, 1996).

6. See, for example: *Kronshtadtskaia tragediia 1921 goda: Dokumenty v dvukh knigakh*, Kn. 1–2 (Moscow, 1999); G. Vasil'ev, "Vosstanie Sapozhkova v Zavolzh'e," *Volga*, nos. 9–10 (1994); S.N. Semanov, "Kronshtadtskii miatezh: Glava iz rukopisi," *Slovo*, no. 10 (1992); V. Tereshchuk, "Miatezh," *Niva*, no. 5 (1992); P.N. Dmitriev and K.I. Kulikov, *Miatezh v Izhevo-Votkinskom raione* (Izhevsk, 1992); I.D. Sanachev, "Krest'ianskoe vosstanie na Amure–kulatskii miatezh ili shag otchaianiia?" *Vestnik Dal'nevostochnogo otdeleniia Rossiiskoi AN*, nos. 3–4 (1992); "Neizvestnyi Kronshtadt," *Rodina*, no. 7 (1993); V. Kozliakov, "'Sluzhba eta byla dlia Rossii...': Iaroslavskii miatezh 1918 g.," *Volga*, no. 3 (1993); "Kronshtadtskaia tragediia 1921 goda," *Voprosy istorii*, nos. 4–7 (1994); "Krest'ianskoe vosstanie v Chuvashii. Ianvar' 1921 g.," *Vestnik Chuvashskoi natsional'noi akademii*, no. 2 (1994); L. Iakubova, "Kulatskie miatezhi ili krest'ianskaia voina?" *Tatarstan*, nos. 7–8 (1992); *Krest'ianskoe vosstanie v Tambovskoi gubernii v 1919–1921 gg.: 'Antonovshchina': Dokumenty i*

materialy (Tambov, 1994); N.G. Tret'iakov, "Sostav rukovodiashchikh organov Zapadno-Sibirskogo vosstaniia 1921 g.," *Gumanitarnye nauki v Sibiri. Seriia: Otechestvennaia istoriia*, No. 2 (1994); "Krest'ianskaia voina," *Voenno-istoricheskii zhurnal*, Nos. 1–2 (1993); G.G. Makarov, "Antisovetskoe vooruzhennoe dvizhenie v Iakutii osen'iu 1921 goda," *Problemy sotsial'no-ekonomicheskoi i obshchestvenno politicheskoi istorii Iakutii* (Iakutsk, 1993).

7. See for example: *Tragediia sovetvskoi derevni: Kollektivizatsiia i raskulachivanie: Dokumenty i materialy v 5 tomakh. 1927–1939.* T. I. *Mai 1927– Noiabr'* 1929 (Moscow, 1999); N.R. Romanets, "Massovye antikolkhoznye vystupleniia krest'ianstva perioda kollektivizatsii kak reaktsiia na agrarnuiu politku sovetskogo gosudarstva," *Totalitarizm i lichnost'* (Perm, 1994).

8. N.A. Cherkashin, *Poslednii parad: Khronika antibrezhnevskogo miatezha* (Moscow, 1992); "Miatezhnyi kapitan," *Rodina*, no. 3 (1993).

9. *Vlast' i oppozitsiia*, 221.

10. I. Mardar, *Khronika neob"iavlennogo ubiistva* (Novocherkassk, 1992); "Novocherkasskaia tragediia, 1962," *Istoricheskii arkhiv*, nos. 1 and 4 (1993). A clear picture of the general circumstances in the country during the riots in Novocherkassk is given by the publication of V. Lebedev, "'Ob"ediniaites' vokrug Khrista—bol'sheviki povysili tseny': Otnoshenie naseleniia SSSR k povysheniiu tsen na produkty pitaniia v 1962," in *Neizvestnaia Rossiia. XX vek.* Vyp. 3 (Moscow, 1993).

11. "Novocherkasskaia tragediia, 1962," *Istoricheskii arkhiv*, nos. 1 and 4 (1993).

12. Ibid., 111.

13. Ibid.

14. F. Baazova, "Tanki protiv detei" [Perepechatka iz zhurnala *Vremia i my*, 1978], *Rodina*, no. 10 (1992); "'Ne dopustim kritiki Stalina': Sobytiia v Gruzii: Mart 1956," *Istochnik*, no. 6 (1995).

15. See, for example, *Soprotivlenie v Gulage: Vospominaniia. Pis'ma. Dokumenty* (Moscow, 1992); I. A. Maksimova, "Zabastovka v Vorkutlage v 1953 g.," *Totalitarizm i lichnost'* (Perm, 1994); A. Makarova, "Noril'skoe vosstanie," *Volga*, no. 1 (1993). To a certain degree, the research of E.Sh. Khaztakhmetov complements these works; see E.Sh. Khaztakhmetov, "Massovye vystupleniia politicheskikh ssyl'nykh Sibiri 1906–1917 gg.," in *Materialy k khronike obshchestvennogo dvizheniia v Sibiri v 1895– 1917 gg.* (Tomsk, 1994). From Western scholarship it is necessary to note the following: A. Graziosi, "The Great Strikes of 1953 in Soviet Labor Camps in the Accounts of Their Participants: A Review," *Cahiers du monde Russe et Sovietique*, no. 4, vol. 33 (1993); M. Kraveri, "Krizis GULAGA: Kengirskoe vosstanie 1954 goda v dokumentakh MVD," *Cahier du monde Russe et Sovietique*, no. 3, vol. 36 (1995).

16. "1959 god. Rasstrel v Temirtau," in Iu. N. Afanasiev, ed., *Sovetskoe obshchestvo: vozniknovenie, razvitie istoricheskii final*, Tom 2. *Apogei i krakh stalinizma* (Moscow, 1997), 273–327.

17. A.G. Lopatin, "Rossiia, kotoruiu my poteriali?: Neskol'ko faktov k Lenskim sobytiiam," *Ekonomika i organizatsiia promyshlennogo proizvodstva*, no. 12 (1992).

18. Iu.I. Kir'ianov, "Massovye vystupleniia na pochve dorogovizny v Rossii (1914– Fevral' 1917 g.). Ulichnye besporiadki i vystupleniia rabochikh Rossii: Po dokumentam Departamenta politsii. 1914–Fevral' 1917," *Istoricheskii arkhiv*, nos. 4, 5/6 (1994).

19. "Smiatenie oseni sorok pervogo goda: Dokumenty o volneniiakh ivanovskikh tekstil'shchikov," *Istoricheskii arkhiv*, no. 2, 1994.

20. Ralf Dahrendorf, "Toward a Theory of Social Conflict," in *Social Change: Sources, Patterns and Consequences* (New York, 1964).

21. See also V.A. Kozlov, "Sostoianie dukhovnoi zhizni obshchestva kak kategoriia sistemnogo izucheniia istorii sovetskoi kul'tury," in *Sistemnyi podkhod k istorii sovetskoi kul'tury: Sbornik nauchnykh trudov* (Novosibirsk, 1985).

22. Lewis Coser, *Continuities in the Study of Social Conflict* (New York, 1967).

23. See A.S. Akhiezer, *Rossiia: kritika istoricheskogo opyta. V 3–kh tomakh* (Moscow, 1992).

24. A.V. Obolonskii, *Drama rossiiskoi politicheskoi istorii: sistema protiv lichnosti* (Moscow, 1994), 11.

25. Ibid. The word "System" is used by A.V. Obolonskii not in the political sense, but in a broader context. He proves that "in and of itself the changing of political systems in our country has not brought a principled transformation of the System in terms of the social relations between people."

26. See the preface of M.A. Barg to the Russian edition of the work of the historian Dzordzha Rude (George Rudé), *Narodnye nizy v istorii. 1730–1848* (Moscow, 1984), 12.

27. "O massovykh besporiadkakh s 1957 goda. . . ," *Istochnik*, no. 6 (1995), 143–53. This is a publication of the Russian Federation Presidential Archive.

28. "Novocherkasskaia tragediia, 1962," *Istoricheskii arkhiv*, nos. 1 and 4 (1993).

29. "'Ob"ediniaites' vokrug Khrista.'"

30. See "'Ne dopustim kritiki Stalina': Sobytiia v Gruzii: Mart 1956 g.," *Istochnik*, no. 6 (1995).

31. P.P. Siuda, "Novocherkasskaia tragediia," *Karta: Nezavisimyi istoricheskii zhurnal*, no. 1 (1993).

32. F. Baazova, "Tanki protiv detei."

33. RGANI, f. 2, op. 1, d. 329, l. 30–41.

Part I: Social Conflict in the USSR After the Death of Stalin, 1953–1960

Chapter 1. Mastering Territories in Kazakhstan and Siberia

1. GARF, f. R-9401, op. 2, d. 234, l. 349.
2. See ibid., d. 450, l. 168–69.
3. Ibid, f. R-8131, op. 32, d. 3288, l. 64–65.
4. Ibid., f. R-9401, op. 2, d. 466, l. 93.
5. See ibid., d. 481, l. 255–56.
6. Ibid., l. 102–3.
7. Ibid.
8. Ibid., f. R-8131, op. 32, d. 5602, l. 44–45.
9. Ibid., l. 45.
10. Ibid., f. R-9401, op. 2, d. 498, l. 348.
11. Ibid., d. 499, l. 196.
12. Ibid., op. 1, d. 4553, l. 201.
13. Ibid., l. 194.
14. Ibid., l. 282.
15. Weapons were used to suppress a fight in the city of Taiga in the Kemerovskaia

Oblast and in the village of Astrakhanka, Akmolinskaia Oblast, of the Kazakh SSR.
See ibid., d. 500, l. 164.

16. See Ibid., d. 506, l. 225–26.
17. Ibid., f. R-8131, op. 31, d. 86920, l. 2–3.
18. Ibid., l. 61–68.
19. Ibid., l. 63.
20. Ibid., l. 68.
21. Ibid., l. 170.
22. Ibid., l. 162.
23. Ibid., f. R-9401, op. 2, d. 506, l. 266–67.
24. Ibid., f. R-8131, op. 31, d. 86920, l. 94–97.
25. Ibid., l. 213.
26. Ibid., l. 81–83.
27. Ibid., f. R-9401, op. 2, d. 506, l. 335–36.
28. RGANI, f. 89, per. 6, d. 10, l. 4.
29. Ibid., l. 4–5.
30. Ibid., l. 5–6. For more information on the political ramifications of the events
in Temirtau, see "1959 god. Rasstrel v Temirtau."
31. GARF, f. R-9401, op. 2, d. 507, l. 32–34.

Chapter 2. Unrest in the Military

1. Included in this conditional concept are cases of mass hooliganism, collective
fights and disturbances, the participants of which were military personnel and conscripts in the Soviet army.
2. Twenty-one out of forty-four documented cases.
3. Sixteen cases or 36.3 percent of all documented cases.
4. Six episodes or 13.6 percent of all cases.
5. GARF, f. R-9401, op. 2, d. 105, l. 85–91.
6. Ibid., l. 340–43.
7. See ibid., d. 66, l. 9–10; d. 168, l. 26–30; and others.
8. Ibid., f. R-8131, op. 32, d. 2231, l. 57.
9. Ibid., l. 59.
10. See ibid., d. 2233, l. 235, 236–37.
11. Ibid., l. 236.
12. Ibid., f. R-9401, op. 1, d. 4160, l. 84.
13. Ibid., f. R-8131, op. 32, d. 2235, l. 207.
14. Ibid., f. R-9401, op. 1, d. 4553, l.181.
15. Ibid., l. 310.
16. Ibid., op. 2, d. 491, l. 278.
17. Ibid., op. 1, d. 4320, l. 118–118 *oborotnaia storona stranitsy* (on the back side
of the page, henceforth abbreviated "ob.").
18. Ibid., f. R-8131, op. 32, d. 2232, l. 1–3.
19. Ibid., l. 8–9.
20. Ibid., d. 2235, l. 237.
21. Ibid., f. R-9401, op. 2, d. 481, l. 298; d. 499, l. 184.
22. Ibid., op. 1, d. 467, l. 223–25.
23. Ibid., op. 2, d. 498, l. 393–94.

24. Ibid., f. R-8131, op. 32, d. 2235, l. 122.

25. Ibid., l. 120–24.

26. Ibid., f. R-8131, op. 32, d. 3286, l. 43–47.

27. Ibid., d. 3287, l. 13–14.

28. Ibid., d. 3286, l. 107.

29. Ibid., d. 3287, l. 13–14.

30. Ibid., l. 14.

31. Ibid., f. R-9401, op. 1, d. 4320, l. 1–2.

32. Unfortunately, clear information on this episode is not available. Judging by the existing information, the conflict had more of a mass character, but it seems that the suppression of the disorders did not include a confrontation with the police. See ibid., d. 4321, l. 21–22.

33. This mindset is reflected in the advice once given by the poet Alexander Pushkin to a young colleague. Pushkin told him to put a small dash between the words "boss" and "enemy" (boss-enemy) since the words are synonomous. See V.V. Veresaev, *Pushkin v zhizni. Sistematizirovannyi svod podlinnykh svidetel'stv sovremennikov s illiustratsiiami na otdel'nykh listakh.* Izd. Shestoe, znachitel'no dopolnennoe. T. 2 (Moscow, 1936), 156.

34. GARF, f. R-9401, op. 2, d. 451, l. 149–53.

35. Ibid., op. 1, d. 4160, l. 97–98; f. R-8131, op. 32, d. 2232, l. 83–85.

36. Ibid., f. R-8131, op. 32, d. 2235, l. 121.

37. Ibid., f. R-9401, op. 1, d. 4160, l. 278–79.

38. Ibid., f. R-8131, op. 32, d. 2230, l. 2.

39. See ibid., d. 4000, l. 140.

40. Ibid., f. R-9401, op. 1, d. 4320, l. 1–2.

41. Ibid., f. R-8131, op. 31, d. 67201, l. 24.

42. Ibid., f. R-9401, op. 1, d. 4320, l. 137.

43. Ibid., l. 134–37.

44. Ibid., f. R-8131, op. 32, d. 4000, l. 251–52.

45. Ibid., l. 140–42.

46. Ibid., f. R-9401, op. 2, d. 463, l. 221–22.

47. Ibid., f. R-8131, op. 32, d. 4000, l. 139.

48. Ibid., l. 142.

49. Ibid., l. 143–45.

50. Ibid., l. 237.

51. Ibid., l. 235–38.

52. Ibid., f. R-9401, op. 1, d. 4320, l. 139–40.

53. Ibid., op. 2, d. 464, l. 262.

54. See ibid., f. R-8131, op. 31, d. 67201, l. 9–11, 42–44.

55. Ibid., l. 32.

56. Ibid., l. 16.

57. Ibid., l. 16–17.

58. Ibid.

59. Ibid., l. 6.

60. Ibid., l. 22.

61. Ibid., l. 30.

62. Ibid., l. 18–19.

63. Ibid., l. 19–21.

64. Ibid., l. 29.

65. Ibid., d. 67680, l. 1–2.

Chapter 3. Violent Conflicts in the Virgin Lands

1. See GARF, f. R-9401, op. 1, d. 4599, l. 9; d. 5402, l. 221.
2. See ibid., op. 2, d. 492, l. 187–88.
3. Ibid., l. 224.
4. Ibid., d. 138, l. 381–82.
5. Ibid., l. 380–81.
6. Ibid., l. 381–82.
7. Ibid., d. 139, l. 378–80.
8. See materials for the series *Narody i kul'tury*. Vyp. 12. *Deportatsii narodov SSSR (1930–1950–e gody)*. Ch. I. *Dokumental'nye istochniki Tsentral'nogo Gosudarstvennogo Arkhiva Oktiabr'skoi revoliutsii, vysshikh organov gosudarstvennoi vlasti i organov gosudarstvennogo upravleniia (TsGAOR) SSSR* (Moscow, 1992), 80–83.
9. GARF, f. R-9479, op. 1, d. 925, l. 125–27.
10. See ibid.
11. Ibid., f. R-9401, op. 2, d. 451, l. 373.
12. Ibid., d. 464, l. 262.
13. Ibid., f. R-7523, op. 75, d. 359, l. 2, 4.
14. In Dzhambul Oblast, above all in the regional center, in April 1957, approximately 5,000 Chechens and Ingush were unemployed—more than 50 percent of the able labor force. In Vostochno-Kazakhstan Oblast there were similar numbers of unemployed. In Karaganda Oblast, where there were 30,000 Chechens and Ingush, a significant number also remained unemployed. See ibid., f. R-9401, op. 2, d. 490, l. 279–80.
15. Ibid., l. 280–81.
16. Ibid., l. 295.
17. Ibid.
18. Ibid., l. 279–81.
19. Ibid., l. 283–84.
20. Ibid., f. A-259, op. 7, d. 9230, l. 27.
21. Ibid., op. 1, d. 910, l. 142–44.
22. See ibid., f. R-9401, op. 2, d. 498, l. 163, 379–80.
23. According to the incomplete data available, in 1960, still awaiting return were 1,131 families out of the number of those who had to return to the territory of Dagestan. See ibid., f. A-259, op. 42, d. 4830, l. 33–35.
24. Ibid., f. R-8131, op. 31, d. 89558, l. 53–53 ob., 77.
25. Ibid., l. 97.
26. Ibid., l. 101.
27. Ibid., l. 5.
28. Ibid., l. 97.
29. Ibid., l. 12–14.
30. Ibid., l. 36.
31. See ibid., l. 16–16 ob.
32. Ibid., l. 2–3, 9.
33. Ibid., l. 34.
34. Ibid., l. 79.
35. Ibid., l. 12–13.
36. Ibid., l. 174–75.

37. Ibid., l. 176.
38. Ibid., l. 5.
39. Ibid., l. 38.
40. Ibid., l. 176.
41. Ibid., l. 4.
42. Ibid., l. 176–77.
43. Ibid., l. 11.

Chapter 4. The Return of the Deported Nations to the Northern Caucasus

1. GARF, f. R-9401, op. 2, d. 491, l. 425.
2. Ibid., f. R-8131, op. 32, d. 4580, l. 124.
3. Ibid., f. 7523, op. 75, d. 359, l. 7–9.
4. Ibid., f. A-259, op. 7, d. 9230, l. 44–50.
5. Ibid., f. R-9401, op. 2, d. 490, l. 111–12.
6. A "Dagestan" ethnic group as such does not exist, but authorities frequently used this collective term in their statistical reports and memoranda in speaking about the multiple peoples of the Dagestan ASSR.
7. GARF, f. R-9401, op. 2, d. 490, l. 111–12.
8. Ibid.
9. Ibid., d. 491, l. 201–2.
10. Ibid., f. A-259, op. 7, d. 9230, l. 75–76.
11. Ibid., l. 90–92.
12. Ibid., l. 88–89.
13. Ibid., f. R-8131, op. 31, d. 84693, l. 17–18.
14. See ibid., f. 9479, op. 1, d. 925, l. 3–20.
15. Ibid., f. A-259, op. 42, d. 4830, l. 33–34.
16. Ibid., f. R-9401, op. 2, d. 500, l. 402–3.
17. See ibid., f. A-259, op. 42, d. 4830, l. 34–35.
18. Ibid., f. R-9401, op. 2, d. 491, l. 122.
19. Ibid., d. 451, l. 427–28.
20. Ibid., f. R-8131, op. 31, d. 84390, l. 20–21.
21. Ibid., l. 21.
22. Ibid., op. 1, d. 4558, l. 58–59 (part 82 of separate pagination).
23. Ibid., f. R-9401, op. 1, d. 4558, l. 86 (part 4 of separate pagination).
24. Ibid., f. R-8131, op. 31, d. 86533, l. 72.
25. See, for example, ibid., f. P-9401, op. 1, d. 4553, l. 19.
26. Ibid., f. R-8131, op. 31, d. 86533, l. 73.
27. Ibid., l. 23.
28. Ibid., l. 23–24.
29. Ibid., l. 33.
30. Ibid., f. R-9401, op. 1, d. 4558, l. 65–66.
31. Ibid., f. R-8131, op. 32, d. 5066, l. 93–94.
32. Ibid., op. 31, d. 84695, l. 7.
33. Ibid., l. 8.
34. Ibid., l. 7–10.
35. Ibid., l. 9.

36. Ibid., f. R-8131, op. 31, d. 84668, l. 11–15.
37. Ibid., f. R-9401, op. 1, d. 4558, l. 28–29 (part 82 of separate pagination).
38. Ibid., l. 77.
39. Ibid., l. 79.
40. RGANI, f. 2, op. 1, d. 329, l. 30–41.
41. GARF, f. R-9401, op. 1, d. 4553, l. 274.
42. In the report of the MVD to the Central Committee, the phrase "Chechen-Ingush nationality" figures prominently. What this specifically meant, or who precisely (Chechens, Ingush, or both) took part in the fight is impossible to tell.
43. GARF, f. R-9401, op. 1, d. 4599, l. 213; op. 2, d. 506, l. 340–41.
44. Ibid., l. 229.
45. Ibid.

Chapter 5. Political Disturbances in Georgia After the CPSU Twentieth Party Congress

1. Baazova, "Tanki protiv detei," 105.
2. GARF, f. R-9401, op. 1, d. 4442, l. 74–75 (part 2 of separate pagination).
3. Ibid., l. 86 (part 2 of separate pagination).
4. Ibid.
5. "'Ne dopustim kritiki Stalina,'" 62.
6. Ibid., 62–63.
7. Ibid., 63.
8. GARF, f. R-8131, op. 31, d. 72093, l. 19.
9. "'Ne dopustim kritiki Stalina,'" 63.
10. GARF, f. R-9401, op. 1, d. 4442, l. 75–76 (part 2 of separate pagination).
11. Ibid., l. 76 (part 2 of separate pagination).
12. Ibid.
13. Ibid., l. 88 (part 2 of separate pagination).
14. Ibid., l. 76 (part 2 of separate pagination).
15. Ibid., op. 2, d. 479, l. 192.
16. Baazova, 106.
17. GARF, f. R-9401, op. 1, d. 4442, l. 78 (part 2 of separate pagination).
18. Baazova, 106.
19. GARF, f. R-9401, op. 1, d. 4442, l. 87 (part 2 of separate pagination).
20. According to other information, the number was around 5,000. See ibid., l. 78 (part 2 of separate pagination).
21. Ibid., op. 2, d. 479, l. 192.
22. Baazova, 106.
23. GARF, f. R-9401, op. 2, d. 479, l. 192.
24. Baazova, 106.
25. Ibid.
26. GARF, f. R-9401, op. 2, d. 479, l. 192.
27. Ibid., op. 1, d. 4442, l. 78 (part 2 of separate pagination).
28. Ibid., l. 189 (part 2 of separate pagination).
29. Ibid., l. 73–74 (part 2 of separate pagination).
30. "'Ne dopustim kritiki Stalina,'" 64.
31. GARF, f. R-8131, op. 31, d. 72093, l. 41–42.

32. "'Ne dopustim kritiki Stalina,'" 65.
33. Ibid., 67.
34. Ibid.
35. Baazova, 106.
36. "'Ne dopustim kritiki Stalina,'" 65–66.
37. GARF, f. R-9401, op. 1, d. 4442, l. 79 (ch. 2 of separate pagination).
38. "'Ne dopustim kritiki Stalina," 65.
39. GARF, f. R-8131, op. 31, d. 99074, l. 5–6.
40. See ibid., f. R-9401, op. 1, d. 4410.
41. Ibid., d. 4442, l. 79 (part 2 of separate pagination).
42. Ibid., l. 188 (part 2 of separate pagination).
43. Ibid., f. R-8131, op. 31, d. 72093, l. 42.
44. Ibid.
45. Ibid., l. 50–52.
46. Ibid., d. 72094, l. 73.
47. Ibid., d. 72093, l. 50–52.
48. Ibid., l. 43.
49. Ibid., l. 42.
50. Ibid., f. R-9401, op. 1, d. 4442, l. 185 (part 2 of separate pagination).
51. Ibid., 189 (part 2 of separate pagination).
52. Baazova, 108.
53. GARF, f. R-9401, op. 1, d. 4442, l. 187 (part 2 of separate pagination).
54. Ibid., l. 183 (part 2 of separate pagination).
55. Ibid., l. 182 (part 2 of separate pagination).
56. Ibid., l. 183 (part 2 of separate pagination).
57. "'Ne dopustim kritiki Stalina,'" 67.
58. Ibid., 68.
59. Ibid., 62.
60. Ibid., 66.
61. GARF, f. R-9401, op. 1, d. 4442, l. 183–84 (part 2 of separate pagination).
62. Ibid., l. 185 (part 2 of separate pagination).
63. Ibid., l. 184 (part 2 of separate pagination).
64. "'Ne dopustim kritiki Stalina,'" 66.
65. Ibid.
66. GARF, f. R-9401, op. 1, d. 4442, l. 82 (part 2 of separate pagination).
67. Ibid., f. R-8131, op. 31, d. 82284, l. 7. The testimony of the witness has not been satisfactorily verified, but merits being mentioned if only as an example of the rumors spreading around Tbilisi.
68. Ibid., f. R-9401, op. 1, d. 4442, l. 187 (part 2 of separate pagination).
69. Ibid., l. 186 (part 2 of separate pagination).
70. Ibid.
71. Baazova, 108.
72. GARF, f. R-9401, op. 1, d. 4442, l. 80 (part 2 of separate pagination).
73. Ibid., l. 187 (part 2 of separate pagination).
74. Ibid., l. 87 (part 2 of separate pagination).
75. Ibid., l. 187 (part 2 of separate pagination).
76. Ibid., l. 192 (part 2 of separate pagination).
77. Ibid., l. 194–97 (part 2 of separate pagination).
78. Ibid., l. 198 (part 2 of separate pagination).

79. Ibid., l. 196 (part 2 of separate pagination).
80. Ibid., l. 200 (part 2 of separate pagination).
81. Ibid., l. 83 (part 2 of separate pagination).
82. Ibid., l. 85 (part 2 of separate pagination).
83. Ibid., f. R-8131, op. 31, d. 96302, l. 3.
84. Ibid., f. R-9401, op. 1, d. 4442, l. 83–84 (part 2 of separate pagination).
85. Ibid., l. 82 (part 2 of separate pagination).
86. Ibid., l. 84 (part 2 of separate pagination).
87. Ibid., f. R-8131, op. 31, d. 96302, l. 3–8.
88. Ibid., f. R-9401, op. 1, d. 4442, l. 58, 85 (part 2 of separate pagination).
89. Ibid., l. 85 (part 2 of separate pagination).
90. Ibid., f. R-8131, op. 31, d. 77022, l. 6, 20–24.
91. See ibid., d. 82494; op. 36, d. 7241; op. 31, d. 83274, 72058, 82683.
92. Ibid., f. R-9401, op. 1, d. 4442, l. 156–57 (part 2 of separate pagination).
93. Ibid., l. 155–56 (part 2 of separate pagination).
94. Ibid., l. 155–57 (part 2 of separate pagination).

Chapter 6. A Hooligan's War or Battles on the Margins

1. GARF, f. R-9401, op. 1, d. 4320, l. 48; f. R-8131, op. 32, d. 5602, l. 37–43.
2. Ibid.
3. Ibid., l. 38–39.
4. Ibid., op. 2, d. 499, l. 175.
5. Ibid., f. R-8131, op. 32, d. 5602, l. 38–39.
6. Ibid., f. R-9401, op. 2, d. 492, l. 34.
7. GARF, f. R-9401, op. 2, d. 482, l. 203–8.
8. Ibid., l. 204.
9. Ibid., l. 205.
10. "Parasite" was a term used in Soviet jurisprudence for a person who was not employed. The implication was that the person was not actively seeking work. In the first six months of 1957, about 25,000 people all over the country were matched with jobs in this way. See ibid., d. 492, l. 34.
11. For example, in the first half of 1957, about half a million (456,000) violators of the passport regimen were uncovered. In particular those disciplined were people in official capacity (managers of buildings, supervisors of dormitories, department heads) "who had allowed citizens to live and come to work who did not have passes and updated passports." See ibid.
12. Ibid.
13. The numbers are taken from ibid., op. 1, d. 4160, l. 55–56.
14. Ibid.
15. Ibid., f. R-8131, op. 32, d. 3287, l. 61–62.
16. Ibid., l. 65.
17. Ibid., f. R-9401, op. 2, d. 464, l. 94–97.
18. Ibid., d. 466, l. 92–93.
19. Ibid., d. 482, l. 134–36.
20. Ibid., f. R-8131, op. 32, d. 6410, l. 37.
21. Ibid.
22. Ibid., f. R-9401, op. 1, d. 4160, l. 139–41.

23. Ibid., f. R-8131, op. 32, d. 2232, l. 133–36.
24. Ibid., d. 5065, l. 144–56.
25. Ibid., d. 2235, l. 137–38.
26. Ibid., f. R-9401, op. 1, d. 4320, l. 312–13.
27. Ibid., l. 318.
28. Ibid., d. 4410, l. 164.
29. Ibid., d. 4439, l. 2–3; ibid., f. R-8131, op. 32, d. 4577, l. 14.
30. Ibid., f. R-9401, op. 1, d. 4444, l. 10–12.
31. Ibid., d. 4410, l. 115.
32. Ibid., d. 4446, l. 124–25; op. 2, d. 482, l. 21–22.
33. Ibid., d. 492, l. 32–33.
34. Ibid., f. R-8131, op. 32, d. 5603, l. 114.
35. Ibid., l. 358–59.
36. Ibid., d. 6190, l. 238.
37. See ibid., d. 5598, l. 8–9.
38. Ibid., d. 6410, l. 36.
39. "O massovykh besporiadkakh s 1957 goda . . . ," 153.
40. GARF, f. R-8131, op. 31, d. 86791.
41. Ibid., d. 81280.
42. See, for example, ibid., d. 86980, d. 88433, and others.
43. Ibid., d. 88902.
44. Ibid., d. 70717.
45. Ibid., d. 45107; f. 9474, op. 39, d. 166.
46. Ibid., f. R-8131, op. 31, d. 43168.
47. Ibid., d. 80420.
48. Ibid., d. 83366.
49. Ibid., d. 66958.
50. Ibid., d. 79928.
51. Ibid., d. 73188.
52. Ibid., d. 84765.
53. Ibid., d. 89507.
54. Ibid., d. 84719.
55. Ibid., d. 84089.
56. Ibid., d. 79484.
57. Ibid., d. 81832.
58. Ibid., d. 81823.
59. Ibid., d. 86941.
60. Ibid., d. 90718a.
61. Ibid., d. 43427.
62. Ibid., d. 87227.
63. Ibid., d. 83645.
64. Ibid., d. 79317.
65. Ibid., d. 84969.
66. Ibid., d. 89379.
67. See ibid., d. 86402.
68. Ibid., d. 78897.
69. Ibid., d. 73678.
70. Ibid., d. 42269; f. R-9474, op. 39, d. 641.
71. Ibid., f. R-8131, op. 31, d. 43126; f. R-9474, op. 39, d. 24.
72. Ibid., f. R-8131, op. 31, d. 79312.

Chapter 7. Orthodoxy in Revolt

1. GARF, f. R-9401, op. 2, d. 451, l. 317–19.
2. RGANI, f. 5, op. 30, d. 321, l. 28.
3. GARF, f. R-8131, op. 31, d. 73934.
4. See ibid., op. 36, d. 4123.
5. See V. Tsybin, *Istoriia russkoi pravoslavnoi tserkvi* (Moscow, 1994), 150.
6. See GARF, f. R-6991, op. 1, d. 1747, l. 12–13.
7. See ibid., l. 18.
8. Ibid., l. 149–50. I will note a very typical phenomenon: I was born in 1950 and was secretly baptized, unbeknownst to my parents, by my Communist grandmother and her nonparty relatives.
9. Ibid., l. 18.
10. Ibid., l. 12.
11. Ibid., op. 3, d. 166, l. 138.
12. Ibid., op. 1, d. 1747, l. 18–19.
13. RGANI, f. 5, op. 30, d. 289, l. 85.
14. GARF, f. R-6991, op. 1, d. 1747, l. 98–99.
15. Ibid., f. R-9401, op. 2, d. 506, l. 206.
16. Ibid., f. R-6991, op. 1, d. 1649, l. 106.
17. Ibid., l. 106–07.
18. Ibid., d. 1747, l. 100–101.
19. Ibid., l. 14–15.
20. Ibid., l. 155.
21. Ibid., f. R-8131, op. 31, d. 93859, l. 1, 3.
22. Ibid., f. R-6991, op. 1, d. 1747, l. 98–99.
23. Ibid., l. 11–12.

Part II. The Crisis of "Liberal Communism"

Chapter 8. The Early 1960s

1. RGANI, f. 89, per. 6, d. 20, l. 1–2.
2. Ibid., l. 3.
3. See E. Panovian and A. Panovian, *Uchastie Verkhovnogo Suda SSSR v vyrabotke repressivnoi politiki (1957–1958 gg.)* (Moscow, 1996), 58–59; *Kornitravy,* 68–70.
4. RGANI, f. 89, per. 51, d. 1, l. 1–2.
5. Ibid., l. 1.
6. Ibid., f. 2, op. 1, d. 626, l. 103.
7. Ibid., f. 89, per. 51, d. 1, l. 1, 3.
8. "Ob"ediniaites' vokrug Khrista," 145.
9. RGANI, f. 5, op. 30, d. 383, l. 30, 32, 47, 66, 72, 102, 105.
10. GARF, f. R-8131, op. 31, d. 90093, l. 23–26.
11. Ibid., d. 94443, l. 35.
12. Ibid., l. 34–35.
13. "Ob"ediniaites' vokrug Khrista," 151.
14. Ibid., 152.
15. Ibid., 152–53.
16. GARF, f. R-8131, op. 31, d. 93517, l. 34–37.

17. RGANI, f. 5, op. 30, d. 351.
18. GARF, f. R-8131, op. 32, d. 6748, l. 85–96.

Chapter 9. Krasnodar, RSFSR, January 15–16, 1961

1. GARF, f. R-8131, op. 31, d. 90228, l. 194.
2. Ibid., l. 47–48.
3. Ibid., l. 29.
4. Ibid., l. 1–2.
5. Ibid., l. 53.
6. Ibid., l. 43–44.
7. Ibid., l. 193.
8. Ibid., l. 46.
9. Ibid., l. 98, 98 ob.
10. Ibid., l. 98 ob.
11. Ibid., l. 47.
12. Ibid., l. 54.
13. Ibid., l. 193.
14. Ibid., l. 44–45.
15. Ibid., l. 50.
16. Ibid., l. 49.
17. Ibid., l. 37.
18. Ibid., l. 32.
19. Ibid., l. 33.
20. Ibid., l. 32–33.
21. Ibid., l. 33.
22. Ibid., l. 2.
23. Ibid., l. 75.
24. Ibid., l. 76.
25. Ibid., l. 132.
26. Ibid., l. 69.
27. Ibid., l. 72.
28. Ibid., l. 74.
29. Ibid., l. 69.
30. Ibid., l. 72.
31. Ibid., l. 34–35.
32. Ibid., l. 70.
33. Ibid., l. 6–7.
34. Ibid., d. 92788, l. 50–50 ob.
35. Ibid., d. 92786, l. 16.
36. Ibid., l. 46.
37. Ibid., l. 47–49.
38. Ibid., l. 52–53.
39. Ibid., l. 48.
40. Ibid.
41. Ibid., d. 90228, l. 51.
42. Ibid., l. 204–205.
43. Ibid., l. 7.

44. Ibid., l. 207–208.
45. Ibid., l. 207.
46. Ibid., l. 41–42.
47. Ibid., l. 3.
48. Ibid., l. 45.
49. Ibid., l. 3.
50. Ibid., l. 16.
51. Ibid., l. 86.
52. Ibid., l. 87–88.
53. Ibid., l. 89.
54. Ibid., l. 90.

Chapter 10. 101 Kilometers from Moscow

1. GARF, f. R-8131, op. 31, d. 91127, l. 1–2, 8–9.
2. Ibid., l. 2.
3. *Muromskii rabochii*, August 13, 1961, 4.
4. GARF, f. R-8131, op. 31, d. 91127, l. 12.
5. Ibid., l. 11–12.
6. Ibid., l. 12.
7. Ibid., l. 150–50 ob.
8. Ibid., l. 150 ob.
9. Ibid., l. 148.
10. Ibid., l. 70.
11. Ibid., l. 56.
12. See ibid., l. 16–17.
13. Ibid., l. 44–45.
14. Ibid., l. 57.
15. Ibid., l. 27.
16. Ibid., l. 22, 148–48 ob.
17. Ibid., l. 73.
18. Ibid., l. 65.
19. Ibid., l. 17.
20. Ibid., l. 46.
21. Ibid., l. 151 ob.
22. Ibid., l. 46.
23. Ibid., l. 150–50 ob.
24. Ibid., l. 17.
25. Ibid., l. 19.
26. Ibid., l. 15.
27. Ibid., l. 58.
28. Ibid., l. 1.
29. Ibid., l. 4.
30. Ibid., l. 30.
31. Ibid.
32. Ibid.
33. *Muromskii rabochii*, August 13, 1961, 4; *Prizyv*, August 13, 1961, 4.
34. *Sovetskaia Rossiia*, August 17, 1961, 4.

35. GARF, f. R-1831, op. 31, d. 91127, l. 53.
36. Ibid., l. 52.
37. RGANI, f. 5, op. 30, d. 373, l. 40.
38. GARF, f. R-8131, op. 31, d. 91241, l. 2.
39. Ibid., l. 103.
40. Ibid., l. 276–77.
41. Ibid., l. 287.
42. Ibid., l. 47–48.
43. Ibid., l. 27.
44. Ibid., l. 27–28.
45. Ibid., l. 48–49.
46. Ibid., l. 4–5.
47. Ibid., l. 28.
48. Ibid., l. 290, 277.
49. Ibid., l. 52.
50. Ibid., l. 251–52.
51. Ibid., l. 38.
52. Ibid., l. 112.
53. Ibid., l. 125.
54. Ibid., l. 35, 284.
55. Ibid., l. 45.
56. Ibid., l. 82.
57. Ibid., l. 249–50.
58. Ibid., l. 32.
59. Ibid., l. 2.
60. Ibid., l. 32.
61. Ibid., l. 28.
62. Ibid., l. 6.
63. Ibid., l. 10–11, 29.
64. Ibid., l. 43.
65. Ibid., l. 51–52.
66. Ibid., l. 36–37.
67. Ibid., l. 304 ob.
68. Ibid., l. 92.
69. Ibid., l. 98.
70. Ibid., l. 42.
71. Ibid., l. 34–35.
72. Ibid., l. 61.
73. Ibid., l. 34–35.
74. Ibid., l. 45.
75. Ibid., l. 275.
76. Ibid., l. 19, 281.
77. Ibid., l. 282.
78. Ibid., l. 275–76.
79. Ibid., l. 19–21.
80. Ibid., l. 9.
81. Ibid., l. 2.
82. Ibid., l. 56.
83. Ibid., l. 297 ob.

84. Ibid., l. 116.
85. Ibid., l. 47.
86. Ibid., l. 297 ob.
87. Ibid., l. 73.
88. Ibid., l. 8–9.
89. Ibid., l. 11–13.
90. Ibid., l. 30–31.
91. Ibid., l.13.
92. Ibid., l. 2–3.
93. Ibid., l. 13.
94. Ibid., l. 200.
95. Ibid., l. 201.
96. Ibid., l. 291–92.
97. GARF, f. R-8131, op. 32, d. 7031, l. 200–201.

Chapter 11. Biisk—1961 or The Uprising on Market Day, June 25, 1961

1. GARF, f. R-8131, op. 31, d. 91265, l. 43–44.
2. Ibid., l. 90.
3. Ibid.
4. Ibid., l. 91.
5. Ibid.
6. Ibid., l. 96.
7. Ibid., l. 90, 97–98.
8. Ibid., l. 97.
9. Ibid., l. 39.
10. Ibid., l. 46.
11. Ibid., l. 5.
12. Ibid., l. 46.
13. Ibid., l. 7.
14. Ibid.
15. Ibid., l. 91.
16. Ibid., l. 100.
17. Ibid., l. 40.
18. Ibid., l. 39.
19. Ibid., l. 46.
20. Ibid., l. 45.
21. Ibid., l. 93.
22. Ibid., l. 42.
23. Ibid., l. 93.
24. Ibid., l. 6.
25. Ibid., l. 14.
26. Ibid., l. 9 ob.

Chapter 12. The Phenomenon of Novocherkassk: Part One

1. See information on the KGB in *Istoricheskii arkhiv*, no. 1 (1993): 111–18, and no. 4 (1993): 170–72; Lebedev, "Ob"ediniaites' vokrug Khrista."

2. *Istoricheskii arkhiv*, no. 1 (1993): 122–23.

3. Mardar, *Khronika*, 5–6.

4. *Istoricheskii arkhiv*, no. 1 (1993): 126.

5. Mardar, *Khronika*, 6.

6. GARF, f. R-8131, op. 31, d. 93661, l. 7.

7. *Istoricheskii arkhiv*, no. 1 (1993): 113.

8. Ibid., 112.

9. Mardar, *Khronika*, 8.

10. *Istoricheskii arkhiv*, no. 1 (1993): 123.

11. GARF, f. R-8131, op. 31, d. 98328, l. 10.

12. Ibid., d. 93662, l. 106 ob.

13. Ibid., d. 93661, l. 192–93; d. 93662, l. 105–6.

14. Ibid., l. 105 ob.

15. *Istoricheskii arkhiv*, no. 1 (1993): 123.

16. GARF, f. R-8131, op. 31, d. 98328, l. 10.

17. *Istoricheskii arkhiv*, no. 1 (1993): 132.

18. GARF, f. R-8131, op. 31, d. 98328, l. 10.

19. Mardar, *Khronika*, 9–10.

20. Ibid., 10–11.

21. GARF, f. R-8131, op. 31, d. 93661, l. 8.

22. Ibid.

23. Ibid., l. 18–19.

24. Ibid., d. 95432, l. 73–74.

25. Ibid., l. 74.

26. Ibid., l. 70–71.

27. Ibid., l. 67, 74.

28. Ibid., l. 67.

29. Ibid., l. 8.

30. Ibid., l. 41.

31. Ibid., l. 77.

32. Ibid., l. 68.

33. Ibid., l. 66, 70.

34. Ibid., l. 70.

35. Ibid., l. 69.

36. Mardar, *Khronika*, 9.

37. GARF, f. R-8131, op. 31, d. 93661, l. 8.

38. Siuda, "Novocherkasskaia tragediia," 17.

39. GARF, f. R-8131, op. 31, d. 98328, l. 11.

40. Ibid., d. 95895, l. 46.

41. Ibid., d. 98311, l. 2.

42. Ibid., d. 95432, l. 119.

43. Ibid., l. 10.

44. Ibid., l. 51.

45. Ibid., l. 75.

46. Ibid., l. 66.

47. Ibid., l. 9.

48. Ibid., l. 76–77.

49. Ibid., d. 98309, l. 3–4.

50. *Istoricheskii arkhiv*, no. 1 (1993): 125.

51. GARF, f. R-8131, op. 31 d. 93940, l. 12.
52. *Istoricheskii arkhiv*, no. 1 (1993): 125.
53. Ibid.
54. GARF, f. R-8131, op. 31, d. 93661, l. 8–9.
55. *Istoricheskii arkhiv*, no. 1 (1993): 125.
56. GARF, f. R-8131, op. 31, d. 93661, l. 19–20.
57. Ibid., d. 95895, l. 45.
58. Ibid., d. 93661, l. 207.
59. Ibid., l. 207–208.
60. *Istoricheskii arkhiv*, no. 4 (1993): 147.
61. GARF, f. R-8131, op. 31, d. 95432, l. 19.
62. Ibid., d. 93661, l. 20.
63. *Istoricheskii arkhiv*, no. 1 (1993): 125.
64. Ibid.
65. GARF, f. R-8131, op. 31, d. 95895, l. 44.
66. Ibid., d. 93661, l. 251–52.
67. Mardar, *Khronika*, 13–14.
68. Ibid., 13.
69. *Istoricheskii arkhiv*, no. 1 (1993): 125.
70. Ibid.
71. Mardar, *Khronika*, 13–15.
72. *Istoricheskii arkhiv*, no. 4 (1993): 147.
73. Ibid.
74. Ibid., 147–48.
75. GARF, f. R-8131, op. 31, d. 93661, l. 250; d. 93662, l. 30.
76. Ibid.
77. Ibid., d. 93661, l. 255.
78. Ibid., l. 251; *Istoricheskii arkhiv*, no. 4 (1993): 148.
79. GARF, f. R-8131, op. 31, d. 93661, l. 251.
80. Ibid., l. 161.
81. Ibid., l. 295–96 ob.
82. Ibid., l. 175.
83. Ibid., l. 166.
84. Ibid., l. 162.
85. Ibid., l. 253.
86. GARF, f. R-8131, op. 31, d. 98328, l. 11.
87. Ibid., l. 9–10.
88. Ibid., d. 98304, l. 2–3.
89. Ibid., d. 98302, l. 3.
90. Mardar, *Khronika*, 15–16.
91. GARF, f. R-8131, op. 31, d. 95432, l. 69.
92. *Istoricheskii arkhiv*, no. 1 (1993): 125.
93. Mardar, *Khronika*, 17.
94. GARF, f. R-8131, op. 31, d. 93661, l. 9.
95. Ibid.
96. *Istoricheskii arkhiv*, no. 4 (1993): 148.
97. Ibid.
98. Ibid., 148–49.
99. GARF, f. R-8131, op. 31, d. 93661, l. 164.

100. Mardar, *Khronika*, 17.
101. *Istoricheskii arkhiv*, no. 1 (1993): 122.
102. GARF, f. R-8131, op. 31, d. 93662, l. 71–73.
103. Ibid., d. 93661, l. 232.
104. Ibid., d. 95895, l. 49.
105. Ibid., d. 98299, l. 5–6.
106. Ibid., d. 95895, l. 47.
107. Ibid., d. 98329, l. 2.
108. Ibid., d. 98326, l. 14.

Chapter 13. The Phenomenon of Novocherkassk: Part Two

1. *Istoricheskii arkhiv*, no. 1 (1993): 126.
2. GARF, f. R-8131, op. 31, d. 95342, l. 76.
3. Mardar, *Khronika*, 28.
4. *Istoricheskii arkhiv*, no. 1 (1993): 126.
5. GARF, f. R-8131, op. 31, d. 95432, l. 68.
6. Ibid., l. 72.
7. Ibid., d. 93661, l. 130.
8. Ibid., l. 131.
9. Ibid.
10. Ibid., 143–44.
11. *Istoricheskii arkhiv*, no. 4 (1993): 149–50.
12. GARF, f. R-8131, op. 31, d. 93661, l. 133.
13. Ibid.
14. Ibid., l. 134.
15. Ibid., l. 143–44.
16. Ibid., l. 228.
17. Ibid., d. 95895, l. 28–30.
18. Ibid., d. 93661, l. 242.
19. Ibid., l. 245.
20. Ibid., d. 98308, l. 6.
21. Ibid., l. 7.
22. Ibid., l. 6.
23. Ibid., l. 7.
24. *Istoricheskii arkhiv*, no. 1 (1993): 126.
25. GARF, f. R-8131, op. 31, d. 93661, l. 10.
26. Ibid.
27. Mardar, *Khronika*, 31.
28. *Istoricheskii arkhiv*, no. 1 (1993): 126.
29. Quoted from Mardar, *Khronika*, 32.
30. GARF, f. R-8131, op. 31, d. 93661, l. 242; Mardar, *Khronika*, 32.
31. GARF, f. R-8131, op. 31, d. 93661, l. 243.
32. Ibid., l. 61–66.
33. *Istoricheskii arkhiv*, no. 1 (1993): 150–51.
34. GARF, f. R-8131, op. 31, d. 93661, l. 78–80.
35. *Istoricheskii arkhiv*, no. 1 (1993): 153.
36. GARF, f. R-8131, op. 31, d. 93662, l. 102.

37. *Istoricheskii arkhiv*, no. 4 (1993): 151–52.
38. GARF, f. R-8131, op. 31, d. 93661, l. 149.
39. *Istoricheskii arkhiv*, no. 4 (1993): 152.
40. Ibid., 153.
41. GARF, f. R-8131, op. 31, d. 93661, l. 179.
42. *Istoricheskii arkhiv*, no. 1 (1993): 130.
43. I. Mardar unjustifiably rejects police claims that they had to lock up several rioters in the police department premises. In his opinion, all of the policemen ran away in cowardly fashion (see Mardar, *Khronika*, 34). As we have seen, such an episode really did take place.
44. GARF, f. R-8131, op. 31, d. 98327, l. 95–95 ob.
45. Ibid., l. 9 ob.-10 ob.
46. *Istoricheskii arkhiv*, no. 4 (1993): 152.
47. Ibid.
48. GARF, f. R-8131, op. 31, d. 98327, l. 33.
49. Ibid., l. 35.
50. Ibid., d. 93661, l. 107–9.
51. Ibid., l. 111.
52. *Istoricheskii arkhiv*, no. 4 (1993): 154.
53. GARF, f. R-8131, op. 31, d. 93661, l. 111–12.
54. Mardar, *Khronika*, 33. Several sources, including the report on B.N. Mokrousov that was compiled by the procurator Shubin even before the final formulation of the case, propose another version of events. Mokrousov, as he called for the creation of a delegation, already knew about the shooting and was protesting specifically against it (GARF, f. R-8131, op. 31, d. 93661, l. 109). However, this version did not end up in the indictment.
55. Mardar, *Khronika*, 36.
56. Ibid.
57. Ibid., 36–37.
58. Ibid., 37.
59. Ibid.
60. Ibid., 36.
61. GARF, f. R-8131, op. 31, d. 98326, l. 15.
62. Ibid., d. 98310, l. 5–6.
63. Ibid., l. 4–5.
64. Ibid., l. 6.
65. *Istoricheskii arkhiv*, no. 4 (1993): 153.
66. GARF, f. R-8131, op. 31, d. 98895, l. 45.
67. Ibid., d. 98285, l. 14.
68. *Istoricheskii arkhiv*, no. 4 (1993): 151.
69. *Istoricheskii arkhiv*, no. 1 (1993): 130. There were very few among the strikers and demonstrators who had prior anti-Soviet views. Besides Otroshko, there was V.G. Kuvardin, an unemployed man who took part in the attack on the party committee building. But even in his case, the organs of state security had only vague information about anti-Soviet attitudes and an intention to establish contact with the American embassy.
70. GARF, f. R-8131, op. 31, d. 93661, l. 13.
71. *Istoricheskii arkhiv*, no. 1 (1993): 126.
72. Ibid., 119.

73. Ibid.
74. Ibid.
75. Ibid., 119–21.
76. Ibid., 121.
77. Ibid., 126.
78. GARF, f. R-8131, op. 31, d. 93661, l. 14.
79. *Istoricheskii arkhiv*, no. 1 (1993): 130.
80. Ibid., 130–31.
81. GARF, f. R-8131, op. 36, d. 97726, l. 9–10.
82. Ibid., l. 10.
83. Ibid., l. 11–12.
84. Ibid., d. 1808, l. 5–6.
85. Ibid., l. 7.
86. Ibid., l. 6.
87. Ibid., l. 10.
88. Ibid., op. 31, d. 98285, l. 13–14.
89. Ibid., d. 93662, l. 16.
90. *Istoricheskii arkhiv*, no. 1 (1993): 122.
91. GARF, f. R-8131, op. 31, d. 95432, l. 47.
92. Ibid., d. 93661, l. 162.
93. Ibid., d. 95432, l. 52.
94. Ibid., d. 93661, l. 210.
95. Ibid., 148–54.
96. Ibid., 152.
97. Ibid., d. 98327, l. 38, 58.
98. Ibid., d. 93662, l. 106 ob.
99. Ibid., d. 95895, l. 1 ob. –2.
100. Ibid., d. 95432, l. 123 ob.
101. Ibid., l. 9.
102. Ibid., l. 93 ob.
103. Ibid., d. 95895, l. 111.
104. Ibid., d. 95432, l. 40–41.
105. Ibid., l. 33.
106. Ibid., l. 36–37.
107. Ibid., d. 98327, l. 43–44.
108. Ibid., d. 93661, l. 164.
109. Ibid., l. 152–53.
110. Ibid., l. 61.
111. Ibid., d. 95432, l. 41.
112. Ibid., l. 52 ob.–53.
113. *Istoricheskii arkhiv*, no. 4 (1993): 176–77.
114. Ibid., 173.
115. Ibid., 175.
116. Ibid., 173.
117. Ibid.
118. Ibid., 175.
119. Ibid., 176.
120. GARF, f. R-8131, op. 31, d. 95895, l. 155.

Chapter 14. Rear-Guard Battles of the Late Krushchev Era

1. RGANI, f. 5, op. 30, d. 454, l. 111.
2. GARF, f. R-8131, op. 31, d. 93517, l. 25–28.
3. Ibid., l. 13.
4. Ibid., l. 27.
5. Ibid., l. 10–12.
6. Ibid., l. 25.
7. Ibid., l. 28.
8. Ibid.
9. Ibid., op. 32, d. 7068, l. 35.
10. Ibid., d. 6589, l. 123–24.
11. Ibid., d. 6913, l. 75–78.
12. Ibid., l. 78.
13. Ibid., l. 78–79.
14. Ibid.
15. Ibid., d.7069, l. 98.
16. Ibid., op. 31, d. 96438, l. 5.
17. Ibid., l. 7.
18. Ibid.
19. Ibid., l. 8.
20. RGANI, per. 6, d. 27, l. 1.
21. GARF, f. R-8131, op. 31, d. 96438, l. 26.
22. Ibid., l. 27.
23. Ibid., l. 28.
24. Ibid.
25. Ibid., l. 4–5.
26. Ibid., l. 36.
27. Ibid., d. 97328, l. 1–2.
28. Ibid., l. 4–6.
29. Ibid., l. 8.
30. Ibid., l. 9.
31. Ibid., l. 11.
32. Ibid., l. 11–12.
33. Ibid., l. 15.

Chapter 15. Social Unrest and Symptoms of Decay in the Brezhnev Years

1. GARF, f. R-8131, op. 32, d. 7528, l. 101–102.
2. Quoted from ibid., d. 7658, l. 63.
3. "O massovykh besporiadkakh s 1957 goda...," 147.
4. GARF, f. R-8131, op. 32, d. 7528, l. 42.
5. Ibid., op. 36, d. 1782, l. 1–2.
6. RGANI, f. 89, per. 6, document 29, l. 1–3.
7. GARF, f. R-8131, op. 36, d. 1486, l. 1–3.
8. RGANI, f. 89, per. 51, document 3, l. 7.
9. Ibid., per. 16, document 10, l. 3–5.

10. GARF, f. R-8131, op. 32, d. 9102, l. 21.
11. Ibid., l. 22.
12. RGANI, f. 89, per. 11, d. 138, l. 1.

Conclusion

1. See the preface of M.A. Barg to the Russian edition of the work by the historian George Rude, *Narodnye nizy v istorii. 1730–1848* (Moscow, 1984), 12.
2. See V. Dal', *Tolkovyi slovar' v chetyrekh tomakh*, T. 4 (Moscow, 1991), 239. The second and most complete edition of this work was published in 1880–1882. The word *smuta* literally means discord or sedition.

Index

Vladimir A. Kozlov is a 1972 graduate of Moscow State University. He received his candidate's degree (equivalent to a Ph.D.) in 1980 in the field of Soviet history, and is currently the deputy-director of the State Archive of the Russian Federation and head of its Center for Research and Publication of Documents. Dr. Kozlov has been a visiting professor and lecturer in the History Department at the University of Bologna in Italy and in the Sociology Department at the University of California at San Diego. He has published extensively on Soviet history and historiography, and his work has been translated into English, German, Italian, Japanese, and French. Besides this publication, he has authored or co-authored seven books and edited numerous document collections, including the four volume series *Neizvestnaia Rossiia, XX vek (The Unknown Russia, Twentieth Century), The Last Diary of Tsaritsa Alexandra,* and the forthcoming *Kramola (Sedition): Anti-Governmental Opposition in the USSR, 1953–1982.* His current research, funded by a grant from the Guggenheim Foundation, focuses on the social history of the Gulag system after the death of Stalin.

Translator and editor **Elaine McClarnand MacKinnon** is associate professor of Russian and Soviet history at the State University of West Georgia. She is the author of several scholarly articles on Soviet historiography. Her current projects include a study of the Soviet historian I.I. Mints, a monograph on Soviet historians and debates over Stalinism during the Gorbachev era, and a textbook on Russian and Soviet history, *Searching for Russia's Past*, Volume II.